D1022393

NOT
ABOVE
the
LAW

———————————————

NOT ABOVE THE LAW

THE BATTLES OF WATERGATE PROSECUTORS COX AND JAWORSKI

A Behind-the-Scenes Account

by James Doyle

WILLIAM MORROW AND COMPANY, INC.
New York   1977

Printed in the United States of America.

2   3   4   5   6   7   8   9   10

Library of Congress Cataloging in Publication Data

Doyle, James (date)
    Not above the law.

    Includes index.
    1. Watergate Affair, 1972-   —Personal
narratives. 2. Doyle, James (date)
3. Jaworski, Leon. 4. Cox, Archibald, 1912-
I. Title.
E860.D68   345'.73'052   77-1501
ISBN 0-688-03192-7

BOOK DESIGN   CARL WEISS

FOR ANNIE

WITH LOVE

CONTENTS

TO THE READER

This book is a piece of the puzzle we call Watergate—a journalist's eye-witness account from behind the doors of the Watergate Special Prosecution Force.

When the special prosecutor was first appointed, I was a national correspondent for the *Washington Star*. I agreed to become spokesman for the effort, with the understanding that I would write about it afterward. That was in June, 1973.

For two years I worked inside the sealed-off compound on the ninth floor of 1425 K Street, four blocks as the crow flies from Richard Nixon's White House. I made contemporaneous notes of what transpired when that was feasible, and each night as I drove home alone in my car, I dictated into a tape recorder, reconstructing quotes and recounting the things that would have faded with time—incidental remarks, anecdotes, attitudes, and anxieties that hid behind each day's black headlines.

In May, 1975, I left the government and began interviewing the principals in this drama, doubling back over the events, researching the records. I also began writing this book. I was blessed with an enormous degree of cooperation from those who appear within these pages, some of them in less than favorable light.

Many who have cooperated with this effort will disagree with the result —with the author's judgments and with his methods as well. Lawyers generally take a conservative view of what is the proper amount of disclosure of the public policy debate within the inner circles of government, and especially a prosecutor's office.

Archibald Cox told the court, at the outset of the tapes case: "An aide is likely to speak more candidly, more openly to his superior if he has a reasonable degree of assurance that what he says will not be spread out in public for criticism, debate, or misunderstanding. . . . An executive himself is freer to make policy wisely if he has the ability to put it colloquially, to think out loud, to advance ideas tentatively, to put them out, to have them knocked down, again without the danger that it will all be spread in public for debate, discussion, and possible misunderstanding."

True. But the goings-on in the prosecutor's offices will not remain sealed forever. Fear of criticism is no reason, at this time after the events, to deprive the nation of information on how decisions were made. Since it was a most personal process, the recounting of it becomes personal, too.

There are individual accounts of what happened at 1425 K Street during those two years. I have tried to transcend the memoir form by using my reporter's training and my access to all the participants. I believe this will stand as something more than one man's account. In the end the judgments had to be mine, informed by my own experience living those two years behind the lines. But I have tried to infuse the book with the perspective and knowledge of various participants, including many who were at different vantage points during that time.

In his argument before the court at the outset of the tapes case, Archibald Cox added this: "The confidentiality that encourages free discussion and candid views is surely not the only value in our society, or even the supreme value. At times the interests advanced by confidentiality must yield to other important interests that conflict with them." He was proven right —vindicated in and out of court for the history books. It is for those same pages that I write.

This book is mine, from its conception to its execution, through more painful adversity than expected. For several months it seemed reduced to nothing more than an item in a literary divorce settlement. There was for a time a real danger that it would not be published, and I learned first-hand A. J. Liebling's observation that freedom of the press is for him who owns one. But the book, and I, recovered. For that I owe thanks to Hillel Black of William Morrow and Company, who believed in this book when others did not.

That is the lovely part of the story of *Not Above the Law*. It exists now because of the extraordinary generosity of a large number of people. Their help and encouragement have been a gift of great value indeed.

Foremost among them is Henry Belber, shipmate and friend, whose support has been constant and total. Then Francis J. O'Donnell, one of the promising journalists of the new generation, my companion in this effort for most of a year, organizing mountains of research, reporting, checking my recollections, catching my mistakes, bringing good humor and energy to long days and nights. And then Ronald Ostrow of the *Los Angeles Times,* friend, colleague. We have been through much together. More than anybody else, he was present at the creation.

And then there is the special story of Bob Woodward of the *Washington Post.* After my dispute with a first publisher and while his own book, *The Final Days,* was receiving unprecedented affirmation, he asked to read the manuscript. "This book has got to be published," he said simply, and then he and I spent several months in a collaboration that revived my spirits and, just as important, reminded me that my responsibility was as a journalist; that pulled punches didn't become me or my manuscript. We have become friends, and that is great reward in itself.

My bureau chief at *Newsweek,* Mel Elfin, has been patient, kind, and understanding during a taxing year. Without that help this book could not have been completed. I owe him and *Newsweek*'s top editors a special debt.

The community of journalists is a special one, its members generous to one another. I take note of all those newsmen who shared with me their insights and their notebooks and their differing vantage points during the two years I was out of the business. I cannot name them all, but some I must.

Anthony Lewis of *The New York Times* has been extraordinarily kind to me. Brock Brower, whose account of Leon Jaworski's boyhood in Waco first appeared in *Esquire* magazine, offered me not only all of that material but the professional help of an author familiar with the vagaries of publishing. His editorial advice and his encouragement during the dark days are not forgotten. Anthony Marro, now of *The New York Times,* offered detailed criticism of each chapter and recounted for me his own reportorial experiences during Watergate, as we worked together at *Newsweek* during 1976. Columnist Joseph Kraft and Adam Clymer and Stan Carter of the New York *Daily News* offered me information that was otherwise unavailable, concerning some of the players. Several of my colleagues from the prosecutor's office read and corrected the manuscript, saving me from embarrassing mistakes.

Three public information officers were especially helpful. Dean St. Dennis of the Justice Department deserves an extra thanks because he established the special prosecutor's press office before I arrived on the scene, and advised me well in my early days. And as I wrote this book, St. Dennis was the one Justice Department press officer always able to answer my questions concerning the department, its history, and its operations. My former colleagues John Barker and Dan Rosenblatt of the Watergate Special Prosecution Force were generous with their time and expertise in furnishing facts and filling gaps in my data.

S. Linn Williams and Les Hyman are two lawyers, and friends, who were very generous to me, and I owe a special debt to Linn Williams for so much time and advice. Hillel Black and Bonnie Donovan of William Morrow offered me invaluable editorial guidance, and Sterling Lord found Hillel Black for me, no small accomplishment.

I owe thanks to Abby Schaefer of William Morrow & Company, Professor Lewis Wolfson of American University, and my former colleague at the *Washington Star,* Ann Sausedo. And I remain indebted to Bill Donnelly, Mel Ryder, and all of their associates at the Army Times Publishing Company whose facilities were available to me throughout this project.

This is my first book. Hereafter, I will never again wonder why it is a tradition to thank those who helped. Books are even more magic than I had thought, and writing one means constantly being surprised by the generosity of friends and strangers.

Which brings me to the final acknowledgment. I owe the greatest debt to Mary Cassie and Joe Doyle, who worked harder than anybody and at greater sacrifice to see that the author turned out all right.

J. D.

Bethesda, Maryland
December 16, 1976

INTRODUCTION

by Anthony Lewis

It was very likely the most profound constitutional event in our history: the dethroning of a President. Appropriately, it involved all three parts of the governmental structure created at the Constitutional Convention of 1787. The legislative branch acted in the Senate Watergate investigation and the House Judiciary Committee's impeachment proceeding. The judicial branch was involved from start to finish, from Federal District Judge John Sirica to the Supreme Court of the United States. The executive branch investigated itself through the extraordinary device of the Watergate Special Prosecution Force. And that quasi-constitutional element in the American system, the press, goaded the formal machinery to act.

None of those institutions alone could have succeeded in bringing Richard Nixon to book for his wrongs. But one was decisive: the special prosecutor. Underlings were exposed in various ways, but only the special prosecutor brought the corruption home to its principal author so conclusively that there was no escape. Without the work of the Watergate Prosecution Force the impeachment inquiry would have got nowhere, because it relied almost entirely on the prosecutors' investigations for evidence. Without the unrelenting pressure of the special prosecutor's search for truth, Richard Nixon would not, in the end, have destroyed himself.

Self-destruction did have much to do with Nixon's fall; that he recorded his own conspiracies and allowed at least some of the recordings to survive remains an astonishing fact. But with the vision of hindsight, some tend to assume that the Nixon tapes were part of an inevitable series of events—that they would have been obtained for use as evidence against the President one way or another. That is the opposite of reality. It took enormous determination, professional skill and personal integrity to wrest the tapes from Nixon. The crucial part was played by Archibald Cox, the first special prosecutor. If he had not done what he did, I am certain that the tapes would have been kept from the process of law, and that Nixon would have stayed in office.

Alexander Butterfield told the Senate Watergate committee about the White House taping system on July 16, 1973. Archibald Cox and his staff immediately began the legal research necessary to make a case for production of some tapes. On July 18 Cox wrote to the President's lawyer requesting eight tapes of specific conversations that he showed might contain material relevant to the investigation. On July 23 he got the answer: No. That afternoon he announced that he would subpoena the tapes, "in the impartial pursuit of justice according to law."

Nixon's lawyers advised him that any suit to obtain material from presidential files would fail, and at that stage the advice was reasonable. It had been nearly two hundred years since a court of the United States had subpoenaed papers in a President's possession, and no court had ever insisted on enforcing such a subpoena to the letter against determined resistance. Moreover, judges are traditionally deferential to Presidents, reluctant to get into battles with them, respectful of presidential demands for secrecy.

Those were some of the obstacles that Archibald Cox faced in his suit for White House tapes. He overcame them by persuading judges that there were sound professional reasons in this case for overriding the presumption in favor of Presidents—not generalized political arguments but particular reasons of law and fact, which are more likely to move judges. He explained specifically why the eight conversations he wanted to hear were likely to be material; for example, White House logs pinpointed the meeting of March 21, 1973, between the President and John Dean at which, Dean had testified, he described the Watergate cover-up and warned of a "cancer on the Presidency."

Some luck was involved in the strength of Cox's argument. Before the existence of the tapes was known, Cox had asked the White House counsel, J. Fred Buzhardt, for a good deal of material, especially the logs showing the times of presidential meetings. Buzhardt stalled. One day Cox decided to introduce his newly assembled staff at a press conference. Buzhardt heard that there was to be a conference and telephoned James Vorenberg, assistant to Cox, to ask what was up. Vorenberg took the occasion to remind him of the backed-up requests and said the special prosecutor's patience was running out. Just before the press conference, Buzhardt sent over a package of White House logs—which were of critical importance later in selecting tapes for subpoena.

But even luck has its reasons. Cox chose a remarkable staff of lawyers, who knew where to look for the facts and understood the movement of the law. Perhaps most important was a factor that Nixon and his men never could understand: Archibald Cox and his staff were genuinely determined to decide issues on the merits. They were not out to get Nixon for political reasons—as Nixon assumed, reading his own motives into others. That was doubtless one explanation of Cox's unusual persuasiveness with judges: They knew that he was seeking the public interest.

The turning point in the long Watergate story was a matter of character. When Cox persuaded Judge Sirica and the U.S. Court of Appeals to enforce his subpoena, Nixon tried to escape by an extra-legal device: a unilateral "compromise" that would have given the special prosecutor mere summaries of the taped conversations and barred him from any further presidential evidence. Immense pressure was put on Cox to accept —pressure of a kind hard for outsiders to appreciate. He was operating on his own, without a political base, without advice beyond that of his young staff, and he could not be sure that holding out was the right thing for the country. But his commitment was to the law, and he rejected the attempt to bypass it. His principles, explained in simple terms at a televised press conference on October 20, 1973, awoke the country—and changed its history. When he was fired that night, the public reacted so passionately that Nixon was forced to do the one thing he had wanted above all to avoid: turn over the tapes.

That was the beginning of the end. The public outcry led the House to start the impeachment process. Nixon sought to cushion the effect of the tapes by publishing trimmed transcripts, but even they disgusted the country and spurred the impeachment inquiry. Cox's successor, Leon Jaworski, proved as determined as Cox to get the evidence. He subpoenaed more tapes, and he pressed his case on to the Supreme Court. Its unanimous judgment forced the delivery of another incriminating tape, and within days Richard Nixon had withdrawn to San Clemente.

Americans who lived through the two years of Watergate have its outlines etched on their minds. But James Doyle describes in this book, as no one has before, the hidden internal drama that I think determined the outcome: the workings of the special prosecutor's office. It *is* drama as he tells it, with clashes of principle and personality, with mystery and morality and humor. If anyone doubts that great events are made by human beings, not fate, he will find correction here.

Even the tapes, those central inanimate elements in the story, take on a new significance here. Leon Jaworski heard the first in December, 1973; he knew at once that there had been criminality in the White House, and he was convinced that Richard Nixon had to go. On December 21 Jaworski went to the White House chief of staff, Alexander Haig, who had recruited him for the job of special prosecutor with the argument of patriotism. He told Haig that the tape of March 21 showed the President in conspiratorial discussion of blackmail payoffs and clemency for the Watergate burglars. Haig's eyes filled with tears. But a few hours later, Doyle says, Haig telephoned Jaworski excitedly and said "there was no overt act" after March 21. General Haig, the patriot, had evidently been given a lesson on conspiracy by some White House lawyer—incorrectly on the facts, as it happened—and was now defending the President of the United States in terms of the criminal law.

One of the remarkable features of the story is that the Watergate prosecutors knew for months what the tapes showed but not a word leaked. During that time they studied and debated the central problem of their work: how to deal with a sitting President when there is evidence that he has committed crimes in office. Should he be indicted? Could he, constitutionally? Alternatively, could a prosecutor properly take evidence acquired by a grand jury and turn it over to a legislative committee for purposes of impeachment? The questions were difficult, and history gave no certain answers.

Doyle's account of this debate inside the prosecutor's office in the winter of 1973–74 provides extraordinary insights into the legal mind and into our constitutional values. He gives us the staff memoranda, and they are of very high quality. In the end Leon Jaworski decided not to seek an indictment of the President. When the grand jury charged his associates, it named Nixon as an unindicted co-conspirator. And it took the decisive step of forwarding the evidence to the House Judiciary Committee. Readers will be able to form their own judgment on the arguments among the lawyers. But I think few will doubt that the issues were explored with intellectual rigor by serious men and women dedicated to finding the right answer for the United States.

Not that James Doyle's tale is a saga of nobility. It has its share of rogues. One important function it performs is to throw light on the behavior of presumably respectable people when they come within the distorting aura of the President of the United States. The book provides numberless examples of how ideals and judgment may be subverted in the service of power.

Henry Petersen, a career attorney in the Department of Justice who rose to Assistant Attorney General, was in charge of the Watergate investigation until superseded by the special prosecutor. Archibald Cox questioned him about his frequent meetings with Nixon in the spring of 1973, wondering what they had talked about. Petersen assured Cox that he had not given the President any "grand jury information." He knew it was a violation of the Federal Rules of Criminal Procedure for a prosecutor to do so. But Henry Petersen had told Nixon about evidence before the Watergate grand jury. That became clear from the tapes, which showed Nixon passing the information on to his co-conspirators.

Alexander Haig and Fred Buzhardt, we learn from Doyle, played a curious role in the case of Spiro Agnew. They put heavy pressure on Attorney General Elliot Richardson to drop his demand that the Vice President acknowledge his crimes as part of his plea bargain. Haig and Buzhardt also misled Senator John Stennis into thinking that the role he accepted in the proposed tapes compromise was to verify summaries for the Senate Watergate committee only, not the special prosecutor.

Haig asked Solicitor General Robert Bork to become Nixon's chief Watergate lawyer—hinting crudely that the reward would be a seat on the Supreme Court. (Bork said he would have to hear the tapes. Haig said no, and so did Bork.) Haig repeatedly told Attorney General Richardson to control Cox, and later he himself put pressure on Leon Jaworski. On February 1, 1974, after Jaworski had warned him of the criminality shown on the tapes, Haig told him: "If Nixon falls, Brezhnev will fall shortly afterwards and the entire world will become unstable." Before transcripts of the tapes were published, Haig showed Senator Hugh Scott, the Republican leader, summaries so laundered that poor Scott told the world they showed Nixon to be innocent. On June 4, 1973, before he knew that the actual record would come out, Haig counseled Nixon on how to deal with the terrible facts of March 21: "You just can't recall. It was in a meeting."

James St. Clair, the noted Boston lawyer who took over the Nixon defense, said repeatedly that he never listened to any tapes. But before the transcripts came out he stated publicly—and falsely—that tapes supplied to Jaworski contradicted John Dean and supported "what the President has said." St. Clair vouched for the accuracy of the tape transcripts issued by the White House, and he never withdrew that assurance when he learned—if he had not known before—that incriminating passages had been deleted.

The judges who dealt with Watergate were not all paragons. George L. Hart, Jr., chief judge of the Federal District Court in Washington in succession to John Sirica, gave pungent evidence of bias. He went easy in sentencing corporate offenders, and once he asked a lawyer from the special prosecutor's office when they were going to bring in some Democrats and unions. Richard Kleindienst, the Attorney General who lied to the Senate, was sentenced so lightly by Judge Hart—and praised at the same time—that some compared the scene to the award of a Congressional Medal of Honor.

The sentences passed on Watergate defendants, taken as a whole, were not uniform models of fairness. Of twenty-seven corporate executives convicted of illegal contributions in the 1972 campaign, none went to jail—not even George M. Steinbrenner III, of the American Ship Building Co. and the New York Yankees, who badgered his employees to lie to the FBI about his misdeeds. Petty men at the bottom of the pyramid drew harsher sentences than more powerful and more responsible malefactors above. And of course the man at the top was pardoned.

How to deal with Richard Nixon after he resigned was the last great question to face—and divide—the special prosecutor's office. The staff felt that as a matter of equal justice he should be prosecuted, as his underlings were. Leon Jaworski inclined otherwise, because of doubts about the possibility of a fair trial and general reluctance to proceed criminally against a fallen President. Jaworski met alone with Alexander Haig on August 8, the day before Nixon resigned. Jaworski has said that no promises were asked or given, but doubts remain about what might have been implied if unsaid. Jaworski may well have let slip his distaste for the idea of prosecution—enough to let Haig believe that there would be time for a pardon to be worked out before any decision to prosecute.

Important factual questions were left unanswered by the special prosecutors—not because they were part of a cover-up themselves, as some fanciful radical critics have suggested, but because investigations could not find sure answers. There was never enough evidence to prosecute anyone for the cooking of the White House tape transcripts; the original typescripts had been destroyed, and no one would say who gave the orders for the deletions. The prosecutors could not prove who made the famous eighteen-minute erasure in the tape of June 20, 1972. One is left with the suggestive question that John Dean asked one of the lawyers: "Who in the White House had the most to gain? And who has two left hands? Who hasn't driven a car in years? Who has trouble taking the top off his fountain pen?"

Then there was the puzzle of Bebe Rebozo and his money, including two $50,000 packages of $100 bills he got from Howard Hughes—and returned, he said. On a tape of April 17, 1973, Nixon said there was a way he could get two or three hundred thousand dollars with "no strain. . . . I told B-B-Bebe, uh, basically, be sure that people like, uh, who have contributed money over the contributing years are, uh, favored, and so forth in general. And he's used it for the purpose of getting things out, paid for in check and all that sort of thing."

That was never explained. Much never was. But a great deal was explained, and was changed—more than this country had any reason to expect. The reason was the Watergate Special Prosecution Force.

"The President is not above the law. Nor does he contend that he is."
  —James D. St. Clair, to the United States Supreme Court, July 8, 1974

CAST OF CHARACTERS

PHILIP J. BAKES, JR.— Assistant prosecutor, the Plumbers task force.

JOHN F. BARKER— Deputy spokesman, Watergate Special Prosecution Force.

RICHARD H. BEN-VENISTE— Number two lawyer, cover-up task force.

WILLIAM O. BITTMAN— Howard Hunt's criminal lawyer.

ROBERT BORK— Solicitor general who dismissed Archibald Cox.

CHARLES R. BREYER— Number two lawyer, Plumbers task force.

STEPHEN G. BREYER— Harvard law professor, associate prosecutor.

ALEXANDER P. BUTTERFIELD— White House aide, first custodian of the tapes.

J. FRED BUZHARDT— Special White House counsel for Watergate.

DONALD E. CAMPBELL— Assistant U.S. Attorney; one of three original prosecutors.

FLORENCE L. CAMPBELL— The special prosecutor's secretary.

DWIGHT L. CHAPIN— White House aide; guilty, making false statements to a grand jury. Ten to thirty months. Served six months.

CHARLES W. COLSON— Counsel to the President. Guilty, obstruction of justice. One to three years. Served seven months.

JOHN B. CONNALLY— Treasury Secretary. Indicted on two counts, accepting an illegal payment. Found not guilty by jury.

JOSEPH J. CONNOLLY—	Head of the ITT prosecution task force.
ARCHIBALD COX—	Special prosecutor, May 25 to October 20, 1973.
RICHARD G. DARMAN—	Personal aide to Elliot Richardson.
RICHARD J. DAVIS—	Head of the "dirty tricks" and later the ITT prosecution task forces.
JOHN W. DEAN III—	Counsel to the President. Guilty, conspiracy to obstruct justice. One to four years. Served four months.
JOHN DOAR—	Counsel, House Judiciary Committee Impeachment Inquiry.
JAMES S. DOYLE—	Spokesman, Watergate Special Prosecution Force.
JOHN D. EHRLICH-MAN—	Assistant to President Nixon for domestic affairs. Guilty, conspiracy to obstruct justice, obstruction of justice, making false statements to a grand jury, conspiracy to violate the civil rights of Dr. Lewis Fielding, making false statements to the FBI. Two and a half to eight years. Began serving October, 1976.
SENATOR SAM ERVIN—	Chairman of the Senate Watergate committee.
CARL B. FELDBAUM—	Assistant to deputy prosecutor Henry Ruth.
GEORGE T. FRAMPTON, JR.—	Assistant prosecutor, cover-up case.
LEONARD GARMENT—	Counsel to the President.
SEYMOUR GLANZER—	Assistant U.S. Attorney. One of three original Watergate prosecutors.
GERALD GOLDMAN—	Assistant prosecutor, cover-up case.
L. PATRICK GRAY III—	Acting Director, FBI.
ROBERT P. GRIFFIN—	Senate minority leader, President Ford's confidant.
GEN. ALEXANDER M. HAIG, JR.—	White House chief of staff.
H. R. (BOB) HALDE-MAN—	White House chief of staff. Guilty, conspiracy to obstruct justice, obstruction of justice, perjury. Two and a half to eight years. Appeal pending.

GEORGE L. HART, JR.— Chief Judge, U.S. District Court for the District of Columbia.

GEORGE A. HEARING— Florida accountant. Guilty, fabricating and distributing illegal campaign literature for Donald Segretti. One year. Served ten months.

PHILIP B. HEYMANN— Harvard law professor, associate prosecutor.

E. HOWARD HUNT— White House aide. Guilty, conspiracy, burglary and wiretapping. Thirty months to eight years. Served thirty months.

JAKE JACOBSEN— Dairy industry lawyer. Pleaded guilty to making an illegal payment to Treasury Secretary John Connally. A jury found Connally not guilty of receiving the payment.

LEON JAWORSKI— Special prosecutor, November 5, 1973, to October 25, 1974.

THOMAS V. JONES— Chairman, Northrop Corp. Guilty, willfully aiding and abetting a government contractor to make illegal campaign contributions. Fined $5,000.

HERBERT W. KALMBACH— President Nixon's attorney. Guilty, promising federal employment as a reward for political activity, violation of Corrupt Practices Act. Six to eighteen months. Fined $10,000. Served seven months.

RICHARD G. KLEINDIENST— Attorney General. Guilty, refusal to answer pertinent questions before a Senate committee. Thirty days and $100 fine, both sentences suspended.

JOHN G. KOELTL— Assistant prosecutor, campaign finance task force.

PETER M. KREINDLER— Legal assistant to Cox and Jaworski, then counsel to Ruth.

EGIL KROGH, JR.— White House aide. Guilty, conspiracy to violate the civil rights of Dr. Lewis Fielding. Two to six years, all but six months suspended. Served four and a half months.

PHILIP A. LACOVARA— Counsel to the special prosecutor.

FRED C. LARUE— Aide to John Mitchell. Guilty, conspiracy to obstruct justice. One to three years. Served four and a half months.

G. GORDON LIDDY— White House and campaign aide. Guilty, conspiracy, burglary, and wiretapping; refusal to testify before Congress; conspiracy to violate the civil rights of Dr. Lewis Fielding. Seven to twenty years, six months (suspended), and one to three years concurrent. Presently in prison.

THOMAS F. McBRIDE— Head of the campaign finance prosecution task force.

JEB S. MAGRUDER— White House and campaign aide. Guilty, conspiracy to wiretap, conspiracy to obstruct justice. Ten months to four years. Served seven months.

ROBERT MARDIAN— Assistant to John Mitchell. Charged with conspiracy to obstruct justice. Conviction reversed and new trial ordered. Charges dropped.

WILLIAM H. MERRILL— Head of the Plumbers prosecution task force.

HERBERT J. (JACK) MILLER, JR.— Attorney for Spater, Kleindienst, Bittman, and finally citizen Richard M. Nixon.

JOHN N. MITCHELL— Attorney General. Guilty, conspiracy to obstruct justice, obstruction of justice, perjury, making false statements to FBI. Two and a half to eight years. Appeal pending.

JONATHAN MOORE— Personal aide to Elliot Richardson.

JAMES F. NEAL— Head of the Watergate cover-up prosecution task force.

RICHARD M. NIXON— President. Unindicted co-conspirator, conspiracy to obstruct justice. Resigned August 9, 1974. Pardoned by his appointed successor, Gerald R. Ford, September 8, 1974.

KENNETH W. PARKINSON— Attorney, Committee to Re-elect the President. Found not guilty by jury in Watergate cover-up case.

MARK B. PEABODY— Special prosecutor Ruth's driver.

HENRY E. PETERSEN—   Assistant attorney general who supervised first Watergate investigation.

HOWARD E. REINECKE—   Lieutenant governor, California. Convicted of perjury before Senate. Conviction reversed on appeal.

ELLIOT L. RICHARDSON—   Attorney General, May 25 to October 20, 1973.

PETER F. RIENT—   Assistant prosecutor, cover-up task force.

DANIEL N. ROSENBLATT—   Special Prosecutor Jaworski's driver, then a spokesman for the Watergate Special Prosecution Force.

WILLIAM D. RUCKELSHAUS—   Deputy attorney general.

CHARLES F. RUFF—   Number two man, campaign finances prosecution task force; special prosecutor, October 11, 1975, to present.

HENRY S. RUTH, JR.—   Deputy special prosecutor; special prosecutor, October 26, 1974, to October 10, 1975.

JAMES D. ST. CLAIR—   President Nixon's criminal lawyer during the last seven months of his Presidency.

DONALD H. SEGRETTI—   Attorney. Guilty, conspiracy, distribution of illegal campaign literature. Six months. Served four and a half months.

EARL J. SILBERT—   Assistant U.S. Attorney, headed the original Watergate prosecution team.

JOHN J. SIRICA—   Chief Judge, U.S. District Court for the District of Columbia.

J. T. SMITH—   Personal aide to Elliot Richardson.

GEORGE A. SPATER—   President, American Airlines, the first company to plead guilty to an illegal Nixon campaign contribution.

MAURICE H. STANS—   Nixon campaign finance chairman. Guilty, violations of financial reporting requirements and acceptance of illegal contributions. Fined $5,000.

GEORGE M. STEINBRENNER III—   Chairman, American Ship Building Co. Guilty, conspiracy to violate the campaign finance law;

	being an accessory after the fact to an illegal campaign contribution. Fined $15,000.
GORDON C. STRACHAN—	White House aide. Indicted in cover-up case, then severed from other defendants. Charges dismissed by special prosecutor.
JILL WINE VOLNER—	Assistant prosecutor, cover-up task force.
JAMES VORENBERG—	Harvard law professor. Cox's executive officer during start-up of Watergate Special Prosecution Force.
ROGER M. WITTEN—	Assistant prosecutor, campaign finance task force.
CHARLES ALAN WRIGHT—	The President's constitutional lawyer in the first tapes case.
DAVID YOUNG—	White House Plumber, granted immunity for testimony and documents incriminating Ehrlichman.

PROLOGUE:
NIXON JUSTICE

The traditions of Anglo-Saxon history have it that neither king nor president can stand above the law. Until Richard Nixon that tradition was more folklore than fact. Before Richard Nixon no American President ever delivered himself into the hands of an executioner as powerful and as efficient as the Watergate special prosecutors.

It seemed unlikely to happen on that Saturday in June, 1972, when five burglars were caught inside national Democratic headquarters at the outset of a campaign in which the incumbent President seemed assured of reelection. However shaky their commitment to the law of the land, Richard Nixon and his aides were not fools, everyone thought. As the trail of Republican campaign money led to the burglary, as the connections to the Nixon White House became known, there were a few calls from Democrats for the appointment of an independent prosecutor. But even the Democrats seemed not to accept the implications of the unfolding evidence, or to believe that much could be done about it. "It's just politics," the Nixon people said. "They all do it." Much of the country accepted this view.

In his 1968 campaign Nixon had talked a great deal about lawlessness, exploiting a theme that had existed in American politics since the nineteenth century, when the great migrations turned the nation's cities into breeding grounds for violent crime. With calculated shrillness he blamed street crime and the breakdown of authority on Ramsey Clark, the incumbent attorney general; on softheaded administrators and fainthearted judges; on mincing civil libertarians who worried too much about technical due process and too little about locking up criminals and throwing away the key.

One day in 1968, as a political reporter with the *Boston Globe,* I watched with distaste and fear as Nixon whistlestopped across Ohio, pausing in each city and many towns, raising the bloody specter of violent crime, of cities gone mad with rapists, of judges and prosecutors too unmanly to care.

In the town of Deshler a few of us were interviewing the police chief as Nixon spoke from the rear platform of the train. In the forty-five minutes it had taken him to get there from Lima, he was saying, there had been so many rapes—he gave the exact numbers—so many murders, so many crimes of violence. When he was elected, he would see that there would be a new attorney general in the Justice Department, and the forces of law and order would once more be strengthened against the forces of crime and disorder.

The police chief was telling us that he knew of no rape or violent crime ever committed in Deshler in his lifetime. The biggest problem Deshler had, he thought, was the migration of its young to the cities for jobs. A little girl held up a sign: "Bring Us Together." And on election night the most divisive President of our time remembered the little girl's sign in Deshler and promised to heed it.

Nixon's vague rhetoric had raised high the country's expectations, but in office his law enforcers were just as confused by the crime rate, the chaotic court and prison systems, the political violence.

His campaign rhetoric had been that of the privileged, and the administration of his Justice Department would be for the privileged. He did indeed replace Ramsey Clark—with the bond attorney who had been his campaign manager. John Mitchell and his new assistants would politicize Nixon's Justice Department, so that the head of an airline or an oil company or a multinational corporation would have no doubt who was in charge of the really important law enforcement questions, those in the areas of commerce.

By the time Commerce Secretary Maurice Stans began raising an unprecedented sixty million dollars in "contributions" from American businessmen for the reelection campaign, the Justice Department had done very little for the people of Lima or Deshler, Ohio, but somewhat more for ITT, for Jimmy Hoffa, for the never-indicted president of a Texas bank who happened to be an old friend of the head of the criminal division. His bank had failed because, according to the Securities and Exchange Commission, he led a scheme to illegally manipulate the price of unregistered stock. When indictments came, the bank president was allowed to testify against his co-conspirators under a grant of immunity.

That was something a bond attorney could understand. Under John N. Mitchell there were to be congressional investigations, resignations in protest, and a decided smell of lawlessness about the Nixon Justice Department that would leave it with little moral authority when Watergate took hold.

The deputy attorney general, Richard G. Kleindienst, ran the department, and one of his early directives illustrated his mentality. He ordered all attorneys to fill out daily records describing their work for each quarter-hour segment of the day and listing each of their telephone calls.

The telephone record would discourage attorneys from talking to the press or to critics of the department. The quarter-hour diary is a device used in law firms as a billing technique. In some firms the junior lawyer who is able to bill the most hours to clients each week is the one who shows promise; an average of sixty hours a week is considered quite acceptable.

This ordering of one's life around institutional greed was exactly the thing that had driven many of the department's lawyers out of private practice and into government. It made no sense to set up such a system at Justice, except to make the paper shuffler king. After a brief time the quarter-hour logs were quietly dropped.

It turned out that Kleindienst's own reporting was not very good. In a 1971 bribery-conspiracy trial in New York he testified that he hadn't reported an offer from Robert T. Carson, a Republican aide on Capitol Hill, of a fifty-thousand-dollar "contribution" to Nixon's campaign in return for Kleindienst's intercession in a stock fraud case. Kleindienst hadn't considered it a bribe offer until he discovered that the FBI had had Carson under electronic surveillance at the time.

Kleindienst talked tough. His private language was spicy; he occasionally acted boorish with departmental secretaries; he leveled broadsides at his predecessors. But he and Mitchell left the department rudderless. Each division operated on the strength of its career people, well or badly according to their talents. The White House intimidated division heads. If Kleindienst's daily logs had been kept, they would have shown numerous calls from John Ehrlichman and his assistants, reminding the division heads of White House "interest" in various cases. The pressure was not subtle.

The politization of Justice under Nixon was well known in Washington and suspected across the nation. It had no effect on his electability. He traveled to Peking and Moscow. His henchmen disrupted the Democratic primaries. Henry Kissinger said peace was at hand on the eve of the election. Nixon was returned to office in an unprecedented landslide, albeit a lonely one. Republicans lost at the courthouse and the statehouse, in the Senate and the House. Nixon carried every state but one.

In January, 1973, the four Cuban-Americans and E. Howard Hunt pleaded guilty to the Watergate burglary without implicating anyone else. The lawyer for the Cubans withdrew from the case to protest his clients' guilty plea. The trial went on anyway, with G. Gordon Liddy and James McCord as defendants.

On January 20 Richard M. Nixon was sworn in for a second term. The trial recessed for the day, and the sequestered jury watched the inaugural parade on television.

The trial would continue for ten more days. On January 28 *Los Angeles Times* reporter Robert L. Jackson caught its mood in this dispatch:

A clubby atmosphere has prevailed in federal court during the three weeks it has taken government prosecutors to present their case in the Watergate bugging trial.

The questioning of Republican officials and others has been more polite than penetrating. Entire areas have been left unprobed.

In corridor discussions, prosecutor Earl J. Silbert has been asked repeatedly by newsmen why he has not posed additional questions to witnesses or called higher Republican officials to the stand.

Silbert's contention is that the government is submitting only evidence that is necessary to prove charges in its indictment of the original seven defendants last September.

There is no evidence of a wider conspiracy, he has told reporters. Additional testimony could be immaterial and irrelevant, he has said.

Not only have the prosecution's questions been limited but the defense attorneys at times have even waived their opportunity to cross-examine officials of President Nixon's campaign.

That same weekend, with the terms of the peace settlement in Vietnam made public, George Gallup polled the American people. He found Richard Nixon's favorable rating at 68 percent, the highest since 1969.

During the trial the Congress had returned to Washington. Senate Majority Leader Mike Mansfield of Montana met with Senator Sam Ervin of North Carolina, who agreed to head a special investigating committee on the 1972 campaign. It would concentrate on the Watergate incident.

On January 30, after deliberating for ninety minutes, the jury found McCord and Liddy guilty on all counts of illegal wiretapping, illegally planting eavesdropping devices, and stealing documents. Sentencing was scheduled for March. A few days later Judge Sirica told reporters he was not satisfied that the full Watergate story had been disclosed. He expressed the hope that the Senate Watergate committee would be granted power to get to the bottom of the case.

On February 7 the Senate voted unanimously to appoint four Democrats and three Republicans to investigate the case. The seven members were quickly appointed and began gathering a large staff.

All of this was prelude. The events that led quickly to the establishment of a Watergate special prosecutor began on the morning of March 20, when James McCord walked into Judge Sirica's chambers holding an envelope in his hand.

As witnesses recalled it, the two men barely spoke, hardly met each other's eyes. McCord, the bland, middle-class businessman who seemed to wear a trace of a smile on his face through much of the trial; "Maximum John" Sirica, the dark-browed, short, muscular old man who had scowled throughout the trial. McCord wanted to see the judge. If Sirica met alone with one of the convicted defendants, the appellate court might find the meeting improper. What was in the envelope?

Early in the case McCord, a former CIA man, had telephoned the Chilean Embassy, knowing that his call would be recorded by U.S. intelligence agents. Then his lawyers moved to have the Watergate charges against him dismissed, charging that the government had overheard McCord on an illegal wiretap. The government attested that no evidence in the case came from such activity and told the judge of McCord's call. Was McCord trying once again to get charges against him dismissed on a technicality?

Sirica sent McCord to the floor below to his probation officer. Then he summoned the probation officer, two law clerks, a bailiff and a court reporter. He had the probation officer unseal McCord's envelope and read its contents, which the court reporter took down.

In the hope of gaining leniency at sentencing, McCord was surrendering. He confirmed the judge's suspicions. There had been "political pressure" on the defendants to plead guilty and remain silent; witnesses had perjured themselves; higher-ups had been protected by this perjury. There were no specifics. McCord asked for a private session with the judge after sentencing. This was necessary, he said, because he knew he could not trust the FBI or the prosecutors.

Three days later John Sirica sat expressionless at his bench while spectators filled every seat in the courtroom. It was sentencing day. He announced that he wished to read a letter from one of the defendants, then dropped his eyes to the paper before him. A pain built in his chest as he read the words. By the time he finished, the pain was sharp and intense.

He announced a twenty-minute recess and the courtroom exploded with reporters rushing toward the swinging doors. Sirica went to his chambers and lay down. Later his doctor would examine him and tell him he was a victim of fatigue, anxiety, and indigestion.

He returned to the bench fifteen minutes later, and by then the Watergate cover-up had begun to unravel. Nixon and his men had been busy. They thought Howard Hunt was the threat and they had been paying his blackmail demands. Now, as McCord's letter rattled across the teletype machines of Washington, there was panic. Dean tried to reach Ehrlichman and could not. Magruder tried to reach Dean and could not. Tape recorders were brought from desks and attached to telephones. Memos disappeared from files. Defense lawyers got calls.

Within a week two liberal Republican senators, Charles Mathias of Maryland and Robert Packwood of Oregon, called for the appointment of a special prosecutor. The idea seemed more interesting than it had when Lawrence O'Brien, the Democratic chairman, and George McGovern, the Democratic standard-bearer, broached it the previous summer.

Two weeks later the senior New Jersey Republican, Clifford Case, spoke before the prestigious New York City Bar Association, his subject the creation of a Watergate special prosecutor. The Illinois Republican senator, Charles Percy, proposed it on the American Broadcasting Company's Sunday show, *Issues and Answers*.

By this time Dean and Magruder were talking to the prosecutors, who had been so insistent with the press that no higher-ups were involved. The prosecutors were now arguing among themselves. On April 15 the prosecutors went to the attorney general, Richard Kleindienst, to tell him what they were learning about the Watergate cover-up. Kleindienst went to see the President.

There were days of furious activity as the Nixon men sought to recoup. The press and the public wondered but knew little. On April 19 the White House counsel, John Dean, issued an unusual statement. He announced that he had no intention of becoming a scapegoat.

On Saturday, April 28, Defense Secretary Elliot L. Richardson was in McLean, Virginia, at the Madeira School visiting his daughter. Secretary of State William P. Rogers telephoned. Haldeman, Ehrlichman, Kleindienst and Dean are about to be fired, Rogers said. The President wants you to become attorney general.

On Sunday Richardson took a helicopter from the Pentagon to the upper reaches of the Catoctin Mountains in Maryland, to Camp David. It was a beautiful spring day. He met with Richard Nixon on the terrace of Aspen Lodge. The President was strained but "impressive." Richardson made notes afterwards. Richardson was instructed to pursue the investigation wherever it might lead, "even to the Presidency."

Nixon mentioned the idea of a special prosecutor. He would leave it to Richardson. He mentioned three possible names. One was a retired appeals court judge from New York, Joseph Edward Lumbard. Another was John J. McCloy, the lawyer at the pinnacle of the Establishment. He was seventy-eight years old. The third was Willmot Hastings, a bright young Boston lawyer. Hastings had been a loyal and discreet lieutenant of Richardson's throughout the latter's political career.

Richardson would remember a moment of intensity just before his meeting on the terrace ended. Richard Nixon leaned forward and said, "I had no knowledge of any of this. . . . You must believe that or you can't take this job."

1

ARCHIBALD COX

"I thought it would be fun."

On April 30, 1973, President Richard Nixon announced the resignation of aides John Dean, John Ehrlichman, and H. R. Haldeman and of Attorney General Richard G. Kleindienst, all of whom had been swept into the tides of the Watergate scandal. He appointed Elliot Lee Richardson Attorney General. "If he should consider it appropriate," Nixon said, "he [Richardson] has the authority to name a special supervising prosecutor for matters arising out of the case."

What the President had in mind was something less than an independent special prosecutor. He had first raised the idea with H. R. Haldeman on April 15 after they got the bad news from Kleindienst. Haldeman had been alarmed at the prospect, but Nixon reassured him.

"This is not to prosecute the case," said Nixon's voice on the White House tapes. "A special prosecutor to look at the indictments, to see that the indictments run to everybody they need to run to. So that it isn't just the President's men, you see."

Haldeman was beginning to understand. "In other words," he said, "he is above Silbert rather than replacing Silbert?"

"Oh no. Silbert runs the case and that's all," Nixon said. "But he is just there for the purpose of examining all this to see that the indictments cover everybody."

Haldeman understood. "Uh huh," he said. "Well, that does protect you a lot. Because if they don't indict some of us, then you have a cover-up problem. If you have that guy, then you have a basis . . ."

Nixon interrupted. "Then he goes out and says, 'I have examined all of this, and now, let's stop all this. These men are not guilty, and these men are not indictable, and these are.' "

Elliot Richardson knew nothing of this conversation. He knew only that after three brief months as secretary of defense his President had called upon him for another crucial assignment. He was reluctant to leave the Defense Department so soon, but Nixon had cast him as the symbol of integrity needed to save the administration at a time of crisis.

By coincidence, or Nixon's intuition, Richardson's intentions for a special prosecutor dovetailed neatly with the President's. Richardson thought the new appointee should be an assistant attorney general answerable to him.

To the President, Richardson must have seemed the perfect choice for such a delicate role. He had proved his loyalty to Nixon time and time again in the past four years and had enjoyed any number of successes in the bureaucratic politics of an administration where he was essentially an outsider. Nixon knew that Richardson believed himself capable of becoming a great President if ever called to the task. Richardson's many admirers felt the same and believed the call must come soon if it was to come at all. Richard Nixon understood that. He knew what it had taken to become President. He read Elliot Richardson as a man of great and indiscriminate ambition, and at this time Nixon needed such men.

Elliot Richardson had come willingly—hungrily—to serve the Nixon administration in 1969. He had been working his way up the political ladder in Massachusetts, aiming for the governor's chair. His career in state politics had been spotty, his reputation divided between those who thought him brilliant and highly principled, and those who thought him brilliant and highly ambitious.

Richardson once said that successful men in Washington rely on "those random currents of air to get up, stay up, and get where they want to go."

This was often quoted to explain Richardson's political navigation. At age fifty-two he had held thirteen government posts in Washington and Boston, none for more than two and a half years. Everyone agreed this was a first-rate mind, committed to excellence. His critics complained of his soul. What was the commitment there? they asked.

In his first year in the administration Undersecretary of State Richardson endured the secret bombing of Cambodia without protest. When Cambodia was invaded in late April, 1970, the rumor coursed through political and academic circles in Massachusetts that Richardson would resign in protest. In fact there was never any indication of this, and it would not have been Richardson's style. But his classmates and political supporters wanted to believe that among the top administration officials Richardson would be the one sensitive to the legal and moral implications of Cambodia. When he didn't resign one of them wrote to him, "On the basis of the record to date you will be remembered as one more over-educated, morally constipated Boston Yank. . . ."

In June of 1970 he was promoted to the Cabinet as secretary of health, education, and welfare. He discovered that in important matters John Ehrlichman ran his department. Despite some embarrassments, including public repudiations by the White House on a busing plan, a comprehensive health maintenance program, and a welfare reform program, Richardson stayed on. Once he faced the White House press on the lawn at San Clemente to explain that he really had shared the President's reservations about busing and thus was not chagrined at his own busing plan's being scuttled. He was, he would explain, a team player who believed in loyalty to the President.

The post of secretary of defense had been his reward. Like Henry Kissinger, Richardson seemed content to make his own way, disregarding the moral atmosphere around him. There was never any indication that either man had reservations about the Nixon administration. One sought the Nobel Peace Prize, the other, whatever ride he could get on those "random currents of air" that just might lead to the Presidency.

Richardson spoke out when he was appointed attorney general. "A kind of sleaziness has infected the ways in which things have been done," he said, "and this has touched agencies that have been concerned with law and law enforcement almost inevitably."

Then he moved over to the great office that had been occupied by John

Mitchell and then Richard Kleindienst. The man who had been at the top of his class at Harvard Law School, who had clerked for the great judge Learned Hand, who had served with distinction as U.S. Attorney for Massachusetts, settled down to the task of returning excellence to the Justice Department.

He appeared before the Senate Judiciary Committee for what he thought would be a routine hearing on his nomination. Chairman James Eastland opened the proceedings.

"Did you ever hear of the Watergate affair?" Eastland began. "All right, now if you are attorney general, what are you going to do about it? What about a special prosecutor?"

Richardson had already begun canvasing the legal community for an experienced prosecutor who would be appointed an assistant attorney general and given a free hand. He was chagrined to discover that eight of the sixteen committee members found such an arrangement unacceptable. They wanted Richardson to disqualify himself completely from the Watergate case. They suggested guidelines for the prosecutor that would give him "final authority" over the case. Richardson objected.

"The attorney general must retain ultimate responsibility for all matters falling within the jurisdiction of his department," he told the committee.

They skirmished for a week, Richardson trying to turn away the hard questions with assurances that the problems were only semantic. The special prosecutor would have "full authority," he said, but not "ultimate authority."

It became clear that Richardson's nomination was in trouble. Sam Ervin, a student of history, himself immersed in the Watergate case, was a senior member of the Judiciary Committee. He warned Richardson that his intransigence "might tempt Congress to follow the precedent it adopted in respect to the Teapot Dome matter."

In that single previous example of a successful special prosecutor the Department of Justice had been bypassed completely. Congress had forced Calvin Coolidge to name two independent prosecutors, Owen Roberts and Atlee Pomerene, with the advice and consent of the Senate.

Richardson told the committee he would not interfere with the Watergate prosecutions and would not fire the prosecutor unless his actions were "arbitrary, capricious, and unreasonable." Senator Birch Bayh of Indiana spent much of a day trying to get Richardson to define those terms.

Senator John Tunney of California suggested a clearer guideline: "The special prosecutors shall have charge and control of such litigation, anything in the statutes touching the powers of the attorney general or the Department of Justice to the contrary notwithstanding." Richardson was appalled at the suggestion, pointing out that it would make his appointment meaningless. Tunney noted that the wording was taken directly from the joint congressional resolution passed at the time of Teapot Dome.

During the second week of Richardson's confirmation hearings Senator Adlai Stevenson of Illinois introduced a resolution on the Senate floor which would have created a Teapot Dome-type special prosecutor. Senator Robert Byrd of the Judiciary Committee, one of its "swing" votes between the conservatives and the liberals, and one of the committee's more influential members, served notice that Richardson's attitude disturbed him greatly and that he was on the verge of leading a fight against the nomination and in favor of a new attorney general with no previous ties to the Nixon administration.

To save the situation Richardson had to do two things: acquiesce on guidelines that would render the special prosecutor independent; and find an appointee who would be applauded by Democrats and Republicans alike, and especially by the members of the Senate Judiciary Committee. Richardson began writing a set of guidelines and looking hard for a man to fill the bill.

Archibald Cox was at the University of California delivering the annual Thomas Jefferson Lectures on his favorite subject, the Warren Court. The audiences at the law school had been large and appreciative. But on his third morning in Berkeley, Wednesday, May 16, 1973, the day before his sixty-first birthday, Cox awakened to discover that he was totally deaf in one ear.

He didn't know what to think. Was he getting old? He was tall and robust and had worked hard every day of his adult life, mostly at the law. His life had been committed to the law—practicing it in court, teaching it in class, administering it in government posts, interpreting it as solicitor general of the United States. But even when he was relaxing in the garden or chopping wood or hiking, Archie Cox worked hard.

His staffs were always devoted to him although he pushed them mercilessly and worked even harder himself. His students at Harvard called him "arrogant," a word used to account for his combination of shyness and insistence on unmitigated excellence in scholarship. Cox was brilliant (and he knew it), but the real secret to his relentless success—in academia, in government, and as an arbitrator in labor disputes and student uprisings— was that Archibald Cox got up earlier and worked harder than his rivals. Newspaper biographies always repeated a line he uttered years before, "The central tragedy of life is that there are only twenty-four hours in the day."

When he received the telephone call from Elliot Richardson on that Wednesday morning, Cox was interested immediately. He wanted to become the Watergate special prosecutor. "I guess I knew there would be headaches, and heartaches as well, but I thought it would be fun," he would recall.

Attorney General-designate Elliot Richardson didn't actually offer Cox the job. He asked whether Cox might be available.

"I think you have to ask yourself whether I am qualified. I have no recent trial experience," Cox said.

Richardson had been trying for an experienced trial lawyer, one who would set aside a comfortable position and put his reputation on the line. Four men had turned him down.* By the second week of the search trial experience seemed less important. "I think what is more important now is that you will be acceptable to the legal community, and you have some very strong supporters on the Hill, on both sides of the aisle," Richardson said. "You can hire assistants who are trial men."

Cox had taught labor law to Richardson at Harvard a generation earlier. He was a Kennedy Democrat often rumored as a Supreme Court nominee during that administration, and as solicitor general he had gained a reputation as one of the best constitutional lawyers of his time. He was also known as a skilled negotiator.

As a young man during World War Two, Cox had served as counsel to Labor Secretary Frances Perkins and had since held a number of jobs in which his talents as an arbitrator were noted.

He headed the Wage Stabilization Board briefly under Truman, until

* Federal District Judge Harold Tyler of New York, former Deputy Attorney General Warren Christopher of Los Angeles, retired Appellate Court Judge David Peck of New York, Justice William H. Erickson of the Colorado Supreme Court.

Truman overruled a Cox wage settlement in the coal industry because of pressure on the President from John L. Lewis. Cox resigned in protest. He had served as the public member on any number of arbitration boards in the textile and railroad industries during the fifties and sixties. As Senator John F. Kennedy became more dominant in the Senate Labor Committee, Cox became his adviser and wrote most of the labor bills that enhanced Kennedy's reputation and effectiveness.

Then in the late sixties, after his time as solicitor general, Cox's reputation as a peacemaker spread into more visible fields. When the first major student rioting on the east coast broke out at Columbia University, Cox was called upon to head an investigation and seek a solution. The riots spread to Harvard a few years later and President Nathan Pusey's mishandling threatened disaster. Cox became the official who, for a two-year period, was the president of Harvard in all but name when it came to dealing with insurrections.

There had been a famous incident one night during that period when the Young Americans for Freedom were holding a pro-Vietnam War "teach-in" in the Sanders Theater and the Students for a Democratic Society drowned out the speakers. The "arrogant" Archibald Cox strode to the stage, tears in his eyes before he was through, and over the din spoke to the mob:

> Freedom of speech is indivisible. You cannot deny it to one man and save it for others. . . . History is filled with examples of the cruelty inflicted by men who set out to suppress ideas in the conviction of their own moral righteousness. . . . You seem to say, "We are scared to let others speak for fear the listeners will believe them and not us." Disruptive tactics, even by noise alone, start us on the road to more and more violence, because each group will come prepared the next time with greater numbers, ready to use a little more force until in the end, as in Hitler's Germany, all that counts is brute power.

Cox was hooted off the stage, but the moral force of his words had taken hold. At the campus demonstrations and the building occupations, as the man in the gray brush cut confronted the students, trying to ease tempers and find solutions, the chant would go up, "Cox, Cox, Cox, Cox," shouted as an epithet. Yet there was a quality of both respect for the man's courage and fear of his intellect. In the end he had won the day.

Richardson, who had been a distant friend of Cox's then, knew of his reputation as a distinguished lawyer, as a troubleshooter, and as an independent man. Some of those who had come to respect Cox during his Senate staff days—Philip Hart, Edward Kennedy, and Roman Hruska, for instance—were influential members of the Judiciary Committee. Cox's appointment was likely to diminish the growing resistance to Richardson.

So Richardson and Cox talked and negotiated on that Wednesday and the next day as well, Cox holding the telephone to his left ear, wondering why he could hear absolutely nothing through the other.

Richardson read the guidelines for something called the Watergate Special Prosecution Force, which would be under the attorney general but would have a great deal of latitude on all but the final decisions. The special prosecutor would be hired by the attorney general and could be fired by him, but the guidelines said this could only be done if the prosecutor was guilty of "extraordinary improprieties." Neither Richardson nor Cox spent much time on this provision. After all, Archie Cox had never been accused of an extraordinary impropriety in his entire life, and Elliot Richardson was not likely to fire his friend and fellow Boston Brahmin.

Cox did want certain things spelled out further. He knew that trouble would come if he had to lean on the White House. He thought there should be a sentence in the guidelines saying that the special prosecutor had full authority to investigate members of the White House staff and presidential appointees. Richardson wrote the sentence.

They talked about "executive privilege," a phrase that does not exist in the Constitution but which had become very important during the Nixon administration. Before he joined the Supreme Court, William Rehnquist had spent much of his time at the Justice Department expanding the frontiers of this doctrine, which allowed Presidents to withhold information from Congress and the courts.

Just a month before Richardson and Cox talked, Kleindienst had told a Senate hearing that Congress didn't have the power to compel anyone in the executive branch—all 2.5 million federal employees—to testify or produce documents if the President forbade it. Senator Edmund Muskie had raged at Kleindienst, called his assertion frightening, and said Nixon was exercising power like a monarch.

"If Congress feels he is exercising power like a monarch," Attorney General Richard Kleindienst said calmly, "you could conduct an impeachment proceeding."

Richardson did not believe that Nixon would try to hinder the Watergate investigation by hiding the evidence behind executive privilege. But to reassure the Senate he had already written into the special prosecutor's guidelines a sentence which said the appointee would have the authority to contest in court all claims of privilege by the Nixon administration. That was satisfactory to Cox.

There remained the central problem for the Senate, how to assure Cox's independence. Cox suggested that the problem could be solved by simply stating in the guidelines that it would be up to the special prosecutor to decide to what extent he would inform or consult with the attorney general before making a decision or bringing a prosecution. Richardson agreed to the addition.

Finally, Cox was worried about the conflict between his legal and political roles. Prosecutors are supposed to be very closemouthed and to do their talking in the secrecy of the grand jury. They aren't supposed to go public until they do so in a court of law with an indictment.

But Cox thought it would be important to keep public opinion mobilized on his side and that this would be difficult to do if he was secretive about the most notorious criminal conspiracy in American political history. The essence of the crime was cover-up, and it would be important to establish early with the press and public that Cox was not part of the cover-up.

He was far less confident than Richardson that the White House would cooperate with his investigation. If it did not, Cox would have a powerful weapon in public opinion. More than anything else it was public opinion that had forced the appointment of a special prosecutor, and it would be public opinion that would compel cooperation with him.

Cox suggested that Richardson add a paragraph to the guidelines specifically authorizing the special prosecutor to report to the public from time to time on the progress of his work and, when he was finished, to make a final report to Congress. Richardson added the paragraph.

After two days of telephone negotiations Richardson formally offered Cox the job. Cox said he needed to think about it overnight and talk to a few people. He also told Richardson that something seemed to be wrong with his hearing and he wanted to have it checked before he gave his answer.

Cox delivered the final Jefferson lecture at Berkeley early that evening and flew back to Boston. He drove from Logan Airport to the old farmhouse in Wayland where Phyllis Ames Cox, his wife, had been born. She was waiting. They talked until morning, both of them excited at the prospects, although Phyllis Cox has deep roots and takes to transplanting even less than her husband. The move to Washington was not appealing.

He would recall his feelings that day. "I thought, it's a no-win job. But somebody has to do it. Who better than a sixty-one-year-old with a secure chair at the Harvard Law School and no ambitions?" He doubted that the special prosecutor would ever be able to prove to the satisfaction of the country that Nixon was either innocent or guilty. The results were likely to be inconclusive. "Some would say I've sold out, that I should have found him guilty; others would say that if I wasn't prejudiced against him I would be satisfied he was innocent."

Shortly after 8 A.M. Cox was at Harvard talking to his close friend, Derek Bok, the new president of the university. Cox laid out all the obstacles, as he had for Phyllis.

"You're going to take it, Archie," Bok said. "So go ahead and take it."

With Bok's help, Cox tracked down the best ear specialist at the Massachusetts General Hospital and was in the doctor's office before eleven. The doctor told him he had a rare, virus-caused condition. Hearing in the affected ear could not be restored, but the chances of the disease occurring in the other ear were infinitesimal. Cox should have no difficulty functioning as special prosecutor.

At 3:30 P.M. that day, May 18, 1973, in Washington, Elliot Richardson announced his intention to appoint Archibald Cox as special prosecutor.

"Is he any relation to Tricia Nixon's husband?" a reporter asked. Richardson, annoyed, started to say no, of course not, and then caught himself. He flushed slightly. "I forgot to ask," he said.*

The President's men were angered and shaken to discover that Elliot Richardson had chosen as special prosecutor an intimate of John F. Kennedy, a man who wrote legislation for Kennedy in the Senate and speeches for him in the presidential campaign, and who was given a high-ranking legal appointment in the Kennedy administration.

There was of course nothing that Richard Nixon could do about it. He was not much in control of the government and spent these days trying to salvage what he could.

* Archibald Cox and Edward Finch Cox are not related.

The appointment seemed to mollify the Congress. Richardson went through two more days of extensive questioning, with Cox at his side, before the Senate Judiciary Committee approved the nomination. Cox's independence seemed assured.

Robert Byrd asked if Cox was ready to pursue his task no matter what federal officials might be involved.

"I can promise the committee that, sir," Cox responded.

Byrd pressed. "Even though that trail should lead, Heaven forbid, to the Oval Office of the White House itself?"

"Wherever that trail may lead," Cox said.

On Friday, May 25, Elliot Lee Richardson was sworn in as the seventy-second attorney general of the United States in the gilded formality of the White House East Room, with President Nixon and his Cabinet looking on. After Chief Justice Warren Burger administered the oath, Richardson told the gathering, "This is a time when the institutions of our government are under stress . . . not because their structure is not sound. If there are flaws they are in ourselves, and our task therefore must be one not of redesign but of renewal and reaffirmation, especially of the standards in which all of us believe."

Then President Nixon invited the two hundred guests into the State Dining Room for a brief reception. "The attorney general would be happy to see those of you who do not have any matters pending before the courts at the moment," the President said to laughter and applause.

Two hours later in the muted blue reception room of the solicitor general's office, Archibald Cox took his oath in a brief and informal ceremony. He was sworn in by the senior judge of the District of Columbia appeals court, Charles Fahy, whom Cox had served when Fahy was solicitor general under Franklin Roosevelt. "I asked to have the ceremony here because this office means a great deal both to me and Judge Fahy," Cox said. "It represents traditions of candor, honor, human sensitivity, dedication to justice, and unswerving rectitude, without, I hope, the taint of self-righteousness." These qualities, he said, would be needed in his present task.

Among the guests were two old friends of Archie and Phyllis Cox— Mrs. Ethel Kennedy, who sat on a couch beaming as the oath was sworn, and Senator Edward M. Kennedy, who stood in the rear of the room, having come in a little late. This friendship with Nixon's political opponents was seen as proof of Cox's independence.

On Saturday the Coxes were back in their farmhouse in Wayland, now accompanied by a United States marshal. Cox spent much of the weekend reading grand jury transcripts in his living room. The marshal sat across the room, refusing all invitations to read a book or watch television, just watching Cox read.

The following Monday, Memorial Day, I met Archibald Cox for the first time. The Society of Nieman Fellows was holding a reunion at Harvard, and a few of us convinced Cox to meet with us off the record. There were newsmen from *The New York Times,* the *Boston Globe,* the *Los Angeles Times,* the *Washington Post.* I was from the *Washington Star.* We waited for Cox in a faculty lounge in the deserted law school.

A tall, athletic-looking Yankee in a crew cut, bow tie, and suede Wallabees walked in and greeted us. He sat down on a couch and we drew chairs in a ring and listened.

Prosecutors are supposed to have the instincts of a shark; this one seemed more the dolphin. High-pitched voice. Very intelligent. Every time a question was asked he would look toward the ceiling, his eyes darting furiously, focusing on nothing in particular. "There are two considerations there," he would say. Then almost invariably he would add, "Perhaps three." Then he would tick them off.

The reporters asked about names and tactics. Cox talked about the conflicting legal principles that must be reconciled. They asked whether "national security" could be a proper defense for the commission of crimes by government officials. That was a complex question, Cox said, and would require a good deal of legal research and specific facts about the case in point before it could be answered. Cox was very friendly and articulate but he was cautious. He said nothing specific.

The only spark Cox showed was when he was asked about stories in the weekend newspapers that could only have come from the original Watergate prosecutors—Earl Silbert, Seymour Glanzer, and Don Campbell. Cox was outraged by the stories, which spoke of the theory under which the Watergate prosecutors were proceeding.

"When you see stories about the 'theory of the prosecution' you can discount them completely. I promise you they will not have come from me or my assistants," he said. Yet he refused to say whether Silbert's team would be kept on the case.

In the midst of the session Cox said, "This is a bit awesome. In a way, I'm being asked to play God."

Someone asked how long Cox thought the job would take. "Owen Roberts was at Teapot Dome for six years," he said. "It's impossible to guess how long this will take. I could envision it being over relatively quickly. On the other hand I could spend the rest of my working life at this."

I made a note that Cox was just sixty-one and looked as though his working life would be a long one.

Cox had asked two of his faculty colleagues to join him at Harvard that Memorial Day weekend. They would be going to Washington for the summer to help with the organization of the new office and recruitment of a staff. James Vorenberg was forty-five and wealthy, the heir to a Boston department store fortune. He had been active in criminal justice politics: first director of the Office of Criminal Justice under Robert Kennedy, executive director of President Johnson's famous Crime Commission, on the board of the Police Foundation, director of Harvard's Center for Criminal Justice.

In 1972 Vorenberg wrote position papers on crime for presidential candidate George McGovern. If McGovern had won, Vorenberg would not have turned down a high government post, preferably attorney general. He was tough and ambitious, and knew his way around the circuit of prosecutors and criminal justice administrators.

The second man was Philip B. Heymann, forty, bespectacled, friendly, with an unusual quality to his voice. It was by nature soft, but he seemed always to be projecting it loud and clear, as if he were constantly at oral argument. This was Heymann's way of compensating for Archibald Cox's new deafness.

Heymann had trained under Cox at Harvard Law and had worked for him in the solicitor general's office. Cox's own son, Archibald, Jr., had broken a long family tradition and had gone into finance rather than law. Phil Heymann, now a faculty colleague, was as close to Archibald Cox as a son.

Shortly after the Nieman Fellows left, another visitor from Washington arrived at the law school. Vorenberg had arranged for a briefing from a young man who had followed Watergate developments with interest from the beginning and had begun a Senate committee investigation that was never to get off the ground because of partisan considerations. His name was James Flug.

Flug was counsel to Edward Kennedy's administrative practices subcommittee, a bright, abrasive lawyer who had served in the Justice Department under Nicholas Katzenbach and been in the thick of every Senate Judiciary Committee fight since then, including the defeat of Nixon's two Supreme Court nominees, Clement Haynsworth and Harold Carswell.

He had done an impressive report on the ITT scandal of early 1972. When Gerald Ford succeeded in getting a House investigation of Watergate shut off, Flug began investigating for the Senate. He had collected a lot of information, but the idea of staff from a Kennedy subcommittee doing the inquiry was considered suspect and it never got off the ground.

Flug's theory was hardly a novel one in late May of 1973, but he made his argument persuasively. The Watergate break-in bore a relationship to the earlier break-in at the office of Dr. Lewis Fielding, Daniel Ellsberg's psychiatrist, which was committed by some of the same men. Both of these events were related to the financing of the Nixon political campaigns and the general flow of money around the Nixon White House. A series of seemingly discrete and disparate incidents all fell within the ring of White House and Nixon campaign committee activities, so that a man like Howard Hunt, who worked for the White House, had direct ties to the two burglaries and ties as well to Donald Segretti, the dirty trickster, who had ties to Herbert Kalmbach, Nixon's lawyer and bag man.

As Flug talked the three Harvard professors jotted down notes and tried to diagram events; Flug was describing interrelationships but he had not suggested a clear and definable pattern.

One could not really distinguish between the White House Plumbers and the Committee to Re-elect the President; between John Mitchell—who entertained Plumber Gordon Liddy's burglary–bugging–b-girl proposal of "intelligence operations" for the Nixon campaign—and Charles Colson and John Ehrlichman—who had employed Liddy and Hunt as White House agents at the time of the Fielding burglary. One could not be sure of the connections between Nixon lawyer and bag man Herbert Kalmbach, who bankrolled Segretti and was in touch with Hunt; and Maurice Stans, whose finance committee bankrolled the Watergate job; and H. R. Haldeman, who took $350,000 from his White House safe to pay Hunt the blackmail money for the cover-up.

One of the prosecutors who attended the session with Flug saved his notes, and they contained a tangle of lines that looked like a spider web, with the names of the various principals and the suspected criminal activities slicing back and forth like the lines on an organization chart—for an organization gone mad.

The next morning, Tuesday, May 29, the Watergate Special Prosecution Force began to assemble in Room 1111 of the Justice Department. It wasn't much of a force. The members were outnumbered by the reporters standing in the hallway outside.

The previous week Vorenberg and Heymann had been on the telephone recruiting a few good lawyers—known quantities who were completely trustworthy—to help get the show on the road. There was great suspicion about the handling of the case up until then. Cox was unsure of Silbert, Glanzer, and Campbell.

When Cox appeared before the Senate Judiciary Committee Charles Morgan confronted him during a break. Morgan was a lawyer for the American Civil Liberties Union who had taken on a private client, Spencer Oliver, the man whose phone at the Democratic National Committee had been tapped. Morgan wagged his finger in Cox's face and said, "As long as any of the present prosecuting staff continues in the investigation we will not consider it untainted."

Cox was not impressed with Morgan's approach. A few days later, while he was still waiting for the Judiciary Committee to act, Cox had his first meeting with the three prosecutors—and was even less impressed by them.

He had picked up the *Washington Post* that morning and read that the prosecutors were threatening to resign because Cox had not consulted them. The story quoted unnamed sources as saying that more indictments were ready to be handed down but that if Cox appointed a new staff there would be months of delay. Although he had not yet been sworn in, Cox called U.S. Attorney Harold Titus and asked him to bring the three prosecutors to Cox's temporary office that afternoon.

The meeting lasted two and a half hours. The demands of the three men were never stated as demands but they were clear. Unless Cox gave them a quick vote of confidence and announced publicly that they would remain in charge of the cover-up case, they planned to resign.

Cox told the three men he expected them to stay at their posts until relieved. To make sure that there would be no misunderstanding, he put it in writing:

"The public interest requires you as honorable and responsible public officials to carry on while I am familiarizing myself with all that has been done; and at that time we can see what is most appropriate for the future."

When the next day's *Post* carried a story saying the three men had been given Cox's vote of confidence, Cox made public his letter to them. His private response was to call Jim Neal in Nashville.

James F. Neal is a short, barrel-chested man who smokes large cigars, wears hand-tailored clothes, and doesn't like to lose, at tennis or at trial. Archie Cox first met him in the early sixties, when Neal was handling one of the more important cases in the Justice Department. James Neal was the man who in 1964 won a conviction of James Hoffa on charges of jury tampering and put the labor leader in jail. Afterward Hoffa presented Neal with an accolade that has followed him in all his press notices. Hoffa called Neal "the most vicious prosecutor who ever lived."

In the spring of 1973 Jim Neal was prospering in his own Nashville law firm, which represented a range of clients from singer Johnny Cash to local pinball dealers. As the chief trial man in a small firm, he was indispensable.

"Jim, I desperately need a trial man to get on top of this case," Cox said. Neal said it was impossible. Cox said he would like to start the FBI background check needed for Neal's appointment in any case; perhaps Neal could help him out of the immediate emergency. When the conversation was over, Neal had signed on for two weeks—which were to stretch out indefinitely.

Neal arrived at Room 1111 the first day and received simple instructions: Inform yourself completely about the Watergate case; ride herd on Silbert's team; make sure they don't do anything without the special prosecutor's knowledge.

Three other new lawyers showed up that day to scout the Cox operation and see if they wanted to join. One was Thomas F. McBride, forty-four, who was the number two man at the Police Foundation, a private organization that tries to get federal and foundation money to improve law enforcement. Tom McBride was a restless man who had had tours of duty in the New York City district attorney's office, the organized crime section of the Justice Department, the Peace Corps and the Law Enforcement Assistance Administration. McBride thought the criminal justice system was a roulette wheel. But he cared about it and kept trying.

Peter Rient, thirty-five, walked down the corridor from the criminal division to Room 1111 at the request of Jim Vorenberg. Unlike Neal and McBride, Rient was not a personal friend of Cox or the other Harvard professors. But he came highly recommended by everybody they talked with. He was a tall, dark man with a full beard. He was very quiet.

George Frampton, twenty-eight, a graduate of Yale and of Harvard Law School, had been clerking for Supreme Court Justice Harry Blackmun when his old professors sought him out. He was an activist who had worked for VISTA and the Center for Law and Social Policy, and had written speeches on criminal justice for Sargent Shriver in the 1972 vice presidential campaign. His academic record was first-rate.

Room 1111 was actually a suite. The lawyers milled about in the anteroom, using the one available desk, or the mantelpiece, or the coffee table for their papers. Their only files were the daily newspapers. Their schedules each day consisted of whatever emergency cropped up from minute to minute. Outside, the press gathered, wanting to know what was going on.

An inner office used by Cox was an island of calm in this sea of confusion. He was able to hold conferences, conduct interviews, and take telephone calls in relative peace. His office was normally used by the assistant attorney general in charge of administration, but that post was now vacant. Cox inherited the last man's secretary, a senior woman in the department named Florence Campbell, who had left her native Salem, Massachusetts, years before but retained a strong New England accent. Most visitors presumed that this efficient woman with the Boston accent had come down from Harvard with Cox, but in fact she was a veteran of the Justice Department who knew how to get things done, which smoothed Cox's way those first weeks.

((53))

In another office off the anteroom was Glenn E. Pommerening, the department's acting administrator. He was a handy resource for anyone trying to create an entire agency in a hurry.

Vorenberg sat in Pommerening's office that first week discussing the start-up task, surrounded by pictures of Nixon, Mitchell, and Kleindienst. "This is the first case I've worked where the potential defendants' personally autographed pictures are on the office walls," he said. Pommerening winced.

Cox and Vorenberg asked Henry Petersen, the head of the criminal division, to stop by Room 1111 for an interview on their first evening in the office. They arranged for a stenographer to be present.

Petersen was a short, rugged man who had started as an FBI file clerk. He had been a Marine sergeant in World War II, had returned to the department and put himself through night law school. In the department he was the blunt, tough-talking prosecutor who would show his disdain for politics and politicians. Yet he was good at departmental politics. He had become the first career man in the criminal division, the flagship division, to be given a presidential appointment as assistant attorney general. It was a politician's post, above the career bureaucracy that he had navigated so carefully for twenty-five years. It was said that Petersen revered the two men who had so honored him—John Mitchell and Richard Nixon. John Dean had announced Petersen's loyalty to Richard Nixon in the privacy of the Oval Office weeks earlier, and his assessment was recorded by the White House tapes.

Petersen had been responsible for the Watergate investigation from the first day. Silbert had reported to him almost daily, kept him informed, and followed his directions. The Nixon administration had used Petersen's career reputation as proof that the investigation was both thorough and impartial.

The meeting with Cox and Vorenberg was awkward. Cox began by suggesting that Petersen run down the case chronologically. He realized that there would be a great deal of information and evidence in the files that would not be worth summarizing. Perhaps Petersen could concentrate on the key developments. Cox added casually that he would be particularly interested in conferences Petersen might have had with the attorney general, the director of the FBI, or the President which might not have been fully described in the files.

Petersen answered questions for two hours. He would get ahead of his chronology or off on a detour, and Cox would quietly interrupt to slow him down or to get a point clear. Vorenberg's questions were sharper, more in the character of a cross-examination, and Petersen would often react to them.

At this point nobody outside of a few White House aides knew anything about the Nixon tapes. Since Petersen was an eyewitness to some Oval Office conversations, Cox was especially interested in those meetings. They started with April 15, the day that Petersen and Kleindienst discussed with the President what Silbert and his men had told them the night before. Petersen gave a very sketchy report on the meeting, revealing nothing.

Cox wondered why the session had taken two hours. Was Petersen reviewing the Dean and Magruder testimony with Nixon? No, Petersen answered, he had simply given a summary of the Magruder and Dean allegations. It was meager information at that point, and a few days later he had reduced it to writing and submitted a one-page memorandum to the President.

"What took you a couple of hours, Henry, at that first meeting?" Cox asked.

"I don't know. It's hard to say. It certainly wasn't all substance. On this thing, for two weeks I saw the President more, probably—I'm guessing—than most Cabinet officers see him."

Vorenberg asked for a copy of the one-page memorandum.

Petersen said, "I don't think it's material at this point to disclose in those explicit terms what passed between me and the President of the United States."

"Well, I guess I do," Vorenberg replied.

"Well, too bad," Petersen said. "That's all I can say. We disagree."

Vorenberg said he might make a formal request for the memo at some point, and Petersen replied, "You may make a formal request right now. Write it down, and I'll write back and say no. I don't know what the hell that gets us."

The memorandum was hardly material to any investigation, Petersen said. He would be happy to describe its contents. "I reduced it to writing for his [the President's] convenience, but I'll keep the writing unless it becomes material."

Cox was willing to drop the subject, adding, "I think when you read the guidelines you will see that I'm entitled to it."

Petersen defended his behavior, saying he was acting according to his personal responsibilities. Cox voiced his concern about the fact that Petersen would not show him the memo, then returned to the question of why the meeting with Nixon—about which Petersen was still being sketchy—had taken two hours. He asked for more details of what had transpired. Petersen recalled he had recommended that Nixon get the story firsthand by meeting with Dean. The President agreed to do so.

"Did you ever get a report from the President of what Dean told him?"

"That report is on tape, but I didn't want to hear it. The President said I could hear it if I wanted to, but I couldn't listen to that tape because we were dealing with Dean and his counsel."

Cox repeated this new fact as if he didn't believe what he had heard. "Do you mean Dean's conversation with the President is on tape?"

"So I've been told," Petersen said.

The President had once told Petersen he knew the prosecutors were offering Dean immunity—that Dean had told him that was the case. When Petersen denied that this was so, Nixon said, "It's on tape. You can hear it if you want to." Petersen had declined.

Vorenberg asked if Petersen had made notes of his talks with Nixon. He had not.

Petersen made an analogy between his relationship to the President and that between an attorney and his client, saying he did not feel free to reveal confidential conversations with Nixon "until such time as I reasonably believe that the President of the United States is in violation of the law. . . . I do think there are obligations of fundamental privilege that are involved there, and it seems to me that something further must arise in order to permit me to broach that privilege to any substantial degree."

"Well, this brings me back to the part that was puzzling me before," Cox said, "because every time you say that, I begin to wonder how complete your account is."

"Fine, I don't blame you," Petersen said. "Do whatever you choose. I mean how complete can the account be? You know I didn't record it."

Petersen insisted that he was giving a full account to the best of his recollection, and he did not mean to leave the impression that he was withholding some dramatic details. But he repeated his reservations about detailing the specifics of a presidential conversation which he felt was a privileged communication. Finally, he agreed to hand over the memorandum and submit to a second interview on specifics if the President had no objection. He did so a few weeks later. Nothing new came of it.

It is a violation of Rule 6(e) of the Federal Rules of Criminal Procedure for a prosecutor to disclose grand jury testimony outside of court. It is also a very unwise thing to do if you don't want to blow your case. Cox and Vorenberg were very interested in whether Henry Petersen had considered the President of the United States an exception and had shared grand jury information.

"I had a number of meetings with him which were, frankly, desultory, awkward," Petersen said. "He wanted reassurance. It's a terrible thing to say about the President of the United States but it was kind of, 'You believe me, don't you?' A lot of BS, to put it frankly. A lot of generality. We had agreed that I would not give him grand jury information, so that meant I was reduced to ultimate conclusions."

Petersen kept saying "frankly." However, when the White House tapes were published a year later, it turned out he wasn't as frank as he might have been.

"I couldn't turn and give him grand jury information," he told Cox. "We both agreed on that."

But on the White House tapes, there was Nixon getting Petersen to tell what was happening in the grand jury; to tell, for example, that Mitchell's aide, Fred LaRue, had broken down inside the grand jury room. There was Nixon reassuring Petersen that he knew the rules, and promising that he would not pass on the grand jury information. Then a few hours later Nixon would tell the whole story to Haldeman and Ehrlichman.

The tape of that April 15 meeting of Petersen, Kleindienst, and Nixon was never published. It was among the missing.

As Petersen talked with Cox and Vorenberg on this night in May, he was upset, defensive. By now it was clear that the man who had been his favorite attorney general, John Mitchell, was deeply implicated in the crimes Petersen's men had been investigating for a year. It was also clear that the President of the United States was not above suspicion. Petersen admitted to having suspicions about the President, saying he was a little ashamed of them.

Petersen said, "I told Elliot Richardson, I'm not very good at cross-examining Presidents."

"No," Cox said, "I doubt that any of us are."

2

COX'S ARMY

"The President will fight."

The task ahead of Archibald Cox was enormous. To accomplish it he would need a cadre of his own attorneys, men and women loyal to him and to the integrity of the investigation.

A few days after the Petersen meeting James Vorenberg sat down with Glenn Pommerening, the Justice Department administrator, and sketched out an organization of task forces to handle the known cases and whatever arose in the future. By guesswork he computed the number of lawyers needed for each task force, allowing for a range of experience and salary levels. Pommerening projected the cost for such a staff: $1.2 million a year. "Now add fifty percent to that," Vorenberg said. Pommerening winced. He wrote down $1.8 million, proposed budget for personnel. Vorenberg had him add another million dollars for offices, equipment, operating costs. Within a few weeks the Justice Department and then the Congress had approved the $2.8 million without objection.

Cox was to put together a staff of lawyers larger than all but six of the ninety-four United States Attorneys' offices across the country. This would be the greatest effort ever by the executive branch to investigate and prosecute a political scandal.

Pommerening sought suitable space for this fledgling organization in the warehouse of government buildings that is downtown Washington, D.C. Cox was not anxious to end up in the Justice Department main building or one of its many annexes, even if room could have been made for a staff of eighty or ninety persons. The trappings of independence were important to him.

By mid-June two floors of a temporarily empty private office building had been located a few blocks from the White House, at 1425 K Street. Cox told the security officer for the Justice Department, "I want it to be as secure as the inner reaches of the FBI."

The special prosecutor and his assistants pored over the facts already developed. The cases seemed to fall into several groups. The Watergate break-in and cover-up would take precedence, and Jim Neal had already begun to monitor the performance of Silbert, Glanzer, and Campbell. Cox cautioned Neal to be sure that Silbert made no decisions that were not cleared by the special prosecutor. Soon Cox would have in place his own lawyers to reinvestigate the case and proceed with an obstruction of justice prosecution. The only uncertainty was the extent of the conspirators' ring.

Then there were the Plumbers cases—the break-in at the offices of Daniel Ellsberg's psychiatrist, and an almost endless list of leads and rumors about other burglaries, telephone taps, and efforts to subvert government agencies from the Internal Revenue Service to the Central Intelligence Agency. Most of these leads pointed toward John Ehrlichman or Charles Colson, and the strange group that had gathered in the basement of the Executive Office Building, Room 16, where a blue Bakelite plaque on the door said simply, "Plumbers."

Next came the trail of money from the Watergate burglary, which had merged with a wider flow of transactions that led to the Nixon reelection effort. Tom McBride had already begun to examine the campaign finance laws and to assemble evidence of massive violations.

At Elliot Richardson's bidding, Cox took jurisdiction over the International Telephone and Telegraph Corporation investigation, which had been sitting moribund at the Justice Department for a year, ever since the highly suspect testimony of John Mitchell and Richard Kleindienst before the Senate Judiciary Committee in the spring of 1972.

Then there were the "dirty tricks," the disruptions of the 1972 Democratic primary campaigns, apparently masterminded by the White House and carried out by a small young man named Donald Segretti.

Any one of these investigations might have required the services of the best lawyers in a U.S. Attorney's office.

By the third week of June recruits were passing through the doors of 1425 K Street along with the IBM Selectrics, the Xerox machines, and the empty file cabinets.

Finding a quality typewriter is, unfortunately, easier than finding a quality lawyer. Cox needed about forty who would be trustworthy beyond question, wise beyond their years, and well disciplined.

The special prosecutor, Vorenberg, and Heymann had been working on the staffing problem from the day Cox was named, relying at first on people they knew personally. They wanted lawyers to start work immediately, long before the FBI could finish background checks on them. The best way to avoid embarrassing mistakes would be to have people known to be trustworthy. Cox had one confidant screen West Coast applicants and another examine the large pool of attorneys practicing in Manhattan. Vorenberg spent most of his time on the personnel problem, convincing lawyers to come, then convincing their employers to let them begin work immediately. Henry S. Ruth, Jr., an old acquaintance of Vorenberg who had been his deputy at the Crime Commission, called from New York to suggest some names. Could Ruth himself come? No, he said. He could not make his family suffer another move.

Vorenberg is a crafty bureaucrat who had staffed President Johnson's Crime Commission. He had a pretty good idea what was needed and how to reach into his and Cox's network of contacts to get bodies. He needed five lawyers with long trial experience to run the task forces, a dozen middle-rank men and women who had handled complicated investigations and had a record of successful prosecutions, and about twenty foot soldiers —lawyers recently out of law school, with brains and judgment, who would work the sixteen-hour days in the back rooms just for the experience.

Of course one doesn't hire a lawyer without endless negotiations. Good prosecutors are as rare as precious stones, and like jewels they look best under a spotlight. Every experienced prosecutor wanted to work on the Watergate case; that's where the spotlight would be.

Three of the five task force leaders were to come from private practice. Two—James Neal and Joseph Connolly—never moved their families to Washington. For more than a year they commuted from other cities.

The oldest task force leader was William Merrill, aged fifty, tall, graying, distinguished, with a soft voice and kind eyes. He had been a prosecutor in Detroit and was in private practice there, but anxious to make a change. He checked out the Cox operation with friends, then wrote a letter saying, "I have to be in Washington on business in a few days, and I will drop by."

William Merrill did not have to be in Washington on business. He was interested in Democratic politics. He had worked in Bobby Kennedy's presidential campaign. He had run for Congress, and lost, in 1966. Some day he wanted to run for the Senate or the Michigan governorship. Merrill wanted to work on the Watergate case. Vorenberg hired him on the spot. Merrill and Neal worked together for about three days on the Watergate case. Merrill did not have shark instincts. Neal, who was forty-three years old, kept referring to Merrill as "a nice boy," but he had reservations about working with him. Merrill decided that he wouldn't mind heading the Plumbers task force instead.

Tom McBride had once had shark instincts, as any number of grand jury witnesses will testify. In his forties, he was mellower, still endowed with moral outrage but no longer able to get mad at human targets. McBride was small, about five foot seven inches. He had a soft voice, a finely honed sense of humor, and a distinct gentleness. On Christmas Eve, Tom McBride would take the neighborhood kids caroling. He liked adventure, and every so often he would climb a mountain in South America or go skin diving in dangerous waters. Once when Washington got an unusually heavy snow, McBride skied down Massachusetts Avenue to the office.

The day Cox began operations in Room 1111, McBride showed up out of curiosity. After a few days he said, "I'll stay. I like Archie." The first task force director to sign on permanently, he took over the investigation of presidential campaign finances.

Richard Ben-Veniste was thirty years old and he too was small, perhaps not quite five foot seven. He had a sense of humor and was a pleasant man to talk to, but anybody who had ever seen him in the courtroom would tell you that he could have starred in *Jaws*. Vorenberg offered Ben-Veniste his own task force. Ben-Veniste said he wanted to work on the Watergate cover-up. He would take the number two position there, behind Neal, who might not be staying.

Jill Volner was also thirty years old, a striking woman. She could have been a lawyer on television, and ABC tried to hire her to do that later. She was a criminal trial lawyer in the Justice Department, specializing in labor cases. Many people were prepared to dislike her when they met her and to believe she got ahead because she was a pretty strawberry blonde. Jill Volner got ahead because she worked hard.

Philip Allen Lacovara was a very old twenty-nine, an intellectual cop. He was one of those people who finished everything—high school, college, exam papers, legal briefs—in half the time it took other people. He got married when he was a teen-aged college student, and by age twenty-seven he had seven children. His wife was very beautiful and looked like she was a senior in high school despite the seven kids. Lacovara had been a Goldwater supporter when he was in law school and later he became counsel to the New York Police Department. He had practiced law, taught at Columbia, then joined the Justice Department. He had become deputy solicitor general. Vorenberg knew about Lacovara because he had tried to hire him for the Harvard faculty. Archibald Cox looked at Lacovara's record and at some legal work he had done. He told Vorenberg to hire him.

Vorenberg offered Lacovara one of the task forces. No, Lacovara said, he should be counsel to the special prosecutor, which would give him a chance to work as the lawyer's lawyer on all the cases. Lacovara described this job as just below the deputy special prosecutor. "I am number two and a half in this office," he would tell visitors. Vorenberg agreed that this would be a splendid idea. Lacovara was also under five foot seven.

Richard J. Davis was twenty-seven and had worked in the U.S. Attorney's office for the Southern District of New York along with Ben-Veniste and several others whom Vorenberg would hire. Davis was quiet, methodical, cerebral, balding before his time. He was also under five foot seven. He became the head of the dirty tricks tasks force.

Joseph Connolly was thirty-two, the only lawyer in the office who had much experience with corporate law. He had been a staff man for Robert McNamara at the Pentagon, then a staff member at the Crime Commission, and later an assistant to Solicitor General Erwin Griswold. Connolly was a Republican, the son of a former member of the House of Representatives from Philadelphia's Main Line. That was an added recommendation, because the office needed as many Republicans as were willing to investigate Richard Nixon.

All of the task forces were plunging ahead, organizing investigations at the same time that they recruited lawyers and hauled witnesses before the grand jury. By the time the staff was assembled, some were beginning to wonder about the "Napoleon complex" theory of prosecution. Out of thirty-eight lawyers fifteen were below average in height. Charles Breyer, a talented prosecutor who was then with the district attorney's office in San Francisco, remembers being puzzled when he was telephoned by Bill Merrill and Phil Bakes of the Plumbers task force to see if he was interested in working with them. During the conversation Bakes asked, "How tall are you?" Breyer is five foot six. Bakes and Merrill are six-footers.

Finding a deputy for Cox was taking a lot of time. Cox had virtually promised the Senate that he would appoint a number two man who had considerable trial experience. Of course if Jim Neal stayed to try the big case, that would fit the bill. But Neal kept signing on for one more week at a time and worrying aloud about his slowly disintegrating law practice.

Vorenberg and Cox searched hard for an experienced prosecutor who was also a distinguished Republican. They were turned down by Whitney North Seymour, Jr., who had recently retired as U.S. Attorney for the Southern District of New York; by Roswell Perkins of New York, a private lawyer who had been an official in the Eisenhower administration; and by a Boston Republican who had made his name as an understudy to Joseph Welch during the Army-McCarthy hearings, James St. Clair. A fourth Republican, William Ruckelshaus, then serving as acting director of the FBI, was named deputy attorney general before Cox could get to him. And a fifth, John Doar, didn't seem to solve the problem. Cox was being criticized for hiring too many Kennedyites. Doar's connection to Robert Kennedy would probably loom larger than his Republicanism.

Hank Ruth, who had worked with Vorenberg on President Johnson's Crime Commission, agreed to come down and talk about the job. He and Cox met at a downtown restaurant, with Vorenberg acting as the marriage broker. It did not begin as a love affair on either side. Cox, the ramrod, with a high-pitched, clear voice and an athletic manner, could hardly hear this soft-spoken, intense, slack-shouldered man who seemed to be casually chain-smoking his way through life. Cox was looking for a trial man, and Ruth had not done any trial work for years, although he was an expert on criminal law and possessed a good deal of experience as an administrator. Cox tends to be all optimism and dogma in his conversation. Ruth, who has a penchant for irreverent one-liners, spices his idealism with a dose of cynicism. The two men shared one bond: Both thought the job was a loser, and both thought it had to be done.

Shortly after the restaurant meeting Ruth agreed to become deputy special prosecutor.

There was no problem in recruiting junior attorneys. It seemed as though every law review editor and Phi Beta Kappa within a thousand-mile radius of Washingtoin wanted to work on the Watergate case. By mid-June, new ones were arriving every day, straight kids with trimmed hair and serious faces. Many had studied at Harvard under Cox, Vorenberg, or Heymann, and had done well. A number had just finished a year's duty clerking for a federal judge.

Vorenberg would show them the top of the mountain, impress on them the importance of their work, and then send them to the "boiler room." A converted conference room at the far reaches of the offices, it was jammed with young lawyers who had been handed transcripts of Senate Watergate committee or grand jury hearings and told to summarize the testimony on index cards so it could be cross-referenced.

This was automaton work, but Jim Neal insisted upon it. Until all the facts in the case were mastered, he said, it would be impossible to make any headway. Later a group of paralegal researchers would take over this job and program the material so it could be computerized, but during June and July the work was a strictly manual operation that made necks sore and minds numb.

Vorenberg would ask the new lawyers to choose the task force they wanted to work on. Invariably they would hesitate in answering. Then he would suggest that they work in the boiler room for a short while until he could arrange to place them. About once a week there would be a rebellion in the boiler room and the young attorneys would request a meeting with Vorenberg. Those who had been imprisoned the longest would then be transferred to a task force, and the others would be promised that relief was on the way.

During this period the prosecutors were operating with a public information officer borrowed from a government agency. He was swamped with press requests and telephone calls, working long hours and six-day weeks with no staff. Vorenberg and Cox were also distracted by the press requests.

I was covering the Senate Watergate hearings for my newspaper, the *Washington Star*, when one day in mid-June an old friend, Ron Ostrow of the *Los Angeles Times*, sat down next to me at the press table. "Archie Cox is looking for a spokesman," he said. "They asked me about you. I told them you wouldn't be interested."

I looked at Ostrow sitting at the table next to me while a witness droned on. "Call them back and tell them I might be interested," I said.

That afternoon I visited Cox at his new quarters. It seemed a nondescript place until you stepped out of the elevator on the ninth floor. Across the expanse of government-issue gray carpet, all the doors were unmarked except for one at the end of the corridor that belonged to a private firm. There were two television cameras mounted on the ceiling surveying the corridor. A blue door across from the elevators contained a small sign with an arrow: "Push Bell."

A uniformed guard buzzed the door open, presented me with a card to fill out, and demanded positive identification. Then he gave me a red plastic tag on a chain to be worn around my neck. "Must Be Escorted," it said.

As I waited in the tiny entryway for an escort, I faced a huge L-shaped panel containing twenty-seven control switches—burglar alarms, ultrasonic movement alarms, and fire alarms monitoring every door, window, and exterior wall on the floor. There were two television monitors on the guard's desk, each equipped with suction cup sensors that detected motion on the screen. Every time the elevator door opened or anybody moved through the hallway, the sensors reacted.

For weeks we had been hearing about "bag jobs"—not just at the Democratic National Committee, but at Daniel Ellsberg's psychiatrist's office and the Chilean Embassy—as well as unexplained burglaries at reporters' homes. Cox wanted to make sure that if the Plumbers were alive and well and living in Washington, they would not pull a bag job at his offices.

Cox's office was unbelievably austere—government shabby. There was a big wooden desk, with its decaled serial number visible; Cox was in a tall chair behind it. There was a conference table with a half-dozen chairs. The white walls were bare. The room had six windows, and all had blinds drawn and drapes pulled: The Justice Department security man suggested this be done in all rooms where sensitive matters would be discussed or sensitive papers placed on desks. "With a thousand millimeter lens, someone could photograph these documents from a nearby rooftop," he said, and added that laser beam surveillance devices could transmit voices through closed windows.

Was it paranoia? Cox had asked Petersen during their interview whether he had been aware of any "bag jobs" relating to Daniel Ellsberg. "No sir, absolutely no," Petersen had answered. Then Petersen had given a little speech:

"You know, one of the things that eternally plagues us—I mean this has been going on in history since the flood. It is no secret that this government—whether you know about it explicitly or not—that so-called covert operations are carried out in connection with national security. You know, under all Presidents and under all administrations they've been going on. Now, you know, the great American public has blinders on with respect to it, but it happens. And there is no foreign office in the world, in my humble judgment, can run according to the Ten Commandments. It doesn't bother my mind at all that some Russian espionage agent is going to be the victim of a 'bag job,' so they say. It doesn't bother me a bit. I would like to think there is some discrimination, some discriminating judgment involved as to where in hell they are utilizing these techniques."

I was not sure it was a good idea to join this operation as the press man. In his two weeks in Washington, Cox had already gained a reputation. At one of his first news conferences he released a letter to Senator Sam Ervin, whose hearings were the first indication to the country that anyone in Washington cared about the Watergate cover-up. Cox wanted Ervin to call off the Watergate hearings.

He had a point. With nationally televised exposure it would be hard to empanel an impartial jury. Ervin planned to grant immunity to some of the guilty parties, like John Dean. This would get the facts out but make it difficult to prosecute those who testified against themselves under Senate grants of immunity. And all the other conspirators would be listening to the hearings. They could tailor their own versions when they appeared before the grand jury.

Unfortunately Cox had failed to mention any of these reservations about the hearings when he appeared before the Senate a few weeks earlier. Senator Ervin told the press, "Professor Cox's request is extraordinarily arrogant."

The press interpreted Cox's move against the Ervin Committee as illustrative of his two glaring weaknesses—personal arrogance and political naïveté. The columnists and commentators had a field day. A few saw more than just arrogance behind Cox's move. Martin Nolan of the *Boston Globe* wrote, " 'Pre-trial publicity' is to alibi artists among lawyers what 'national security' is to scoundrels among patriotic politicians."

"How do you think you're doing with the press?" I asked Cox.

"I made an unpopular decision that I think was right," he said. "In the end, when we go to trial, we'll be glad that we tried to head off all the publicity. But if I could have handled it better, then I'm concerned."

The next day I became the Special Assistant for Public Affairs for the Watergate Special Prosecution Force. I was more than qualified. I am five feet seven and one half inches tall.

In the summer of 1973 the press was running the Watergate show. Once James McCord's letter was published, exposure of the facts had been unrelenting. There was no longer any question that there had been at high levels of the government a conspiracy to obstruct justice. The *Washington Post* continued to lead the race, but every other news organization was now committed to the story; and that commitment increased the pressures, caused more of the Watergate dominoes to fall, and created a favorable climate for both the Senate Watergate committee and the Watergate Special Prosecution Force.

The Senate committee was the main event for reporters but they held a proprietary interest in Cox's operation as well. How they perceived Cox and his staff would decide the extent of public support we got, and I found that reporters and editors had mixed emotions about us.

They understood the need for secrecy if a prosecutor was to proceed fairly, without arousing prejudice against prospective defendants. But they were also determined to pierce this security if possible. They wanted to help Cox succeed, but they were unwilling to give him a free ride. Most important of all, the press wanted to be dealt with. Cox could not retreat within his fortress any more than Ehrlichman and Haldeman had been able to hide when they were at the White House.

Cox was completely cooperative with me in my new role as ambassador to the press corps. It was up to me to perform the balancing act between submitting to public accountability and maintaining the confidentiality of the investigations. I soon discovered what a pain in the ass reporters could be.

There were, for example, the trash forays. Despite all of our elaborate security precautions we had been in business only a matter of weeks when John Hanrahan of the *Washington Post* called and started reading major portions of a memorandum written by Jill Volner. It was clear that the memorandum, a sensitive one discussing some minor witnesses in the cover-up, was in front of Hanrahan as he spoke The next day Hanrahan had a story in the *Post* based on the memo. Soon thereafter I received a score of calls from reporters accusing the prosecutors of leaking self-serving stories to the *Post*. Hanrahan also called again and recited another memo based on witness interviews in the cover-up case. Neither memo contained much in the way of hard news. But it was clear to the readers of the *Post* that the newspaper had breached Cox's security systems.

After a hurried investigation we determined that the last time anybody remembered seeing the memoranda, they were on the desk of a young lawyer working with Mrs. Volner. The immediate suspicion was that a member of the cleaning crew had stolen the papers and delivered them to the *Post*.

Chagrined, Archie Cox telephoned editor Ben Bradlee of the *Post* to ask for help.

"If you ever tell anyone I told you this, I'll deny it," Bradlee said. "But Archie, you've got a trash problem."

We had been told by the security man that all the office trash was taken to the Justice Department and incinerated. A quick check showed that in fact the waste baskets were emptied into large, transparent plastic bags, which were then brought to the loading platform to await pickup by a commercial refuse company. Somebody who spotted the distinctive memorandum letterhead of the Watergate Special Prosecution Force had handed the bits and pieces of two memoranda to the *Post*. For the next week trash piled up inside the prosecutor's office while we awaited arrival of one of Shredmaster Corporation's largest paper shredders.

The incident inspired Jack Anderson to commission a woman to bring him some of the prosecutor's trash. She brought him a pile of what appeared to be sensitive teletype messages torn in small pieces. Anderson's staff spent several hours piecing the messages together before they realized it was ordinary trash from the Passport Division of the State Department, also housed at 1425 K Street.

One of the young researchers in the office, Tom Martorelli, met another Anderson agent named Bob Owens at a party. They had lunch a few days later. "We've got a number of good sources in your offices already," Owens told the startled researcher, "but we'd be glad to have one more. You'll be able to shape events much more directly, and you'll have the thrill of seeing your own work in a column that appears all over the country."

Martorelli immediately reported the incident, and we held a formal session in the office to interrogate the young man. Then we had Martorelli send Owens a copy of his remarks, without comment.

That kind of espionage angered the lawyers in our office, who considered it unprofessional, if not unethical, to attempt to suborn a government employee and perhaps wreck a legal case in the process.

But Anderson's staff could be helpful, as well. George Clifford, who has ghostwritten some of Anderson's books, gave us an invaluable lead. He had gotten a tip that Maurice Stans was spotted at a New York storage warehouse removing and shredding documents stored there by the Committee to Re-elect the President. By the time Clifford got to the warehouse the owners were saying nothing and the elevator operator was too scared to talk. Without confirmation Anderson could not use the story. Clifford turned over the details to the prosecutor's office, and by subpoenaing witnesses and questioning them under oath, Cox's staff was able to verify that Stans had indeed entered the warehouse and that a number of documents had been shredded. No crime was proved, but the information was valuable when a case was being prepared against Stans.

James Polk, then of the *Washington Star,* gave the campaign contributions task force its first leads into the activities of George M. Steinbrenner III, the American Ship Building Company owner and part-owner of the New York Yankees. Polk's information helped uncover one of the more flagrant violations of the campaign finance laws, and Steinbrenner eventually pleaded guilty to a felony. An accommodating judge in Cleveland let him off without jail time.

A reporter's stock-in-trade is access to sources, and reporters who may have valuable information to offer find it easier to establish a rapport with investigators. The best reporters slowly cultivated the prima donnas and some of the more eager lawyers on the staff, using them in emergencies to add to their information. They also knew that as long as they did not abuse the privilege, John Barker, my assistant, and I would give them "negative guidance," advising when a story they were about to print was untrue.

Carl Bernstein of the *Post* abused this privilege. He called frequently and persistently, often on fishing expeditions, until he began to have trouble getting his calls returned. Then he would tell my secretary that he was calling on a personal matter. I would get on the line, and Carl would explain that he was planning to go away on vacation and before he could leave he had to have an idea whether indictments would be handed down while he was gone. That kind of negative guidance is unwise to give. If you do so once and then say "no comment" the next time, the reporter can assume indictments are about to be handed down.

Once Bernstein called "on a personal matter" and asked me if I could confirm that President Nixon had ordered the Secret Service to tap his brother Donald's telephone. ("That's very personal," Bernstein said.) The story seemed so outrageous that I told Bernstein I would call him back with negative guidance as soon as I had a chance to check. The story was true, and the prosecutors were investigating it. I called Bernstein back, as I had promised, but said only that we had no comment. When the *Post* reported the next day that the story had been confirmed by two sources, I knew that I was one of them.

That sort of ploy is typical of investigative reporters, who are sometimes handed stories through leaks but more often get them bit by bit from a number of sources over a period of time. They are used to conducting open-ended conversations with a number of law enforcement officials, defense lawyers, hoods, and other investigative reporters, "saving string," as they put it, until they have a ball of yarn.

The most dangerous reporter to talk to on the phone is Seymour Hersh of *The New York Times*. He has an uncanny knack for victimizing people on the telephone—catching them off guard and eliciting a devastating quote; or using long paragraphs of quotes, including telltale colloquialisms and slang, which make it clear to insiders whom he talked to even if the person isn't named in the story. Sometimes Hersh uses this device to throw readers off the scent of his true source. Sometimes it is his way of exposing his source while never naming names.

Hersh also had an ability to get through to people on the phone despite their fears about talking to him. He would tell their secretaries, "Tell him I'm writing a story about that son of a bitch he was involved with," or "I have information that will have a direct effect on his career." A combination of fear and curiosity would then get the most prudent to respond.

I was worried about talking to Hersh and yet knew that I would have to do so on a regular basis. I chose psychological warfare. The first time he wrote a story with indications that it had leaked from our office, I called him up. When he picked up the phone, I shouted a four-letter word at him. Hersh was taken aback. "What did you say? I don't believe this," he said. "What are you saying to me?"

For weeks afterward Hersh would recount the story to friends and ask, "What the hell's the matter with Doyle?" But from then on I was able to turn aside his questions with gentle banter; he saved the rough stuff for other potential sources, and we never had a serious confrontation over a story.

I had a different problem with Ron Ostrow of the *Los Angeles Times*. I had to be sure I knew when he was calling on official business and when he just wanted to shoot the breeze. Ostrow was the one reporter with whom I sometimes discussed my problems. He never violated a confidence, even when at times it meant that he was beaten to a story by the competition.

A more important problem concerned the suspicion Washington's high priests and priestesses of journalism had of Cox. I was never able to pin it down exactly, but it seemed to stem from his early days with Jack Kennedy. Cox had been an issues man and speech writer in the 1960 campaign. He had done a first-rate job of organizing an important segment of the intellectual community, coordinating briefings for the candidate on issues, and preparing a series of well-received position papers. But he was not good at the inevitable campaign jostling by the press.

Cox was not a good source for reporters. He did not traffic in the gossip political reporters live by and he came across as stuffy. Furthermore he had little use for two of Kennedy's closest advisers, Ted Sorensen and Dick

Goodwin. Sorensen and Goodwin ended up "with the body"—traveling on the campaign plane "Caroline" with Kennedy. Cox stayed in Washington heading up the speech writing effort. His link to the campaign plane was a young journalist turned speech writer who had made a name covering the war in Algeria: Joseph Kraft.

As always, there were deep and sometimes bitter disagreements between the speech writers in Washington and the aides on the plane, who by virtue of proximity could have the greatest influence. At times the bitterness showed. On one trip, with Cox along, he had an angry confrontation with Sorensen in front of the press corps.

Sorensen and Goodwin missed few opportunities to abuse Cox before the reporters traveling with Kennedy, and some of this feeling apparently lingered thirteen years later despite Cox's distinguished career.

When I told my colleague Mary McGrory that I would be leaving the *Star* to work for Archie Cox, she expressed her reservations, noting that Cox seemed quick to play into the White House's hands by condemning the leaks of prosecution material to the press by Silbert, Glanzer, and Campbell. She thought that was a strange way for Cox to establish himself as his own man and wondered if he was too naïve to do the job.

Author Theodore White expressed similar reservations. "Archie Cox is a bit of a softie," he said, referring to what White thought was his mishandling of student demonstrators at Columbia and Harvard. "You'll find," White said, "that he gets pushed around by his staff."

These comments were in the back of my mind when I met Philip Geyelin, the editor of the *Washington Post*'s editorial page, at a picnic on July 4. "Don't you think it's a little unwise for your boss to be holding news conferences and talking about possibly supoenaing presidential documents?" Geyelin said. I sensed the same theme in all of these comments, perhaps a residue from the recent battle with the Senate Watergate committee: These people were not sure that Cox was the man for the job.

Up until July Cox had been almost inaccessible to reporters and columnists. He was working fifteen-hour days, taking a sandwich at his desk for lunch and retreating to a hillbilly greasy spoon across K Street for a brief dinner with members of the staff.

A few exceptions only reinforced the feeling that Cox did not have sufficient stature with the pundits. Joseph Alsop had invited Cox to his Georgetown home for breakfast. When Cox arrived he was greeted by the maid who ushered him into the presence. Alsop was seated at a breakfast table in the atrium. He never rose—just looked Cox's way and extended his hand.

I decided that Cox had best change his habits. We had breakfasts, luncheons, or dinners with the editors of the *Washington Post* and *The New York Times, Newsweek* and *Time;* with John Chancellor and David Broder, Peter Lisagor and Robert Novak. Cox held background sessions with the reporters who covered the office, but they were of a different kind, with legal issues often discussed in detail, Cox wearing his professor's cap a bit too obviously. The sessions with the high priests and priestesses were more basic; these powerful men and women were allowed to challenge Cox directly and make up their own minds about his capacity to do the job.

These contacts did not change the day-to-day news coverage. Johnny Apple of *The New York Times* still wrote his "news analysis" indicating that Cox's top team of lawyers included a large number with connections to the Kennedys, an oversimplification that haunted us and increased the paranoia in the White House. Apple could just as well have written that the defense lawyers representing Nixon's aides had the same connection to the Kennedys: Both sides had worked in the Justice Department in the early sixties.

The major benefit of the sessions with top newsmen was to scotch rumors that Cox was both arrogant and naïve in his attitude toward his job. He convinced most of his listeners that he was fully aware of the task ahead and facing it with an open mind.

Most of the sessions were "off the record," meaning that nothing in the conversation was to be reported in any way. But I always reminded Cox as I drove him to the homes or offices of the journalists we visited, "Nothing in Washington is ever really off the record. They won't write about it, but they'll gossip about it, and eventually it will end up in print, probably distorted."

There were two incidents early that summer which were seriously to affect Cox's relations with the White House. The first was an innocent-seeming and entirely friendly interview with Hays Gorey in *Time.* In the course of it, Gorey asked Cox how long he expected to be at his task. It was a frequent question, and Cox usually answered it by saying that on the one hand, given some breaks, it might be over with very briefly, but on the other, it had taken Owen Roberts more than six years to clean up Teapot Dome.

His answer was roughly the same on this morning, but Cox was in a philosophical mood, and he expanded upon it slightly. He told Gorey that his was a job for an older man with no ambitions for the future since it was likely to ring him in permanent controversy. That was all right, he said, but he regretted another likelihood—that he would not have the time to complete a major work of scholarship during his remaining active years. Any professor hoped to be remembered by his scholarly contributions.

Gorey wrote of the interview, "The Special Prosecutor has clearly taken on the task of investigating just about anything he chooses. As Cox, 61, looks ahead, he recalls that the Teapot Dome investigation took six years, and adds, 'I rather expect to spend the rest of my working life in this role.' " The article convinced the White House that Cox was vindictive.

When Cox saw the interview, he suggested that I might want to correct the impression that he saw his role as a quasi-permanent one. "Forget it," I said. "It will be forgotten in a week." It was not.

The second incident grew out of a news conference on June 18, where Cox was asked whether an investigation of the financing of Nixon's home in San Clemente and the lavish improvements made on it fell within his jurisdiction. He replied that he hadn't yet formed an opinion and didn't know the facts. The next morning he asked Peter Kreindler, his executive assistant, to gather material on the funding of La Casa Pacifica, Nixon's San Clemente home. Two weeks later he asked Kreindler again.

Kreindler asked me if I could get him all the newspaper clippings on the subject. That was risky, I said. The *Washington Post* or the *Star* would be alerted if I asked them for past articles, and a news story might result.

"I'll ask my friends at the *L.A. Times,*" I said.

I had lunch with Jack Nelson and Bob Jackson, two investigative reporters for the paper. By the time lunch was over it was clear to me that Nelson would write a story indicating the prosecutor's interest in San Clemente. I offered no objection and thought little more about the subject.

What didn't register until the next day was that Richard Nixon was at San Clemente with the White House press corps. A story in the *Post* or the *Star* would have had less effect than one in the newspaper whose circulation area included San Clemente. Reporters started asking Ron Ziegler for comment on the story before his breakfast. By then Richard Nixon was transported with rage.

Elliot Richardson was holding a meeting with federal prosecutors from Maryland, who were telling him for the first time about the felonious conduct of Spiro Agnew. Three times telephone calls from Alexander Haig about the purported Cox investigation drew Richardson away.

On K Street Cox had already informed the press, through me, that at this stage-his investigation was nothing more than a request to a newspaper for back clippings on the subject.

Haig's third telephone call to Richardson had been interrupted when Nixon picked up the phone and ordered the attorney general to get a retraction from Cox within a half hour, or Cox would be fired.

Richardson called Cox three times as well. The first call was an amiable discussion in which Cox told Richardson what had happened. But when Richardson called for the third time, I heard Cox say, "Elliot, do you really think it's proper for you to call me up like this? What about our arm's length relationship? It will do neither of us any good if you advertise the fact that you called me the first time that something hostile to the President appeared in the press."

He rejected Richardson's suggestion that the two men put out a joint statement saying there would be no investigation. That would be for him to decide once he knew the facts, Cox said, and that was why he had asked his staff to get the facts.

Richardson doubted that such an investigation would fall within Cox's jurisdiction in any case. "Well, I think I disagree," Cox said, "but I'm at a disadvantage since I don't know the allegations or the facts." He agreed to issue a formal statement, under his own name, which would say what I had been telling reporters. Richardson had his secretary take Cox's statement over the telephone. He issued his own press release, consisting of Cox's press release on a Department of Justice letterhead.

That night, Bob Jackson's house in the District of Columbia was burglarized. The intruder punched a hole in a window sash, leaving a teaspoon of sawdust and no other signs of a break-in. About thirty dollars in cash, visible on a table, was taken. Nothing else of monetary value, including a fur coat in a closet and two portable tape recorders lying on beds, was touched. But Jackson's notes on the San Clemente story, lying atop his dresser, had been examined, he says. Police said the burglary appeared to be the work of juveniles.

The incident left everyone shaken. Cox was uncomfortable at the intrusion of Elliot Richardson. I was upset at myself for ineptly handling a simple request for newspaper clippings.

In another part of Washington that night Cox and I were dining with the editors of *Newsweek* at the home of Washington Bureau Chief Mel Elfin. He could see we were uptight.

As we seated ourselves at the table, Elfin said, "Nobody is here to work tonight. Everything is off the record. We are here to enjoy the paella."

"Paella," I said from the other end of the table, looking at Cox. "That's Spanish for interview."

The editors of *Newsweek* never violated a Cox confidence. But the danger of an indiscretion or a lapse in security that would embarrass the office was a constant one.

People tended to view some of the office security precautions as a bit exotic and Winslow Joy, the Justice Department security officer, as a genuine eccentric. Still, there were times when we were glad for the guards with their guns. One day during a meeting Cox's private phone rang. He said hello, arched his eyebrows, hung up and announced, "That fellow threatened to bump me off."

One Friday evening George Frampton walked out of the office with a big black leather case, the kind that salesmen call sample cases and lawyers call evidence bags. Frampton's was filled with grand jury transcripts.

When Frampton got to the corner, a meth freak approached him and asked for money.

"Take off, buddy," Frampton said.

The man was persistent. Frampton felt the weight of the evidence bag in his hand and wondered what would happen if the junkie went for it. He turned around and started walking back toward the office.

The man jumped him. Frampton, who is about six feet tall and in pretty good shape, shook the man off his back and started running. The junkie looked at this dapper man running from him and was sure he was about to make a score. He came up beside Frampton and landed a punch on the right side of his face. Frampton kept running, saying to himself, "You son of a bitch, if I didn't have half the evidence in the Watergate case with me, I'd land you in that goddamned gutter."

He ran inside the lobby at 1425 K Street. The junkie followed him. Frampton ran past the guard and lunged for the elevator. "Stop that ass- hole," he said to the guard. As the elevator doors closed, Frampton saw the guard kneeling on the junkie's shoulders and pointing the barrel of a .38 Smith and Wesson service revolver at the man's right eye. The junkie was beginning to settle down.

I was on the elevator, trying to leave to spend a quiet night with my family. Frampton almost knocked me over. As the doors closed and we started ascending, he looked at me and said only one word, "Shit."

Winslow Joy tried to have the meth freak committed to St. Elizabeth's Hospital for psychiatric cases, but the Watergate Special Prosecution Force refused to press charges. After that the lawyers were more selective about the evidence they took from 1425 K Street.

The neighborhood was not the best. Around the corner on Fourteenth Street there were a number of strip joints, and there always seemed to be tired-looking young ladies in very short skirts standing around. One night Maureen Gevlin, a pretty red-headed lawyer, was standing in front of 1425 K Street waiting for her husband to pick her up when two men in a white car waved to her. They went by three times. The third time one of them rolled down the window and said, "Baby, you ain't gonna get any business if you just stand there."

The stringent security discouraged reporters from hanging around out- side the office and soon convinced the press that Archie Cox meant business when he said his investigation would be conducted in strict confidence. It also had a psychological effect on the people inside the wall of security.

Under Richard Nixon 1600 Pennsylvania Avenue had become an island, its inhabitants physically, psychologically, and emotionally removed from the rest of Washington. When the Watergate siege began, the White House became a bunker.

Something like that happened at 1425 K Street as well. Once inside that wall of security devices, the prosecutors were living a life apart, legal Carthusians in their monastic cells, shutting out the world. Sometimes the whole city would be in an uproar over the latest developments at the Senate Watergate committee or the latest revelation in court. Behind the doors at 1425 K Street it was as isolated as a nuclear submarine under the North Pole.

The work was progressing, and Cox was mastering the case. On Monday, June 25, the day John Dean began his public testimony before the Senate Watergate committee, Cox told Silbert and his assistants that he would accept their resignations with gratitude for their help. There followed a week of negotiations over phrases to appear in an exchange of letters.

Silbert's letter to Cox noted that he and his assistants had volunteered to withdraw when Cox was appointed, but that Cox had asked them to stay on during a transition period. "The transition now, in our view, is basically complete," the letter said, and "we renew our request to withdraw from the case. . . ."

In five pages Silbert defended the conduct of the original investigation and the motives of the trial team. The letter ended by noting, "During the past month we have worked closely and cordially with Mr. James Neal, the member of your staff whom you have placed in charge of the Watergate case. He has on many occasions expressed confidence in the way we handled the case."

Neal insisted that this last sentence be deleted, or he would repudiate it. In fact he was confident that they had handled the case properly, but he felt in no position to say so after the short time he had spent examining the records. Cox was expected to make a careful and deliberate judgment on that very question.

Cox's letter to Silbert, Glanzer, and Campbell was one page of cordial but reserved thanks. "You acted in a highly creditable fashion in acceding to my request that you put the interests of the Watergate investigation ahead of your own wishes and give us the benefit of your knowledge and experience during a period of transition," it said. "Your help has been invaluable. Without it we would be weeks behind. Even now the loss of your assistance may slow us down somewhat, but not enough to justify my over-ruling your own wishes."

It was Cox's final paragraph that caused anguish and anger in Silbert's team, and there were intense efforts to get Cox to change it.

"Perhaps I may add in closing that I realize this has not been an easy time for you," Cox wrote. "I am aware of various criticisms of your earlier conduct of the investigation and prosecution of seven defendants. Lawyers often differ on questions of judgment, and there are points on which my judgment would have varied from yours, *such as the Segretti matter.* [Emphasis mine.] Thus far in the investigation, however, none of us has seen anything to show that you did not pursue your professional duties according to your honest judgment and in complete good faith."

For three days Cox refused to delete the reference to Segretti's questioning in the grand jury, where Silbert had cut off grand jurors' questions. Finally, on Friday, June 29, he took the reference out, and the resignations were announced.

Silbert's team had done a much better job with the reopened investigation of the Watergate cover-up than they had with keeping it confidential. Many of the details of the cover-up that finally emerged in the Senate hearings, or a year later at the second Watergate trial, were developed by Silbert, Glanzer, and Campbell between March and late May.

If their successors tended to glide over those difficult questions left from the first investigation and trial, it could be ascribed to a general sympathy with the no-win position in which the three men had found themselves. As they ended their own phase of the case, Silbert, Glanzer, and Campbell were disheartened and embittered. Watergate would cast a shadow on their careers. Glanzer left the government shortly before the second Watergate trial to become an expensive lawyer with Chuck Colson's old firm. In January, 1974, after long controversy and delay, Silbert became United States Attorney for the District of Columbia. Don Campbell, after considering abandoning the law altogether, continued as a trusted Silbert aide.

The three departing prosecutors enjoyed the sympathy of their successors, and in many cases the professional admiration as well. But relations between the two groups continued to be a source of aggravation. From their new seats in the grandstands, the original prosecutors frequently became commentators on the cases. The substance of Silbert's eighty-page prosecutive memorandum was leaked to Daniel Schorr of CBS News, who reported on July 4 that according to the original prosecutors' status report to Cox, the cover-up case was 85 percent completed, that it called for the indictment of Haldeman, Ehrlichman, Mitchell, and Dean; guilty pleas from L. Patrick Gray and Gordon Strachan; and immunity for Herbert

Kalmbach. Schorr's report quite accurately reflected the Silbert memo and caused a number of defense attorneys to serve notice on Cox that their clients had been irreparably damaged by this prejudicial publicity. Cox sought sworn depositions from everyone who had access to the memorandum, including Titus, Silbert, Glanzer, and Campbell, and publicly condemned the "gross breach of professional ethics" on the part of the leaker.

Archibald Cox was very anxious in his early days as prosecutor, worried that it was taking too long to get organized and that he was not himself personally on top of the cases. He left the staffing and organization to Vorenberg, while he determined to stay ahead of the testimony that was cascading in each day from the Senate and the grand jury.

He was also digesting the volumes of testimony gathered before his arrival on the scene. Each morning he would insist on a stretch of undisturbed time to read, and he kept a notebook based on his reading. He strained at the endless meetings Vorenberg held to decide organizational questions, but his manner before the staff was relaxed and low-key. Everybody worked from 8 A.M. until near midnight, taking lunch at their desks and adjourning for a quick dinner at a restaurant across the street called Robin Hood's, which will not make the Michelin Guide.

Phyllis Cox was in Maine. Cox was living alone in a borrowed house near Rock Creek Park where he ended each day reading the final exam blue books from his Harvard classes until midnight. He finished grading them just in time for the fall reopening of school.

Each day's developments on Capitol Hill and in the grand jury brought forth the need to make more decisions, and they could not be made from ignorance. Cox would not depend on the original trial team's judgment in Watergate cover-up matters, and Jim Neal was not committed to a lengthy stay, so Cox felt he must personally be on top of that case in all its details.

The special prosecutor was uncomfortable with the idea that he was involved with a case in which he did not know every available fact, and he had an uneasy feeling that developments would take him by surprise because he was unprepared. In June he wrote a letter to Buzhardt asking for written answers from President Nixon to John Dean's public charges. He also asked for an interview with the President at an early opportunity.

Cox told his staff, "The worst thing that could happen to me now would be a quick summons from the White House for that face-to-face with the President. I'm not prepared to ask the right questions."

One morning I was in his office with Rick Ben-Veniste and I inquired after the special prosecutor's health, since he looked especially tired and drawn. "I'm afraid I didn't sleep much last night," he said. "I was worrying about witness Nixon."

Ben-Veniste looked at Cox. "If you think you had a bad night, imagine what kind of nights he's having."

"I suppose you're right," Cox said. "The two of us should get together some morning around three at the Lincoln Memorial and talk the problem over."

From his interview with Henry Petersen, Cox had gotten two leads, and he arranged a session with Nixon's lawyers to follow up on them as quickly as possible. Petersen's one-page memorandum to the President did not seem that promising, but it pointed up a fact that Cox had already calculated: The key to his investigation lay somewhere within the White House files. The more enticing lead was Petersen's reference to tape recordings. Might the President have recordings of his actual meetings with John Dean? Cox meant to find out.

While he was still in his temporary offices at the Justice Department, Cox arranged for a visit by the President's lawyers. It was held on Wednesday, June 6.

Leonard Garment, the "house liberal" of the White House staff, was very quiet. Charles Alan Wright, the University of Texas expert on Constitutional law, was slightly imperious, curt. J. Fred Buzhardt, a new lawyer General Alexander Haig had just brought over from the Defense Department to the White House staff, seemed to be in charge. He was courteous.

Cox told the three men he wanted to make arrangements for access to White House files pertinent to his investigation.

That would be impossible, Buzhardt said. The files ranged over too many subjects and were too sensitive.

Well, Cox said, it would be unreasonable to expect him to be very specific until he could get an idea of the files and how they worked. He certainly didn't want to see anything he wasn't entitled to see.

Cox wanted to get the lawyers to agree to an inventory of White House files. There was a good chance, he thought, that they already had such an inventory. It would show how the White House worked, where he should be looking. He didn't mention his idea; not yet.

There were limits, Charles Alan Wright said, to what Cox could reasonably request. Every President since George Washington had asserted exclusive control over presidential files.

Leonard Garment added that what Cox had in mind would be a bad precedent.

No, Cox said, it would hardly be much of a precedent at all. It seemed unlikely that anything like the present situation would arise again very quickly.

There was a momentary silence. Vorenberg reminded the White House lawyers that Elliot Richardson had been confirmed as attorney general only after the Senate was assured that Cox would be given the cooperation of the Nixon administration. Vorenberg made a specific request. How about the logs showing visits and calls between the President and John Dean between, say, June, 1972, and May, 1973? Buzhardt made a note of the request.

Cox then went over the background of his recent session with Petersen. He asked for access to Petersen's memo to the President and wanted the lawyers to instruct Petersen not to hold back information because of any cited "privilege." Buzhardt made more notes.

Then Cox asked for the Nixon-Dean tape of April 15, which he said the President had mentioned to Petersen. Buzhardt made a note, giving no sign of surprise, nor any indication whether such a tape existed.

Vorenberg added that the prosecutors wished to request, as well, all tapes, notes, or memoranda of conversations between Nixon and Dean.

"There are limits to this," Charles Alan Wright said. "Many of the President's papers are too sensitive for his own lawyers to see."

Cox said he was not interested in seeing anything to which he was not entitled as part of his work. But it was not reasonable, he said, for the White House to deny him sufficient access to the files for him to determine which were likely to be pertinent. I want assurances, Cox said, that I can have reasonable access to the White House files.

"The President is being forced into the role of defendant," Buzhardt replied. He said it quietly, matter-of-factly. "The President will fight."

CHAPTER

3

THE PRESIDENT'S MEN

"You just can't recall. It was in a meeting."

Four days after Nixon recruited Elliot Richardson as the new attorney general, Alexander Meigs Haig, Jr., was dining with the senior officers of Fort Benning, Georgia. He was a four-star general, the Army's vice chief of staff, and generally considered the next chairman of the Joint Chiefs. That evening, May 2, 1973, Haig was summoned to the phone to talk with President Nixon.

The President urgently needed a chief of staff to replace Haldeman and Ehrlichman, and to bring some order out of the chaos that followed their forced resignations. General Haig did not want the job but he could hardly refuse his commander-in-chief. President Nixon had been extraordinarily helpful to Haig's military career.

Haig was a colonel when he came to the White House in 1969 as Henry Kissinger's senior military adviser. He came highly recommended. Fritz Kraemer, the Pentagon's resident intellectual, who years before had spotted Henry Kissinger and James Schlesinger and helped them toward the top, suggested Haig to Kissinger. Joseph Califano, former counsel to the Department of the Army and later President Johnson's right-hand man, warmly endorsed the idea. Califano told Kissinger that Al Haig "is one of the new breed of Army officers who knows politics, international affairs, and people."

Henry Kissinger is a poor administrator and Al Haig is a brilliant one. Henry Kissinger has a towering ego and a frail sense of self. Al Haig is sure of himself. He manipulates people more by charm than guile, a reversal of Kissinger's style. The two worked well together, Haig the loyal lieutenant who got out of bed in the middle of the night and drove to the White House situation room, nursing some crisis until Kissinger arrived in the morning to be briefed. Kissinger fought the ideological battles. Haig was more conservative, holding the conventional views of a West Point-trained senior military man. He cared less about ideology. He implemented.

He had the staff man's ability at modest self-promotion. Nixon was made aware that it was Al Haig who put together the ten or twelve pages Nixon saw each morning summarizing security conditions throughout the world. Nixon told Ron Ziegler, "When you see the lights burning late in Doctor Kissinger's office, it's usually Al Haig."

When Vietnam threatened to fall apart during the year before the 1972 elections, Haig moved in and out of Southeast Asia for Kissinger and Nixon, propping up Lon Nol in Cambodia, preventing Nguyen Van Thieu from sabotaging negotiation efforts from Saigon. Then he did the advance work for Nixon's trips to Moscow and Peking, which had been such stunning political successes back home. As Nixon was rewarded with an unprecedented landslide of votes, so Haig was rewarded as well.

By March of 1972 the colonel was wearing two stars. After the election Nixon promoted him again, and this time Haig skipped three-star rank altogether, vaulting over 240 more senior officers to become a four-star general. Few doubted that before Nixon left office, Alexander Haig would be the highest-ranking man in uniform. Haig's classmates at the United States Military Academy, where he ranked 214th in a class of 310, would not have predicted his success. Haig had been turned down by West Point when he first applied, and spent a year at Notre Dame while an uncle with congressional contacts worked on the appointment. The key to his later successes was there in that mixture of persistence and political pull; Al

Haig would work hard, charm his adversaries, and do what was needed to get what he wanted.

Al Haig was ten years old and living in Bala Cynwyd, one of Philadelphia's wealthier suburban communities, when his father, an assistant city solicitor, died. Haig's brother Frank, a Jesuit priest who teaches at Loyola College in Baltimore, remembers that Al worked for a living from then on as he completed his schooling. He delivered newspapers, worked in the post office, served as a floor walker for a department store. "He had a normal adolescence," Father Frank says. "I say that because as an adult he's had so much drive he can seem like a machine."

In 1949, two years out of the academy, Lieutenant Haig was assigned to General Douglas MacArthur's staff in Japan. Haig learned in a peacetime army that the qualities of soldier-statesman could be more coveted than those of combat leader. He was to become mostly a staff man—diplomat, politician, manager, public relations expert—spending the required amounts of time in the field to avoid being passed over as a line officer.

Haig saw combat in Korea and in Vietnam, where he commanded the 2nd Brigade, 1st Infantry Division, and was highly decorated. Later, when he became a public figure, there was confusion over the decorations. According to Army records, his commander, General James Hollingworth, had put Haig in for both the Distinguished Service Cross and the Distinguished Flying Cross for two separate actions in different commands on the same date, March 31, 1967. It was an administrative error, apparently, and Hollingworth later explained that the two actions had occurred one day apart.

Haig's combat record was impeccable and he was proud of it. Shortly after Nixon asked him to become chief of staff, Haig told Henry Kissinger that he could not refuse, that he had "risked a bullet in the heart in Vietnam" and saw this new job, too, as a mortal risk, at least professionally, but one he must take for his honor. He was often to talk this way, telling reporters that the courage of those locked in political battle compared favorably to professional soldiers in combat, which, he would intimate, was his much preferred line of endeavor.

There was a good deal of criticism from the military when Al Haig catapulted over his superiors to become vice chief of staff, and there was more when he let it be known he saw the White House job as temporary and did not plan to resign his commission. After all there was a law governing these things—Section 973(b), Title 10, United States Code. It said that no active duty military man "may hold a civil office by election or appointment whether under the United States, a territory or possession of a state." To do so, the law added, automatically terminated that person's military commission. At first the general counsel for the Department of Defense ruled that the law did not apply, that Haig was simply a military officer on detail to the commander-in-chief. This so upset Congress, including staunch and needed White House allies like Senator Barry Goldwater, that Haig backed down and agreed to resign his commission, effective four months after accepting the White House assignment. The August resignation would increase his retirement pay by $3,300 a year.

This, too, caused criticism. Representative Les Aspin of Wisconsin denounced Haig for not resigning, saying, "The General Accounting Office has already ruled that Haig is illegally serving in a civilian office while continuing on active duty. For General Haig an extra $3,300 booty in his own pocket is more important than obeying the law."

Haig took over at the White House on May 6, apparently in the belief that he would have nothing to do with the management of the Watergate crisis. That did not last very long.

Four days after he became White House chief of staff, Al Haig installed J. Fred Buzhardt as Nixon's chief Watergate lawyer. The job had been vacant since the departure of John Dean, although several White House staffers, headed by Len Garment, had been trying to prepare defenses against the coming Senate Watergate committee hearings. Like Haig, Buzhardt was a staff man noted for hard work and follow-through. He, too, was an early postwar West Point graduate. He also finished in the middle of his class. But Buzhardt chose the Air Force. He resigned after his obligatory tour of duty because an ear dysfunction made it clear he would be grounded and would not have the potential of an unlimited career.

Buzhardt graduated first in his class from the University of South Carolina Law School in 1952 and returned to his hometown, McCormick, South Carolina (population 1,850), where he joined his father's small practice of general law. A few years later his father's close friend and law partner, Senator Strom Thurmond, invited Fred Buzhardt to become a legislative assistant in Washington.

These were Strom Thurmond's fire-eating days, when he played the role of premier Washington racist and anticommunist. Later, age and the Voting Rights Act would moderate Thurmond's racial stands; and his shift to the Republican Party and allegiance to a détente-seeking Nixon would temper the force of his anticommunism. But in the fifties he was an admixture of Theodore Bilbo, Joseph McCarthy, and the coming George Wallace. Fred Buzhardt became a trusted aide and an ideological comrade as zealous, his coworkers reported, as the senator himself.

Thurmond was then a member of the Senate Labor and Public Welfare Committee, which had before it reform legislation submitted by Senator John F. Kennedy and drafted in large part by his adviser, Archibald Cox. Since Kennedy's entrance into the Senate in 1953 he had become the champion of moderate reform within the labor movement, much to the annoyance of Republicans and southern Democrats. The Wagner Act of New Deal days had provided organized labor with economic and political power, but corruption within the unions and a resurgence of conservative strength in Congress had given antilabor forces an opportunity to gut the Wagner Act and return some of that power to business. With Cox's help Kennedy became the voice for moderate change. In doing so the Massachusetts senator displeased many labor leaders but angered the antilabor forces even more.

Another member of Thurmond's staff at this time was Robert O. Dupre, an Anderson, S.C., lawyer. He was interviewed late in 1973 by Rudy Abramson of the *Los Angeles Times,* and he recalled that in 1956 Buzhardt proposed a plan to keep Kennedy and Cox under surveillance. According to Dupre, Buzhardt was seeking to uncover Communist influences in the labor movement. Dupre rejected Buzhardt's proposal, the *Los Angeles Times* reported, "to shadow Kennedy and Cox to keep up with their contacts in labor organizations." At the time, Archie Cox didn't know that Fred Buzhardt existed.

The passion that burned within J. Fred Buzhardt was invisible to those who did not know him. He neither smoked nor drank. He was a deacon of the McCormick Baptist Church. But those who worked with him knew that he made warm friends and bitter enemies on the basis of his political beliefs.

During the sixties Buzhardt became Thurmond's military adviser. His big issue concerned the Kennedy administration's "muzzling" of the right-wing political statements of senior military officers who fulminated for

God, Country, and the John Birch Society during the Eisenhower-Mc-
Carthy years. Buzhardt was in the background of Thurmond's fight to
maintain military indoctrination programs that made use of Birch Society
literature.

Following his father's death, Buzhardt returned to McCormick, in 1966,
to carry on the family law practice. When Nixon won the 1968 presidential nomination with the help of Thurmond, and the Presidency with the
help of the southern strategy, Buzhardt returned to Washington. At first
he was simply a middle-level Pentagon lawyer. Within a year he was
Defense Department general counsel, handling such matters as the Pentagon Papers and later the Daniel Ellsberg case. To those not watching
closely he was just a simple country lawyer making good.

Buzhardt seemed mild-mannered, but friend and foe found him deceptively skillful at mortal combat. Harry Dent, a colleague on Thurmond's
staff and later at the White House, once said admiringly of Buzhardt, "He
would have been a great director of the CIA. He does like intrigue."

A friendly profile of Buzhardt ran in the *Charlotte Observer* at the time
of his White House appointment, anonymously quoting former members
of Thurmond's staff who were not fans: "He's the kind of guy who could
steal your underwear without ever disturbing your pants," one said. Another called him "a very decent individual [but] a man with a very vivid
imagination about all kinds of conspiracies. . . . His views of national
and international problems were extremely narrow . . . a lot of cloak and
dagger thinking." The piece noted that among opponents he was often
referred to as "Buzzard" or "The Bird."

These two men, Alexander Haig and J. Fred Buzhardt, became the
architects of Richard Nixon's new Watergate defenses. They were quite
different from their predecessors—Haldeman, Ehrlichman, Dean, and
Colson. But the system, the expectations, and the results would be the same.

Like all government officials each had sworn an oath to uphold the
laws and the Constitution of the United States. Each saw his duty more
narrowly: to be loyal to the man who held the office of the Presidency.
If either man examined the evidence against Nixon, it was only to prepare a defense, not to advise him of his duty, or even of his options.

When the White House tapes were made public, the voice of Alexander
Haig was heard on one made June 4, 1973, less than a month after he
assumed his new duties. Nixon was listening in a state of depression and

shock to the devastating self-incrimination recorded during the March 21 meeting of the conspirators. Haig is heard to say to Nixon, "You just can't recall. It was in a meeting."

It was Buzhardt who dealt regularly with Archibald Cox. His first line of defense was a standard one for Washington lawyers: diversion and delay.

Buzhardt had a way of hunching himself up which made him appear smaller, bowed as if by a great burden. His eyes stared out passively from behind wire frame glasses. He was courtly. Many members of Cox's staff became acutely suspicious of him. He gave them the impression he suffered silently, that his hair shirt bothered him.

Archibald Cox dealt with Buzhardt constantly. He considered him earnest, and probably as obliging as it was possible to be. "I think he's a conscientious lawyer who can't control his client," Cox would say.

Elliot Richardson meanwhile kept telling Cox of Buzhardt's expressed admiration for the special prosecutor. Richardson had known Buzhardt for some time. "Fred is an honorable man," he told Cox.

The White House furnished no document or other information to Cox in his first month. Cox put his requests in writing, and a series of letters flowed back and forth between Buzhardt and Cox during June. Buzhardt said it was the President's view that his conversations with Henry Petersen were protected by executive privilege because they were confidential communications with the chief executive. Nevertheless Nixon would waive the privilege and allow Petersen to cooperate and testify fully.

As to the tape of a Nixon-Dean conversation of April 15, Buzhardt suggested that such did not exist. "The tape which the President referred to in his discussion with Mr. Petersen was a tape on which the President dictated his own recollections of that conversation after it was finished. It would, of course, not be appropriate to produce the tape," Buzhardt wrote.

Given the facts that later developed, Buzhardt's answer was an outrageous deception. Lawyers have been held in contempt or disbarred for such obstruction of an investigation, but not often.

However, it was not a provable lie. The letter was carefully worded. It served its purpose, deceiving Cox into dropping his pursuit of White House tape recordings, at least as a first order of business. Buzhardt did not actually deny the existence of a tape of a Nixon-Dean meeting; he asserted simply that the President had not been referring to such a tape in his talks with Petersen.

The trouble with this tactic was that it bought time but offered no solution to the President's problem. Buzhardt was sticking his fingers in the Watergate dike, but the cracks were too many for him.

Shortly after putting off Cox about the tapes Buzhardt granted a lesser request. It was to be a fatal mistake. Cox's staff was anxious to see the White House logs of presidential meetings, particularly those between Nixon and his top aides during the months when the Watergate cover-up was developing. It would help establish the relationship between the President and Dean, and it might show other patterns or leads as well. Buzhardt never turned down the request for these logs but he stalled for weeks. Then in mid-June an incident occurred which shed a good deal of light on the White House counsel's methods.

By then Cox had assembled the top members of his permanent team and was anxious to show the public a sense of momentum in his investigation. One Monday on the spur of the moment, he informed the news services that he would hold a news conference in two hours. Cox intended nothing more than to announce his new staff and introduce a few of us to the press, but the impromptu flavor of the event caused a reaction at the White House. No sooner had the wire services announced the Cox press conference than Buzhardt was on the phone with an urgent call to Jim Vorenberg. Are there developments I should know about? Buzhardt asked. Vorenberg immediately turned the conversation to the many unfulfilled requests for information. The special prosecutor was running out of patience, Vorenberg said. Well, tell him to be patient a little longer, a package is on its way, Buzhardt said.

Twenty minutes before the scheduled news conference, as Cox was heading out the doors of his offices, a messenger arrived from the White House carrying an envelope containing the logs listing meetings between Nixon and Dean from June 15, 1972, through April 30, 1973. It was a fraction of what had been requested, but important. Two lawyers from the Watergate task force, Gerry Goldman and George Frampton, constructed a picture of Dean's dealings with the President showing that Dean had almost no access to Nixon except during times of intense activity in the Watergate case. Within a short time the logs became a devastating legal tool. Once the existence of the tapes became known, Cox had no

trouble being quite specific, as the courts require, in writing his subpoenas.

On the afternoon of July 16 a group of the young lawyers were clustered around my desk peering at the screen of the small television set I
kept tuned to the Senate Watergate committee hearings. Nixon's personal
lawyer and bag man, Herbert Kalmbach, was due to begin testifying. Instead Alexander Butterfield took the stand and disclosed publicly for the
first time that since late 1971 Richard Nixon had taped every conversation
held in his Oval Office and in his hideaway office in the Executive Office
Building, as well as those held on some of his telephones and some held
in the Cabinet Room.

One of the young men standing behind my desk was Peter Kreindler,
a rangy lad, mustachioed and bespectacled, who had been an Olympic style
speed skater while growing up in Liberty, New York, where his father
was a manager at Grossinger's resort hotel. His cousins are the owners of
New York's posh "21" Club. Kreindler, who had given up ice skating for
law, ranked at the top of his Harvard Law School class. He had just
finished a tour as law clerk for Justice William O. Douglas. Cox had
hired him as his executive assistant—his own law clerk.

Peter Kreindler was tamping the tobacco in his pipe. He stood there
listening to Butterfield, the pipe in one hand and a pipe tool in the other,
his mouth slack. "Can you believe that?" he said. "Can you *believe* that?"

A few minutes later Archibald Cox stood in his office with Kreindler
and Philip Lacovara. Cox was puffing out his cheeks, letting the air escape,
then puffing his cheeks again, a habit of his when measuring a problem.

Charles Alan Wright had been correct when he said that every President
since George Washington maintained control over his own presidential
documents. In recent years they had taken them along when leaving
office, decided which to make public and which to conceal. But President
Nixon had tapes of actual conversations, magnetic ribbons that might tell
the story of the President's involvement in Watergate and the cover-up
with more precision than any document. At least they would disclose who
said what inside the Oval Office, and whether Dean or Ehrlichman or
Haldeman was lying.

Besides the logs showing exactly when Dean had met with Nixon the
prosecutors had also received, voluntarily, the desk diaries of Ehrlichman

and Haldeman, showing the times of their meetings with Nixon. Goldman and Frampton had been poring over these papers, establishing the patterns of Nixon's meetings with his aides on the days of Watergate developments. The logs and diaries would now be a devastating tool for purposes of discovery if it came to a court fight over Cox's access to the tapes. And it would surely come to a court fight. Nixon would give no ground voluntarily. The case would go all the way to the Supreme Court.

Cox knew that he had to look down a long road before he took the first steps. There were real doubts whether the Supreme Court would order Richard Nixon, who had appointed four of its members, to release the tapes; whether the justices would take the case at all; whether Nixon would honor a decision by the court if it did rule against him.

Butterfield's revelation left Cox no real choice. He had told the Senate he would follow the evidence wherever it led. He turned away from Lacovara and Kreindler and started walking back to his desk. "Let's get started," Archibald Cox said.

The first great English law books were compiled by Henry de Bracton in the thirteenth century. De Bracton wrote, "The king ought not to be under any man, but he is under God, and the law." And at least since the time of Magna Carta, this had been the clear tradition of English-speaking peoples. Americans had a simple phrase for this secular belief that was as strong as any religion: "No man is above the law." But aphorisms did not answer this question: How do the courts enforce the law against a defiant President? In 184 years of American jurisprudence, it had never come to a final test.

Cox worried about this question. He thought he knew what the courts would say to any claims of executive privilege when it came to evidence of possible criminality in the White House. But he knew, perhaps better than any of the participants, the dangers of forcing the confrontation to the ultimate testing point. The court of last resort, the Supreme Court of the United States, was home to Archibald Cox. He had served the court with deep commitment as solicitor general. He cherished it as an institution and as a shrine to the law, to which he had devoted his life. In the words of historian Daniel Boorstin, the court had become the American conscience, a "secular papacy," which acted in each generation to stir in us the dream of the Founding Fathers for equal justice. The other two branches were supposed to reflect the will of the governed. In good times and bad the court was to guarantee the rule of law. But like the papacy, the court had no troops to enforce its decisions.

It was difficult to predict how the President would react to a court challenge, and doubly difficult to chart the course in the courts. There were no clear-cut precedents. The traditions of the law, and especially the criminal law, were on the side of the prosecutor. But the issue of a chief executive's privilege, his exemption from the normal criminal process in such a case, had not arisen before in a clear and definitive way. The courts would have to weigh, depending on exactly what came before them, whether they should decide these questions in the present atmosphere.

Cox saw the great danger in starting down this road. First, whenever one sues in court, there is a fair chance of losing. Better to reach a compromise if possible, to be patient and accept less than all the available evidence at first in hopes of more later. Nothing would be lost except time. A protracted court fight would mean the possibility that the President's position would be upheld and the evidence lost forever. And there was a greater danger, the possibility that Nixon would defy a subpoena and the courts would lack the courage to enforce it.

Judge Sirica might find the subpoena faulty, or simply unwise, and refuse to enforce it. Or the appellate court might do the same. Or the Supreme Court might find a way to dodge the question, which would be far worse than losing on the merits. Besides assuring that the prosecutors would see no more evidence from within the White House, it would invite future mischief within the executive branch and cause a fatal erosion of judicial sovereignty, perhaps permanently damaging the branch of government Cox honored most.

Before Butterfield's revelation there was a practical problem in proceeding to court. Cox did not know what evidence he was seeking from Nixon and the White House files. Buzhardt had put him off when he requested that an inventory of the files be drawn up. Cox would have to make a forceful public case that the specific things he was requesting had a direct relationship to some criminal conduct. That was impossible when Cox didn't know what was in most of the files.

Cox had given signals of his growing impatience but had hardly threatened to go into court. He had planned to "go public" first, to lay out at a news conference the details of his many requests over the past two months and the lack of White House response. He hoped to build public support for his case before taking the drastic step of legal process against a President.

Part of his preoccupation during this period was with the mental state of Richard Nixon. Cox, a negotiator, liked to study the parties to a controversy. How was Nixon likely to respond to the special prosecutor's thrusts? During these weeks Nixon was a man in seclusion. He had not held a news conference in four months, since before James McCord started talking. He appeared before the cameras of the White House press corps only when long planned public occasions required it. He fled the White House at every opportunity, staying at nearby Camp David, returning by helicopter to meet a foreign head of state, departing for Key Biscayne and the seclusion of Robert Abplanalp's Grand Cay. Rumors circulated that the President was drinking heavily and depending more and more on sedation.

"Do you think the President is unwell?" Cox asked me one morning after we had reviewed the day's news. Some of the stories had recounted Nixon's mood swings, from outbursts of public activity and bellicose statements of defense to further escape and isolation from all but two or three aides. "He must be, by now," I said.

"Well, if he is, it's going to be hard to get any response out of him, isn't it?" Cox said.

The day after Butterfield testified, Cox asked Buzhardt for the precise location of all the tapes and the name and title of the person who held legal custody. Buzhardt said the tapes were "locked up under the protection of the Secret Service," but that they were in the President's sole custody, and that nobody had access to them without Nixon's specific authority. Buzhardt was sharpening the point of executive privilege, making it clear that any legal process would have to be directed to the President. In the last great confrontation between the executive and the courts, when President Truman seized the steel mills during the Korean War, the controversy had been indirect. The injunction and the ultimate court order were directed to the Secretary of Commerce.

The prosecutors tried to interview Butterfield the next morning, only to find that he had departed for the Moscow Air Show. Ben-Veniste suggested radioing his aircraft in midair and directing him home, but Cox decided to wait until Butterfield returned to probe deeper into the operations of the taping system.

The immediate problem was to pinpoint a small number of tapes that the courts would be hard-pressed to deny the special prosecutor. Frampton and Goldman began combing the chronology to see exactly which tapes should be subpoenaed. The trick was to pick not those tapes which common sense told you would be most revealing but those which would help make a strong but narrow point in court—that these conversations were important criminal evidence in the cover-up investigation and ought to be turned over despite the normal traditions of presidential confidentiality.

There was a certain inescapable logic to the choices Frampton and Goldman made. The first tape demanded was of a long meeting of Nixon, Haldeman, and Ehrlichman on June 20, 1972, the first time they were together in Washington after the Watergate break-in. It would beggar the imagination of the most unimaginative judge to suggest that they didn't talk about the Watergate break-in at this first meeting.*

The others chosen were of a kind: meetings that looked inherently suspicious and in which at least one of the participants had already talked publicly about it, weakening any claim of confidentiality. The later choices, in September, 1972, and spring, 1973, were meetings in which Dean was present and about which he had given lengthy details under oath. Cox could argue that the tapes were needed for an obstruction charge if Dean had testified truthfully, or a perjury charge if the other participants were right.

The list had to be kept small. Once you convinced the courts that some of these tapes were indispensable to justice it would be easier to go back for more.

On Wednesday, July 18, as the Senate Watergate committee began talking publicly about the possibility of subpoenaing tapes, Cox sent a letter to Buzhardt requesting the eight tapes selected by Frampton and Goldman. He noted that these conversations were material and important evidence quite apart from anything they might show about the President. Second, he said, furnishing these tapes involved none of the issues of separation of powers that were raised by furnishing them to the Senate. Furnishing them for a grand jury would set no precedents damaging to the executive branch.

Charles Alan Wright was in Scotland when Butterfield testified. The

* This tape, when furnished, had an 18¼-minute erasure in it.

White House found him two days later in London, and he rushed back, arriving on the nineteenth, to deal with Cox's letter and the Senate's simultaneous public demand for the tapes. Wright later told columnist Robert Novak that he had suggested to the other White House lawyers that some compromise be explored with Cox, and they rejected it out of hand. According to Wright he brought back with him an editorial from the *Times* of London urging such a compromise, and pointed out that no newspaper in the world had been more supportive of Nixon. Garment replied that it was too late to worry about newspaper editorials. The other parties to this conversation have said that Wright's remarks were made casually and in a political, not a legal, context, and that they do not contradict his subsequent assessment to the White House staff that Nixon was a sure winner in the suit.

The prosecutors assumed that the tapes would not be destroyed at this point and decided there was no need to issue the subpoena until the following week, after the White House had a chance to consider the written request and the public had a chance to absorb the importance of this evidence.* Nevertheless, the Butterfield episode made everybody uneasy.

Cox and many others in the office were disappointed and angered by the Senate hearings. Witnesses like John Dean seemed to be escaping without the kind of hard cross-examining that would test their credibility and expose holes in their stories. Bernard Barker was before the committee for four hours relating descriptions of the patriotism of the four Miamians who entered the Watergate offices. He told the committee they broke into the Democratic headquarters because they thought Senator Edward Kennedy—the millionaire whose brother had launched the Bay of Pigs invasion—was getting money from Castro. The committee members did not probe deeper into Barker's reasoning on this dubious proposition, and no one asked how the Watergate burglary money had gotten from the Nixon campaign committee into Barker's bank account.

* Pat Buchanan today believes there were two principal reasons why the tapes were not destroyed. "I think they were looked upon as the most presidential of documents," he told me. "If anything was privileged it would be these meanderings of the President. Later I think they were not destroyed because the situation had changed so. He [Nixon] didn't believe he could survive their destruction. I think he could have. There would have been another fire storm and it would have been over. The tapes would have been gone."

At the same time Cox felt the committee was mindlessly prejudicing the rights of potential trial defendants, by the televised sessions and the way they were conducted, and by the material that was leaking out of committee staff meetings. "Why hasn't the American Civil Liberties Union spoken out about this outrage?" Cox asked one day. "The ACLU isn't the group it used to be," he concluded.

Yet Alexander Butterfield's revelation about the tapes showed that the committee was doing a thorough enough job despite its limitations of time and format. It was embarrassing that the prosecutors, who could operate quietly and presumably more patiently and thoroughly, hadn't discovered the tapes for themselves despite Henry Petersen's clue to their existence in late May. Nobody talked much about these things. They were preoccupied with individual tasks and worried about the outcome of the investigations. An incident at a staff meeting on Thursday, July 19, reflected the uneasiness.

Cox held senior staff meetings at least once a week so that each task force would have a sense of what the others were doing and would not create conflicts, since many of the witnesses and suspects overlapped from one case to another. They were like seminars. The lawyers would be talking about prospective prosecutions that threatened to bring the government down around them, yet the voices were so subdued they might have been discussing some obscure point in a graduate thesis.

That mood was broken on this Thursday afternoon when an aide came into the room with a wire service bulletin reporting that Senator Ervin had been informed the President would turn over the tapes to the Watergate committee. Three days after the initial shock of learning of the tapes' existence they appeared to be slipping from the prosecutors' hands. Cox was stunned by the news and tried unsuccessfully to hide his disappointment. Hank Ruth, who was normally quiet at these meetings, spoke first. "Archie," he said, "Buzhardt has been giving you the runaround. You ought to call him up right now and have it out with him." Vorenberg, Lacovara, and Kreindler agreed.

The details of the story had now come over the ticker. Ervin had announced that he had received a telephone call from Treasury Secretary George Shultz during the committee's luncheon recess informing him that Nixon had decided to make the tapes available. Kreindler remarked that while Cox had been dealing exclusively with Buzhardt, apparently others, such as Shultz, had been the real advisers to Nixon. Once the tapes left the custody of the President and were delivered to the Senate, Lacovara said, the prosecutors' legal problems would be multiplied; the courts might throw out the tapes as evidence unless the chain of custody could be carefully established. The prosecutors would have the burden of proof that there had been no physical changes made in the tapes. Vorenberg echoed Ruth's remarks. "I think you ought to get Buzhardt on the phone right away," he said.

"Oh, I don't know, Jim," Cox said. "Why not wait and see what develops? I'd prefer that he call me to explain this. It happened on the lunch hour. Let's give Fred a chance to find out the details and call me." He was defensive and very much alone. The others were angry. They began to speculate aloud as to whether the tapes had been an elaborate trap set to destroy both John Dean and the Senate committee. I sided with Cox.

"Why should we let Buzhardt know how upset we are?" I asked. "What's the difference between calling him now and calling him in a couple hours? We should have at least until the end of the day to make that decision. We don't know whether Buzhardt even knew about this."

"It seems obvious that he didn't," Lacovara said.

"Well, in any case, he knows now," Kreindler said.

An aide came into the room with a new bulletin. Senator Ervin had interrupted the afternoon hearings to announce the caller was a fraud. "I have been hoaxed," he said, and cursed the day that the telephone, "this instrument of the devil," had been invented. Cox laughed in delight.

The other staff members were uncomfortable now. "Glory, Senator Sam must be mortified," Cox said. The incident was dismissed. But it stiffened Cox's faith in his own judgment that caution was, for the present, the best course, and that he should continue to cultivate Fred Buzhardt. Later that evening he climbed into my car as we headed off to a dinner together. "Lawyers!" he said in mock exasperation. "I wonder how anybody can stand dealing with them all day."

Cox expected President Nixon to respond to the Senate's public request for the tapes early the next week and to ignore the letter from him as a piece of insubordination not worthy of a reply. Cox planned to hold a news conference on Tuesday or Wednesday, making public not only his request for the tapes but all the correspondence to and from the White

House over two months, to show the lack of cooperation with his investigation. Then he would issue the subpoena. Over the weekend the office was unusually busy with the preparations. On Sunday I took my two daughters, Kathy and Becky, to the office to reacquaint them with their father. Becky was in Cox's office opening and closing the venetian blinds (an infraction for which the security man might have had her arrested) when I noticed that Archie was reading an antique, leather-bound law book which turned out to be the case of *United States* v. *Burr*.

The treason trial of Aaron Burr in May, 1807, was the only known previous occasion when a President was subpoenaed by a court, and it was a confusing precedent. The politics in that situation were even more bitter than in the present case. Burr had conspired with the Spanish ambassador to raise an army to bring about the secession of the Louisiana Territory. Even before Burr was indicted, President Jefferson had publicly declared him guilty of treason. The judge at the trial was Chief Justice John Marshall, sitting in circuit in Richmond.

While waiting for the government's principal witness to arrive from New Orleans, Burr's attorneys asked Judge Marshall to issue a subpoena duces tecum (literally, bring it with you under penalty) to President Jefferson, compelling his appearance at Richmond with a number of government documents and specifically a letter sent to Jefferson by General James Wilkinson, a confessed conspirator with Burr and the man now awaited as star witness. The letter, which informed Jefferson of Burr's plot, also included Wilkinson's suspicions about a number of prominent citizens of New Orleans who might be involved with Burr. The defendant's lawyers apparently hoped to embarrass the Jefferson administration and use the names as a means of making Burr's plotting more respectable. There is evidence that they also expected some War Department memoranda to show that Jefferson had expressed the feeling that it would be all right if Burr were not captured alive, but no such documents were ever turned up.

"That the President of the United States may be subpoenaed, and examined as a witness, and required to produce any paper in his possession is not controverted," Marshall ruled. Having issued the subpoena, however, he was wise enough not to insist on its enforcement, since there was every indication that Jefferson would refuse to come to Richmond. The record is unclear and controversial at this point, but it appears that Jefferson supplied the War Department memoranda and a copy of the Wilkinson letter with what he said were irrelevant parts—including the names of the other citizens—deleted. Since Burr was acquitted, the issue was never pressed. In his argument to the court about Nixon's tapes Cox was to stress both Marshall's sweeping language and the fact that Jefferson complied with the court's wishes even while he declined the exact terms of the subpoena. The White House always held that Jefferson had done exactly what Nixon proposed, that is, decide for himself what the courts should have and what could be withheld. This oversimplified the case, since Jefferson had offered to testify by deposition and did not question the court's powers to seek his testimony. But it was a strong point nevertheless. Against Marshall's grand language, Charles Wright could cite the reality of Jefferson's actions. In his private letters Jefferson stated that he would resist a subpoena for his personal appearance by force, noting that the Constitution had conferred upon him the force necessary. But Jefferson never said this publicly, much less to the court.

Later on that sunlit Sunday I watched Archibald Cox walk to his aging blue Falcon and drive away, the tattered leather volume of the Burr case under his arm. He was about to make the same kind of history.

The next morning, July 23, Elliot Richardson received a telephone call from Alexander Haig informing him that the President was about to refuse Cox's request for the tapes.

"The President is uptight about Cox. He wants a tight line drawn. No further mistakes, or we'll get rid of Cox," Haig said, according to Richardson's testimony three months later.

Richardson met with Cox shortly after the telephone call and made a number of legal arguments as to why Cox should curtail his activities. But he never mentioned the threat from Haig.

At one point in their conversation Richardson casually mentioned that he was considering issuing instructions to Cox telling him not to pursue an investigation of possible illegal wiretapping within the administration. Richardson argued that it was outside Cox's jurisdiction.

"I think you are heading for trouble if you take that position, Elliot," Cox said. "Before you issue any instructions, you might want to carefully review your testimony before the Senate."

A few hours later Cox received the President's answer. For Senator Ervin and the Watergate committee there was a letter signed by Richard

Nixon invoking the Constitutional doctrine of separation of powers. The President would refuse to turn over the Watergate tapes in the best interests of Congress, the President, and the people. He had listened to a number of the tapes, Nixon said, and found them "entirely consistent with what I know to be the truth and what I have stated to be the truth. However, as in any verbatim recording of informal conversations they contain comments that persons with different perspectives and motivations would inevitably interpret in different ways." It was the first hint since John Dean's testimony that the tapes probably contained incriminating comments.

For Cox there was only a letter from Charles Alan Wright. It noted Cox's requests for tapes dating back to June 20, a month before the Butterfield testimony, and said they were rejected for the same reasons in general as the Senate request. As for Cox's argument that separation of powers was inapplicable since he was, like the President, a member of the executive branch, Wright declared, "If you are an ordinary prosecutor, and thus a part of the Executive branch as well as an officer of the court, you are subject to the instructions of your superior, up to and including the President, and can have access to Presidential papers only as and if the President sees fit to make them available to you." Potentially this was Wright's strongest legal argument. Stated simply it said that Cox had no standing in court to sue his superior, the President, that such a suit did not in truth represent a legal conflict between two separate entities. But perhaps the argument seemed politically too explosive because Wright added that aside from this consideration, Cox wanted the tapes for the grand jury and "questions of separation-of-powers are in the forefront when the most confidential documents of the Presidency are sought for use in the Judicial branch."

Wright's letter arrived at lunchtime. Cox's staff gathered in his office, sandwiches in hand. Everyone agreed that the proper response was to announce immediately that Cox would subpoena the tapes. At 3:00 P.M. he walked out on the stage at the Department of Commerce Auditorium and read a prepared statement saying a subpoena was necessary in "the impartial pursuit of justice according to law. None of us should make assumptions about what the tapes will show. . . . In seeking and obeying a constitutional ruling with respect to these papers and records, we would promote the rule of law essential to both liberty and order."

Cox left the stage and disappeared while I tried to assuage fifty reporters who were left somewhat bewildered by this low-key performance. They were confused, and eager for answers to a variety of technical legal questions. Nobody quite knew what would happen next.

Don Rothberg of the Associated Press telephoned a bulletin to his office, which immediately relayed the news to Mike Putzel, a talented and aggressive young reporter who was covering the Senate Watergate committee. Putzel had been standing by on a telephone in Senator Lowell Weicker's office, directly across the hall from Sam Ervin's office, where the committee was gathered. For several days the committee members had been trying to decide what they would do if the President rejected their request. They had postponed the beginning of that afternoon's hearings while they thrashed out the issue.

Herman Talmadge of Georgia had no doubts a subpoena was necessary. Sam Ervin had grave doubts about the likelihood of success and worried about the damage to the legislative branch that a failure would bring. Howard Baker of Tennessee pushed for one last effort at a compromise that would give the Senate the substance of the tapes, if not the tapes themselves.

As soon as he heard the bulletin, Putzel streaked across the hall and, breaking the normal rule, brushed past the other reporters, entered Ervin's anteroom and passed the word of Cox's action to the committee through a staff member. It resolved all doubts. In a few minutes the members emerged, and Sam Ervin announced over national television that the committee by unanimous vote had decided to issue a subpoena to the President of the United States. Sam Ervin signed the Senate's version on national television while Lacovara and Kreindler were still perfecting the language of Cox's subpoena and researching the proper way to serve it.*

In his subpoena, Cox added three items not mentioned in his recent letter to Buzhardt. One was a ninth tape, for an afternoon meeting of March 21. The second was a two-paragraph memorandum, dated March 30, 1972, ten weeks before the break-in, from W. Richard Howard to Bruce Kehrli, two White House functionaries, indicating that Howard Hunt was off the White House payroll. Its importance to Cox was that a copy of it had been supplied to the FBI during the original investigation,

---

* The one Ervin signed on television was faulty and never got served. Two others, one overly general and one requesting five specific tapes, were drafted later and signed off camera.

sharpening Cox's point that executive privilege had been waived in this case. The third item was for the political matters memoranda sent by Gordon Strachan to H. R. Haldeman between November of 1971 and election day, 1972. These memos, which dealt among other things with raising funds and granting ambassadorships, would help make the point that some White House documents by their nature dealt with the President's political life, which should not be covered by any executive privilege.

The special prosecutor's counsel, Philip Lacovara, meanwhile was negotiating with William E. Hall, deputy director of the United States Marshal Service, to have the subpoena served in the normal procedure. Hall said that while the marshals sometimes served subpoenas within the White House compound in civil cases, they would prefer to skip this one. Lacovara made plans to serve the subpoena himself. It was important to Cox to maintain control of events by moving his own case into court quickly. He did not want to see his case become a tagalong, preempted by the Senate in a court battle.

Shortly after 6:00 P.M. Kreindler and Lacovara hopped into a taxi, the subpoena in Lacovara's hand, and alighted at Blair House across the street from the White House. They crossed at the light and walked unrecognized through a crowd of reporters and cameramen who were waiting in front of the Executive Office Building for emissaries from the Senate. Inside, the two young attorneys were escorted to Room 188½, and there greeted by J. Fred Buzhardt.

They were nervous, but Lacovara was determined that no technicality would mar this event. Sometimes a court case can revolve around the issue of whether a subpoena is validly served. Lacovara had never seen J. Fred Buzhardt before in his life and wondered how he could someday attest in an affidavit that the man behind the Empire desk in the lofty room in the Executive Office Building was personally known to him to be Buzhardt. Lacovara had served as deputy solicitor general while Buzhardt was general counsel to the Pentagon, so "partly to break the ice but also so I could say the man was known to me," Lacovara recalled, he began discussing Defense Department legal cases. They talked about the suit of a pregnant WAF whom the Air Force tried to discharge. Then they talked about the Ellsberg case. After about ten minutes, Buzhardt said, "What is there I can do for you?"

"I have something for you, a subpoena," Lacovara said.

"I expected you would," Buzhardt replied. He took it and a copy, and on the back, where it says "Marshal's Return," Buzhardt wrote, "Received by J. Fred Buzhardt, special counsel to the President."

Lacovara looked at it. "Would you have any objection to adding, 'on behalf of the President'?" he asked. Buzhardt's face was solemn. He added the phrase, thereby cutting down the possibility the White House might later say, as part of its argument, that Cox *didn't* serve a subpoena on the President.

Once outside, the two lawyers headed for a telephone booth to call me so that I could inform the press that the second subpoena in history had been served upon a President. Lacovara had to wait for a television crew member who was on the telephone to his office. "There hasn't been anybody go in or out yet," he said into the phone. "Nothing at all has happened here."

Two days later, Cox knew what to expect. To the Senate Nixon wrote declining to supply the five tapes listed in the narrow subpoena and judging the other one too broad to be complied with. If Ervin's staff would be more specific he would try to comply, as long as presidential documents were not involved. To Cox's subpoena he replied with a letter to Judge Sirica. It would be "wholly inadmissible" for the President to seek to compel some particular action from the courts, and it was equally inadmissible for the courts to do that from him. He would, he said, turn over the Howard-to-Kehrli memorandum, which was enclosed, and would make available the Strachan political memos as well.* "I have always made relevant material available to the courts except in those rare instances when to do so would be inconsistent with the public interest," he concluded.

Cox had the grand jury standing by and within an hour he went before them and read the President's letter, explained the background to the controversy and why he felt they needed the nine tapes to complete their work. At his suggestion they voted unanimously to have him petition Judge Sirica for an order directing the President to "show cause why there should not be full and prompt compliance" with the subpoena. Sirica brought the grand jury into his crowded courtroom, where only the defense

* In fact the White House withheld these documents from the prosecutors for two more months.

table was empty. The twenty residents of the District of Columbia (three were absent) each attested that they sought this action from their instrument, the prosecutor. They stood—mostly black, mostly middle-aged, most of them women—as the clerk called their names. Their foreman, a thin, gray-bearded archivist from the Library of Congress named Vladimir Pregelj, stepped forward to help the deputy clerk pronounce the names. When the simple proceeding had ended, they filed back to their grand jury room and Sirica signed the order.

Outside before the cameras Cox was asked for his comment on the President's refusal to honor the subpoena. "I'm sure it was made in good faith but I think it's quite wrong," he said. Then he walked through the crowd to where his government car should have been waiting, but was not. He stood there waving for a taxi as 150 newsmen surrounded him, a scene often repeated during that summer. Archibald Cox perhaps could command a President, but he had poor luck with government drivers.

The afternoon the subpoena was issued Elliot Richardson told reporters he did not believe that Cox was necessarily entitled to obtain the President's tape recordings. He told Sanford J. Ungar, then the Justice Department reporter for the *Washington Post,* that Cox was in the Justice Department and expected ultimately to follow the chain of command within the executive branch. Cox's investigation of a crime "doesn't by itself confer right of access" to the President's confidential papers, Richardson said. He added that it was possible that before the controversy ended there could be several competing voices arguing in court, and he named Solicitor General Robert Bork along with Cox and White House lawyer Charles Alan Wright.

About an hour later Richardson issued a formal statement on the case. It said, "The President's decision to protect the confidentiality of presidential conversations rests, in my view, on substantial legal and Constitutional foundations. The separation of powers argument seems to me to be particularly persuasive with reference to the Ervin committee. It is also my view that Mr. Cox, in seeking access to the tapes, is acting in full accord with the requirements of his job. In the interests of justice, it seems to me important to try to work out some practical means to reconciling the competing public interests at stake."

The next day, *The New York Times* reported that Richardson had sided with Cox in the controversy with the White House. The *Washington*

Post reported that his remarks indicated he was coming down on Mr. Nixon's side in the confrontation.

Cox was asked about it at a news conference. "Mr. Richardson was your student. Do you think you taught him well?"

"I taught him labor law," Cox said.

CHAPTER

4

STORM CLOUDS

"No further mistakes, or we'll get rid of Cox."

Elliot Richardson tried to stay away from the Watergate investigation, to concentrate his efforts on the demoralized Department of Justice. But Richard Nixon and Alexander Haig thrust him into the role of middleman between the White House and the special prosecutor. Richardson played the role with finesse.

Early in July, 1973, the *Los Angeles Times* reported that Cox was investigating the financing of Nixon's San Clemente home.* Within a week Richardson and his staff requested a meeting with Cox and his staff to discuss which matters fell within the special prosecutor's jurisdiction and which were the claim of the Justice Department proper.

From Cox's point of view this was a legitimate gray area that needed to be discussed. Cox was receiving a flood of leads and allegations, many of them only tentatively related to Watergate yet easy to construe as falling under Cox's broad and vague jurisdiction. Many of the tipsters and complainants, including congressmen and congressional committees, had no

* See Chapter Two.

confidence that the Justice Department would vigorously investigate the matters.

For Richardson the meeting also served a second purpose. Afterward he was able to send a memorandum to Alexander Haig, in response to Haig's pressures, assuring him that Cox was not roaming at random through the bureaucracy looking for criminal activity on the part of the Nixon administration.

Richardson continued to get heat from the White House. In late July Buzhardt called to complain that Cox had sought to interview former White House aide Tom Huston, the author of an admittedly illegal plan for gathering intelligence, and two Secret Service agents (the Secret Service had tapped the telephone of President Nixon's brother Donald without a court order). Richardson passed on the complaint, saying the White House felt Cox was conducting an unlimited investigation of all the intelligence activities of the Nixon administration. Henry Ruth, who took Richardson's call in Cox's absence that day, assured Richardson that this wasn't true and that the interviews were necessary to establish what official policy was in the area of electronic surveillance so that activities counter to that policy could be investigated.

Richardson was becoming more or less a transmission belt for complaints from the White House, but he was always careful not to pass on the threat that usually accompanied a complaint from Buzhardt or Haig. His aides later reported that at least once—during the San Clemente episode—Richardson had contemplated resigning over the White House pressures. Such feelings were not long-lived. Elliot Richardson wanted almost desperately to remain attorney general.

To his critics within and outside the Justice Department Elliot Richardson seemed to be playing on two teams, trying to be both a hero of Watergate and a loyal Republican ally of Richard Nixon. To his supporters he was simply doing his job. To Richardson himself it was a case of following Justice Louis Brandeis' dictum that a lawyer's responsibility always is to the situation, not the narrow interests of a client.

Richardson could have no illusions about life in Nixon's universe; he had been there too long and seen too much. But he fancied himself a Thomas More, traveling the road of compromise when possible but maintaining personal standards whatever might be the whoring of the king.

Archibald Cox held him in respect and affection but he was unsure just what to expect from Elliot Richardson. Much later he would be asked how sure he had been of the attorney general. "I was always eighty-five percent sure," he said. That was the atmosphere as Cox headed toward a courthouse confrontation with the President of the United States.

At Harvard Archibald Cox had a reputation for making unreasonable demands on his students. When he was solicitor general he was known for mercilessly revising the work of his subordinates, no matter how good. Both reputations were deserved.

From mid-July until mid-August Cox, Lacovara, and Kreindler were consumed with preparation of the tapes case. Most mornings they would meet in Cox's office and discuss the legal arguments, debating the proper strategy for handling each issue that arose. Then Kreindler would go back to his office, which he shared with another lawyer, and resume writing. As he finished a section of the brief he would give it to Lacovara and the two men would talk more. Lacovara might change phraseology or sharpen an argument. Then they would give it to Cox, who would recommend further changes.

The broad framework of the case was simplicity itself, the clash of two traditions of American law. Cox would point to the early law books of Henry de Bracton, the Burr case in Jefferson's time, and the steel seizure case during Truman's Presidency to show that even a President must submit to the needs of the law. Charles Alan Wright could point to the entire history of the American Presidency to show that no President had ever been compelled to turn over his most secret papers, that no court had gone so far as to interpose itself between a President and his personal judgment of state secrets or of what must remain confidential.

But within those two traditions were all the unresolved questions. Did the courts have jurisdiction? Was Cox, a member of the executive, able to bring a true case against the President before the courts under the terms of Article Three of the Constitution, which set forth the judicial powers? Would disclosure of Nixon's conversations establish a precedent in criminal law so destructive that the confidentiality of the Presidency would not survive? Was Cox's subpoena legally correct? Had he shown sufficient cause for its issuance?

Cox and his two assistants drained the law books of every available precedent. Lacovara had a staff of lawyers to research specific points. Their memoranda were turned over to Kreindler, who would then incorporate the favorable cases in his brief and show the inapplicability of the unfavorable ones.

The broad context of the law was on Cox's side, but hard cases are not won because the petitioner is right. The procedure must be flawless as well, so the judge finds no reason to delay a decision on the merits.

Throughout August the three men worked until time was a blur and they seemed to be living in a slightly different world from the rest of us. We would come to work and go home, take a day off, kiss our spouses, mow the lawn. They would be there, using up secretaries, persisting, writing and rewriting. They disagreed on minor points of interpretation and strategy, in some cases to the bitter end.

The brief was due in court on Monday, August 13. The Justice Department printer required it no later than Sunday morning. It was finished on Friday. Then, in a fit of nervous energy that would have been familiar to those who worked for him in the solicitor general's office, Archibald Cox decided the brief wouldn't do. He tore it apart. He and Kreindler and Lacovara spent the final forty-eight hours before the printer's deadline rewriting the brief once more, the two younger lawyers laboring in a silent fury.

On the morning of August 13 the special prosecutor and Charles Alan Wright, the President's lawyer, stood across from each other in the fluorescent glare of the courtroom on the sixth floor of the U.S. District Courthouse. In the sight of three hundred newsmen, law clerks, visiting judges, congressmen, White House aides, and assistant prosecutors they shook hands tentatively and then retreated to the company of their respective counsel tables. Overlooking this scene from the massive gray marble wall behind the judge's bench were the statues of four men whose lawmaking endured: Moses, Hammurabi, Solon, Justinian. The clerk pronounced the litany of the American courthouse, "God save the United States and this honorable court," and the familiar figure of John J. Sirica emerged and took the bench.

Wright began, portraying the case as broad and precedent-making. He quoted Justice Cardozo, "We must not throw to the winds the advantages of consistency and uniformity, to do justice in the instance." The court was being told, he said, that it had the power to substitute its judgment for the President's on whether to disclose his most private documents. No court in 184 years of the country's Constitutional history had ever undertaken such a thing. In another time it would not be contemplated, Wright said, but popular legal opinion had been distorted by "the hydraulic force arising out of that sordid and unhappy episode" called Watergate.

Cox responded that it was a grave and dramatic case, but one whose ramifications would be limited if it were decided according to law. "The great strength of our legal system is that it is not influenced by drama or mystique," Cox said. "When one approaches the present case in the simple, direct spirit of the law—indeed, when one looks for the consistency of legal principle to which my brother referred at the opening of his argument—it becomes clear that this case is governed by settled legal principles and precedents."

Cox, too, could quote Cardozo. In *U.S.* v. *Clark* the great justice had written that the normal sanctity of secret jury deliberations must yield to judicial scrutiny when there is reason to believe those deliberations included wrongdoing. "We think this case is precisely similar," Cox said. "There is not merely accusation, but stronger reason to believe that the integrity of the executive office has been corrupted, although the extent of the rot is not yet clear."

Each man cited his precedents and dismissed those of his opponent. Wright argued that if the President's conduct itself was suspect, this was the wrong place to seek a remedy, that an impeachment proceeding of the Congress was the only proper forum. Short of that, the President's judgment must be accepted on the need for confidentiality.

Cox pointed to Charles Alan Wright's own work, his monumental volumes on federal practices and procedures, to reject the argument. Citing page and paragraph, Cox quoted Wright's conclusion that it was for the courts to determine claims of executive privilege.

Wright was incensed. "I think this is a matter of much too grave moment for us to attempt to make debater's points by ad hominem argument against opposing counsel." He noted that despite his top level security clearance as a lawyer for the President, "in one of the tapes that is the subject of the present subpoena there is national security material so highly sensitive that he does not feel free even to hint to me what the nature of it is. This is the kind of material that will necessarily be made public, at least on demand of defendants, if these tapes were ordered produced."

The tension in the room did not dissipate as the judge adjourned the court.

A week later to the day, John Sirica ruled. It was the peculiar quality of his legal opinion that both sides thought they had lost.

Lacovara and Kreindler raced to the courthouse in Cox's government car. They called from the phone in the car as it headed back to K Street. Flipping to the order attached to the back page of the opinion, Lacovara said into the phone, "The President has been ordered to turn the tapes over to the judge within five days."

But by the time they got to the office Lacovara and Kreindler had read the opinion. "It's a disaster," Kreindler told Cox. "Sirica tried to walk a tightrope."

Lacovara added, "And he knocked both parties off."

Sirica had accepted Cox's arguments and adopted much of his language but he had drawn back from the conclusion that the tapes were evidence that must be turned over to the grand jury. "The court," Sirica said, "is extremely reluctant to finally stand against a declaration of the President of the United States on any but the strongest possible evidence." Sirica would examine the tapes himself and decide whether they were privileged. He set down no standards for such a judgment but added a sentence that chilled the prosecutors, "If privileged and unprivileged evidence are so inextricably connected that separation becomes impossible, the whole must be privileged and no disclosure made to the grand jury."

The wire services and networks were already broadcasting Sirica's decision as a victory for Cox. To Cox, Lacovara, and Kreindler it looked like a false victory that put the White House in a position to litigate for months, bringing new cases to decide each of the standards for disclosure, which Sirica had neglected to spell out. Cox would have to defend the decision in the higher courts, yet it omitted the argument he thought would be most impressive to the Supreme Court: that Nixon had waived any claim of executive privilege when he authorized the participants in the taped conversations to testify about them under oath.

Cox decided that he would wait for the White House to appeal the decision, then he would quietly file his own appeal to reinstate his best arguments and to pry from the higher courts a more decisive order to the President.

In San Clemente Ron Ziegler announced that the President would not comply with Sirica's order. "White House counsel are now considering appellate review or how otherwise to sustain the President's position," the statement said. Was Nixon considering defiance of the court order? I called members of the press corps in San Clemente. They believed the President was indeed considering such a move. The White House press office was not discouraging such speculation.

Cox had scheduled a meeting of the senior staff, as he did each Thursday afternoon. All the lawyers were in agreement that if Nixon rejected Sirica's order and refused to appeal to a higher court, Cox must ask the district court to hold the President of the United States in contempt. There were penalties available that would not mean jail or disruption of executive leadership. Nixon could be subjected to a fine for each day he was in defiance. The courts could order his salary attached. They could place liens on San Clemente and Key Biscayne if it went that far. And, Lacovara noted, the laws provided that a lawyer in contempt could be stricken from the rolls of attorneys, disbarred.

I alone disagreed. "If we let the public reaction set in, the political pressure will cause him to back down within a few days of the order's effective date," I said. "We won't have to escalate the confrontation."

Cox looked at me. "Why, Jim, I'm surprised," he said. "You are the one who always says we should do what's legally right, and eventually the public will come to agree. We'll follow your general rule."

At the end of the meeting Tom McBride, the head of the campaign contributions task force, took a paper bag from beneath his chair. "Archie, we wanted to celebrate your victory with you today, so I went to the store to get some champagne," McBride said. "But on the way I read the decision." He pulled out a bottle of Boone's Farm Strawberry Hill Wine, with a prominently displayed sticker which said "97¢."

As we sipped it from plastic glasses, Rick Ben-Veniste examined the bottle. "March," he said. "That was an excellent month."

Nixon did appeal, and Cox plunged once again into the preparation of a legal brief for the appellate court. All that would be needed was a supplementary brief to counter the worst effects of the Sirica decision. Charles Alan Wright, publicly resentful that the appellate court decreed an expedited schedule for hearing the case, announced that despite the short time, he would prepare and file a new brief.

"By God, if Charlie Wright can write a whole new brief, so can we," Cox announced to Lacovara and Kreindler four days before the papers were due in court. After some discussion he admitted that he had less to gain and abandoned the idea.

The members of Lacovara's task force were still ferreting. In the microfilm of the National Archives they found, among the records of the judge advocate general's office, another subpoena to a President which had been obeyed. In 1818 a Dr. William Burton had subpoenaed President James Monroe to testify at his court martial at the Philadelphia Navy Yard. Monroe's attorney general, William Wirt, advised the President that under Marshall's ruling in the Burr case, the subpoena was valid. Monroe begged off going to Philadelphia but submitted written answers to the court's questions. It was a small point, but the supplementary brief would note that two previous Presidents had been subpoenaed, and both had submitted to court process.

Cox continued to flog Kreindler for more of the same. One day I heard him ask, in his tentative, indirect way, whether Kreindler didn't think that some research should be done on a specific point of executive privilege from cases before state courts.

"In the ideal world I would say yes," Kreindler responded, "but I don't think it will make any difference."

Cox reared. "Well, Peter, let's strive for the ideal world. I have an open enough countenance so that I look blank when my mind is blank. I don't want to look blank if one of the judges' law clerks has done a good job."

Kreindler left the room to bury himself in obscure cases from state courts. "I have trouble getting these young lawyers to perform as I did when I was their age," Cox added.

"Well," I said, "it's a little difficult to produce perfection."

"It was always assumed when I was a young lawyer," Cox replied.

On Labor Day my wife, Ann, and I went to dinner at Hank and Tina Ruth's. I was sitting in the garden drinking a gin and tonic. The women were in the house.

"Did you see the *Newsweek* item?" Ruth asked. He was puffing method-ically on a Kent.

"Yes."

"Do you buy it?"

"No. I don't know."

It had been a single paragraph:

After vaguely hinting that it might somehow sidestep or even ignore the normal judicial process, the White House announced that it has decided to continue its fight over the tapes in court after all, beginning with a motion for review this week in the U.S. Court of Appeals for the District of Columbia. But that quick response, *Newsweek* learned, may be little more than the open-ing feint in a protracted strategy of delay designed to prevent a final decision in the Supreme Court until the President feels he has got his shattered majority back together again. At that point, White House sources said, Mr. Nixon would be prepared openly to defy anything short of a unanimous or near-unanimous Supreme Court ruling—and to purge both Attorney General Elliot Richardson and Special Prosecutor Archibald Cox in the process.

Ruth sat there puffing.

"If it is true," I continued, "the rest of us have got a bigger job to do." I remembered what Cox used to say whenever we suffered a setback. "Keep chopping wood."

"There's a problem with that," Ruth said. "If Archie is fired, nobody has the power to sign an indictment. We might end up serving Nixon's purpose. Harmless window dressing."

Ruth was wondering what he should do, I thought. "My guess is that it would be like the Office of Economic Opportunity," I said. "They an-nounce they are going to abolish it, and then the political fight begins. Congress gets involved. If we stay put and continue investigating, he'll have to back down."

Ruth said nothing. He smoked. The subject shifted.

The day before the appellate court arguments in the tapes case John Connally spoke in Washington to the officials of his newly chosen party at a meeting of the Republican National Committee. He told reporters he thought President Nixon could well be justified in ignoring any Supreme Court decision that went against him in the tapes case. "We're leading ourselves into believing the Supreme Court is the ultimate arbiter of all disputes," he said, "and I don't believe it. I think there are times when the President of the United States would be right in not obeying a decision of the Supreme Court."

The next day fellow Texan Charles Alan Wright was in a bad mood. So was everyone else in the courtroom. The line outside was longer than it had been in August. (With court set to begin at 1:00 P.M. some of those in line had waited since 8:00 A.M., but few were to be admitted.) Inside there was a large showing of judges' wives, law clerks, and celebrities. Seven commercial artists were present to sketch the scene for newspapers, magazines, and television. Over to one side near the jury box stood Senator John Stennis, the seventy-two-year-old Mississippi Democrat who had returned to the Senate only the week before after being near death from gunshot wounds sustained during a mugging. He stood to the side talking to an old friend, J. Fred Buzhardt. Reporters asked him for his opinion of the case, but he demurred, saying he hadn't studied the issues.

At the bench there were seven tall black leather chairs. Two of the conservative judges had disqualified themselves. Roger Robb, appointed by Nixon in 1969, chose not to take part because he had once been a law partner to Kenneth Wells Parkinson, the attorney for the Committee to Re-elect the President. Edward A. Tamm, once a close aide to J. Edgar Hoover who was elevated from the district court by President Johnson in 1965, gave no reason for disqualifying himself. Wright's task had become more difficult and some detected a note of sarcasm in his soft voice as he began his argument.

"We have read much in the press about whether it is a liberal or a conservative position that I have taken or that my friend, Mr. Cox, has taken. I am certain that considerations of that sort are the last things that are in the mind of this court," Wright said. "It is not a question of whether we are Republicans or Democrats, admirers or opponents of President Nixon. The decision the court is called on today to make is one that will have tremendous and lasting impact on the American Presidency, no matter what the name of the incumbent at any particular time may be."

He expanded an earlier metaphor: "Once there is a hole below the waterline of a ship, no matter how small, the tremendous hydraulic pressure of the sea quickly broadens the gash and the ship is in danger. It will be that way, too, if the hydraulic pressures of Watergate are thought to permit to tolerate even a very limited infraction on the confidentiality that every President since George Washington has enjoyed."

Chief Judge David Bazelon asked if there was any circumstance in which these tapes could be demanded by the courts.

"In my submission, Mr. Chief Judge, there is none," Wright said.

Could Wright imagine any circumstances where the President would agree to make the information available?

"Of course, Mr. Chief Judge," Wright said. Nixon had voluntarily produced a great deal of documentary information when he could have claimed executive privilege. But the recordings were "the raw material of life," the ultimate example of what the President must be allowed to hold confidential. And if it were ever established that any part of these tapes was not privileged, then any participant in any one of the conversations would have an absolutely clear right to hear the entire tape of every conversation in which he had participated without excisions.

Judge Bazelon asked if the executive privilege would be available to a President in an impeachment proceeding. "I am inclined, Judge Bazelon, to think that it would not be," Wright said. "But since I have never contemplated the possibility of impeachment, I must honestly say that I have not done independent research on it."

Judge Harold Leventhal noted that Wright maintained there must be an assumption that executive privilege has not been abused. What if it had been, if "a common law fraud" had been discussed in the Oval Office, according to a party to this fraud?

Wright answered, "My position, Judge Leventhal, would be that the privilege would stand." The matter would be beyond the reach of a grand jury, since the President was involved. "It seems to me that so long as the President is President, so long as he has not been impeached, that when the President says, 'I participated in these in the exercise of my constitutional duty and not as part of a cover-up, not as part of a criminal scheme,' that it is not for the courts, the grand jury, the special prosecutor to say, 'Mr. President, we don't believe you. We think you are a criminal.' I think that if there is reason to suspect the President of criminal conduct, that it is necessary to go to the one remedy that the Constitution has provided for this purpose."

Like his opponent, Cox began much as he had in the district court. It was a "grave and dramatic case" and only twice before (he now added the Monroe example) had a subpoena been so issued to a President. But the court could be guided by settled principles. "To state the precise question here requires care and analysis and more attention to the facts than my brother seems willing to give them," Cox said.

Perhaps it was my imagination, but the language on both sides seemed a bit sharper than it had in the first court arguments, and with a more personal edge to it.

Judge Bazelon asked Cox, "Assuming that the President is not subject to punishment for contempt, what significance would that have to the question now before the court?"

"I think no real relevance, Your Honor," Cox responded. . . . "The question of the court's duty to decide is determined not by its power to enforce its decrees but by whether the issue is one that lends itself to adjudication." It was a textbook answer, but the question was one that had given Cox more anguish than any other before he decided to proceed, and he was still unsure of where this case was leading.

Cox concluded, "Our country is blessed of course, Chief Judge Bazelon, by the fact that Presidents, when the time came, have always bowed to a decision of the Supreme Court and complied with it. . . . I at least have every confidence that the same spirit which has characterized our history would prevail here, both with respect to this Court, or the Supreme Court, if the case should go higher."

The questioning of the judges and the attitude of Charles Alan Wright had the press guessing that Cox would win this round. It seemed logical. Judges, like anybody else, prefer to avoid crises if they can. They would like to avoid broad and troublesome precedents. Cox's strategy had been to distinguish this case from others, to reassure the judges that one like this was unlikely to arise again in a hurry and that the enforcement of a subpoena in this case would set only a narrow but important precedent which would reaffirm the principle that in the United States no man is above the law.

Wright, on the other hand, seemed to offer the court only two choices. It could go against the tendency toward judicial conservatism and issue a broad ruling that granted absolute secrecy to presidential records. Or it could concede that the judicial branch had no legal jurisdiction over the question, an even broader change in the Constitutional balance of powers.

Two days later the clerk of the court called Lacovara to say that a memorandum on the case was about to be issued. As a lawyer dashed to the courthouse, Cox paced his office. "This doesn't seem good," he said.

When he saw the memorandum, his spirits lifted. It was the unanimous view of the seven judges that "the issues dividing the parties might be susceptible of resolution by procedures other than those set forth in either District Judge Sirica's opinion or the briefs of the parties." Since the caliber of counsel was high on both sides, and both men were agents for the executive branch, a solution seemed possible, the court said, which would allow examination of the tapes by the President or his delegate, assisted by both Wright and Cox. If some such procedure could not be worked out, the court would discharge its duty. It asked for a report one week later, on September 20.

"Charlie will have to tell the President that while this is only a suggestion, he must expect that an order to this effect will follow if they ignore it," Cox said.

Approval of the court's suggestion was not unanimous in the legal community. Yale law professor Fred Rodell wondered publicly whence came the new doctrine whereby courts seek resolutions without a Constitutional ruling. "I would say the doctrine is the other way," he told reporters. "There is a principle that the federal courts cannot hand down advisory opinions." If the appeals court memo was not an advisory opinion, "it was damned near one," Rodell said.

Four days later Fred Buzhardt made an offer to Cox. He would provide Cox with written summaries of the tapes containing brief snatches of direct quotes but for the most part summarizing the subject matter and presenting each party's conversation rewritten in the third person.* Cox told Buzhardt he was almost certain that the courts would never accept any summaries as evidence. Still, thought Cox, Buzhardt's opening proposal was not hopeless.

During the next five days Cox walked to the Executive Office Building several times to hold negotiating sessions, first with Buzhardt, then with Buzhardt and Garment; finally he and Lacovara saw Buzhardt, Garment, and Charles Alan Wright.

* One has to wonder, in retrospect, how such presidential phrases as, "For Christ's sakes, get it," and "I don't give a shit about the lira" would have come out of Buzhardt's blender.

In the midst of these conversations Cox asked me, "What would the public reaction be to our accepting less than the actual tapes?"

"Massive suspicion," I said. "The press will decide you've been had. But we can live with that if you're comfortable with it, and if it will work in court."

"I'm not at all comfortable with it," he said, "but I'm not sure we'll get any more than this from the courts."

He was talking about partial transcripts, along with an affidavit from a third party that the untranscribed portions of the conversations were not relevant.

On Thursday morning, September 20, Cox had a written proposal ready to present to the White House. Buzhardt had summoned Charles Alan Wright to answer some of the legal questions Cox had posed. A meeting was set for 11 A.M. Cox's proposal was going to be a disaster with the public, I thought.

Cox's top advisers—Ruth, Kreindler, and Lacovara—agreed that he should make the proposal, although nobody was very happy about it. They were convinced that if the case went to the Supreme Court, they might get no evidence at all from the President.

A key element of the proposal was the identity of the third party. Cox was leaning toward William P. Rogers, who had just resigned as secretary of state. He had considered two other cabinet officers—Treasury Secretary George P. Shultz and Defense Secretary James R. Schlesinger—but rejected them because they were not lawyers. Some would argue that they were Nixon appointees without any expertise at deciding what was evidence. He also mentioned J. Lee Rankin, the former solicitor general. I urged him to propose that name. Rankin had no real ties to Nixon.

At the meeting in Buzhardt's office Cox kept his proposal in his pocket but asked the three White House lawyers if they had considered the idea of a third party arbiter. They had.

One of them said they had been throwing around such names as Republican John Sherman Cooper and retired Supreme Court Chief Justice Earl Warren. (At this suggestion Len Garment rolled his eyes toward the ceiling.) Cox seized on Cooper's name. They had been friends during Cox's previous tours in Washington, and he had immense respect for the recently retired senator from Kentucky. Cox said he thought either would be fine.

As it approached one o'clock, Cox pulled his proposal from a pocket and laid it before the three White House lawyers. He began a long introduction. This wasn't a firm offer, simply a suggestion. The name proposed, J. Lee Rankin, was of course subject to negotiation. But the proposal reduced to a bare minimum what Cox believed the courts would demand.

The three looked at Cox's six-page document. Garment remarked that the special prosecutor had been busier than they had thought. Charles Alan Wright said, "Who is going to go in and tell the President that he won't be believed? Nobody is going to do that."

Cox said, "Well, sometimes someone ought to do that with Presidents. I know what it's like to work with Presidents who don't want to listen to reason, but sometimes they have to be told."

The three men said they would take the proposal under advisement and let Cox know. He left the Executive Office Building around 1:15 P.M. and walked back to the office trailed by reporters and photographers, since rumors of an impending compromise had begun to circulate. In less than an hour, around 2:00 P.M., Buzhardt called Cox. "The answer is no," he said.

Cox's proposal had been complicated enough so that any person making a good faith effort to consider it would have needed more than forty-five minutes. The abrupt rejection made it clear that Cox had never been even close to reaching any agreement with his White House counterparts. And Charles Alan Wright's remark raised doubts whether the President was informed of the proposal in more than a perfunctory way.

The details of the September negotiations were not made known to the public, to the disadvantage of Archibald Cox. Had they been revealed, they would have shown the lack of good faith on the part of the White House and the perhaps too generous penchant for compromise on the part of Cox. They would also have prepared official Washington and the country for the surprise proposal of the next month and given everyone—especially Sam Ervin and Howard Baker—a chance to ponder the ramifications.

One of the few men who was informed of the details of the negotiations was Senator Robert Byrd of West Virginia. "Well, you've offered to give ninety percent of it away," he said to Cox.

The White House and the special prosecutor informed the circuit court that they were unable to reach a compromise. It would be three more weeks before the court handed down its decision.

CHAPTER

5

RECKONING

"I just had the most Byzantine discussion with Elliot."

As the familiar rhythms of autumn settled over the capital in 1973, Richard Nixon could sense, perhaps better than any man, that his time of decision approached. He settled back into the White House for his first long stay there since spring. Also, for the first long period since spring, Watergate seemed to recede from the front pages.

The biggest developing news story was the sudden decline and fall of Spiro Agnew, the administration's moralizer, exposed as a petty grifter by the federal prosecutor in Baltimore.

Agnew had been Nixon's hand-picked choice for the Vice Presidency, supposedly the symbol of middle-class morality, and the revelation of his hypocrisy was embarrassing. But this was an event Richard Nixon could control. His Watergate handlers, Haig and Buzhardt, were now spending more and more time with Elliot Richardson, overseeing the Agnew prosecution. The White House was leaking damaging information about Agnew in a drill familiar to White House aides, a squeeze meant to force the Vice President's resignation. The press and the public awaited each day's developments and once again it was to the White House that people looked for initiatives, for leadership out of a possible Constitutional crisis.

As summer ended, the problems of the world crowded in on Washington. The bloody coup in Chile against Salvador Allende's three-year experiment with Marxism-cum-democracy raised nagging questions about the United States' involvement. In North Africa Libya nationalized its oil companies, raised prices, and refused American dollars in payment. In Cairo the Arab leaders met to discuss oil and Israel, and showed unusual unity. Off the coast of Syria Israeli jets shot down thirteen Syrian MIG-21s.

At home the nation was preoccupied with crushing inflation brought on by the oil squeeze, a worldwide food and fiber shortage, and the obvious drift in Washington. Americans were once again thinking about the increasing difficulties of their everyday existence, after a summer that seemed to be devoted to constant speculation about the legal, moral, and physical health of their President.

The same newspapers and broadcasts that reported the bad news brought images of Nixon returning to normal routine. He sent to Congress a "second State of the Union Message" calling for action on more than fifty previously submitted legislative proposals. He signed a bill that would ban football blackouts on television when a stadium is sold out. He reappointed Nancy Hanks as chairman of the National Foundation for the Arts, and teased her, for the benefit of the cameras, on her success in getting a 900 percent increase in her congressional appropriation. In a more solemn ceremony he presided over the swearing-in of Henry Kissinger as secretary of state. He announced plans to visit Europe in October or November. As *Newsweek* reported, "Behind the President's facade of purposeful activity there was an undeniable reality of purposeful activity, and few in Washington doubted that that was where his salvation lay."

He was perceptibly regaining control of the government, restoring his authority, once again using the unlimited visibility of his office to establish an agenda of priorities. To succeed, he needed desperately to move Watergate to the bottom of that agenda.

On the afternoon of September 20, after Nixon's lawyers had rejected Cox's proposed tapes compromise with almost no study, Elliot Richardson held a long session on the Agnew matter with Buzhardt and Haig at the White House. The two men aggressively prodded the attorney general to drop his demand, made during plea bargaining with Agnew, that the Vice

President make a public acknowledgment of his guilt in a long and specific list of criminal acts. Although Richardson does not recall any specific mention of Cox during this session, he called Cox the following Monday, September 24, and told him, "I'm afraid that there is going to be an explosion. It will be bad for you, bad for the President, and bad for the country." At this point Richardson's aides say they knew that Buzhardt and Haig were dealing with Agnew's attorneys behind Richardson's back, apparently offering to pressure Richardson to relent in return for a promise of Agnew's quick departure. These aides say that they speculated, on the basis of Haig and Buzhardt's attitude, whether Nixon planned to fire Richardson for some misstep in the Agnew affair and then fire Cox once Richardson was gone.

On Tuesday, September 25, Richardson met with Nixon personally on the Agnew situation and at the end of the meeting Nixon told Richardson he wanted to get rid of Cox once the Agnew problem was resolved.*

At this time, although the Middle East was extremely tense, American intelligence was predicting there would be no outbreak of hostilities. One need not believe that the Nixon administration helped create the crisis to realize that, once it existed, Nixon decided to take advantage of it to solve his Watergate problems.

Archie and I talked that week about the forthcoming "explosion," and he speculated that if he were fired, he did not believe Nixon would succeed in dismissing the rest of the lawyers in the office. "I think it will be up to Hank to carry on and up to everybody else to stay at their posts," he said.

"Hank and I have already had this conversation," I said, "and I think he's convinced."

Cox did not talk about this much during the next month, and he said nothing at all to Hank Ruth until a few days before the Saturday Night Massacre. But every so often during these weeks Cox and I would sit around and try to figure out whether the White House would fire Richardson first and then Cox, or would somehow convince Richardson that Cox had committed an "extraordinary impropriety" and get him to fire Archie.

---

* Richardson later told two slightly different versions of this conversation to the House and Senate, fixing it as "late September or early October." In both versions he had the President saying he wanted to get rid of Cox now that the Agnew matter was settled. It was not yet settled on Tuesday, September 25, but the notes of one of Richardson's aides fix the conversation on this date and in the context I have related. This was the only date in this period when Richardson met with Nixon. Their next meeting was on October 20.

We were never able to guess what would happen.

To any number of observers—defense attorneys, prospective defendants, hostile witnesses—it was clear that Cox was getting uncomfortably close to the marrow in a number of his investigations. In late August a second grand jury had been convened for his exclusive use, and a month later the two grand juries were very busy and ready to act.

The first grand jury, which had been sitting since the Watergate break-in, had been through two sets of prosecutors and tended to be wary, aggressive, and thorough in questioning witnesses. The leaders did not much care about the stature of either the witness or the prosecutor who appeared before them. In sixteen months they thought they had seen it all, and they would trust only themselves to do the job.

The second grand jury was still filled with the excitement of it all. The jurors were hearing an array of witnesses from different investigations —the Fielding break-in, the ITT case, the campaign contributions cases. One day in September the second grand jury heard a number of witnesses from one corporation telling how they had been prodded into joining a scheme to transfer corporate money to the Committee to Re-elect the President. It was clear that all the witnesses were scared to death of the corporation's president, who had set up the scheme. They were being quite vague about just how central he had been to the conspiracy. When one of the witnesses finally blurted out a sentence that summed up the importance of this Mr. X, the grand jurors burst into applause.

The White House was to claim later that it was the predominance of blacks and Democrats on the grand juries that created a hostile attitude toward the Nixon administration. In fact, the few white middle-class Republicans on the panels were often the best educated and most aggressive in questioning both the witnesses and the prosecutors. Judge Sirica almost invariably chose a middle-aged white male as foreman of these juries, and there was always a marked degree of white leadership. After a while, though, the grand jurors fought among themselves like members of a family, and in those cases it was frequently some of the articulate middle-class, middle-aged blacks who were the voices of moderation, holding back the others who thought the prosecutors were not aggressive enough. Between September 20 and October 19 these two grand juries listened to a steady parade of witnesses as the jurors prepared to make the decisions that would draw the ring around Richard Nixon's men. After their months of rehearsing stories with their lawyers, of maneuvering, of hoping, these men knew. Some of them chose to go before the juries themselves, unable to face the thought of pleading their Fifth Amendment privileges. Others heard from associates what was taking place on the sixth floor of the Federal District Court. There were no news stories, no photographs of the witnesses coming and going. But in the subculture of Watergate suspects, everyone knew. They wondered only how bad it might be when it happened, how many would be drawn inexorably into the grand juries' ring.

Everyone waited. Cox waited for the tapes. The suspects and their lawyers waited to be called. And at the White House Richard Nixon waited, too, for his last chance to survive.

Even now it is difficult to sort out the jumble of events that took place in this short span, but one can discern certain threads that made the pattern. In the last week of September Spiro Agnew was getting ready to trade the Vice Presidency for a walk away from prison. The Arabs were getting ready to attack Israel on Yom Kippur. And the Watergate Special Prosecution Force was getting ready to take decisive actions that might break open a number of its cases. In all of these matters the President of the United States took a decided interest.

For the prosecutors, there was first the case of John Dean. For months Dean had been refusing to cooperate, holding out for immunity from prosecution. Charles Shaffer, Dean's lawyer, argued persuasively that the evidence against Dean had been tainted by the murky discussions between Dean and the three original prosecutors the previous spring. No court, Shaffer predicted, would allow the special prosecutor to charge Dean on the basis of information he had volunteered during a process of negotiation —information the original prosecutors had promised not to use or to pass on, but some of which in fact had been given to Richard Nixon.

Peter Rient, a bearded, taciturn young man who had joined the special prosecutor's office on its first day, combed through the available information about Dean's dealings with Silbert, Glanzer, and Campbell. He interviewed the three prosecutors at length and then analyzed Dean's testimony before the Senate and the information about him available from other witnesses.

Rient concluded there were two areas where he had committed provable crimes that Dean had never mentioned to Silbert. First, on June 26, 27, and 28, 1972, Dean had met with General Vernon Walters, deputy director of the Central Intelligence Agency, and asked Walters to supply some of the agency's covert funds to pay off the men who had been implicated in the Watergate break-in. Walters declined to do so without specific approval of President Nixon. In January, 1973, after Dean received word that James McCord might start talking, he dispatched John Caulfield to meet with McCord and promise him executive clemency if he remained silent.

Both of these acts amounted to obstruction of justice. Through a lucky break the original prosecutors' files contained undisputed proof that the evidence of those acts was not tainted.

During May, when Dean and the original prosecutors were fighting over his status, Shaffer had complained to Glanzer that his client had been completely candid with the prosecutors and deserved better treatment. Glanzer responded that Dean had not been completely candid. He mentioned the two incidents, which by then had been related by Walters and Caulfield. Shaffer then wrote a letter to the prosecutors in which he asserted that Dean's failure to relate these two incidents had been completely inadvertent. In any taint hearing Shaffer's letter would be proof to a judge that the government was not using Dean's own testimony against him.

Armed with this analysis, Jim Neal went to Charlie Shaffer in September and gave him the bad news. "We are going to indict your man, and sooner or later we are going to convict him, Charlie. That's a firm decision that has been made. Before you and I are through, the case against the higher-ups may be ruined; they may get off the hook. I will take that chance. We are not going to let John Dean off the hook."

Shaffer knew the conspiracy laws well enough to understand the continuing value of his client as a cooperating witness. But he also knew Jim Neal and he realized his prediction contained no bluff. Shaffer had until the third week in October at the latest to decide whether Dean would take the offer of a guilty plea to a single felony count—with the certain knowledge that, first offender or no, Judge Sirica would send Dean to prison.

The Plumbers task force had a similar problem, and in the last week of September they focused on Egil "Bud" Krogh as the solution. In terms of evidence and legal theory Archie Cox did not believe the indictments of Ehrlichman, Colson, Krogh, and the other Plumbers in the Fielding break-in case were ready to move. There was the national security problem, which he had promised to discuss with Richardson before he acted. There was the lack of a cooperating witness above the level of David Young, the former Kissinger aide, whose memory was so bad that you wondered how he got all those degrees from all those schools.* And there was the special problem that the theory of prosecution—a federal civil rights violation—had to be carefully thought through in advance.

On the other hand there were two strong cases, plain and simple perjuries, existing within the evidence, including the documents David Young had turned over. One was against John Ehrlichman, for whom bigger things waited. The other was against Egil Krogh, who had lied to the original Watergate grand jury in August of 1972.

The Plumbers task force was prepared to convict Krogh on the perjury charge while moving their big case through the grand jury. Once Krogh was convicted, they could immunize him and use him as a government witness during the conspiracy trial. There was no hope, in Krogh's case, that he would agree to a felony plea without the indictment; but there was the possibility that, confronted with certain conviction after he was indicted, Krogh would agree to cooperate for some reduction in charges. Unlike Dean, Krogh really believed at this point that he had done no wrong. He was going to need the reality therapy of a trip through the criminal justice system.

Bill Merrill was dubious about a separate attack on Krogh, not because he thought the case was weak. He thought the perjury was an integral part of the Fielding break-in case, and he worried that the break-in case would never be brought to trial. He feared that the dynamics would be exactly the opposite of what others predicted; that once Krogh was convicted, it might seem safer to drop the conspiracy charges, indict Ehrlichman for perjury, then bring individual cases against the Miamians, or drop the break-in charges in favor of other more pressing cases in the office. The Fielding burglary, he feared, would never be tried in a federal court, despite the criminal outrage that it represented. But the consensus of the

---

* After the trial Young's memory apparently improved, because he was allowed to resume an academic career at Oxford University.

task force was to move against Krogh. Phil Bakes and Chuck Breyer prepared a draft indictment, and the case was ready to go in a matter of days.

On October 1 Donald Segretti pleaded guilty to three counts of distributing illegal campaign literature and Richard Davis' dirty tricks task force began work on an indictment of Dwight Chapin for perjury. Tom McBride's campaign financing task force had the cases of a half-dozen cooperating illegal contributors ready to move into court, and McBride was about to indict George Steinbrenner, head of the American Ship Building Company, for obstruction of justice, obstruction of a criminal investigation, and aiding and abetting an individual to make a false statement to agents of the FBI, as well as with an illegal corporate campaign contribution. Steinbrenner had been the first such executive found to be resisting the investigation in an active, criminal manner, and McBride meant to send a message to the business community that such conduct would not pay.

Joseph Connolly's ITT task force was paving the way for perjury indictments against some of the witnesses who had testified before the Senate Judiciary Committee in March, 1972. One of the key figures in that case, former Attorney General Richard G. Kleindienst, came to the office on September 28 and disclosed President Nixon's direct order to him not to press the antitrust cases against ITT, an order he had denied receiving during his sworn testimony before the Senate. Kleindienst's disclosure was another link in the ever-lengthening chain of evidence against Richard Nixon and his administration.

There was more. McBride was poking into several agencies where there were indications of quid-pro-quo activity—favors or punishment in return for campaign contributions or the refusal of same. The dairy industry case was big enough to require a separate prosecution team, and Hank Ruth began to set it up.

And there was the case of Charles G. Rebozo. Until now the prosecutors had been slow in pursuing this case for a number of reasons. Rebozo was not a member of the administration. His hometown of Key Biscayne was so overcrowded with Senate Watergate committee staff members and investigative reporters looking into his affairs that no inquiry could have been conducted with the secrecy we wanted and usually achieved. Until now Tom McBride had contented himself with asking the Internal

Revenue Service to check out Rebozo's bank's books and some other documents, to follow up allegations which linked him with dirty money being funneled to Nixon by way of gambling casinos. But in September the Senate committee unearthed the story of Howard Hughes' post-election $100,000 cash contribution to Nixon via Rebozo, and the case took on a new importance in the eyes of Archibald Cox.

Cox's brother Maxwell was a New York lawyer, and one of his firm's partners was Chester Davis, Hughes' lawyer. If there was a suspicious Hughes-Rebozo connection, Cox wanted to be sure that we were especially diligent in checking it out. On September 28 he wrote a memo to McBride telling him to get busy on the Rebozo case. He told McBride to make all decisions without consulting him, to use Hank Ruth for advice and any necessary decisions. Only if Cox could facilitate the progress of the investigation by helping with other government agencies or the attorney general, he told McBride, should he be called upon.

On October 9 Elliot Richardson forwarded to Cox an FBI report indicating that Rebozo had used the special agent in charge of the Miami office of the FBI to inventory some bills in a safe deposit box. Rebozo said the money was being returned to Hughes. Cox immediately wrote another note to McBride: "This falls in your bailiwick. In view of the relationship between Hughes and my brother's law firm we should be sure to do a prompt and vigorous job of investigating these areas." A few days later he asked me to call McBride to be certain that the investigation had begun.

If the President did not know that Jim Neal was closing the net around John Dean, he almost certainly did know, or soon would, about the other dominoes ready to fall—Krogh, Chapin, Kleindienst—and about the investigative activity involving CRP, several executive agencies, Rebozo and his bank, and the dairy industry contributors. It is thus no wonder that a reporter told me, on September 28, that someone described as "a middle-level White House guy" had remarked that day, "Over here they talk about how to get Cox all the time."

The activities of Cox's various task forces formed the discordant background music for Nixon. In the foreground was the cry of Vice President Agnew, who on Saturday, September 29, began to attack the Justice Department for persecuting him as a way to save face over its failures in the Watergate investigation. Agnew began with a full-throated attack on Henry Petersen, who had been brought in to supervise the Agnew case partly at the Vice President's suggestion. Buzhardt, who was in daily contact with Agnew and his lawyers, told Richardson and his aides that there would be a staged escalation of the attacks, reaching up through the echelons of the Justice Department and then into the White House, unless the Agnew case was dropped.

On October 6 the Middle East erupted in war.

On October 10 Spiro Agnew appeared in a federal court and admitted the truth of a forty-page bill of particulars prepared against him by the Baltimore prosecutor. Despite enormous pressures from Haig and Buzhardt, and the astute maneuvering of Agnew's attorneys, Richardson had refused to budge on this acknowledgment of guilt. As the other part of the bargain, the judge, who had been in on the plea negotiations, gave Agnew a fine and a suspended jail sentence. Moments before the court proceeding an Agnew lawyer had handed the Vice President's resignation to the secretary of state.

For Elliot Richardson this was the end of a difficult period when he had frequently doubted his own wisdom in prolonging a Constitutional crisis by insisting that Agnew acknowledge his guilt. There was no precedent for the situation, and Richardson wondered whether he was insisting on a formality rather than an act of substance. Agnew finally backed down. Many critics were to say that this was another example of unequal justice, of the powerful escaping punishment. But to those involved at the time it looked like a good bargain for the government, which has traditionally reduced a felon's criminal liability when he could offer the government something in return, whether it be testimony or a less congested court docket. Agnew had more than that to bargain with—a Constitutional office. Had he refused to resign, the government would have been left indefinitely with its two highest offices under a cloud, and no clear executive leadership.

Richardson had no doubts about the value of what he had just done for his country and his administration, and he was filled during those days with a strong sense of his accomplishments. One day, after Agnew's resignation, he sat in Al Haig's office and listened to Haig compliment him on his adroit performance in the Agnew case. As he got up to leave, the subject of the President's increasing displeasure with Archibald Cox came up. "It reminds me of the first hard thing I had to do on D-day," Richardson told Haig, who had been a cadet at West Point at the time. Richardson had left school to join the Army as a medic, and went ashore on Utah Beach that day as the platoon leader for a team of litter-bearers.

"We had just gotten behind the dune line," he said, "and there was a guy whose foot had been blown off by an antipersonnel mine, lying in a field of barbed wire just over the crest of the dunes. I didn't want to take anybody else in. The sand was blown—there was no way you could see signs of another mine. So I just walked in putting one foot in front of another, picked him up and carried him out, one step at a time. Al, all we can do is take one step at a time."

The day after Agnew resigned, Richard Nixon, just returned from Key Biscayne, flew to Camp David with the announced purpose of choosing a new Vice President. Richardson held a news conference, carried on live television, to explain the Agnew negotiations and bask a bit in the success of the endeavor. His department, under attack and suspicion for weeks, had been vindicated, he thought. Afterwards, to celebrate, he and two close aides, Richard Darman and J. T. Smith, repaired to a French restaurant for a leisurely meal and a moment of self-congratulation. When they returned to the office, they got the news that Cox had moved the Plumbers case into court by indicting Egil Krogh for perjury.

The Krogh indictment took Richardson completely by surprise and signaled the possible onset of a new crisis with the White House. Richardson thought he had a specific agreement with Cox that none of those cases involving the national security question would be moved to the indictment stage without prior notice to him, so that he could make whatever arguments he considered pertinent (including, presumably, ordering Cox not to proceed because the matter was outside his jurisdiction under Richardson's interpretation).

Richardson had recently reassured Buzhardt and Haig that he and Cox had reached an understanding and that there were to be no more surprises in this area. Now Buzhardt was on the phone demanding an explanation. Richardson summoned Cox to his office the following afternoon, October 12.

The attorney general's meetings with Cox were always friendly and low-key, even when Richardson was maneuvering toward some obscure point.

This day was no exception, although the meeting opened on a tense note. Richardson suggested that there had been a serious lapse on Cox's part, that the Krogh indictment had been counter to their express understanding. Cox was surprised and defensive. He was quite certain, he said, although he had no notes or memorandum on the point, that he had specifically excluded from the understanding any case of perjury.

Richardson reached into his drawer and extracted his notes from the meeting of September 17, where the subject had been discussed. At the top of the single sheet of yellow legal paper it said: "Cox, 9/17/73. Perjury—no apparent national security problem. Will not otherwise prevent go-ahead w/o working out best we can."

The attorney general apologized to the special prosecutor, confessing that he had completely forgotten that part of the conversation. They talked more about the Krogh case and the overwhelming evidence against him. At the time of Krogh's deposition, Cox said, he believed that Silbert already knew that Hunt and Liddy had been involved in the break-in at Dr. Fielding's office. Whatever the national security interest, even if it applied to the break-in itself, it could not apply to a false answer to the question of whether Krogh knew that Hunt and Liddy went to California.

Richardson was in a strange mood, playing the role of philosopher-king. Without actually referring to the Agnew case Richardson said he had "learned a great deal in recent weeks," and had been "forced to examine what was important and what was not" when one had to make a big decision. Cox didn't have any idea what Richardson was talking about. Richardson recalled afterward that he was turning over in his mind his own situation and how it compared to Thomas More and his problem with King Henry VIII over his divorce from Catherine of Aragon. Richardson had seen Robert Bolt's *A Man For All Seasons* and had found it hard to decide whether More was risking his life for an important principle or a formality. Richardson identified with More.

"We are heading into a difficult period," he said to Cox. "There will be times when I will have to push you. I will never push you on matters of principle, but there will be times when I have to push."

Richardson paused, then said, "It wouldn't seem to me that it would be good for the country if I were fired or if I had to fire you." He paused again. "Sometimes it's better to lose your hat than your head."

The two men parted. Cox returned to his office and called me in. "I don't want to mention this to any of the others," he said, "but I just had the most Byzantine discussion with Elliot."

He started telling me about the conversation. Peter Kreindler and Phil Lacovara burst into the room.

"The appellate court has a decision," Kreindler said.

6

A WEEK IN OCTOBER

"We are heading for a horrendous confrontation. . . .
I just thought you ought to know."

Despite the building tensions, the days before the appellate court decision were good ones at the office. There was a momentum to the developing cases, and the many signs of progress gave the place a renewed sense of purpose. John Dean and Egil Krogh seemed on the verge of becoming government witnesses, Richard Kleindienst and Donald Segretti had talked, and Tom McBride's nets were filling with corporation executives who admitted illegal contributions to Maurice Stans' finance committee. The big fight—the legal struggle for the tapes—was going well and would soon move to its final stage. One night in early October Cox and I drove along Maryland Avenue beside the Supreme Court, where some of the office lights were still burning although it was close to midnight. "Well, there it is, Jim," he said. He expected to be inside that building very soon, before the bench where he had spent some of his most productive years, once again arguing and winning a historic case.

The day Krogh was indicted, one day before the appellate court announced its ruling, Cox began the weekly staff meeting by presenting Bill Merrill with a large badge imprinted "Office Hero," in mock celebration of his accomplishment as the first lawyer to bring in an indictment. The badge had been Hank Ruth's idea and it was accompanied by an amount of jeering unusual to these rather staid sessions. Egil Krogh was an earnest young man and within the office he was regarded (with a few suspicious exceptions) as the most decent of the people we were dealing with, certainly the one with the best public image. As a devout Christian Scientist, a family man, and a midday jogger, Krogh was viewed by the press as Nixon's answer to Jack Armstrong. Indicting him was hardly reeling in a big fish, and nobody was more aware of this than Merrill. Jim Vorenberg, who was down from Harvard for the day, summed up the atmosphere at the meeting when he walked in late with a wide grin on his face and said, "Congratulations, Bill, you finally ran Egil Krogh to the ground."

That mood changed in the next days. Richardson's enigmatic warning to Cox was followed very quickly by the news of the appellate court's decision and the signals that this time the White House had a clearer idea of how to proceed.

The court had rejected all of Charles Wright's absolutist arguments and had drawn the case in terms narrow enough to make it palatable to all but the die-hard Nixon partisans. The opinion acknowledged that a privilege existed in some areas, such as state secrets and certain types of internal government documents. Presidential conversations, it said, are normally presumed to be privileged. But such presumption "must fail in the face of the uniquely powerful showing made by the special prosecutor in this case," that the tapes were evidence "peculiarly necessary" to the grand jury's decision-making duties. The President could not rely on some "incantation of the doctrine of separation of powers" to claim an absolute privilege.

The appeals court noted that Mr. Nixon had decided against invoking executive privilege to prevent aides from testifying about these conversations, and this testimony permitted Cox to show the importance of those conversations. The judges "freely assumed" that the President was only carrying out his Constitutional duties when he held the conversations, but where it was proper to testify about them, tapes of the conversations became even more important evidence, the court said. Mr. Nixon could withhold portions of the tapes relating to national defense or foreign relations and ask Judge Sirica to schedule arguments as to whether private inspection of this material was necessary. All other material was to be submitted to the judge along with an analysis of why particular items shouldn't be disclosed. This analysis was to be furnished to the special prosecutor so that he could assist the judge in determining what material was relevant to the grand jury investigation.

The decision was per curiam, unsigned by its author, and thus representing the disembodied view of the five-man majority. Only Judge George MacKinnon dissented strongly, arguing that the President's privilege was indeed absolute. Judge Malcolm Wilkey wrote a separate dissent in which he argued that the courts were not the proper authority to decide the issue, that it was uniquely the province of the executive.

We were "very pleased," this time, both privately and publicly. The White House would say nothing more than that the decision was being studied. Unlike the confusion following the Sirica decision, there was no further public hint of what was in the President's mind. He was showing more confidence in his relations with the rest of the government and seemed more in control of events.

The Middle East War was a week old when the court decision came. The Israelis had pushed their way back onto the Golan Heights, the Syrian Army was in full retreat, and Israeli soldiers were within eighteen miles of Damascus. In the Sinai Desert the tanks battled throughout each night, and the Egyptians continued to send men across the Suez Canal. The situation there was confused, and while a full resupply of the Arab armies was underway from Moscow, Washington hesitated before doing the same for Israel, hoping to avert an escalation that might destroy Kissinger's prized détente. The huge Cargomasters left U.S. airbases each day to stage supplies nearer the front, but the decision for a large-scale resupply was deferred.

It was unsettling. This was pennant race time in America, a traditional time to relax and enjoy the sports pages while easing back to winter cares. In a capital still ravaged by Vietnam the Mideast war seemed especially grave. And in the midst of that first week of war, as Israel's fate seemed in the balance, the Vice President had resigned.

Three hours after the appellate court decision there appeared on the nation's television screens an extraordinary example of the mood in Washington, the fragility of the government, and the anxiety of its leaders. Since the resignation of Spiro Agnew two days earlier, Richard Nixon had orchestrated a highly public search for a replacement. Although this should have been a somber occasion, pointing up as it did another stain on the administration, Nixon acted out a charade reminiscent of his choice of Agnew in 1968. He canvassed the members of the House and Senate, and had one of his political operatives, Anne Armstrong, call Republican leaders around the country for the names of men and women to be put forward as candidates. This was to be the first appointed Vice President in history, under the new terms of the Twenty-Fifth Amendment. As such it seemed a time for careful precedents and guarded responses.

While the names were still pouring in and before most of them could be digested, Nixon flew back from Camp David and staged a live television show in the East Room, where he promised to name his choice before his invited guests. Members of Congress, the Cabinet, and the diplomatic corps joined White House aides in what looked like a small political convention, except that it was markedly bipartisan. Of the congressional leaders only Mike Mansfield declined to join the show, as did members of the Supreme Court. The President, smiling broadly and savoring the moment, gave a convention-type speech, extolling the virtues of his candidate while hiding the name until the final moment. As a loyal, friendly teammate from Congress, Gerald Ford was a great favorite with this audience, and they cheered and celebrated when he was named. It was one of the more vulgar shows ever broadcast from this room. As the late Bruce Biossat, a wise and fair Washington columnist, wrote shortly afterward, it was a strange exercise in unreality. Nixon's demeanor was such that "one half expected to see King Faisal coming along close behind, here to tell us that the Arabs and Israelis had settled their long conflict and the Arab nations were pledging 35 percent more oil production per year to the United States."

The name of Spiro Agnew never passed the lips of those gathered in the East Room. For at least a moment they had a symbol and an event they could rally around, and the good fellowship these men and women longed for had returned.

On Sunday, October 14, Archibald Cox drove his Falcon over beyond Front Royal, Virginia, and spent much of the day walking the Appalachian Trail alone. He did this many Sundays, either near Front Royal or closer to Washington on the trails above the Potomac, along the Chesapeake and Ohio towpath. Elliot Richardson, more distracted, was at his brother's home in Brookline, Massachusetts, relaxing with the Sunday papers.

In several newspapers that Sunday there were full-page advertisements, sponsored by the American Civil Liberties Union, headlined, "Why it is necessary to impeach President Nixon. And how it can be done." The copy underneath the headline began, "Richard Nixon has not left us in doubt. He means to function above the law. If he is allowed to continue, then the destruction of the Bill of Rights could follow. If, after all the Watergate revelations, we allow him to continue, we are accomplices to that destruction." The 1972 Democratic presidential candidate spoke to the Detroit chapter of the ACLU the same day and told his audience that Congress was not ready to impeach. Said Senator McGovern, "The White House has retreated in some respects and the Congress is slowly moving to reaffirm its power, but at present we do not even have the necessary majority to override presidential vetoes."

Elliot Richardson was summoned to the phone by a call from Alexander Haig, who wondered if Richardson could come by to see him first thing in the morning. He talked about the appellate court decision, but mostly about the Middle East war and how it was preoccupying the President. There was the suggestion that the war would be the subject of the conversation. He asked Richardson to come alone.

What preceded that telephone call remains in controversy. After his triumphant Friday evening in the East Room, when the Congress seemed to forget about Watergate and Agnew, President Nixon decided that the tapes case should be resolved outside of the Supreme Court, and that it should be done within the week. That much is agreed to. Haig and Buzhardt, who were present when that decision was made on Saturday, were to say later that the President wanted an accommodation with Cox. But the private statements of these men indicated that what the President decided on Saturday was to seize this moment to discharge Archibald Cox in the hope that Jerry Ford and the Mideast war would blunt the political reaction, and the incriminating tapes would be forever hidden from the courts.

Many months later, when he was reviewing his notes of this period with a fresh eye (he was preparing testimony for the House impeachment committee), Elliot Richardson concluded that the week-long exercise that began unfolding with this Sunday telephone call was conducted by Haig and Buzhardt as a means of getting rid of Cox without losing Richardson. Richardson would act as a buffer for the attacks on the Nixon administration which were sure to follow Cox's dismissal. Alexander Haig's role in this process was central, and he had the complete trust and respect of Elliot Richardson. Yet within two weeks Richardson would learn that Haig was telling people, with no foundation in fact, that Richardson's actions during this week were the result of drinking. (The rumor that he was a drunkard had plagued Richardson for years. It was based on two serious traffic violations he committed when he was in his twenties. A Massachusetts district attorney, whom Richardson had investigated and almost indicted, convinced Drew Pearson to publish the arrest sheets and to embellish them when Richardson was first named an undersecretary of state in 1969. The rumors had stopped circulating since then, but Haig attempted unsuccessfully to revive them after the Saturday Night Massacre.)

The second principal in the week's events was J. Fred Buzhardt, who also enjoyed Elliot Richardson's confidence. Richardson had frequently praised Buzhardt to Archibald Cox, which may have caused Cox to have more faith in or tolerance for him than he would have had otherwise. Again, only when the week was over would Richardson remember what a predecessor at the Pentagon had told him, "If you ever need a job done with no traces, Fred Buzhardt is your man. He can bury a body six feet under without turning a shovelful of dirt."

At 9:00 A.M. Monday, Richardson arrived at the spacious corner office from which Alexander Haig directed much of the government. Fred Buzhardt was to join them later. These three men had met frequently in the past two months, usually over the Agnew plea bargaining, and it had always been a two-to-one affair. Still, they were engaging fellows, Buzhardt rather courtly in his soft-voiced manner, Haig always forceful and exuberant, the decision-maker, wanting to end every meeting with the matter resolved. The former general began with a military survey of the Middle East. The Jordanians had joined the Syrians in the east and blunted the Israeli push, but Israeli artillery was in range of Damascus. The Egyptians had launched a fresh attack in the Sinai after a brief lull, but the Israelis were holding. The Russians were airlifting everything into the area, while they charged the Americans with resupplying Israel with tanks, planes, and even pilots. Jordan's entry could escalate matters and diplomatic efforts were getting nowhere. The situation was precarious and bordering on the first steps of nuclear confrontation.

Richardson was intrigued. Much of this information had already been in the newspapers, but he was flattered to get it first hand and to know the White House still valued his judgment in foreign policy. Richardson hoped some day to be secretary of state. Then Haig began a line of analysis that Richardson had heard before. The Egyptian attack was rooted in the world's perception that the President's authority had been weakened by his domestic troubles. Archibald Cox was weakening the President's authority. He had to go. The President wanted to exercise the so-called "Bickel option," named after the renowned Yale Law School professor who died in 1975. The President would himself prepare transcripts for the district court, and he would authenticate them. Then he would fire Cox, mooting the pending court case.

Alexander Bickel's argument had actually been slightly different. For one thing, he did not believe the tapes were privileged and argued that they should be turned over to the Senate. With the special prosecutor, however, he argued that the courts should not take jurisdiction in the case. Bickel's point was that when one man sues another, and the second man can end the suit by issuing an order, then it is not a justiciable court case; it is wholly within the hands of one party to settle. The President could order Cox to desist at any time, and remove him if he chose to. Thus, Bickel argued, Cox had no real standing against the President in court.

The courts ruled indirectly on Bickel's point when they agreed to hear the tapes case. The issue was never addressed head-on by Wright, who argued repeatedly that the President intended to let Cox exercise complete independence. When his argument once hinted of something close to Bickel's point, Cox had responded that the executive could not have it both ways, that if the President chose to assert his power to dismiss Cox and moot the case, he would have to exercise that power explicitly and accept the consequences. It was this that Haig seemed now to be proposing.

Richardson was taken aback by the proposal. Each time he discussed the special prosecutor with Haig and Buzhardt he found himself explaining once again the mandate that had been written for Cox and the commitment that had been made to the Senate. Haig didn't really seem to understand these, but he would accept Richardson's explanation of why he could not order Cox to do whatever it was that Haig wanted done. It was clear that Buzhardt was an active advocate of the Bickel option as the answer to all of Haig's problems. For more than two hours Richardson tried to explain why firing Cox would be seen as a disastrous breach of faith on the part of the Nixon administration, with the most serious consequences on Capitol Hill and in the country. Richardson thought the plan unacceptable.

What were the alternatives? Haig asked. The President wanted to end this controversy now and he was in no mood for a protracted Supreme Court case. Buzhardt mentioned the possibility of a third party to authenticate the tapes and noted that Cox had agreed to this idea a month earlier. Later in the day, when Richardson asked to see the proposal Cox had agreed to a month earlier, Buzhardt said he was not authorized to show it to anyone. The whole thing had fallen apart, Buzhardt said, over the names Cox proposed. This was an odd claim, since Cox's proposal said, "The President will appoint Honorable J. Lee Rankin (or some other mutually acceptable person)," and since in presenting it Cox had emphasized that the name was negotiable. In fact when Garment or Buzhardt had mentioned retired Senator John Sherman Cooper, Cox had seized upon the name and made clear Cooper would be more than acceptable.

Richardson said that a third-party review of the tapes was the best solution for everybody and urged it upon Haig. Richardson thought he might be able to prevent the President from inflicting a serious wound upon himself and the country, which would jeopardize Richardson's own tenure as attorney general. Those who saw Richardson in these days attest that one of the strongest motivations he displayed was the desire to remain as attorney general.

When he left Haig at 11:30 A.M., Richardson wasn't sure whether the plan was to fire Cox outright, or whether something more reasonable might be worked out. He returned to his office and immediately summoned his new deputy, William Ruckelshaus, to tell him the bad news. "We've got a problem that may be worse than Agnew," Richardson said.

Ruckelshaus, a big open man, responded, "Good Lord! How can that be?"

Richardson told him the White House wanted to fire Cox, and Ruckelshaus said, "They're not going to do that. That's just talk. When it comes right down to it, they can't do it because they know how bad the public reaction would be." Then the deputy attorney general left for three days in Grand Rapids, where he was to supervise some seventy FBI agents who were making an emergency background check of Gerald Ford before his confirmation hearings.

Within a very few minutes—at 12:10 P.M.—General Haig was on the telephone. He wanted Richardson to know that he would try to persuade the President to go along with this idea of third-party review—it almost sounded like Richardson's idea, the way Haig expressed it. Haig said that he was going to recommend Senator John Stennis as the third party, and he and Buzhardt would try to convince the senator to take on the task. The President had a lot of respect and affection for Stennis, Haig noted. Richardson immediately endorsed this sudden idea of Al Haig's, who hung up, supposedly to go sell it to the President.

When the events of the week were over, there was to be a great deal of confusion about the timing of this initiative. Some reporters were told by White House aides that the President decided to seek an out of court accommodation on Saturday, discussed it with his legal counsel over the weekend, and came up with the Stennis plan. According to these reports, which were based on a chronology prepared by White House aides, it was the President himself who proposed the name of John Stennis. This discrepancy with what Richardson was told on Monday could be a misunderstanding or a simple misstatement. But it raises the possibility—considered a strong one by those who watched this process during the fateful week— that Alexander Haig deliberately misled Richardson, threatening the cataclysm, then seeming to back away to a far more moderate position as an "accommodation" with Richardson. There was a great deal of misunderstanding during this week, and it seems that some of it came about because Haig and Buzhardt were once again playing the game with less than a full deck of cards.

One hour after proposing the Stennis plan, at 1:15 P.M., Haig called Richardson again. He had been to see the President, who was extremely reluctant to accept the Stennis plan but agreed with two provisions. First, Richardson was to tell Cox that "this was it," meaning that he would get no further evidence from the White House and was not to seek it. Second, Richardson must agree to fire Cox if the latter balked. Richardson hesitated, and Haig told him to call the White House in an hour with his answer. Richardson's own resignation, clearly, was in the balance. Yet when Richardson called back to say that he could not fire Cox on those terms,

Haig simply accepted Richardson's statement and said he would contact Stennis and seek his cooperation. The President's two demands were forgotten and were not mentioned again until Friday.

Haig and Buzhardt visited Stennis in his Senate offices sometime after 2:30 P.M. Monday. Haig had worked with the Armed Services Committee chairman often in recent years. Buzhardt was an old friend, close to Stennis since his early years in Washington. As they explained the plan to him, Stennis was to perform a judicial function relating only to the Senate Watergate committee. Cox was not mentioned. Stennis was left with the impression that he could work without publicity and that there would be no dispute over his performing this task. Still, he resisted and said he would not be able to do the job alone. He finally agreed when Fred Buzhardt promised that he would assist the senator to whatever degree necessary, a suggestion that brings to mind all sorts of possibilities in light of events.

At 4:00 P.M. Richardson returned to the White House to meet again with Haig and Buzhardt. They gave him the impression that the Stennis proposal was practically identical with Cox's September proposal, which they still did not show him. The Stennis proposal was not in writing. Richardson endorsed it, nevertheless, and agreed to propose it to Cox.

Cox arrived at Richardson's office around 6:00 P.M. To Richardson, perhaps, this was a new situation, but to Cox it was a continuation of the "Byzantine" discussion of the previous Friday. Richardson tried to deflect his real meaning with indirect language, but Cox understood that the Stennis plan represented an ultimatum on the part of the White House. They could be bluffing, but Cox saw that Richardson was worried he would be fired if he failed to get an agreement. Cox had lots of questions.

First, he thought that standards for the job of editing the President's conversations should be specific in terms of what it would be proper to exclude, rather than what should be included. Richardson agreed and accepted Cox's suggestion that the two of them prepare a memorandum on standards for exclusion.

Second, Cox said, the person reviewing the tapes should work with a full transcript as well as the edited transcript, because otherwise the meaning of phrases could be twisted.

Third, why did it have to be Stennis, a man who only recently returned from his sick bed? Cox's aides were to say many times during the week that Stennis could be expected to bend toward the President, who was both a personal friend and the holder of a position revered by the senator from Mississippi. Richardson explained that Stennis was best qualified to assess the national security implications of the tapes; he had arbitrated touchy questions before in the Senate and was a former state judge in Mississippi; he was a Democrat who had great prestige within both political parties on Capitol Hill.

Cox asked, what about things other than tapes? As an example he mentioned the extensive notes that John Ehrlichman took at meetings he attended. Then there was the President's habit of dictating memoranda after his meetings with Dean. Supposedly many of these remained on the dictating belts, never transcribed. There were other written materials concerned with these conversations.

And then, Cox wanted to know, where would he stand on other "presidential" papers and other recordings? Two weeks earlier Cox had heard from Kleindienst how the President had ordered him to drop the ITT appeals. That conversation with Kleindienst had been "off the record" and Cox would not disclose it to Richardson. Instead he reminded the attorney general that during his Watergate committee testimony, Ehrlichman had said he was in the Oval Office on one occasion when the President told him to call Kleindienst and tell him to drop a case. When Kleindienst objected to the call, the President had gotten on the line and ordered Kleindienst to drop the case, according to Ehrlichman. Cox said he could guess what case that was from when the incident occurred. In his notes of this meeting, Richardson wrote, "ITT." Cox said, "It's hard for me to believe that I wouldn't want that tape at some point."

Next, Cox said, where would things be left with respect to the inevitable motions by defendants, once the indictments were filed? If the court left the government with the choice of producing the original tapes or dismissing the indictments, the originals would have to be produced, he said. He asked Richardson why he had not looked at the proposal Cox submitted in September, which was a carefully thought-out proposal employing the same principle of a third-party verifier. Richardson said Buzhardt had mentioned such a proposal but had said it was confidential. Cox offered to supply Richardson with a copy of it, providing Buzhardt had no objection.

"When it comes to sanitizing the President's language," Cox said, "what do you do about parts where the meaning may turn on the tone of the remarks?" Cox would have to rely on Stennis to convey the meaning. "That may do for me," Cox said, "but what about the defendants?"

Cox returned to what for him was the essential question: How could he get evidence in the future if he abandoned his thus far successful fight for a court order? He mentioned John Dean's testimony that the President had discussed clemency for the Watergate defendants. Those conversations had not been subpoenaed. If it turned out that the subpoenaed tapes showed Dean as truthful, Cox would want these tapes and would take steps to get them. "It would be most reprehensible of me if I did not," he said.

Suppose, Cox said, that Egil Krogh was convicted of perjury and then forced to testify under a grant of immunity from further prosecution. Suppose he was then to testify about conversations with Ehrlichman in which Ehrlichman referred to incriminating conversations with the President. "How does one keep from seeking those tapes?" he asked. It would be a dereliction of duty if he gave up the right to such evidence in advance.

As this conversation continued, Richardson, who had been taking notes and executing ornate, detailed doodles on a yellow pad, became more and more restless. He was expected at the White House for a dinner in honor of retiring Secretary of State William Rogers, the first social invitation he had received from the President since before he became attorney general. He began to move around the room, to get dressed in his formal suit, as the conversation continued. The two men had never been close friends but they were from the same Brahmin circles of Greater Boston, trained in the same social graces and service to the law. They were both graduates of "The Law School," as Harvard is called by its own, and both alumni of a smaller distinguished group, those who had been honored to clerk for Judge Learned Hand. There was an easy formality between these men. They could be frank but never disagreeable. Both presumed the other's *bona fides,* as Cox might have put it. And at this point neither was ready to expect utter deviousness from a cornered President and his top staff.

The Cox-Richardson meeting lasted about seventy-five minutes, and then Richardson departed for the receiving line at the White House, where he found Richard Nixon in an expansive, ebullient mood, toasting Bill Rogers and giving him the Medal of Freedom.

I had waited at the office for Cox, because I feared the worst from this late summons to Richardson's office. He stopped for only a minute—his wife, Phyllis, was keeping dinner warm for him—to tell me that Richardson wanted to work on a compromise in the tapes case and that he feared he would be tied up with this subject quite a bit in the next few days. I noticed nothing unusual about Cox's manner except that he was in a hurry to get home.

Later that night I got a puzzling telephone call from an old friend, reporter Christopher Lydon of *The New York Times*. Chris and I had cut our teeth together as newspapermen in Boston, and we sometimes spoke in the tribal codes of that area. "Hey," he began, "what's up between your guy, El Trick and the big E?" At this point I knew next to nothing except that Cox had seemed normal when he returned from the office of "the big E." I wondered if Lydon knew more than I did. Months later he told me a friend had seen Cox leave Richardson's office "looking like he had just been told to clean out his desk." Cox tried to hide his anxieties from the rest of the staff most of the week, but somebody perceptive obviously had seen him in an unguarded moment. I assured Lydon that there was nothing of note to report on, which I believed at the time. As events developed, Lydon and I became suspicious of each other. Lydon came to think that I had lied to him to cover up the developing crisis. I came to think that Richardson or one of his aides had quickly leaked a version of events to Lydon to increase pressure on Cox to settle the case, and that Lydon had withheld valuable information from me. Such was life among friends in Richard Nixon's Washington.

The choice of Senator John Stennis as "authenticator" was an example of the clever hypocrisy of Richard Nixon's Washington. Stennis was a man with a well-deserved reputation for righteousness. Nobody in the Senate, and few in Washington public life, would find it practical to oppose his choice. Yet he was seventy-two years old, and not well. I had shaken his hand a month earlier at the oral arguments and found him frail and wasted compared to the vigorous man I knew when I covered the Senate. He had been shot on January 30, had been near death, and did not return to his desk until September 5. He would rely on Buzhardt to handle the tedious and exhausting job of transcribing and was unlikely to demand that tapes be played over and over until he was sure of their contents.

John Stennis was a believer in the institutions of the central government, whatever his States' Rights background in Mississippi. He was a "national security" man and for years had presided over the little subcommittee that was supposed to oversee the Central Intelligence Agency but which seldom exercised much oversight. Stennis had rigged many a committee hearing by stacking the witnesses in his favor, and he saw no harm in this. He would not deliberately rig this case for Nixon, but he would be understanding and was likely to take Buzhardt's word on any doubts. Once when Nixon was under attack because the Watergate cover-up was unraveling, Stennis had said to the President, "You worked your way up against adversity and you do not panic when things go the wrong way or when the going gets rough." It would be a terrible precedent to turn the evidence over to Stennis for his individual assessment. But few were likely to oppose him if it came to that. On Friday Nixon had chosen Jerry Ford as his Vice President, and the East Room rocked with bipartisan approval. When he publicly chose Stennis, the Senate would applaud.

On Tuesday morning at 10 Cox went to Richardson's office to continue work on a compromise. Perhaps it was something Richardson had heard the night before, or simply the effects of the glitter of the State Dining Room and the attraction of evenings at the summit of power. For some reason he was now more specific about the ultimatum, more open about his anxiety over being fired. If they did not reach agreement by Friday, he said, "the consequences will be very serious for both of us."

Cox objected to working out such an important plan under this kind of deadline. There was absolutely no need for it. First, if the President went to the appeals court and asked for an extension of time before their order became effective, and told them he was working on a compromise, they would grant it without question and with great relief. If he insisted on keeping the compromise secret until it was ready, he could simply file a notice of appeal with the Supreme Court and Cox and the White House could continue their negotiations. It would be weeks before the Supreme Court would require papers, probably months before they heard the case, and the two sides could withdraw at any time.

The idea of a Friday deadline was absolute nonsense, Cox said. Richardson did not offer any logical explanation for the deadline except the desire to moot the case quickly because of the Mideast war. It seems clear that

((149   ))

the deadline, like so much of the White House maneuvering, was simply a ploy to bring about the expeditious departure of Archibald Cox, who had long overstayed his welcome.

Richardson went through those items on which he thought Cox and he agreed, and those where there seemed to be questions remaining. Cox was annoyed at this redundant way of doing business and suggested gently that the two men would have a clearer focus for discussion if Richardson reduced the Stennis plan to writing. He gave the attorney general, with Buzhardt's approval, a copy of the September 20 proposal which had been rejected so quickly by the three White House lawyers. Richardson agreed to write out his proposal and left. That was the last time Cox and Richardson saw each other until after the events of the weekend, although they talked frequently on the phone in the interim.

Cox came back to the prosecutor's offices to thrash out the Stennis plan with his staff. There was nothing on paper, and the basic idea of a third-party authenticator had been studied in detail a month earlier. I remember that the general reaction to Stennis was unfavorable because of his health and his predisposition as an old Nixon friend. We had been through the arguments before, and everyone agreed that the appearance of a fair, objective investigation was just as important as the reality. Stennis would go over big on Capitol Hill, but what would the country think of this plan? I thought Cox would win comfortably in the Supreme Court, but he was far less sure of his case, and some of the others agreed with him. But the question for us now was whether we could live with this solution.

Cox had agreed to hold a long-scheduled off-the-record background session Tuesday evening for a dozen reporters who regularly covered the prosecutor's office. One of the reporters asked Cox if he was working on any compromise plans. Cox tried to downplay the point but admitted that Richardson and he had been discussing the possibility. This was shortly after the session began at 5 P.M.

A few minutes later the NBC News correspondent excused himself, saying he had work to do. At 6:30 P.M. John Chancellor came on the air. "NBC News has learned that Special Prosecutor Archibald Cox has been approached by Attorney General Elliot Richardson on the matter of the disputed White House tapes," he said. "The story is that Richardson asked Cox whether there is any way to settle the issue, an issue now apparently headed for the Supreme Court. A Justice Department spokesman would say only that the two men met yesterday, and again today. And the spokesman would not rule out the possibility that the tapes were discussed."

NBC had broken the ground rules, and nobody was more upset than Elliot Richardson. The White House, it seemed, wanted complete secrecy surrounding these negotiations. We were used to operating under a lid, of course, and Cox believed the way to get serious negotiations was to have them in total confidentiality. But why should the White House want even the fact of the negotiations to be secret? For that matter, why couldn't Cox and Richardson meet with Stennis or anyone else involved with the plan?

By Wednesday morning we still had not seen anything on paper, and our nerves were beginning to fray from the pressure of negotiating under a deadline. We wondered if the deadline wasn't simply posturing on the part of the White House, but Richardson certainly didn't think so, and in any case we had to make the effort. Cox began holding sessions with individual staff members, so that he could argue all sides of the proposal, and hear all points of view. My turn came when I went to brief him on the day's news. It seemed to me that it would be hard to settle for any proposal where one man became the arbitrary instrument to replace the accepted system of grand juries, judges, and petit juries. Part of our job was to convince the American people that the system operated, and operated with integrity.

Yes, Cox said, but there were some things you just couldn't convince some people about. "Sometimes there are things you have to do because you believe them to be for the best," he said. "I'll turn your own words around on you: You do what's right and have faith that you can make people understand."

Well, I said, perhaps in a democracy such as ours, if a majority of the people refuse to believe in the method you've chosen, then it's not the right method.

"No," he said, "I would never accept that."

"If Archie rejects this plan," Jim Neal said, "many people—maybe not *The New York Times,* but many people—will think that Archie Cox is setting himself up as a Super-President, with the power to do whatever he wishes without any check, to make any demands he wants on the President of the United States." Neal was the first man I heard refer to Stennis as "the Judge" (he pronounced it à la Tennessee—"jedge"), but we were to hear that phrase often in the coming days.

Neal suggested that the courts be brought into the process at the outset by having Stennis appointed a "Special Master" under a court order, a common procedure in arbitration cases, and one which would give the Stennis plan greater legitimacy. The procedural issues, as well as Stennis' health and the desirability of having more than one person perform the difficult auditing task, were all questions more likely to be thrashed out in public if the courts became involved in the selection process.

That morning President Nixon met with the foreign ministers of Saudi Arabia, Kuwait, Morocco and Algeria as representatives of the eighteen foreign ministers from the Arab states. The Saudi minister, Omar Sakkaf, told the press assembled in the Rose Garden, "The meeting and discussions were fruitful, and we think the man who could solve the Vietnam war, the man who could have settled the peace all over the world, can easily play a good role in settling and having peace in our area of the Middle East."

As the ministers met, Richardson completed his draft proposal and handed it to Fred Buzhardt, who took it back to the White House. Richardson then went to the State Department to dine with Henry Kissinger in the secretary's private dining room. Kissinger was called from the table for a report from the President. When he returned he said, "He must really want to get rid of Archie Cox badly. He started talking about it in the middle of our conversation about the Middle East."

That afternoon at federal district court, Judge Sirica ruled against the Senate Watergate committee in its suit for the tapes. The ruling removed any likelihood that the committee would get access to the White House tapes.

At 3:30 P.M. Buzhardt returned to Richardson's office with a redraft of the Stennis proposal. There had been several minor changes, and Richardson got the impression that they were made at the President's order, although Buzhardt did not say this. There was also one major change, which Buzhardt passed off as nothing more than a grammatical refinement. At the end of Richardson's first draft there was a section entitled "Other Tapes and Documents" which said, "The proposed arrangement would undertake to cover only the tapes heretofore subpoenaed by the Watergate grand jury at the request of the special prosecutor." That section was omitted in the redraft of the proposal. It had been put in originally because Cox, of course, wanted a guarantee that if he gave up his court fight he would win agreement on a permanent procedure.

Buzhardt explained the omission of that last section by saying it was redundant; on the face of it the proposal dealt only with the nine tapes already subpoenaed. Richardson accepted this explanation, and the section was deleted. Around 5 P.M. he finished a final draft on plain white paper with no letterhead entitled simply "A Proposal" and dispatched it to Cox by messenger.

At 6:15 he called the special prosecutor to get his reaction. "I think I should respond in writing, Elliot," Cox said. "It would be more careful that way."

At Richardson's house on Chain Bridge Road about twenty people gathered that evening to celebrate Bill Ruckelshaus' recent confirmation as deputy attorney general. Among the guests were *Washington Post* political columnist David Broder and his wife. After the meal Elliot Richardson rose to toast Ruckelshaus. He began by quoting a line from a poem called "McSorley's Wonderful Saloon" which begins, "Here's to the little people," and he grew more and more philosophical as his toast progressed.

After dinner the guests went to Richardson's study, overlooking the lights of the Potomac at Little Falls, and sat in a large semi-circle. Richardson's monologue continued, deeply philosophical and, to at least some of the guests, impenetrable. He was speaking about the role of the government servant, his duties and his obligations and his accountability to "the little people." Almost all the guests were struck by his unusual mood. On the way home David Broder turned to his wife, Anne, and said, "What the hell was going on back there?" She didn't know.

It seemed to one guest who knew Richardson well that he was trying to work out some complex problem that had to do with a clash between his personal ethics and his commitment to government service. "Elliot got very philosophical," this guest said. "I've seen him do that before and since, but not very often, and particularly not at an affair like that. It was obviously going through his head at the time that he might not be in the administration much longer, and he didn't like the thought of that very much. He felt trapped and was trying to bring some perspective to it. He was sort of thinking out loud. He often does that."

As Richardson's party was breaking up near midnight, John Dean sat alone in a corridor within the ninth floor complex at 1425 K Street. He was to remain there for several hours while Charles Shaffer and Jim Neal wrestled over his fate on the other side of the door. Shaffer had come in a few days earlier, having been informed that Dean would be indicted no later than October 24. Dean was ready to plead (and indeed had been for some weeks) but Shaffer was fighting over every dotted "i" and crossed "t" in the bill of particulars to which Dean would plead guilty. Every so often Shaffer would leave the room and hold a conference with Dean.

It was close to 2:30 A.M. when Shaffer brought Dean the final item for discussion, the letter of agreement to be signed by Archibald Cox. In it was a sentence that said, "This disposition will not bar prosecution for perjury should it ever be discovered that your client has given materially false testimony in connection with matters within the jurisdiction of the Special Watergate Prosecutor." Dean had already testified on national television and before the grand jury in great detail about his conversations with the President, and he now could expect that the testimony would be matched with the tapes of the conversations themselves. "When Charlie came back in that door and said, 'He says it's okay,' I knew that John Dean's version of events was accurate, and I knew that Archie Cox was in serious trouble with the President," Jim Neal said.

If Richard Nixon had not already planned to dispatch Archie Cox, the events of this week made it clear that he was running out of time. On Monday Senate Republican Whip Robert Griffin had told a reporter that an impeachment inquiry would result if Nixon defied a Supreme Court order. On Tuesday presidential adviser Melvin Laird said the same thing to a group of political reporters. On Wednesday Judge Sirica dismissed the Senate's suit for the tapes, saying he lacked jurisdiction. This left Cox as the last barrier to Richard Nixon's escape from exposure by tape. On Thursday the Knight newspapers reported that Cox had opened an investigation into Bebe Rebozo's finances, and Edward Kennedy told the Senate that Congress should reject the nomination of Gerald Ford unless he acknowledged the obligation of the President to obey the Supreme Court.

Thursday was a day of decision for Archibald Cox. He had the attorney general's proposal in writing and he had the thoughts of his staff. He was receiving advice from closer to home. When the rumors of a compromise began to circulate in the national news, Cox's youngest daughter, Phyllis, a second-year law student at the University of Denver, telephoned her mother to say, "There is no man in the world with more integrity than my father, no man I respect more. If he compromises on the tapes, I'll lose faith in everything I hold dear." Then Cox picked up *The New York Times* to find a column speculating on the compromise negotiations written by an old and dear friend, Anthony Lewis, whose reporting from the Supreme Court had won him his second Pulitzer Prize. It said:

> All this must put the most extraordinary pressure on Archibald Cox. Just consider the difficulty—legal, moral, institutional—of the choices that he may face . . .
>
> Over this long summer and fall, the tapes issue has taken on a life of its own. It has become a test of the principle that rulers in a democracy, like those ruled, are subject to the law. If that question of obedience to law were now apparently compromised away, would the public or a significant part of it feel cynically betrayed?
>
> I do not know Cox's thoughts on these questions. But I do know what kind of person he is, and that is significant.
>
> Mr. Cox cares deeply about institutions. If he thought the role of the Supreme Court might be genuinely injured by a clash with the President in this case, that would concern him. But it hardly needs to be said that he also cares powerfully for the supremacy of law.
>
> Some in the White House, perhaps ridden by paranoia or guilt, have been putting it about for months that Cox is out to get Richard Nixon. Nothing could be a less accurate reading of the man. He is out to do his job. That sounds pompous, but it happens that Cox has less in him of self-gratification than almost any public man.
>
> He is in a terribly delicate position now. If he gets into negotiations and in the end says no to a compromise—especially one endorsed by the Attorney General—he will risk a White House attempt to do what it has always wanted to do: fire him. And he is essentially alone in all this. He has no institution behind him, no powerful colleagues, no party.
>
> The questions are not easy ones. There is even a factual doubt, after all, about what the tapes may contain. The law is not certain either; it never is in this sort of case. But there is the momentum of the Court of Appeals decision, one that so clearly bespeaks an effort to be cautious, moderate, particular. The only certainty is that Archibald Cox will not yield to pressures or care for his own convenience. He will do what he concludes is in the interest of the law.

For a man who didn't trust emotions these were difficult days. Archibald Cox was deeply affected by his daughter's telephone call—she was the only one of his three children who had chosen to study law—and he was just as moved by Tony Lewis' writing. At midmorning, after receiving a report from Jim Neal about the breakthrough with Dean, Archie Cox sat down to write his response to "A Proposal."

His two-page answer had eleven points. The essential idea of an out-of-court settlement, with no direct access to the tapes by the special prosecutor, was "not unacceptable." He would be glad to sit down with anyone to work out a settlement, if they could. Then he addressed the issue of John Stennis. Cox never analyzed the political problems of Stennis with his aides during this week. He simply listened. But he was to remark afterward that the choice of Stennis had been ingenious on the part of the White House, because it would divide liberals and conservatives and serve to deflect the real issue. He hoped to avoid that. He wrote, "The public cannot be fairly asked to confide so difficult and responsible a task to any *one* man operating in secrecy, consulting only with the White House. Nor should we be put in the position of accepting any choice made unilaterally."

He proposed the idea of "Special Masters," whose names would be disclosed, along with the agreement, before the work began. He found the objective of the proposal too narrow and the standards for omissions too broad, and suggested, "to dispel cynicism," that the tapes be electronically checked for tampering and to enhance any portions that seemed garbled. Finally, he asked what the "practical and political links" would be between any agreement and the demands of the Ervin committee.

Cox and his top staff worked over this draft, making only minor changes but one important exclusion. They deleted a sentence that said, "I can hardly be expected to negotiate these issues with the implicit threat of dismissal hanging over my head, if the negotiations are unsatisfactory to the other party."

It was midafternoon before Cox's driver left for the Attorney General's office with his comments. Richardson carried the draft to the White House around 6:00 P.M., where he found a war council in progress in Haig's office. Besides the former general and Buzhardt, Leonard Garment was there and Charles Alan Wright as well. All of them read Cox's comments as a rejection, and a snidely worded one at that. Wright, who had come to

Washington to finish his petition to the Supreme Court, argued eloquently on behalf of the Stennis proposal, which he was seeing for the first time. He found it far more accommodating than he would have expected and he was outraged that Cox had rejected it. Wright said that Nixon had a "fifty-fifty" chance of prevailing in the Supreme Court at any rate.

Like the others present (except Richardson) he argued that there was now no alternative but to dismiss Cox, and expressed optimism that the American public would find Nixon's position reasonable. Although he was new to this situation, Wright quickly became very excited. Richardson, outnumbered and out-argued, finally said, "Charlie, why don't you call Archie and see if you can sell it to him?" Richardson left the White House in a state of confusion. He thought the Stennis proposal was sound and that Cox was unreasonable to reject it. But he didn't understand the White House insistence that Cox must be fired forthwith for his counterproposal. When Richardson gets confused, he becomes even more analytical than usual. At home he sat down with a yellow pad and wrote across the top of it: "Why I Must Resign." One of his aides was to remark afterward that during this week Elliot Richardson was on an "emotional roller coaster" that sped from euphoria to despondency and back again as the White House manipulated him. Now he would try to sort out the factors.

First, it was a condition of his confirmation that he not fire Cox except for "some egregiously unreasonable action." Second, he wrote, "While Cox has rejected a proposal I consider reasonable, his rejection of it cannot be regarded as being far beyond the pale," justifying his being fired. He was, Richardson noted, being asked to accept significantly less than he won in two court decisions. "Besides," he added, "I really believe that in all my dealings with him he has been honest and fair." Third, there needed to be a special prosecutor. "I don't feel that I could effectively deal with Buzhardt et al in Cox's place," he wrote. "I am in fact loyal to the President and I am by temperament a team player . . ." Fourth, the Agnew situation didn't really prove his independence, he wrote. "On the contrary many people feel that the President's interests were served by the part I played in bringing about the vice president's resignation."

This exercise in self-analysis went on, with seven reasons (and four additional sub-reasons) neatly listed. It concluded: "I do not believe the President's attitude toward Cox is fundamentally valid: many problems and headaches could have been avoided by cooperating with him more and fighting him less. However that may have been, this feeling on my part makes it all the harder for me to justify his firing."

Richardson folded the papers and put them in his briefcase. In the morning he would have his secretary type his notes up, and he would take them to the White House. It was time for Elliot Richardson to demand a meeting with Richard Nixon.

As Richardson was writing, a comedy of errors was taking place between the prosecutor's office and the White House. The White House operator had called to announce that "Marshall Wright" wanted to talk to Cox, who had left to have dinner with his brother's family. As far as we knew, we should be hearing from Richardson or perhaps Buzhardt. *Charles* Wright was presumably in Texas. The name Marshall Wright rang a bell with me, but I thought he was in foreign affairs.* In any case Hank Ruth found Cox and asked him to stand by for a call from Marshall Wright. Cox, who was now suspicious of Charles Alan Wright's motivations and annoyed by his posturing, later wondered if Wright had become a field marshal for the battle of the tapes.

Cox was sitting on the floor, his brother Louis' children jabbering excitedly at the thought of an urgent call from the White House for Uncle Archie. When Charles Alan Wright came on the line, Cox said, "Oh, it's you, Charlie." As Cox remembered the conversation, Wright referred to the "Comments" on the Stennis proposal and said, "There are four stipulations you must make that will be essential to any agreement. You won't agree to these, and there is no sense in continuing conversations if you don't."

The four points were that the tapes would have to be heard by John Stennis and only John Stennis; that there would be no designation as "Special Master"; that no portion of the actual tapes would be provided to the courts or to anyone under any circumstances; and finally that Cox must agree not to subpoena any additional presidential tape, paper or document.

"You catch me in a difficult position, Charlie," Cox said. "I'm sitting on the floor at my brother's house and we're in the middle of dinner.

---

* Marshall Wright was a member of the National Security Council staff and later assistant secretary of state for congressional affairs. Since he was the only "Mr. Wright" on the White House staff at the time, the operator presumed he was placing the call.

There are children running about. I don't think I ought to be put in a position of responding under these conditions, do you? Why don't you dictate the four points and I can look at them tomorrow morning and give you a reply? I don't mean to imply that you should be optimistic."

Although the conversation was polite and tentative, both Cox and Wright knew that Cox was opposed to Wright's proposals.

This was the night of the long phone calls—Cox and his aides sifting Charles Wright's words, Richardson and his aides rehashing the meeting at the White House, Nixon and his aides waiting.

The press was calling with rumors. Throughout the Watergate crisis, periods would come and go when the small town of Washington sensed climactic developments but had no firm information. Rumors always filled the void. This night I was told that Buzhardt had counseled the President not to take the tapes case to the Supreme Court; that a firm compromise was in the air; that the White House was considering making public partial transcripts of the tapes and then sitting back, declining to appeal to the Supreme Court, declining to present the material to the lower courts; that David Broder would have a story in the *Washington Post* saying that Richardson and Cox had met twice the past week to negotiate a compromise; that Linda Charlton would have a story in *The New York Times* saying that Richardson had been meeting with White House lawyers and with Cox during the week, but that no details of those meetings were available.

By the next morning, Friday, October 19, the parties to the tapes controversy were emotionally and physically drained from a week of forced march toward the precipice, led by General Alexander Haig on behalf of his commander-in-chief. Now they had arrived at the brink.

At 8:00 A.M. the three teams—the President's, the attorney general's, and the special prosecutor's—were separately huddled in three conferences a few blocks from each other. It was a magnificent fall day in Washington, but none of these men noticed. For them it was a day that began a three-cornered chess game that would slowly draw to a climax in the next thirty-six hours.

Richardson's men gathered in his office, where he passed out carbon copies of a neatly typed sheet entitled "Summary of Reasons Why I Must Resign—ELR Oct. 19, 1973." It was the document he had written the night before. There was no disagreement with it among his top aides—

Jonathan Moore, J. T. Smith, and Richard Darman. At 8:35 A.M. Richardson telephoned Bill Ruckelshaus to tell him his decision. At 9:15 A.M., he called Alexander Haig and was told that the negotiations with Cox were continuing, that they expected further word from Cox that morning. "If you reach an impasse, I would like to see the President as soon as possible," Richardson said. It was understood that he was asking for an audience to submit his resignation.

As Richardson met with his aides, J. Fred Buzhardt took a phone call from an attorney in the Manhattan federal prosecutor's office, James Rayhill. He wanted to know what he should tell the judge in the Mitchell-Stans case about the availability of the tapes in which Dean and the President discussed Dean's bid for immunity. Buzhardt told Rayhill that there might be "technical problems" with some of the tapes. He would call back. At 9:30 A.M. Buzhardt called to say he had talked to the President of the United States about this matter. He would not say whether such tapes existed. If they did, the President refused to turn them over to the judge *in camera* "at this stage."

In the courtroom the prosecutors told the judge they were "more than willing" to turn over any possible evidence to him for *in camera* inspection, but that the White House took a different view. The government reluctantly asked the judge for a postponement until January, in hope that the Supreme Court or the parties would have settled the issue. The government lawyers did not tell the judge that Buzhardt thought there might be "technical difficulties" with the tapes.*

Around 8:30 A.M. Archie Cox received Charles Alan Wright's letter, which was dated the day before and began, "Dear Mr. Cox: This will confirm our telephone conversation of a few minutes ago." But as Cox and his aides read the letter, they found in it almost no mention of the four demands of the evening telephone call, and especially the most important point—that Cox was to desist from seeking any more evidence from the White House. Rather than an elucidation of the demands of the night before, Wright's letter was an apologia for the "very reasonable proposal" put forth through Richardson. It presumed total rejection by Cox, whose comments on it, the letter said, departed so far from the proposal and its

* Much later both Buzhardt and President Nixon disclosed that they had known two of the nine subpoenaed tapes were missing as early as September.

purposes that the White House could not accede to some of them in any form.

Finally, there was a threat: "If you think that there is any purpose in our talking further, my associates and I stand ready to do so. If not, we will have to follow the course of action that we think in the best interests of the country. I will call you at 10:00 A.M. to ascertain your views. Sincerely, Charles Alan Wright."

Cox read the letter and laid it on the conference table. The rest of us—Ruth, Lacovara, Kreindler, myself—crowded around it. "Very clever lies," Cox said. For him that was strong language.

Cox had no intention of letting Wright's letter remain on the record with no answer except a telephone call. Besides, he was due in court at 10:00 A.M. to witness Dean's guilty plea. He sat down and composed a quick letter. I think he knew that Wright stood on formalities, so he began, "Dear Charlie." Wright's letter was clear, Cox responded, but it required "a little fleshing out" in view of the original phone call that it purported to confirm. He pointed out that in the phone call Wright had made demands that must be agreed to categorically, and he spelled them out. "These points should be borne in mind in considering whether the proposal put before me is 'very reasonable,'" Cox wrote. "I have a strong desire to avoid confrontation, but I could not conscientiously agree to your stipulations without unfaithfulness to the pledges which I gave the Senate prior to my appointment."

As Cox wrote, his staff began preparations for "the course of action" which Wright and his colleagues planned "in the best interests of the country." John Barker went to the bank on the first floor—he was there when the doors opened at 9—and opened up a safe deposit box. While he was filling out the application, Kreindler joined him with an envelope filled with the correspondence with the White House. Ruth and Lacovara left for the White House to deliver Cox's answer.

In the meantime a bulletin rattled over the teletype wires: "The Special Prosecutor's office announces there will be a proceeding in Judge Sirica's courtroom at 10:00 A.M. No details until after the proceeding." We left for court, where the most important guilty plea we would ever take was about to be entered.

When Ruth and Lacovara arrived at the Executive Office Building, they were informed that there was nobody available—not Buzhardt, Wright, Garment, or any of their assistants—to receive an envelope. That bulletin on the wires had been misinterpreted as a move by Cox in the tapes case. The two young lawyers left Cox's letter with a guard at the desk and headed for court. It did not take the White House lawyers long to reappear. At 9:55 A.M., shortly after the letter was delivered, Haig called Richardson and told him Cox had rejected Wright's efforts. Richardson was told to come to the White House. The President could see him right away.

While Haig was summoning Richardson to the White House, Jim Neal, Charles Shaffer, and John Dean arrived in the basement of the courthouse where Dean would enter his guilty plea.* As they walked through the garage, Neal called Shaffer aside. He had waited until the last possible moment. "Charlie," Neal said, "I'm not supposed to talk about this, but you ought to know before we go up there. We are heading for a horrendous confrontation with the White House over these tapes. I just thought you ought to know."

"What do you think is going to happen, Jim?"

"To tell you the truth, I don't think we are going to be around much longer, Charlie."

There was a long pause. Dean stood ten feet away, wondering about this last-minute conference between the lawyers.

"If you don't want to go through with this today, that's okay," Neal said.

"No. Shit, Jim, we've done it. He wants to do it," Shaffer said. They all got on the elevator for the second floor.

---

* Jim Neal resigned from the special prosecutor's office after Dean's appearance in court. Some of the lawyers in the Criminal Division of Justice had been sniping at Neal because he had not resigned his law practice. Although the department had ruled favorably on the propriety of his position as a special consultant, Neal was uncomfortable. He had had to give up some federal criminal cases and postpone others so that his firm, a small one in which he was the major litigator, would not appear to be in conflict. He had become increasingly unhappy in this position. "A prosecutor has to be a guy who doesn't give a damn about anything," Neal told me. "I'm half in and half out. I've got a family in Nashville that needs attention, and a law practice that needs me. I've got to cut out. With Dean brought in it's easier to go."

7

SHOWDOWN

*"I read in one of the newspapers this morning
the headline 'Cox Defiant.'
I don't feel defiant."*

The attorney general and his aides knew that when Elliot Richardson left his office the end was at hand. When he returned he would no longer be attorney general, and they would no longer be his aides. Each of them shook hands with him as he departed.

But at the White House Richardson found Alexander Haig in a more optimistic and conciliatory mood. There was no need to fire Cox, he said. They could simply go ahead with the Stennis plan, which now had the approval of bipartisan leaders of Congress * and was likely to be acceptable to the country and the courts. It was not a necessary adjunct to proposing this plan that Cox be fired, Haig said. This change of position

---

* According to one official this was a reference to the fact that Haig had checked the plan with the chairman and ranking minority member of the Senate Judiciary Committee, James Eastland and Roman Hruska. Philosophically, Eastland and Hruska run the gamut of congressional opinion from A to B.

eliminated Richardson's reasons for resigning, and he was euphoric. They were back to Utah Beach, taking things step by step, and he was a survivor, he thought.

Buzhardt, Garment, and Wright joined the discussion, and all agree that Richardson was enthusiastic about this new approach. Shortly thereafter Haig left the meeting, saying that he was going to persuade the President that it was not necessary to fire Cox.

Richardson remembers being shown the letter that had just arrived from Cox, and reading, "Point four was that I must categorically agree not to subpoena any other White House tape, paper or document."

Richardson now raised the question of Cox's seeking further access to presidential tapes or film.

Buzhardt and Garment were to remember that Richardson suggested that in future cases Cox could be ordered not to seek access to presidential files. They distinctly remember his using the phrase, "Give him an order." Someone asked how Cox was likely to react to such an order, and Richardson said he would resign.

Richardson says this entire conversation had to do with ordering Cox to accept the Stennis compromise, not with desisting from further court cases. He adds that he was inexact with the White House; that he should have said, not that Cox would resign, but that he would not go along, that he would resist in some fashion.

To Richardson this point about ordering Cox not to demand more tapes was raised as a tactic for the future. To the others in the meeting it appeared that Richardson was "coming on board" on the Cox question. Richardson would not have to fire Cox—he would give the special prosecutor an order that would cause him to resign.

It may be that Elliot Richardson was devising a plan for the subsequent departure of Archibald Cox, although his own version is that, in predicting Cox would resign, he meant only to indicate that Cox would not acquiesce. In either case, there was no indication that the morning meeting at the White House had resolved the issue of Archibald Cox, and the subsequent actions of Richard Nixon's staff made clear their plan. Knowing that Richardson would attempt to rescue the situation and save his job, Alexander Haig would present him with a fait accompli, sure that the attorney general would do as he was told. He always had in the past, and the document—"Why I Must Resign"—in his pocket as he left the White

House stated the point well: "I am in fact loyal to the President, and I am by temperament a team player."

John Dean stood ramrod straight before Judge Sirica, an earnest look upon his face, and said he understood the consequences of his act this day; that he was forgoing the right to make the government prove the case against him beyond a reasonable doubt.

He looked like a prep-school boy. James Neal rose and delivered a three-minute summary of the case against Dean, which was as broad as the entire conspiracy had been. "I plead guilty, your honor," Dean said. Then Neal told the judge that he must regretfully resign to return to his neglected law practice. Sirica thanked him and gaveled the session closed. Dean's lawyer passed the press a statement from his client: "Initially I sought immunity from prosecution because I refused to be the Watergate scapegoat," it said. "Events have resolved that matter, and I have confidence I cannot and will not be made the scapegoat."

Dean believed he had "excellent technical and procedural" defenses which probably would have meant dismissal or acquittal in a trial, but he was guilty and wished to admit it to restore a measure of integrity to a tarnished government. "Given the nature of the conspiracy," John Dean added, "and the importance of restoring public confidence in our Governmental processes, to have defeated the Government on legal technicalities would have, indeed, been a shallow victory." He hoped that "others involved will also come forward and accept responsibility for their complicity," and in any case he planned to do all he could "to right the wrongs of Watergate."

The unexpected guilty plea set the town on edge. What other surprises might Cox have in store?

The day before Dean pleaded guilty, Bill Gill of ABC News had introduced an informer to two of the prosecutors, Hank Ruth and Carl Feldbaum. The four had lunch in the public dining room at Mount Vernon, Virginia, and after the meal they walked to a parking lot in the shadow of George Washington's home. There the informant handed Hank Ruth an envelope containing three tiny reels of tape, and a box of documents.

The tapes were conversations between the informant and Franklin DeBoer, vice president and trust officer of Bebe Rebozo's Key Biscayne Bank. According to Gill, who had arranged for them, these tapes were

important allegations concerning a million-dollar private investment port-
folio administered as a slush fund for Richard Nixon. Ruth and Feldbaum
dropped the items in the trunk of Ruth's car and thanked their two
companions. When they arrived back at the office, they locked the tapes
in a safe because they did not have the sophisticated equipment needed to
play them.

That day the *Miami Herald* emblazoned a story across its front page
indicating that Archibald Cox was investigating Rebozo for possible tax
violations because of $100,000 he received in 1969 from the Howard
Hughes operation, supposedly as a campaign contribution. This story
came about because I admitted to reporter Robert Boyd that such an
investigation existed. I did it because Archie's brother was a partner
of Chester Davis, Hughes' lawyer, and I did not want any suggestion that
we were easing up on Rebozo.

On Friday morning, as John Dean pleaded guilty and Elliot Richardson
listened to the White House lawyers, Bebe Rebozo caught a plane from
Miami International Airport for Washington, D.C., to visit his friend
the President. No details of their conversation are available.

Perhaps it was entirely unrelated, but one of the most fateful decisions
of Richard Nixon's Presidency occurred at noon this Friday, when he sent
to Congress a message asking for $2.2 billion for long-term military sup-
plies for Israel. In his message, which figured to please his liberal political
opposition, Nixon disclosed that the United States had already authorized
shipments of $825 million in missiles, artillery pieces, and fighter aircraft
to Israel during the first twelve days of the war. "But prudent planning
also requires us to prepare for a longer struggle," Nixon said, and so
he was requesting the large amount in case the conflict did not moderate
soon.

The diplomats on the Middle East desk warned that this move would
provoke the Arab countries. In the past, when military aid was needed
for a less popular cause, the budget experts at the Pentagon and the State
Department had always been able to make the funds available and then
cover the costs in a later military appropriation bill, without serving
notice to the combatants. Nixon chose to advertise his move this time.

His action came just one day after he had entertained the Arab foreign
ministers at the White House, and the Saudi minister had been especially
complimentary. The situation at the Sinai front was still confused, but

Israel was claiming to have turned the tide, having penetrated fifteen miles into Egypt with two hundred tanks and ten thousand men. The Soviets were beginning to seek an armistice, a sign that the war had turned against the Arabs. Russian Premier Aleksei Kosygin was in Cairo talking to Anwar Sadat, and Communist party chief Leonid Brezhnev had summoned Henry Kissinger to Moscow. Nixon's public move on aid to Israel seemed especially ill-timed. Could it have been a domestic political move to reassure his critics of his importance in international peace?

Whatever its motivation, Nixon's announcement of increased aid to Israel set off a chain reaction among the Arabs. Libya was the first to halt all oil shipments to the United States and to nearly double the price of oil on the international market. A few days later King Faisal of Saudi Arabia, an anticommunist who considered himself a friend of the United States, began cutting oil production and embargoed all shipments to the United States. By then Nixon was in the midst of his "firestorm" and made no response. OPEC, the organization of petroleum-exporting countries, realized for the first time its own strength and continued raising prices throughout the next year. By this one act they drained billions of dollars from the American economy alone (Europe and Asia were hit even worse) and brought on the worst economic slump since the Great Depression.

After John Dean's plea the prosecutors headed back to 1425 K Street to await word from the White House or the Justice Department on the pending Stennis proposal, which Cox had all but rejected. We sat around Archie's office for a while, trying to sort out all that was happening, that which we knew and that which we could only guess about. As a newspaperman I was used to confusion during moments of tension. I was always amazed how, at times of crisis, this small corner office with its gray government-issue carpet and its bare white walls became as calm and as quiet as a monastery. A small shudder of excitement would go up my spine when I realized that we sat here in this place as in the eye of a hurricane, and that I was likely to remember these moments for the rest of my life.

Nothing happened. The telephone did not ring. The news wires brought no further word. After a while people straggled back to their own offices to get some work done. Around 1:30 P.M. Cox said, "Well, I don't see any need for my standing around and waiting. I'm going to walk over to Brentano's to buy something to read this weekend." And he did.

Around 11:00 A.M. General Haig tracked down Senator Howard Baker, who was attending a symposium in Chicago, and gave him a quick summary of the Stennis plan, winning Baker's initial approval. The Tennessee senator agreed to take the next plane back to Washington, where he was to arrive around 2:30 P.M. Haig found Senator Sam Ervin at the New Orleans airport and Ervin, too, caught a commercial flight to the capital. Then Haig called Senator Stennis, who agreed to the announcement of his name as the tapes verifier, although he later disputed the White House assertion that he also agreed to go along without the approval of Cox.

At the attorney general's office Richardson and his top aides were rehearsing the events of the morning and marveling that they were still employees of the Department of Justice. At 1:00 P.M. Haig called to tell Richardson that Senator Stennis was "enthusiasic" about going ahead without Cox, as was Senator Baker. Senator Ervin, he said, was due at the White House around 3:00 P.M. to discuss the matter.

Deputy Attorney General William Ruckelshaus got back from another overnight trip to Grand Rapids and was invited to lunch with Richardson, Moore, Smith, and Darman. He remembers, "A couple of us had the feeling Elliot was a little bit too euphoric about what happened that morning. It looked to me like there were some clouds on the horizon if they were going to do what they said they were going to do." By the end of lunch Richardson had concluded that the move to link the Stennis proposal with an order to Cox not to seek any further presidential documents was ill-advised and that he had better inform the President of his view. The "emotional roller coaster" was on the down side again.

Before he called Haig, Richardson wanted to chat with Cox. His secretary made the call at 2:05 P.M., to be told by Hank Ruth, "Archie's not here." Politely she said, "I presume you would tell me where he is if you know." Ruth responded that Cox had gone for a walk. The secretary, somewhat taken aback that Cox could have disappeared in the midst of the crisis, said, "You mean he simply stepped out for a bresh of freth air?" Ruth responded, "Did you say that right?"

A half-dozen of us headed for Brentano's via every possible route that Cox might take. Ruth and Kreindler ran into him on the street. I reached the store, where I was met by John Barker. As we huddled, a woman came up to us and said, "Are you looking for your boss? He's back at the office and he needs you right away."

When we returned, Cox was on the phone with Richardson, who was being casual. He said he had heard that morning that Cox was about to name President Nixon as an unindicted co-conspirator in an indictment concerning large amounts of money routed to the Nixon campaign by the dairy industry. If that wasn't true, he would like to be able to put the story to rest.

Cox told him that there was no substance at all to such a rumor. Richardson did not give Cox any reading on how things were going that day; but as they talked about the situation, Cox mentioned that if the situation deteriorated he might find it necessary to make public their correspondence of recent days. He hoped that Richardson would not consider that a breach of confidence. No, Richardson said, he thought some of the paragraphs, particularly the introduction to Cox's comments on the Stennis proposal, looked as though they had been written for the public.

"Well, it was sincerely written and sincerely meant," Cox said, "but you must have written many of these letters yourself where you believe they may become public. You say what you think, but you say it in the best possible way."

When the conversation ended, Cox knew that White House paranoia was still high, given the Dean guilty plea and the rumor that Nixon was about to be named in an indictment. And Richardson knew, too, that Cox was not about to quietly fold his tent and steal away into the night if things did not go his way.

Immediately, at 2:55 P.M., Richardson called Haig and told him of his reservations about the "linked proposal," as he called it. He put his objections in terms of what was good for the President; the Stennis plan was reasonable and would be seen as such, but placing limitations on Cox was unacceptable from Richardson's position, and contrary to the President's interest as well. When he hung up he immediately put in a call to Buzhardt to make the same point. He was unable to get through for two hours, but he talked to Buzhardt twice in the late afternoon, at 4:30 and at 5:40, and was left with the impression that both Buzhardt and Haig were sympathetic to his point of view and that nothing would be done to link the Stennis plan with any orders to Cox until they had conferred further.

At Cox's office we went through the rest of the afternoon with no knowledge of the conversations the White House was having with Stennis,

Ervin, Baker, and Richardson. But at 5:23 P.M. a White House messenger arrived with Charles Alan Wright's latest effort at revisionism. The two-page letter, addressed to "Dear Archie," began by saying Wright had concluded from Cox's earlier letter that further discussions would be futile. But "in the interests of historical accuracy, in the unhappy event that our correspondence should see the light of day," Wright wished to clear up two points.

The attorney general's proposal was simply silent on the issue of whether any portion of the tapes would be provided under any circumstances in the future. (That was true, but Cox had heard Wright distinctly say on the phone Thursday evening that this was one of four points Cox must agree to.)

"That would have been an issue for future negotiation when and if the issue arose," Wright said, and the White House believed it would never arise. Wright correctly pointed out that Cox wanted an advance commitment from the White House that any compromise would apply to future requests for evidence as well.

As for Cox's subpoenaing White House documents in the future, when the President's counsel had spoken in his telephone conversation about ending Cox's right to do so, he had in mind only "private Presidential papers and meetings, a category that I regard as much, much smaller than the great mass of White House documents with which the President has not personally been involved." (That comment was put in perspective by the testimony of some White House aides that their personal files had been moved into an area specified as "Presidential files," specifically to keep them from the hands of the prosecutors.)

In a final paragraph Wright repeated that "the differences between us remain so great that no purpose would be served by further discussion of what I continue to think was a 'very reasonable'—indeed an unprecedentedly generous—proposal . . . at a time when the country would be particularly well served by such an agreement." It was signed, "Charlie."

This letter and the telephone call of Thursday night were the first strong indications to us that the White House was carrying on a two-track program of negotiations: The written record was to reflect Richardson's reasonable and restrained approach, while the ultimata and threats were made by "the back channel," as Haig might have referred to it. This was indeed like the Vietnam negotiations with which Al Haig had earned his reputation.

When Cox had finished reading this letter aloud, I said to him, "Mark the time it arrived. Within ninety minutes you'll be fired on live television from the East Room." But we heard no more. The press was by now in a state of creeping hysteria.

The courts had closed for the day and there was still no word of any appeal. Outside observers noted that petitions to the Supreme Court could be filed with the guard on duty anytime before midnight. But there was no word from the White House as to its plans. Earlier in the day reporters had been told there might be a development and to stand by for a briefing. The estimated time of this briefing kept being put off. Then, some time after 5:00 P.M., Gerry Warren, Ron Ziegler's assistant, told reporters that the most likely thing to happen that evening would be the release of a written statement on the court case.

As we waited for further word, somebody noted that Jim Neal had mentioned before he left that we ought to have copies of the prosecutors' memoranda available at some location outside the office. Kreindler and Feldbaum visited each task force and suggested that the lawyers go through their files, pull the most important memoranda, especially those that recommended for or against a specific prosecution, and make copies. The lawyers were told that "it might be a good idea if you took these home over the holiday weekend to review." The Xerox machines worked overtime for the rest of the day, and through Saturday.

Phil Bakes of the Plumbers task force remembers that when he got the guard-your-files instructions from Peter Kreindler, he reached over and wrote on his calendar for October 19 one word, "paranoia."

We waited an hour. Cox had been convinced from the outset that at least part of the motivation for forcing negotiations under a deadline was an attempt to raise our anxiety level and perhaps cause mistakes. He was now in no mood to sit around and wait when it was not his move. So at 6:30 P.M. he announced he was going home, unless somebody had an objection. Nobody did.

This was the beginning of a long weekend, with Veterans Day to be celebrated on Monday. Much of Washington—the journalists covering the White House, the lawyers in our office—had made plans to go away. John

Barker wondered if he should change his plans to join his wife and baby, who were already headed for an inn in the Virginia mountains. My secretary, Judy Rollenhagen, planned to leave for the same area in the morning. It seemed silly to ask people to cancel their plans after the months they had put in without time off, unless there was more substantial evidence than Charlie Wright's veiled threats.

The only additional uncertainty came from Susan Kaslow, a secretary whose close friend worked in the White House press office. She reported that her friend had just been told to cancel any plans for that night. But that could have related to any number of subjects. The press, after all, had been told to stand easy. And it made sense that Nixon could file his appeal petition, and make whatever move he planned, after the holiday. Shortly after 6:30 P.M., the Watergate Special Prosecution Force left its office en masse, many for distant points.

Earlier that day Senator Sam Ervin had arrived at Al Haig's office, where he found Howard Baker and Charles Alan Wright waiting with Haig. They talked about a plan whereby the Senate Watergate committee would get the contents of the Watergate tapes, although not the tapes themselves, and they would be authenticated by "The Judge," John Stennis of Mississippi.

Ervin was mightily pleased. Just two days earlier, as he had feared, the courts had rejected his committee's suit for these tapes. After that setback, this appeared to be a great victory for his committee. Haig and Wright were persuasive, and Senator Baker was enthusiastic. After a short time Ervin agreed to the plan, and the four men went to see Nixon about it. Cox's disagreement with the plan was never discussed. Ervin remembers trying to ask a question about Cox when they were with the President, but Nixon changed the subject.

While this meeting was taking place, Senate Watergate committee chief counsel Sam Dash was getting calls from reporters asking him why his boss, Senator Ervin, was at the White House. "It's impossible," Dash kept saying. "He's giving a speech in Louisiana at this moment." He kept trying to find someone who knew about the senator's whereabouts for certain.

Finally he reached Senator Baker at his home. Baker had just returned from the White House. "Sam," Baker said, "we are going to get lengthy

summaries of the tapes. It's a very good deal from our point of view."
Baker was "ecstatic," according to Dash.

The next morning, when Dash finally reached Ervin at his home in
Morgantown, North Carolina, the senator denied that he had agreed to
accept summaries. "We were guaranteed complete transcripts of all the
Watergate material," Ervin said. "I told them, 'This won't satisfy the
special prosecutor.' " Many Ervin supporters came to believe that the senator was sandbagged, that Baker was "in on the deal" when Ervin arrived at the White House. One committee source said his suspicion was
based on the fact that Senator Baker was always suggesting meetings with
the White House, that he wanted to let Alexander Butterfield go to the
air show in Moscow the day Butterfield testified about the existence of the
tapes, and that he had gone to Butterfield's house the day before and convinced him to inform the White House of the testimony he had given in
executive session the previous Friday and was about to give over television.

At 7:00 P.M. Friday Alexander Haig called Elliot Richardson and mentioned to him for the first time a letter which he said was already on its
way to him from the President of the United States. He read it, including
this paragraph:

> As a part of these actions, I am instructing you to direct Special Prosecutor
> Archibald Cox of the Watergate Special Prosecution Force that he is to make
> no further attempts by judicial process to obtain tapes, notes, or memoranda
> of Presidential conversations. I regret the necessity of intruding, to this very
> limited extent, on the independence that I promised you with regard to Water-
> gate when I announced your appointment.

Elliot Richardson had not expected to receive this instruction. He had
believed he would be consulted before any action. He asked Haig how
such instructions could have come to be issued, given the conversations of
the afternoon. Haig replied that he had twice tried to make Richardson's
position clear to the President, but he had been unsuccessful. Haig was
conciliatory and optimistic. This had been cleared with the bipartisan
leadership on the Hill, he said. And then he repeated a remark he had
made earlier. "This will help you with your constituency, Elliot." By now
Richardson was wondering just what Haig meant by that, so he asked.
"With the Republican Party," Haig said. Richardson could almost see over
the telephone the wink that went with the remark. Alexander Haig, Presi-

dent-maker. In a cold fury Richardson ended the conversation, saying, "Al, given the history of our relationship on this, I would have thought that you would have consulted me prior to sending that letter."

The attorney general hung up, as angry as his aides had ever seen him. At 7:20 P.M. the letter arrived by White House messenger. It had been a busy day for Charles Alan Wright, the author. Richardson called Cox immediately. "I've just received a letter I am going to read to you. You can tell the press I read it to you for your information only." After he finished reading, Richardson told Cox that it was going to be released by the White House around 8:00 P.M. Richardson was planning a press release pointing out the distinction between the Stennis proposal and this order, which, he would say, "seems to me inconsistent with explicit understandings on which I was confirmed." He would add that he planned "to seek an early opportunity to discuss this with the President." Cox was less surprised by the letter than by Richardson's other news—Sam Ervin would support the Stennis compromise.

Cox had barely hung up when I called with word that a White House statement was imminent. "Meet me in the office," Cox said.

When I got back to the office I realized how foolish we had been not to keep the place on a war footing. There were no secretaries, and we had little luck finding them. I reached one, Suzanne Westfall, and for the next two hours she was our only support. The office was deserted except for the guards, Hank Ruth (who brought a thermos of milk with him when he returned), and Archie. Kreindler, Lacovara, and some others drifted in a little later. On Friday night of a holiday weekend I knew that time was of the essence. If the White House succeeded in selling this plan to the press as a genuine compromise (as had been rumored most of the week), then we would lose the propaganda war.

"Ervin and Baker have endorsed it," Cox said, with a look of anger in his eyes. "That is a body blow. Spineless!" he said, and then repeated it: "Spineless!"

The first few paragraphs about the White House statement rattled over the wire service machines shortly after we got back to the office. United Press International was calling it a "compromise settlement" of the tapes issue, but Associated Press was being more cautious. That was a fair beginning. We still didn't know what the President's statement said, and there was nothing on the news wires about a letter to Elliot Richardson. Suzanne Westfall hopped a cab to the *Los Angeles Times* bureau, within a block of the White House, and as soon as their reporter returned from Ron Ziegler's office with the statement, they let her have a copy. Thus were we informed of our orders from the President of the United States.

The statement was mostly about the dangerous situation in the Middle East, which made it imperative to settle the tapes issue now. It outlined the procedure put forth by Richardson, noting that he considered it "a reasonable proposal for compromise." Then it said, "I am pleased to be able to say that Chairman Sam Ervin and Vice Chairman Howard Baker of the Senate Select Committee have agreed to this procedure and that *at their request* [emphasis mine] and mine, Senator John Stennis has consented to listen to every requested tape."

Then, repeating some of the phrases of Charles Alan Wright's letters of earlier in the day, the statement noted "with regret" that Cox had rejected the proposal and that the President was now ordering him to make no further attempts by judicial process to get any more Presidential documents. There was no mention of the letter to Elliot Richardson.

Cox called Richardson at 9:05 P.M. to read him what the White House had actually released, which had not been furnished to the attorney general. This further confused matters for him. Richardson had expected Nixon to release his letter to him, to which the attorney general would then be called upon to respond. Now he was not asked to respond to anything. He was simply listed as an endorser, indeed the author, of the Stennis proposal. "Well, have I got this letter or haven't I?" Richardson inquired of Cox. Cox suggested he ask the White House. The press was not calling him, so Richardson decided he could not issue his press release, at least not this night. Once again he began thinking about saving the situation.

At 8:30 P.M. Richardson had taken a call from Bryce Harlow. "Bryce, I have been treated shabbily by Al Haig," Richardson said. That remark was to have a deeper meaning later.*

---

* General Haig called Richardson at home. He had heard that the attorney general felt he had been treated shabbily. Richardson said, "Well, I'm home now. I've had a drink. Things look a little better, and we'll see where we go from here." (A week later, Haig and Nixon were telling congressmen that Richardson had masterminded this whole plan and then backed away from it at the last moment, and that he had not told the truth when he testified about it under oath before the Senate Judiciary Committee. "But who is going to get him for perjury?" Nixon asked. Some of the congressmen, long admirers and friends of Richardson, were outraged, and demanded that Haig explain how he could make such a charge. Haig told them he couldn't explain Richardson's actions, but he knew that on one occasion he had heard that Richardson accused him of treating him shabbily, so he called to find out what the complaint was, and that Richardson had apologized, admitting that he had been drinking when he made the statement.)

The evening news shows were over and would not be back for two days. The morning newspapers were on deadline and would hardly have time to search for much reaction to the President's move. It would be days before we could catch up, if ever, unless we acted immediately. "I can't write anything out at a time like this, but I could dictate it," Cox said. There were no secretaries to take dictation so we headed down the corridor to my office, where Cox paced back and forth dictating and I took his statement down on a typewriter.

> In my judgment, the President is refusing to comply with the court's decree.
> A summary of the content of the tapes lacks the evidentiary value of the tapes themselves. No steps are being taken to turn over the important notes, memoranda and other documents that the court orders require. I shall bring these points to the attention of the court and abide by its decision.
> The instructions [of the President directing Cox not to seek further tapes, notes, or memoranda of presidential conversations] are in violation of the promises which the Attorney General made to the Senate when his nomination was confirmed. For me to comply to those instructions would violate my solemn pledge to the Senate and the country to invoke judicial process to challenge exaggerated claims of executive privilege. I shall not violate my promise. . . .

I ran upstairs to the law library where a few reporters were waiting. There were two telephones in the room, and I got AP on one and UPI on the other, and dictated the statement. I read it again for the attending reporters to take notes. By then the camera crews from the networks had arrived, and I got Cox to read it for TV.

Then I announced that we would hold a news conference at 1:00 P.M. the next day, although I had no idea where I would find a suitable location. That problem was solved for me later by Adam Clymer of the *Baltimore Sun*. He was an officer of the National Press Club, and his fellow officers were at that moment feting Walter Cronkite at a dinner. He got permission that evening for us to use the Grand Ballroom the next day. By 11:00 P.M. the radio was announcing that Archibald Cox would hold a news conference. By morning the networks (except for ABC, which was carrying NCAA football) were announcing that the conference would be televised live.

Saturday morning Archibald Cox had misplaced the green ID card with his picture on it that usually hung around his neck when he was in the office. Everybody had to wear one, so this Saturday the guards gave Cox a substitute. It was yellow and had no picture. On the front there was only a number and two words: Temporary Employee.

The mood in his office shortly after 9:00 A.M. was one of confusion. For most of the week, the war of the tapes had been waged with only Cox's inner circle taking part. Except for Jim Neal, the task force leaders had been concentrating on their own business with only a moderate awareness of the building tension. Now everyone was around the conference table, including Archie's close friend Phil Heymann, who had flown down from Harvard. There wasn't enough room for everybody. Some people were angry, others despairing, still others just sad. There was a babble of voices and opinions. It was the first time in my memory that I saw confusion in that room.

Someone told Cox to go for broke, that it was all over, and that he should kick Nixon a few times on the way out the door. Others counseled caution. After all, this fight was with the President of the United States, and decorum would be important. People started citing various arguments and incidents that Cox should be sure to raise at his press conference. Cox said the only question in his mind was whether he would have the strength to remain composed, and his voice started to crack. "What the hell is wrong with showing a little emotion at a time like this?" I asked. The others disagreed. Any emotion would surely be seen as weakness.

"All of you can help me most by going back to your offices and writing out the ideas you think should be included," Cox said. "I need a little time alone to compose my thoughts." We left him alone.

Throughout the offices on the ninth floor telephones were ringing unanswered. The Western Union Telex machine, which received messages addressed to Cox directly from the point of origin, had been clattering constantly since the night before. There were a couple hundred messages from citizens expressing support.

It was a scene of busy desolation. Very few of the secretaries had reported to work. Most of the lawyers were in their offices drawing up lists of items they had requested from the White House that had not been forthcoming, or writing memos on points that Cox should consider for the press conference. Cox's own secretary, Florence Campbell, had been out of town, a severe loss at such a time. The telephone on her desk was constantly ringing. Congressmen and senators were calling for information.

Many staff members were phoning every contact on Capitol Hill, seeking support. Representative Michael Harrington of Massachusetts, a liberal Democrat, called me and asked, "Is there anything I can do?"

"Call Elliot and stiffen his backbone," I said. "If he buckles it will be a disaster." Harrington made the call, but Richardson did not speak with him.

Joe Connolly got through to a friend in the office of liberal Republican Senator Richard Schweiker of Pennsylvania and asked him to join the small chorus of voices in Congress, led by Senator Walter Mondale of Minnesota, warning the White House against any moves against Cox.

"He's up next year," the aide said. "We can't get out front on this." Later, when the climate seemed more suitable, Schweiker held a news conference calling for Nixon's resignation.

Cox sat alone at his desk and slowly filled a yellow pad with notes for his news conference. A hand-lettered sign on his door said, "Please Don't Enter. Archie Is Busy."

My assistant, John Barker, had left Washington Friday evening, oblivious to the developing confrontation, and had driven through the night to Graves Mountain Lodge in Syria, Virginia. For safekeeping, he had taken with him copies of some sensitive memos from the office.

Shortly after he joined his family, a caretaker came to their cabin. "A Mr. Doyle called and said he needs you," the man said. Barker took a nap, shaved, and got in his car. At 10:00 A.M. Saturday he was at the National Press Club on Fourteenth Street in downtown Washington. "We're going to need a small table, a blue drape for a background, and a very large American flag," he told the club manager.

At 10:00 A.M., Richardson arrived at his office. His staff members wanted him to tell Nixon he was returning the letter which ordered him to stop Cox. But Richardson rejected the idea. He wanted to work out a compromise, still. Those who saw him this day say that his desire to stay at his job was more evident than on any of the previous days.

Richardson called Haig at 10:20 A.M. and told the general that he was writing a letter to the President, which he would send over that morning. He said it would tell the President that his instructions gave Richardson "serious difficulty," and it would propose a number of steps that might rescue the compromise. Haig was courteous but had little comment. He seemed somewhat puzzled about Cox's impending news conference, which was now the only subject of interest in Washington. Haig did not tell Richardson that the White House was already receiving considerable reaction by telephone and telegram that was unfavorable. A man who knows Alexander Haig well has speculated with me that by this point Haig had told the President that Richardson would squirm and fight but that in the end he would follow orders.

At 11:00 A.M. Archibald Cox walked to the library on the tenth floor, where the whole staff had assembled. Most of the younger people still did not know what was going on. This was the first time the entire staff had met together since the very early days.

Cox walked into the room, a rather small one to handle the thirty or forty people who were there. He leaned against a wall. He was dressed far more formally than usual. He had on his best gray tweed suit and a blue button-down shirt. Instead of a bow tie he wore a somber maroon tie with white regimental stripe. His salt-and-pepper hair was short even for him. He wrinkled his bushy eyebrows in a gesture of nervousness.

Cox gave the staff a short history of the past week and then he told them he would answer the President's order and try to explain the issues at his press conference. He could not predict what would happen then but he did know that it was very important, if the President discharged him, that the rest of the staff stay at their posts at least temporarily and do their jobs. It would be a great misfortune if the office did not continue to move forward, because it was important work for the good of the country.

He told us how much he had enjoyed working with this staff and how he felt it was the most dedicated and professional staff he had ever worked with, even including the solicitor general's office. As he said these things, the ringing of the phone interrupted him. One of the staff attorneys was saying, "No, he's not here. I haven't seen him today. Okay." Both men stopped talking at the same moment. The embarrassment of the interruption added to the tension that everyone was feeling. Near the end Cox's voice had begun to crack. He quickly left the room.

At 12:30 P.M., most of the lawyers and other staff members went to the National Press Club to get seats at the press conference. Shortly after everyone was seated, Cox's deputy, Hank Ruth, collected the task force leaders, along with Kreindler, Lacovara, and Feldbaum. They moved to the back of the room. "I think we should try to reach some consensus on what we will do if Archie is fired after this," Ruth said. "It seems to me that the one thing we all should agree to is not to act individually. We'll need to show complete unity. If they want to fire us, let's make them pick us off one by one." Everyone agreed.

Cox had asked that the rest of the staff go to the press club ahead of him. He wanted to walk over with his wife, Phyllis. She was driving in from McLean and had trouble parking. We were debating whether to leave without her when she walked in. It was a sunny fall day, the temperatures balmy and the air uncommonly dry. Yellow chrysanthemums were standing at attention in the parklands that stretched between the prosecutor's office and the White House. Pennsylvania Avenue was at peace this lazy Saturday.

Elliot Richardson was waiting on the telephone when Cox arrived, less than five minutes before the cameras would go live. He wanted to read Archie the letter he had sent to Nixon so that Cox would know what it said before he held his press conference. Cox, polite to the end, mentioned that the television cameras were waiting, but Richardson read the letter anyway.

Cox and his wife moved through the doors onto live television, both smiling yet looking very grave. Phyllis Cox walked with him to the small table with the array of microphones, where they paused for a moment for the photographers, her hand gripped tightly by him. Then she walked away and he sat down.

"I read in one of the newspapers this morning the headline 'Cox Defiant,'" he said. "I don't *feel* defiant." His voice rose and he smiled as he uttered the last words. "In fact I told my wife this morning I hate a fight. Some things I feel very deeply about are at stake, and I hope that I can explain and defend them steadfastly."

He had worried a good deal of his life, he said, about the problems of imposing too much strain on our Constitutional institutions. He was not looking for a confrontation, and he was certainly not out to get the President. "I'm even worried, to put it in colloquial terms, that I am getting too big for my britches; that what I see as principle could be vanity. I hope not. In the end I decided that I had to try to stick by what I thought was right."

Now he was relaxed, fully under control. That morning Archie had said to Phyllis, "I don't think I can make it through this day." But his appearance to the audience was anything but tense. He was folksy, unpretentious, disarming. He seemed the country lawyer, talking good sense.

He twitched a thumb in and out of his breast pocket as he talked, as though searching for his glasses or a piece of chalk. There were three reasons for calling the press conference, one, two, three. To his mind there were four insuperable difficulties with the President's plan, one, two, three, four. "It is not a question of Senator Stennis' integrity, I have no doubt at all of that. . . . It is terribly important to adhere to the established institutions and not accommodate it by some private arrangement involving submitting the evidence ultimately to any one man."

He spelled out the legal difficulties of going to trial without the best evidence, the vagueness of the White House standards for editing the tapes, the uses of the national security excuse in the past to burglarize Dr. Fielding's office and to tap the telephones of two strictly political White House aides, William Safire and John Sears.

He read the Justice Department order that prohibited countermanding him. "The giving of instructions in this very important respect isn't important because it interferes with Archie Cox. It is sort of embarrassing to be put in the position to say, 'Well, I don't want the President of the United States to tell me what to do.' I was brought up with the greatest respect for every President of the United States. But that isn't what is involved. It is that there is a basic change in the institutional arrangement that was established. . . . It wouldn't be right to continue with the pretense that we have the old arrangement. . . . I am afraid if I acquiesced once in the hopes of avoiding confrontation—and as I say, I don't like confrontations—then I would find myself saying, well, it isn't worth doing this time, either."

He talked about the general White House attitude toward supplying any information to his office and briefly went through the stalling tactics of the summer. Just to find out who met with the President when, hadn't been possible. He was still waiting for such logs, requested months before, on Chapin, Colson, Gray, Hunt, Kleindienst, Krogh, LaRue, Liddy, Strachan, and Young. "I hope my records are accurate," he said.

He told of asking how the negotiations would affect the Ervin committee and getting no answer until the President's statement; of the telephone call from "Marshall Wright" with its four nonnegotiable demands; of having submitted his own carefully drafted six-page proposal in September and hearing only a flat rejection.

"Well, there is the account," he said. "I apologize to you for being so professorially long-winded."

Peter Lisagor of the *Chicago Daily News* rose. "Mr. Cox, you would seem to be in what we would call a nonviable position now. Are you going to wait for the President to dismiss you?"

Cox said he would go about his duties "on the terms on which I assumed them."

In response to Sam Donaldson of ABC News he said that this meant he would be going to court on Tuesday to report that the court's order had not been obeyed. He would explain to the court just what was being offered in lieu of the tapes.

"One form of procedure," Cox said, "would be to seek an order to show cause by the respondent that he should not be adjudicated guilty of contempt. I think it might also be possible, and it might be preferable, to seek a further order clarifying any possible doubt resulting from the President's statement last night."

What if he is fired by the end of the news conference, Patrick Sloyan of the Hearst newspapers asked.

Cox had studied the law and found serious question whether anyone except the attorney general could legally dismiss him. "I do not mean to seem to cling to power or office," he said. "If my personal ease were the test, I would be on the coast of Maine and not here. But I do think it important to do everything I can to emphasize the extent of the departure from the kind of detached, independent public inquiry which the Senate caused to be set up. Once I have done everything I can to make that clear, then I will be happy to relax."

Did he believe Richardson would fire him at the President's order?

"He may. I am not saying that nobody can fire me. Of course, eventually, there are ways of firing me. I do not know what Attorney General Richardson will do. . . . Eventually a President can always work his will. You remember when Andrew Jackson wanted to take the deposits from the Bank of the United States and his treasury secretary said he could not do it, he fired him; then he appointed a new secretary of the treasury and he would not do it so he fired him; and finally he got a third who would. That is one way of proceeding."

Cox added, "All through this week, the attorney general has behaved in a way that makes it just as possible for me to say, with as complete sincerity as I said it to the Senate Judiciary Committee when we were up at the hearings on his confirmation: I have admiration, respect, and affection for the attorney general, and I emphasize that to all of you."

In a small alcove off Elliot Richardson's office, the attorney general was standing with four men—William Ruckelshaus, Jonathan Moore, J. T. Smith, and Richard Darman—watching Cox on television. The room is small and somewhat uncomfortable. The five viewers kept glancing at each other, but nobody said anything. An hour earlier the attorney general had sent his letter to the White House, based on notes he had written at home the night before. The yellow pad with those notes was on his desk now. His wife, Anne, had talked with Richardson the night before about what was coming, and they agreed that Richardson was probably going out in style, although he didn't want to go at all. Using her phrase, he had entitled the notes for his letter "The Mahogany Coffin."

For the second weekend in a row—an unusual record—Richard Nixon was at work in the White House. He was reviewing the critical situation in the Middle East, according to the press office, and meeting with top aides. Secretary of State Henry Kissinger had been dispatched to Moscow in the middle of the night at the request of the Soviet government, "for direct discussion with the Soviet leadership on means to end the hostilities in the Middle East." The announcement added, "Since the outbreak of hostilities in the Middle East, the President and General Secretary Brezhnev have maintained close contact through diplomatic channels." Kissinger's plane had departed from Andrews Air Force Base just before 2:00 A.M. Washington time.

The White House press office declined to say whether President Nixon was watching Archibald Cox's press conference. Alexander Haig, who viewed it along with Buzhardt, Garment, Wright, and some unidentified aides, was to tell reporters afterward that Cox's performance had taken the White House team by surprise. Haig said that in "war-gaming" the possibilities he and the White House lawyers had concluded that Cox had three choices: He could defy the President and go to court on Tuesday, the first day the courts would be open; he could obey the President's order; or he could resign in protest. "We thought—and frankly we hoped—that he would choose to resign," Haig told one reporter who shared his notes with me. The general was shaken and angered by Cox's news conference.

At the National Press Club reporters were becoming more interested in the evolving relationship between Archibald Cox and Elliot Richardson. Ron Ostrow of the *Los Angeles Times* asked Cox to disclose the subject of his conversations with Richardson since the President's order.

"I would rather you didn't press that," Cox said. "I think that is between old friends. I really do not think I am holding back anything that is necessary to your understanding. I feel it would be subject to misunderstanding by him."

Pat Sloyan asked, "Are you under the impression that the attorney general is going to side with you and not the President on this issue?"

Cox said, "I cannot tell you because I do not know."

Clark Mollenhoff of the *Des Moines Register* asked if the compromise was really Richardson's "brainchild . . . or do you feel it was foisted upon him by the White House, the President's lawyers?"

Cox didn't know Richardson's "personal druthers," but suggested that the reporters put the correspondence of the past week, which I was to pass out, next to the President's statement of Friday night, "and draw your own inferences."

Fred Barnes of the *Washington Star* asked whether the courts could move on their own to get the tapes if Cox was dismissed.

"I think the answer is very probably yes," Cox said. "It is even possible that I could be appointed counsel to the grand jury or the court for that purpose." The room exploded in a burst of nervous laughter. Cox quickly added, "Don't carry that too far. The thought went through my mind. Then I concluded, no, I think that would be of very doubtful propriety because it would then turn what ought to be a question of principle into something that somebody would look on as a personal fight, and I don't think this is a question of personalities."

Sarah McClendon, the scold of many a public figure at televised news conferences, stood and said, "Sir, you are rather unique in our history because you personally rebuffed the President of the United States. And you come in here today hand-holding with your wife, and it took a lot of moral courage. . . . My question is, how could you expect to succeed in this job? How could you expect to succeed?"

"I thought it was worth a try," Cox said. "I thought it was important. If it could be done, I thought it would help the country; and if I lost, what the hell."

Mollenhoff, a tough investigative reporter who had left journalism to become an aide to Nixon and then left the administration in disgust, ended the conference by saying, "Mr. Cox, speaking about public reaction to this type of thing, would you think that it would be helpful if there was an outpouring of telegrams, calls and mail on the subject, to let the President have some idea of what the public mood is on the subject? Would you disagree with that?"

Cox smiled and said, "Well, you know more about that than I do."

It ended at precisely 2:00 P.M., the most unusual press conference I have ever attended. The hard-bitten, cynical press corps was rooting for Archibald Cox. So, as it turned out, was the entire country.

CHAPTER

8

MASSACRE

"It's the Declaration of Independence, Angie.
Just stamp it 'VOID' and let me take it home."

At 2:07 P.M. Leonard Garment called Elliot Richardson from Haig's office. Except for Thursday night, when he joined the hue and cry for Cox's firing, Garment had played no part in the unfolding action since September, when he was one of those rejecting Cox's proposal for compromise. Garment had been a utility man for the administration before Watergate, handling "causes" such as Indian affairs, youth programs, and cultural affairs. The one area where he professed no expertise was foreign policy.

Garment had been reading Richardson's letter to the President, which made it pretty clear that the attorney general wasn't going to fire the special prosecutor. He was calling because Alexander Haig was beside himself with anger, confusion, and embarrassment. Apparently Haig had assured the President that Richardson would be "on board" at the crucial moment. The crucial moment was here, and Richardson was not "on board."

Garment told Richardson the President was extremely concerned about the Middle East. It would be a serious blow to his ability to negotiate, with Kissinger just now landing in Moscow, if there was a string of resignations in Washington. Would Richardson be willing to fire Cox and then resign if he felt he must? No, Richardson said, he could not fire Cox before he resigned. He had given his pledge to the Senate.

When Garment hung up, he went back to see the President and told him the bad news. Nixon said, "Well, what the hell can I do? Can I back down?" It was a rhetorical question. Garment told the President he could not back down.

If Richardson had any last-minute doubts about what he should do, they were dispelled by Archibald Cox's press conference. His aides were, and had been, unanimous that Richardson could not fire Cox. He asked Ruckelshaus whether Ruckelshaus could fire Cox. "Hell, no," the deputy attorney general said.

At 2:20 P.M. General Alexander Haig called. The conversation was brief. Haig pointed out that Cox was now in defiance of a presidential order and that there was no alternative but to dismiss him. The President was ordering Richardson to fire Cox, Haig said. "Well, I can't do that," Richardson answered. "I guess I had better come over and resign."

Robert H. Bork had played no role in the events of this week. His only dealings with Archibald Cox had been back in August, when Richardson asked him to draw up proposed changes in Cox's guidelines.

Bork, forty-six years old, was an ideological conservative whose philosophy of law was poles apart from that of Archibald Cox. He had Cox's old job as solicitor general, but he hadn't had much time to practice it. He was named to the post in January, 1973, but the retiring solicitor, Erwin Griswold, had wanted to stay on until the Supreme Court session was finished. So Bork was confirmed during the winter, before the Watergate scandal engulfed everything, but didn't take office until June 26. In the interim he continued to teach his courses at Yale Law School.

Once during the summer Alexander Haig had asked Bork to become the President's head lawyer on Watergate matters. "I guess the President knows you quite well," Haig had said. Bork answered that he had met the President exactly twice.

"Really? Well, he certainly knows your work and is a great admirer," Haig said. Bork later told friends that Haig hinted, rather crudely, that this job would be a stepping-stone to the Supreme Court for Robert Bork. Bork asked for twenty-four hours to think it over and then spent the night with his friend Alex Bickel of Yale, who agreed with Bork that it would be a terrible job. The next day Bork told Haig that if he took the assignment he would have to hear the tapes. Haig told him that was not possible. Bork convinced Haig he was the wrong man for the job.

On this Saturday Bork had gone to his office to work on a Supreme Court brief and to answer a letter on the meaning of the Constitution from a grade school class. The night before he had heard about a tapes compromise on television and had called Richardson to congratulate him. That conversation was his first indication that things were not going well.

At one o'clock he wandered into the department press office and watched Cox on the tube. Masterful performance, he thought, not with admiration. He was standing there talking to press officer Jack Hushen, speculating about the next move, when Richardson's secretary came in. "There you are," she said. "The attorney general has been looking for you."

By the time Bork reached Richardson's office the attorney general was waiting to learn from the White House when he could deliver his resignation. He had called Sol Lindenbaum and Robert Dixon, two top Justice Department officials, to tell them what was transpiring. Nobody really knew what would happen to the department if there was "a string of resignations," as Garment had put it. And it looked like there might be.

As one of the participants in this meeting remembers it, when Bork came into the room he started talking about the brief he had been working on for a Supreme Court case. The attorney general brought him to earth and started to fill him in on the background of the crisis. Richardson handed Bork a copy of the letter the President had sent the night before, which had still not been made public. "Who would write a dumb letter like that?" the solicitor general asked.

Richardson told him that as far as he could tell from the scant research he had done, there was no clear line of succession in the department after Bork, the number three man. "You may have to decide if you are going to carry out his order to fire Cox," Richardson said. Bork, according to a witness, "looked like somebody had just hit him in the face with a bucket of wet shrimp." His first reaction was anger. He said, "I've been here four months; I thought I was going to be the government's lawyer in the Supreme Court of the United States. It's something I've dreamed about all my life. And this is the fourth time in four months I've been faced with whether or not I'm going to resign." Then he started to pace.

As Bork explained it then, he had never agreed with the idea of a special prosecutor in the first place. He thought it was a bad precedent for the department. If he had been asked at his confirmation hearings, he would have taken a stand against it. If he had been Richardson in May, he would have fought it.

Then Bork started talking about the power of a President to discharge an employee. As he saw it, he was simply an instrument of that power. Even if he didn't agree with that particular order, he said, he felt an obligation to carry it out. In the background there was concern about what would happen to the department if the top three men left, but Bork did not articulate that worry at the time. Richardson did.

Archibald Cox was a different man after his press conference. He had done very well indeed, and he sensed it. If anybody had been watching television on such a beautiful day, they had received a thorough lesson in government, theory as well as practice. As he walked along Fourteenth Street with his wife, John Barker, and me, Cox began to wonder aloud what Elliot Richardson was likely to do. He was still uncertain, although he thought he could guess. He told us about the letter Elliot had read to him over the telephone before the news conference.

"I know there is a regulation against spiritous beverages on federal reservations," Cox said, "but I could do with a drink." Barker went to a nearby liquor store and picked up a bottle of Old Fitzgerald and some beer. He noticed that the proprietors were watching a replay of Cox's news conference on television. Apparently it was the football half-time show on ABC.

Phyllis Cox went home, and Archie stopped long enough to have a beer with several members of the staff in his office. Once again he saw no point in waiting around. It was the other team's move. So after one beer and a few minutes of conversation about the news conference he headed home to change clothes and go for a short hike.

Elliot Richardson was kept waiting in Alexander Haig's office; once again he was surrounded. Garment, Wright, and Buzhardt did not say much, although their feelings were clear enough. Haig talked some more about the importance of what was happening to the American position in the world, about the possibility of very serious consequences in the Middle East.

Perhaps (Richardson isn't sure it was at this meeting) Haig showed Richardson a "brutal" letter to the President from Chairman Brezhnev which contained the threats later used as a reason for a worldwide alert of U.S. forces. But there was really nothing for these men to say to each other. There was a great gulf between them now.

Finally Richardson was escorted by Haig to the Oval Office, where the President stood briefly behind his desk and shook the attorney general's hand. Richardson sat in the chair to the right of the desk, Haig in another to the left. Nixon said nothing. It was clear that he was angry. So Richardson, as if he had to explain this visit, told the President he had come to offer his resignation. As Nixon explained it, the Middle East situation was so tenuous at this point that it would be extremely important if Richardson could fire Cox and defer his own resignation until the Middle East cooled. Richardson explained once again why he could not do that.

The President said, "I wish you could see it not in terms of your personal commitments but rather in terms of the national interest." The attorney general said, "Mr. President, we may not see this in exactly the same terms, but I would like at least to be understood as acting in the light of what I believe is the national interest."

There was more conversation, the President of the United States talking in detail about foreign policy, not Watergate. He made it very clear to Richardson, without using the words, that he considered what Richardson was doing to be unpatriotic, even sinister. "Brezhnev would never understand if I let Cox defy my instructions," Nixon said. Finally there was a dramatic pause when the President looked at Richardson's eyes with a glare on his face, saying nothing.

Richardson broke the silence. "Mr. President," he said, "I feel that I have no choice but to go forward with this."

Back at the attorney general's office the atmosphere was charged. Richard Darman said, to nobody in particular, "I'll bet the White House backs down." Ruckelshaus answered, "Maybe Elliot will back down," and he laughed. It was the special quality of Elliot Richardson in this case that those closest to him were not sure of his mind.

Ruckelshaus, on the other hand, was the one man who never had any doubts about what he should do. Afterward when people asked him why he refused to fire Cox, he would say that he had made the same commitment to the Senate as Richardson. Once somebody asked, "What if you hadn't?" Ruckelshaus said, "I still wouldn't have fired him." To Ruckelshaus this was a matter where personal morality, self-interest, and the public good converged. He had decided the previous week that he would never fire Cox.

Bork hadn't thought about it before. "Don't you think I'm in a different moral position than you?" Bork asked Ruckelshaus. The deputy attorney general agreed. He indicated that Bork would have to decide the issue for himself. Bork remembers thinking, Can I survive this professionally?

The solicitor general had no doubts about firing Cox but grave doubts about what to do after that. He began talking about a "murder-suicide"; he would fire Cox and then resign. "I have no desire to be regarded as an apparatchik," he said.

Ruckelshaus disagreed with this plan. He said that if Bork decided it was right to fire Cox, he should then stick by his post. "Elliot and I will say publicly that we urged you to stay," Ruckelshaus said.

Richardson returned looking grave and subdued. "The deed is done," he said. Within minutes Ruckelshaus' secretary came in to tell her boss he had a telephone call from General Haig. Ruckelshaus took the private elevator down to his own office to take the call.

"Bob," Richardson said, "you've got about five minutes to make up your mind." Bork remembers that Richardson then said, "Somebody has got to do it. He is going to be fired. You should do it. You've got the nerve and the brains." Afterwards, when the relationship between these two men became strained, Bork would repeat that line to friends and note that it suggested a certain ambiguity.

On the telephone Ruckelshaus was receiving the Middle East briefing from Haig, as well as Haig's interpretation of the rights and duties of those who take an oath of office as a presidential appointee. "Your commander-in-chief is giving you an order, Bill," Haig said in his most reasonable, unthreatening voice. "You don't have any alternative under your oath of office." He suggested that Ruckelshaus carry out the order, wait a week until things cooled down in the Middle East, and then quietly resign.

"Al, this isn't the first time I've given this any thought," Ruckelshaus said. "I've had a week to think about it and I cannot do it. If it's that crucial, why don't you wait a week to fire Cox? There is no magic in the court of appeals deadline. If you want me to stay around a week I'll be happy to do it, but I won't fire Cox before I go."

Haig lectured for a few minutes more, and it crossed Ruckelshaus' mind that Haig might be putting on a little show for his commander-in-chief. The President hated to become directly involved in this sort of thing, but he probably was listening. Haig said, "Do you understand the consequences of your action?" Ruckelshaus did. Haig asked to speak to Bork. He was very angry. When Ruckelshaus sent over his resignation, Haig ignored it. He announced that Ruckelshaus had been fired.

When Bork got on the phone with Haig, the general did not do his Middle East number. He wanted Bork to come to the White House. Bork asked him to send a White House car.

The next several hours are a blur to Robert Bork. Within minutes he was speeding along Pennsylvania Avenue in the back seat of a limousine, with Len Garment in the right front seat and Fred Buzhardt next to him in back. They whisked him into Haig's office, where Haig told him, "Bob, the stability of the executive branch is in doubt, and the situation in the Middle East right now is one of grave jeopardy. We cannot have the President weakened tonight." Bork interrupted him.

"I've already decided to fire Cox," he said. "The only question is whether I resign after I do it." Bork got the impression that this was not the important question to Haig or the White House lawyers who were in the room.

Charles Wright said, "I'll draft a letter." Bork said, "Make it spare."

Haig's office at this point resembled a military headquarters under siege. Ron Ziegler, Bryce Harlow, Buzhardt, and Garment kept darting in and out. They were taking calls from senators and congressmen, and placing calls all over the country. Buzhardt called Richardson's office and ordered several sheets of the attorney general's stationery. It was driven to the White House by a chauffeur who also carried the resignation letters of Elliot L. Richardson and William D. Ruckelshaus.

Wright passed the finished letter to Bork. It said, "Dear Mr. Cox: As provided by Title 28, section 508(b) of the United States Code and Title 28, section 0.132(a) of the Code of Federal Regulations, I have today assumed the duties of Acting Attorney General. In that capacity I am, as instructed by the President, discharging you, effective at once, from your position as Special Prosecutor, Watergate Special Prosecution Force. Very Truly Yours." Bork signed the letter and was ushered in to see the President.

Richard Nixon was standing by his desk looking tired and very gloomy. The two men shook hands.

"Well, you've got guts," the President said. Then he added, "Do you want to be attorney general?"

It was not a job offer. Nixon was thinking out loud, perhaps wondering about this man he had barely met before.

"That would be inappropriate, Mr. President," Bork said.

"All I want is a prosecution, not a persecution," Nixon said.

The conversation died away. Bork headed back to the Justice Department.

There were reporters at the night entrance and roaming the corridors, but Bork avoided them, heading into the courtyard and then up a back elevator. He sat for a long moment in the stillness of the solicitor general's office, a magnificent, high-ceilinged room filled with its own traditions. Since 1870, when the office was created, the finest lawyers of each generation have aspired to sit in this office, to represent the United States in the Supreme Court of the United States. Tonight the solicitor general had other duties. He was also very tired.

Still avoiding the reporters, Bork went by a circuitous route to the attorney general's office, where he found Elliot Richardson phoning senior officials of the department, urging them to stay at their posts. "I've never worked with anybody I liked better than you, Bob," Elliot Richardson said. "Nor have I, Elliot," Robert Bork said. For a moment the emotions of both men were visible. Comrades, one departing with anguish; one remaining, painfully. The warm feeling would be remembered, although it was to dissipate and then turn cold in the coming weeks.

As Ron Ziegler prepared to announce the events of that evening to the press, Alexander Haig gave an order that made his earlier miscalculations pale in its import. He commanded the director of the Federal Bureau of Investigation—the closest thing the country has to a national police—to seal off the offices of the Watergate Special Prosecution Force.

Why did he do it? reporters would ask in future days. His answer would be that he wished to assure that the orders of the President of the United States would be faithfully carried out. "You would turn the country into a banana republic if you allowed defiance of the President," Haig told newsmen.

It was a still, dark night in Washington. Clouds covered the sky and there was no moon visible. Archie and Phyllis Cox and their daughter Sally waited at his rented home, the guest house of a forty-five-acre estate in McLean, Virginia. Around eight o'clock a White House functionary called. The man simply asked for Cox's address. Archibald Cox understood what was coming. He hung up the telephone and returned to the living room. "I should have warned that fellow about the landlord's dog," Archibald Cox said. "He may get eaten alive."

"They will send another," Sally said.

Angelo Lano is an agent of the FBI, assigned to the Washington Field Office. He has large dark eyes and an innocent face that makes him look very young. He had been assigned to the Watergate investigation from the day of the break-in. On Friday evening, October 19, Lano went home to Cheverly, Maryland, and tuned out Watergate. He started installing a new ceiling in his basement and he worked through the next day. Lano had been out of touch with the world for a full twenty-four hours when John J. McDermott, special agent in charge of the Washington Field Office, phoned around 8:30 P.M.

"Cox has been fired. Richardson's out, Ruckelshaus is out. Bork is acting attorney general."

"And you're full of shit," Lano said.

"Don't you have a television, Angie?" McDermott asked. Lano mildly protested that he had been busy all day.

"We got orders," McDermott said.

"From who?"

"From Kelley. The White House wants 1425 K secured immediately."

"John, you're talking to the wrong guy. I work with those people."

"That's why I think you should go," McDermott said.

"What do you mean by secure?"

"Nothing in or out. The people can come and go, but no outsiders."

"There's not going to be any body searches if I go," Lano said.
"Okay," McDermott agreed.

At 8:30 P.M. Phil Bakes and his date, Sally Willis, were sitting down to dinner at the apartment of Carl and Laura Feldbaum. Carl Feldbaum, twenty-nine, was the oldest son of a successful Philadelphia produce broker. He went to Princeton and the University of Pennsylvania Law School, where he shined in a course called "Problems of Prosecution," taught by professors Arlen Specter and Henry Ruth. When Hank Ruth became deputy to Cox, he asked Feldbaum to join him.

Bakes, twenty-seven, was the son of a Sicilian contractor from the South Side of Chicago. His grandfather had changed the family name, Spichaesi, in the 1920s because it had become associated with rackets figures. Bakes decided at age fourteen that he wanted to be a trial lawyer. Nine years later he finished in the top ten of his Harvard Law School class. Then he dropped out, refitted an old school bus and drove through South America for a year with his girl. He broke his back there and was recuperating in Chicago when he was summoned to join the special prosecutor's office.

Just as the four started dinner the phone rang. "Archie's been fired," Hank Ruth told Carl Feldbaum. "I'll see you at the office." The four of them left for 1425 K Street.

The White House was ablaze with lights and stirring with the traffic of black limousines and news courier motorcycles, but the rest of downtown Washington was quiet. At 1425 K Street there were a few people working on the eighth and ninth floors, which housed the Watergate Special Prosecution Force. The seven floors below and the three above were empty.

Feldbaum parked on the sidewalk around the corner from the office. When the four walked into the lobby, they found the downstairs guard friendly. The normal contingent of three guards was on duty on the eighth and ninth floors. Two of them had been watching the beginning of *All in the Family* when the bulletin came on. They didn't have any other word. Feldbaum opened the safe, removed a small brown envelope containing three tape reels, and handed it to Laura. She put it inside her pants, walked past the guard desk, and went down in the elevator.*

Carl Feldbaum was standing by the elevators waiting for Laura to return

* These tapes of conversations between an informant and an officer of Bebe Rebozo's bank suggested the existence of a Nixon slush fund at the bank, but the allegation was never proved.

when the FBI arrived. He backed toward the guard desk. "What are you doing here?" Feldbaum asked.

"Wait a second," Lano said.

"What are you doing here?" Feldbaum repeated.

"It's not of my choosing," Lano said. "We're under orders from the President to seal this place."

Phil Bakes emerged from the office. Earlier that week he had been working with Lano on an investigation.

"Angie, what the hell are you doing here?" Bakes said.

Lano put his hands up, chest high, palms open. "Please, Phil," he said.

"You're their man, aren't you?" Feldbaum said.

"I didn't want to come down here. We got a friendship going," Lano said.

"Every time they get a job like this, they are going to send you," Feldbaum said.

"Please," Lano said, "just don't take anything out of here. The first thing I want to do is to get the hell out of this building. You will still be here after the guy who gave the order is gone."

"You should leave now," Bakes said. "Why don't you leave."

Both men had tears in their eyes.

"They'd send somebody else," Lano said.

Henry Ruth arrived in the lobby. "You can't go upstairs. They are taking over your offices," the GSA guard told him.

"Let me tell you something," Ruth said. He walked slowly past the guard toward the elevator. "I'm going up there."

"Okay," the guard said.

On the ninth floor Ruth saw the jumble of people and sensed that Phil Bakes was almost out of control. Bakes was big and muscular, and he looked ready for a fight. Lano was standing in the entryway, half blocking it. He was dwarfed by Bakes.

"What are you going to do, shoot me, Angie?" Ruth said. He laughed. Then he took Lano to his office and they called Henry Petersen and other top career officials of the Justice Department. Together they devised a plan to move sensitive files to the most secure safes.

Lano and his men were afraid that the prosecutors would remove original documents from the files. Ruth and his men were afraid that someone else might do the same, or add phony papers to the files that could be used to show that the prosecutors had not been impartial.

Lano asked for the key to the large shredder in the file room. He wanted to see that it would not be used. No one professed to know where the key was. It did not turn up. The shredder was not used, either by the staff or by the new guards.

Frank Martin, a young lawyer on the Plumbers task force, had been working in the office Saturday night when he received a call from Gerry Goldman. Goldman told him where to locate copies of Gordon Strachan's "political matters" memoranda, documents loaded with references to the sale of ambassadorships and similar political subjects. They were the best source available at the time on the systematic corruption of the Nixon campaign.

Martin had gotten only some of the memos photocopied and out of the office before the FBI arrived. For more than an hour, as the confusion at the guards' alcove mounted, lawyers and secretaries kept moving in and out. The men were walking like mummies, very stiff-legged. The women, too, seemed to be walking very slowly and carefully. There were no body searches. The Strachan memos were placed in a safe deposit box in a bank early the next week.

At one point a young lawyer named Kenneth Geller walked past the guards with a newspaper folded under his arm. The guards asked to inspect it. Geller threw the rolled-up paper at the guards and left. There was nothing inside.

Almost from the moment I got home from the office Saturday afternoon my telephone was ringing. Reporters from Washington and around the world wanted comment about The Great Tapes Confrontation, and speculation from me about what would happen. After a while I turned the phone off.

John Barker, unable to reach me by phone, showed up at my home in Bethesda. His family was miles away in the mountains. "This is no night to be alone," he said. We sat in my living room, watching the television news shows, and slowly got intoxicated on good bourbon. At 7:30 a talk show came on, and I heard columnist George Will tell the audience that no one should feel sorry for Archibald Cox; that even if he was fired, his performance would simply mean higher fees when he appeared before the Supreme Court.

I called the television station and asked the show's producer to hand Martin Agronsky, the moderator, a note. I was outraged by George Will's cheap shot. I pointed out that Cox had argued before the Supreme Court *pro bono* in his recent appearances. The most recent had been on behalf of an accused murderer in a famous New Hampshire case. Unlike some of the others involved in Watergate, and in particular Charles Alan Wright, Cox had not made a killing in practice before the Supreme Court and had never tried to do so.

Agronsky read my complaint on the air. Will apologized.

Barker went to get a take-out pizza, and a reporter from the *Washington Post*, Peter Milius, arrived at the door. "We couldn't get through to you," he said. "The FBI has sealed your offices."

I went up to the bedroom to put on a necktie. Milius sat in a bedroom rocker nervously rocking and smoking, as I tied the tie. My wife picked up the telephone and heard Archibald Cox's voice. He wanted to know whether he should go to the office. "I don't think that's wise," I said. "I'll go down there and if there is anything for you to do, I'll call you."

He gave me a statement to give to the press: "Whether ours shall continue to be a government of laws and not of men is now for Congress, and ultimately the American people."

While I was on the telephone, Milius was busily writing down all the phone numbers he could find posted on the refrigerator door, including Cox's private number. When I hung up, my wife was crying. "Jim, this is total war."

Cox had still not received official notification of his firing. The White House messenger was driving around Virginia searching for his house. He finally arrived, a young man in an open-necked shirt. He politely handed Cox his dismissal papers and asked for a signature. Cox signed the receipt, closed the door, and said to his wife, "Couldn't they have sent a chap with a proper necktie?"

I was among the last to get the word that the offices were sealed. I left Milius at my house to call in Archie's statement to the *Post* and headed off in my car. I was beside myself with anger.

I ran the first stop sign I came to and within twenty seconds had a Montgomery County police cruiser on my tail. I showed the two officers my credentials and asked if they could help. "You work for Archibald Cox?" they said. "Follow the cruiser." They escorted me several miles beyond their jurisdiction, almost to downtown Washington.

There was an enormous crowd at the office by the time I got there. The lobby was ablaze with lights. Outside cars were double-parked in random fashion. It looked like the scene of a crime just after the deed has been discovered.

Upstairs a crowd of newsmen filled the corridor that ran along the bank of elevators. The reporters just stared at me. Although many of them were friends of many years, nobody said a word. I walked through the crowd to the unmarked door that led to the office. It was tightly shut. As I waited for the guard to open it, I spotted a reporter who had written disparagingly in that morning's newspaper about the lenient deal we had offered John Dean. It was a perfectly fair story from someone who cared deeply about the role of plea bargaining in criminal justice. "You asshole," I said. As the door opened and I entered, I could hear a spasm of nervous laughter from the reporters behind me. Later I would apologize.

Almost the entire staff was there, milling about. Angie Lano and two other FBI agents, men with the unforgettable names of Peter Paul and John Justice, were trying in as restrained a way as possible to keep everyone cool.

Angie Lano was a good and tough cop who did not lack courage. Some months later he would be sent by the prosecutors to interview Deputy Attorney General Laurence Silberman, a man who could have Lano transferred to Butte, Montana, by pushing a button. Lano began the interview by reading the witness his rights: "Anything you say may be used against you . . ." The witness paled and almost collapsed. He wasn't really a suspect in any crime, but Angie Lano didn't take chances. He went by the book.

Now Lano had to contend with something that required courage: the rage and indignation of people whose respect he had earned in the past. He was just a cop following orders, but he was a tangible target. It would be a long night.

Winslow Joy, the security officer for the Justice Department, showed up. When the FBI agents told him they were now in charge of this office, which he had tended from the first days of its existence, he was outraged. "Go ahead and shoot me," he said to Lano. "I'm staying here to see that you don't mess with any files, and my guards are staying, too."

Nearby, Phil Bakes, in a reference to the recent fate of Chilean Premier Allende's government, answered a telephone. "Santiago North," he said.

Hank Ruth made a number of telephone calls, trying to discover the precise status of the Watergate Special Prosecution Force. He could find nobody who knew. Around 10:00 P.M. he went to the library to face the news cameras. He told reporters how the guards tried to prevent him from entering the offices, saying that there no longer existed an office of the special prosecutor, even though there had been no official notice, departmental order, or any other legal move, just a pronouncement of abolition by the White House. Ruth had asked the guards, what if he had love letters from his wife in his desk? Under the Constitution wasn't he allowed to claim them? No, the guards had replied.

"I must say, I suppose that human emotions take over at this kind of occasion," Ruth said. He looked very close to breaking. "One thinks that in a democracy maybe this would not happen. . . . Everything has happened so suddenly that I can't think through what it all means to the country. . . . I was thinking in the car coming in that perhaps it wasn't *Seven Days in May*. Maybe this is *One Day in October*."

Someone asked me what my plans were. "I'm going home to read about the Reichstag fire," I said.

The "mill-in" continued in the offices for several hours. At one point there were five agents to secure two floors of the building; but since nobody in the crowd was looking for violence, that was enough. The men and women who worked there shared Archibald Cox's reverence for the law and they would recognize the authority of the Federal Bureau of Investigation even when they were convinced that it was being abused profoundly. Violence would not be their remedy.

Late in the evening Ruth asked everyone to gather in a large anteroom in the back of the eighth-floor complex. Here he began what was to be a continual series of meetings over the next weeks, where decisions were made by loose consensus. Ruth seemed to sense that it was not a time to feign vigorous leadership when the organization had no discernible function. Yet he felt strongly, as did most of us, that it should take more than a speech by Ronald Ziegler to make us leave our posts.

"Welcome to Moscow," Ruth began. "I'm your tour guide. I assume all of you will be here Tuesday morning so we can try to continue. We will have to take things day by day for awhile."

He told us that he had talked with Henry Petersen, who agreed to allow the most sensitive papers to be moved into the file safes just outside Cox's office, and that Phil Lacovara had talked to Bork, who said everyone would continue to be carried as Justice Department employees, at least for the time being.

Peter Rient rose to say that he wished to offer a vote of confidence for Henry Petersen. He had worked closely with him and he believed him a first-rate public servant. "There are two men who haven't lied about Watergate," Rient said. "Gordon Liddy and Henry Petersen."

Ruth said, "If there is anyone who will not be at their desk Tuesday, would you raise your hand?" No hands were raised.

The group began to file out. Jim Boczar, an attorney who worked in the research section, walked toward Special Agent Ken Russell with an attaché case in his hand. He refused to open the case for the FBI agent. "You have no authority to search my belongings," Boczar said. "That is a violation of my Constitutional rights." He put the case down in front of the agent. "If you search it, you do so without my permission and against my wishes," he said. Angie Lano inspected the case, which contained only some law books.

A short while later I started to leave with the photographs of my family, some paintings and pictures from my walls, which my secretary had taken down and put in a pile for me. Lano asked me to leave them there until the next week, but I was afraid that they would be damaged, and they were so clearly personal I wanted to make a test case of it. Lano insisted. On the top of the pile was a copy of the Declaration of Independence that had hung in my office. "It's the Declaration of Independence, Angie," I said. "Just stamp it 'VOID' and let me take it home."

Not long after the sun went down, the White House began to get the reaction from across the country. It came, as Republican Senator Mark Hatfield said, like a flash flood sweeping down over pasture land.

Late that evening Henry Kissinger, who was in Moscow, tried to get through to Haig to get a message to the President. Kissinger needed some guidance for his negotiations with Leonid Brezhnev. He had difficulty reaching his former aide, which annoyed him immensely. In no uncertain terms he told the White House operators to get Haig and put him on the line.

"Why are you bothering us?" Haig said when his voice finally came on the line. "We have trouble here."

CHAPTER

9

FIRESTORM

"This President does not defy the law."

By midnight the members of the Watergate Special Prosecution Force had dissolved into the quiet night outside the offices on K Street. There had been tears of confusion and anger. Now there was only a stillness.

Many of the young lawyers and paralegal assistants found their way to a large townhouse in Georgetown that one of them had rented from a family friend. Once it had been a magnificent home. The living room had two huge marble fireplaces and a massive Florentine mirror which dominated the opposite wall. Now the mirror was dark and discolored, its silver backing flaking, so that the images it reflected were gray and incomplete.

The young lawyers and their assistants gathered there, watched the television news specials, and wandered through drawing rooms, which were draped in faded crimson silk. They smoked, drank, recited gallows humor. From the fifth floor of the house there was a magnificent view of Washington toward the Potomac River. Several of the young men and women spent long minutes there, silently watching the blinking city lights. A few ventured to the pretty garden in back, and one or two used the pool there. Through much of that night and all of the next day people who had worked together at 1425 K Street came and went at the house, sharing their anger, talking about the future, communicating to each other a sense of hopelessness.

Task Force Leader Bill Merrill had been at his apartment in the Watergate dressing for a Saturday evening dinner party when he heard the urgent tone of the news broadcasters. Around seven o'clock, on the way to the party, he stopped at the office. He rode the elevator to the ninth floor, opened his safe, filled an attaché case with the most sensitive documents in the Plumbers case, bid the guards good-night, and headed for his evening engagement, with the documents locked in the trunk of his car. After dinner Merrill and his host, a Washington lawyer, drove downtown to the lawyer's office, and for more than an hour they photocopied the contents of the attaché case. Then they locked the copies in the law firm's safe.

Similar scenes went on all over Washington. For months I had been dictating notes for this book into a tape recorder as I drove home from the office each evening. At midnight that Saturday I took all of the tapes, and every other note or document that could be tied in any way to the office, and deposited them in the basement storage room of a neighbor's home.

Tina Ruth told her children to allow no federal law enforcement officers into their home. The children were instructed to telephone the local police emergency number and report intruders if agents came to the door with search warrants.

Sunday dawned a peaceful, sunny day. Archibald Cox had slept poorly, and the telephone resumed its ringing early. He talked with a number of friends and shortly after breakfast set out for a hike along a steep rocky trail on the Maryland side of the Potomac. In his tight-fitting dungarees and sweater he was still a strikingly familiar figure. But despite a large number of hikers he was completely alone, lost in his thoughts, making fast time over the rocks.

"My, you *are* getting too big for your britches," called a voice from behind him. It was Tom McBride, head of the campaign finance prosecutions. The two men met, talked briefly about the events of the last evening, and then parted.

Hank Ruth and Phil Lacovara, both of them depressed and exhausted, spent much of Sunday morning on the telephone—with each other, with other government officials, with friends from Capitol Hill and the press— trying to decide what they, as the senior officials in the special prosecutor's office, should do. Neither was very optimistic about the future. Both expressed some cynicism about the possibility that anyone could or would successfully challenge the President's actions.

Because of the holiday weekend it was difficult to gauge the depth of the nation's reaction. It seemed that Nixon had, in Haig's phrase, turned the country into a banana republic. Newsmen were already referring to it as "the Saturday Night Massacre." With one bold, outrageous stroke the President seemed to have erased the due process of law.

In fact Nixon and Haig had assured their own downfall. By the end of the weekend Haig would be referring to the nation's reaction as a "firestorm," and so it must have seemed to the White House. But the general's image of a Dresden or Hiroshima was inappropriate. Rather, the reaction was reminiscent of an earlier democracy in ancient Greece where the hilltops blazed with signal fires when the Persians attacked—a crude but effective summoning of the citizens to the struggle.

The first visible sign of general protest occurred in front of the White House Sunday morning. A man stood on Pennsylvania Avenue wearing a Nixon mask and convict stripes, holding aloft a sign which said, "Honk For Impeachment."

For two weeks there was to be such a cacophony of horns—from cars, trucks, tour buses—that the President had to flee the White House many nights for the quiet of Camp David. The District of Columbia police department ordered that traffic tickets be issued to the horn-honkers, but the police officers' hearts were not in it. One afternoon members of the Community of Christ congregation noticed as they picketed in front of the Executive Mansion that a police cruiser had joined in the honking.

That was a local symbol of a national feeling expressed in the protest telegrams that poured into Washington from across the country. Western Union was used to handling up to three thousand messages a day to government officials. By Sunday morning the messages were coming at the rate of thirty thousand a day. The telegraph company set up special high-speed printers, called in scores of workers from nearby areas, and reprogrammed its computer to compensate for the unprecedented traffic to one city. In ten days 300,000 telegrams were received by Congress and the executive branch, most calling for Nixon's impeachment.

Congress was out of town until Tuesday, so the reactions of its members were unclear on Sunday. The night before, Cox had said the rule of law was up to Congress and ultimately the American people. That was true, but nobody pretended to know what Congress might do, whatever the outrage felt by some of its members or by the American people. Yet there was a common word in the statements of many of those senators and representatives who did react. The word was impeachment.

At the townhouse in Georgetown the situation was confused. Some of the lawyers wanted the staff to resign en masse Tuesday morning. Others argued that this was exactly what the White House hoped to accomplish and the worst possible course of action. Just before he was fired Cox had asked everyone to stay at their posts, and the task force leaders had told Hank Ruth they would do so.

Others wanted to make public a list of nonnegotiable demands directed to Nixon, calling for him to turn over the subpoenaed tapes, guarantee the independence of the special prosecutor, and pledge himself not to interfere with the Watergate Special Prosecution Force. Others argued for a wait-and-see attitude, but even they didn't really expect to be allowed by the Nixon administration to wait very long or see very much.

My own reaction was seething, barely hidden anger combined with the resolve not to go quietly—to make the dissolution of the prosecution force as big a news story as I could manage, and as uncomfortable for the President as possible.

I went to church with my family that Sunday morning, to a small ecumenical Christian congregation that met in the basement of a brownstone not far from Georgetown. The worshipers offered prayers for Archibald Cox, for Elliot Richardson, for the country, and for the Doyle family. We sat there crying.

Then I drove over to 1425 K Street. The White House would be launching one of its propaganda offensives, I knew, and there were likely to be a number of distortions of the events leading up to the massacre. I would do my best to keep our side of the story on the front page.

There were network news crews standing in front of the office and an FBI agent just inside the lobby. Operating on instinct, I motioned to the crews. "Come on, let's go in," I said. The startled agent, a man named Leary, stopped me, insisting that the building was closed.

It was lost on neither agent Leary nor me that our conversation was being recorded by network cameras. "Of course I can come in," I said. "I work here. Here are my credentials. Let me see yours, please."

Leary suggested that I enter but that the newsmen wait on the sidewalk. "Of course they won't wait on the sidewalk," I said. "I'm the public affairs officer and they are the press. It's for me to decide whether they are welcome. There is a press room on the tenth floor, and they are going there."

"Mr. Doyle, I have my orders," Leary said.

"From whom? You'll have to be more specific. Anonymous orders aren't good enough this morning."

Leary looked at me and then at the whirring cameras.

"Okay, go ahead," he said.

On the ninth floor it was quiet. There were a few FBI agents, who showed me their credentials, and nobody from the prosecutor's staff. I turned on *Meet the Press* and heard Tom Brokaw asking White House adviser Melvin Laird what would happen to the evidence now sealed off by the FBI.

"I would like to tell you that the FBI is not present and has not sealed off those offices," Laird said.

As he spoke the FBI agents were in the hall a few feet from the television set. I asked them if the area was still sealed off, if we were prohibited from removing material. "Yes, sir," one of the agents said. Later in the day the agents were replaced by federal marshals with the same orders. They took over Cox's office briefly, until I booted them out into an anteroom, warning them they were violating the office security arrangements.

Other members of the staff began to show up, and I scheduled a meeting with the press in the law library. As soon as the meeting was announced the attorney general's spokesman, John Hushen, telephoned to ask what I planned to discuss. Hushen, a political appointee at Justice, had outlasted Nixon's first three attorneys general. He was most famous for a press release he composed, in Henry Petersen's name, during the original Watergate investigation. It called the investigation "among the most exhaustive and far-reaching" ever conducted by the department. Hushen had written that the investigation was "carried out by 333 agents operating from 51 field offices in the U.S. and four foreign capitals. The agents developed 1,897 leads, conducted 1,551 interviews and spent a total of 14,098 man hours doing it." Hushen was never able to surpass his performance with that press release.

Hushen was very lighthearted on the telephone. He mentioned casually that Henry Petersen was upset with my remark about the Reichstag fire and a few other quotes in the morning newspapers. Laughing, Hushen said, "You are working for me now."

"I haven't seen any paper on that, Jack," I said. I told him I planned to discuss "housekeeping matters" at the news briefing.

By four o'clock the library was loaded with newsmen and camera equipment. John Barker moved among the reporters giving out an old press release containing staff biographies. "Each one of these has been cleared by a federal marshal," he said.

I announced that the investigations were going to continue and that everybody on the staff had voted the previous night to show up for work on Tuesday morning to resume their inquiries. There would be certain nuisances, I said, such as the federal marshals, who were preventing us from taking evidence from the files out of the office. I added that since some of the evidence would be needed before the grand jury on Tuesday, this could prove a problem.

"What precisely is the status of the office?" somebody asked.

"Well," I said, "supposedly we have been folded into the Justice Department, much as you would fold eggs into a cake. But we've gotten nothing on paper. It really is a very extraordinary situation for Washington, D.C."

"Well, then, how do you expect to be able to continue?" someone asked.

"We are going to try like hell. We have reason to believe that some very serious crimes have been committed, and we are a criminal prosecution force. We are going to prosecute." I added that many of the lawyers were at work that very instant. They had taken copies of the most important prosecutive memoranda home with them over the weekend to study. These would be returned on Tuesday, I said, unless the marshals prevented it.

Did we expect more firings?

"Who knows? Some of us kept hearing footsteps all last week. In one case they turned out to be real," I said.

Finally, in exasperation, one of the reporters said, "Jim, you have been abolished."

"Nonsense," I said. "We are still here. Most of the people who work here are part of the Civil Service system. There are rules that apply before you can abolish an agency. Everything has to be done carefully, with lots of paper work. In the meantime we will be here pressing the case. Somebody higher up has got some hard decisions to make."

One of the reporters said, "The White House has announced that the Watergate Special Prosecution Force has been abolished on the orders of the President. How do you expect to continue here?"

"The White House announced we were abolished," I replied. "But, you know, if they announce the sky is green and you look up and see the sky is blue . . ." I did not finish the sentence.

Monday morning's *Washington Post* would have a front-page headline: "Watergate Prosecutors Vow To Stay." The front page of *The New York Times* would say, "Cox Office Plans To Press Inquiry."

My bravado did not change the gloomy facts, however.

Throughout Sunday Robert Bork sat in the solicitor general's office trying to cope with a crisis he barely understood and for which he was not prepared. He had fired Cox because Cox was in open defiance of the President of the United States. Bork made a distinction between his own position and that of Richardson and Ruckelshaus because they had made pledges of independence for Cox at their confirmation hearings. When Richardson and Ruckelshaus seemed sympathetic to his staying, Bork decided he would remain at Justice. But, he admitted afterward, he had no clear idea of what the real issues behind Cox's fight had been.

Resignations on principle are not commonplace in the federal government. Richardson's was the first at the Cabinet level since William Jennings Bryan. Washington reserves a special place in limbo for the high official who resigns and makes waves while doing so.

Bork had called his wife, Claire, and said, "Should I fire Archibald Cox or resign? You have one minute to decide." She said she would support whatever he did and suggested he call his Yale colleague, Alexander Bickel. Bork tried, but Bickel could not be reached. Afterward Bickel consoled his friend. Few others did.

By Sunday morning Robert Bork was to the world the "apparatchik" he had worried about becoming. The telephones were ringing, the angry messages were stacking up in his In box. He was a shaken man.

Henry Petersen came by for an early meeting, assured Bork he would stay on and manage the Watergate cases, and then departed for his boat on Chesapeake Bay. Some of the other career men on the attorney general's administrative staff stayed around to help.

Of the high officials in the department, Robert Bork was one of the least prepared to assume its leadership. He had concerned himself with Constitutional issues and the Supreme Court, and was out of touch with the department's various divisions and their problems. Now there were rumors that Justice was about to disintegrate, that the number of resignations might have multiplied by the time business started on Tuesday. Bork didn't even know how to check these rumors.

Decisions had to be made. The first was to remove the FBI guards at the attorney general's office as well as at the special prosecutor's. "Why not treat them like any other Justice Department employees?" an assistant asked. Not quite. U.S. marshals were sent to replace the FBI, with orders to search all briefcases.

From South Dakota word came that the Indians at Wounded Knee appeared ready to stage another uprising similar to the takeover that had occurred in the spring. Bork himself had no idea how to cope with the pending crisis. J. Stanley Pottinger, the assistant attorney general in charge of the civil rights division, did know but he, too, was on the verge of resigning. One of the career men contacted Interior Department officials, and they agreed to handle the Wounded Knee problem.

During the afternoon Robert Bork telephoned Archibald Cox.

"This is a very hard conversation to begin," Bork said.

There was a long silence.

"I'm sorry. For several reasons," Bork said.

There was another long silence.

"We would like you to come in and brief us," Bork said.

"Hank Ruth can tell you anything that you need to know. If Hank feels there is anything I'm needed for, I'm sure he'll let both of us know," Cox said.

"I'm sorry you feel that way," Bork replied.

Again a long silence.

"Well, good-bye," Bork said.

"Good-bye," Archibald Cox said.

Although Monday was Veterans Day, the entire senior staff of the Watergate Special Prosecution Force showed up for a 9:00 A.M. meeting to discuss what should come next. When I walked in I could see that the mood was both down and divided.

"Here comes our unguided missile," Ruth said, in a clear reference to my news conference of the day before. He was especially unhappy with my announcement that lawyers had taken home photocopies of sensitive documents, but he decided to let it pass. The level of suspicion was growing. Ruth was afraid that his office had been bugged by the FBI over the weekend, so we adjourned to the sidewalk in front of the building. Joe Connolly suggested we use the conference room of a Connecticut Avenue law firm that was associated with his Philadelphia firm. We walked the few blocks there and reconvened the meeting.

George Frampton, who had been doing some of the best legal work for the Watergate task force, was exercised by the stories in the morning newspapers, which he said made us look as if we had gone over to the other side, almost as if Cox's firing was unimportant to us. "When I left home this morning," Frampton said, "my wife asked me if I was going to the office to work for Richard Nixon."

Phil Heymann, Cox's Harvard colleague, spoke. "The important thing to remember is that the White House is going to abolish this office one way or another," he said. Heymann had a student at Harvard Law School who had worked in the White House for Chuck Colson. He didn't mention this fact but he began to remind us of things White House aides had said about the Cox operation, the deep hostility that had always existed. "They are determined to get rid of you, and it can only be a matter of time," he said. Whether we stayed or went was an irrelevant question. We would be going. "Whatever decisions you make should be in light of that," he concluded.

When we returned to the office we found the staff standing around in corridors, visiting each other's offices, and showing a malaise brought on by the uncertainty and confusion of the situation. It was a holiday; the city was empty, the bureaucracy shut down. Nothing much could happen until the next morning, when the courts would open, the grand juries would show up at their usual time, and members of Congress would begin drifting back to town.

The general consensus was that we would all be out on the street in a matter of days, but there was an argument over how this should come about. Phil Bakes and some of the other young attorneys felt that we should set forth the conditions that must be met by the Nixon administration in order for us to continue and then resign en masse if the conditions were not met.

"This isn't a meeting of Students for a Democratic Society, where you draw up lists of nonnegotiable demands," I told some of the young people in a tense corridor meeting. "That's exactly what they want us to do— posture like rampaging college kids. Our job is to rub their noses in it every day and force them to stop us. If they are going to fix these cases, they should have to do it over our prone bodies. We should carry on and let them make the next move."

Bakes and I represented the emotional extremes. All of us were exhausted and ready to take a long vacation, and the frustrations of the situation melded in this confrontation over tactics. Bakes wanted to take the fight to the White House and force the issue with a public confrontation. I wanted to stand ground and force the White House to enact yet another "Saturday Night Massacre"—if it dared. Much of the rest of the staff was in between, some wanting to find a way to leave and get it over with, others instinctively choosing to stay at their posts. But nobody thought we would be at our posts for very long.

There were two attorneys who had no time to take part in the corridor combat. Jon Sale and Jim Quarles had been wrestling for weeks with an investigation of the dairy industry, and by chance they had scheduled an important witness for an office interview on this Monday despite the holiday. With the entire staff standing around aimlessly and federal marshals searching briefcases as staff members came and went, it did not seem an auspicious time to question a witness whose cooperation was much desired. Sale called the Statler Hilton Hotel and asked the subject if he would mind allowing the interview in his suite. Bob A. Lilly, legislative director of the Associated Milk Producers, Incorporated, agreed.

For weeks Quarles and Sale had been buried in a blizzard of dairy industry investigative leads, and Lilly was one of the first witnesses who might bring a break in the complicated case, which included allegations that huge amounts of illegally raised cash had been funneled into the Nixon campaign. It was understood that if Lilly was relatively clean and delivered a straightforward story, he could get immunity.

Lilly began to relate the details of the dairy industry's illegal contributions to political campaigns, providing names and numbers. After two hours he had given the prosecutors details of a large number of specific incidents, and a clearer idea of the relationship between AMPI and its lawyers and consultants, who were the conduits for the illegal contributions.

Lilly sketched out the relationship between himself, other AMPI officials and Treasury Secretary John Connally, who in 1971 had been instrumental in getting milk price supports lifted against the wishes of Agriculture Secretary Clifford Hardin and Budget Director George Shultz. AMPI's principal contact with Connally was a Texas lawyer named Jake Jacobsen. As they left the meeting Sale noted that they would have to make a date with Jake Jacobsen, and Quarles said yes, if they weren't fired first.

On that Monday, Robert Bork had difficulty reaching Henry Petersen to discuss developments. The director of the criminal division had fallen in love with boating in recent years. Whenever he had the opportunity he would head for Chesapeake Bay. Petersen learned that the President or the attorney general thought little of summoning him back from the bay by marine radio for the latest crisis. Petersen's life had been one long series of crises since the Watergate break-in, and the summonses became more and more frequent. So he got in the habit of turning the radio off as he left the harbor and letting the crises wait until the weekend was over or he had returned to port. On Monday afternoon, as he motored into the harbor at Deal, Maryland, he learned from his radio that Robert Bork wanted him for a Justice Department meeting early that evening.

When Petersen arrived, Bork, Henry Ruth, and Philip Lacovara were waiting for him, sitting around a coffee table in Bork's spacious office. All these men knew each other and had worked together in the past. Ruth and Petersen were good friends. Lacovara had served under Bork for a few months before moving to the prosecutor's office, and their relationship was friendly. But that evening, as the conversation began, the participants could feel the tension crackle.

"I hope you guys have strong cases," Bork said. "If you lose them I'm going to be accused of bagging them." It was meant as a signal that Bork wanted the investigations to go forward.

Lacovara sat back, depressed and tired, and began explaining why the matter wasn't that simple. Philip Lacovara is a young man who does not raise his voice. His anger smolders inside. Sometimes it affects his judgment, but it never affects his tone of voice. As Lacovara talked, Petersen paced back and forth on Bork's plush carpet, seeming, at least to one of those present, to be circling Lacovara, drawing nearer, as if to strike. Lacovara's words had an edge to them.

There were certain facts that were not known to Bork and Petersen, Lacovara explained. First, there were many more items of evidence needed from the White House if the investigations were to continue. Second, the entire relationship between the prosecutor's office and the White House had been a charade, part of the cover-up. The events of the weekend simply made that situation even more apparent. Could anyone really expect to carry out an investigation under those conditions?

Both Ruth and Lacovara raised the question that had caused the creation of a special prosecutor in the first instance—the appearance of a conflict for the department. They reminded Petersen that he was almost certain to be a government witness in the main Watergate case because of Dean's testimony.

But there was more, Lacovara said, cases that Bork and Petersen hadn't even dreamed of, which made it impossible for investigation to be conducted by the department in a way that would gain the confidence of the people.

Petersen asked—challenged, really—Lacovara to be more specific, and Lacovara mentioned a perjury investigation that was under way relating to ITT and concerning a high-ranking department official (not Kleindienst) who had never been mentioned in the press, who enjoyed an enormous reputation in the legal community, and who had worked in the department during the years in question.

Petersen walked up to Lacovara's chair, glaring, and Hank Ruth thought he was going to strike the young lawyer, who sat there, his face accentuated by thin-rimmed glasses and a mustache, his gray eyes staring coldly at Petersen.

"You little squirt," Petersen said, interspersing a bunch of profanities. "You better have hard evidence before you start throwing names like that around in front of me. You couldn't hold his briefcase. Don't pull that bullshit on me, Sonny. I was prosecuting cases when you were still in diapers."

Hank Ruth got up and started pacing. As was his nature at such times, he tried in every way he could to calm the situation, to change the subject. But the meeting, which had been on a slippery slope since it began, glided into uselessness and soon ended.

Lacovara and Ruth returned to the prosecutor's office more depressed than ever. Lacovara told a staff meeting that he expected to be gone by the end of the week, and for the next several days it took greater efforts to keep him from resigning than it did with any other staff member.

On Tuesday morning, the long weekend over, Washington began to return to normal (although the honking horns at the White House were a reminder of events). The building at 1425 K Street was bustling with civil servants on every floor. Only one small group failed to show up.

Under a special arrangement, the Internal Revenue Service had agreed to provide agents to work as investigators for the Watergate prosecutors, and in return the prosecutors had agreed to share their files with the IRS. Very early it became clear that with a few distinguished exceptions, the IRS agents would be of no help to the prosecutors. They had been checking the books of every major American corporation every year but they had never seen anything that would lead to the discovery of the multi-million-dollar slush funds many companies, especially oil and aircraft firms, were maintaining for political bribes at home and abroad. And when the prosecutors sent them out to interview corporate executives, the IRS agents usually turned out to be less perceptive than the job required. After awhile the prosecutors relied mostly on the FBI and one or two IRS agents who were unusually good.

But the other half of the agreement became a massive project. The IRS agents were very proficient in gleaning information from our files. Lawyers noticed that every time they wanted to use the Xerox machines there were

IRS men there making copies. The tax agency spent hundreds of man-hours copying everything its agents could get their hands on. Hank Ruth once said, "Watch those guys. I left my gas bill lying around and I think a copy of it ended up in their files."

After the Saturday Night Massacre the men at the Xerox machines disappeared. For weeks we didn't see them. When they finally showed up and started making copies of our documents once again, we knew that the bureaucrats of Washington had decided it might not be fatal to be associated with us.

Judge Sirica had scheduled a hearing for 10:00 A.M. Tuesday, to examine the weekend's developments, at which he requested the Watergate grand juries to be present. Our staff had met until 10:30 P.M. Monday, trying to decide what approach we would take. Tom McBride had drafted a statement—which his secretary typed and smuggled out of the office in her blouse—spelling out the concerns and desires of the staff that would have to be addressed if we were going to continue. Copies of the statement were produced and given to me to distribute to the press after Hank Ruth had read it at Sirica's hearing.

The statement was never read. When we got to court we found John Sirica unusually stern. He invited no suggestions as to how he should proceed. The courtroom was packed with reporters from across the country, law clerks, students, members of the general public, and defense attorneys, as well as all thirty-eight lawyers from the prosecutor's office and the forty-six members of the two grand juries.

Sirica addressed only the grand jurors. "You are advised, first," he said with a most impressive scowl on his face, "that the grand juries you constitute still function. In this regard you should be aware that the oath you took remains binding."

He read the oath, including the pledge of secrecy and the pledge to indict no one "from hatred or malice," nor leave anyone unindicted "from fear, favor, affection, reward, or hope of reward."

Then Sirica said, "The business before you, you will treat as absolutely sacred and secret, and you will of course permit no one on the outside to talk with you concerning any matter relating to the discharge of your duties. You are at liberty to apply to the court for any needed further instructions."

Then he turned to the courtroom at large and said, "These two grand juries will continue to function and pursue their work."

A law professor seeking to enter the case as an interested party rose to argue that the court should appoint a new attorney to replace Cox as a representative of the grand jury. Sirica cut him off. "If the court feels it is necessary to appoint a special counsel, it needs no outside guidance," he said.

Defense attorney John Wilson, whose client, H. R. Haldeman, was due back before the grand jury that morning, had risen earlier to be recognized. When Sirica called on him now, he told the judge his questions had been answered. He left to instruct Haldeman to continue with his appearance before the grand jury.

Before adjourning, Sirica announced that he would hold a hearing with the concerned parties at 2:00 P.M. to review the status of the tapes case. Then he left the bench.

His clerk informed Hank Ruth that the judge would like to see Ruth and his top lawyers in chambers. When they got there they found the judge calm and reassuring. "The law can take care of this situation," he said. "I appreciate it that you all haven't gone off and made a lot of statements about the situation." He urged the lawyers to continue their work while he decided what to do.

Meanwhile, reports circulated among the press corps that Judge Sirica had his aides looking into questions of contempt of court and that he was likely to order hearings on the question of whether the President was already in contempt and should be so judged.

If the prosecutors began Tuesday in a mood of depression, the White House approached it with false optimism.

On Monday President Nixon had invited Elliot Richardson to the White House for a farewell chat. With Alexander Haig present they carried on a cordial conversation, as if the events of Friday and Saturday had not occurred or were an innocent misunderstanding. Richardson did not raise any question about the actions of Haig and Buzhardt, although that morning's newspapers carried detailed stories, obviously from Richardson or his aides, reporting that the former attorney general had been told to fire Cox on the Monday before the massacre and detailing some of the gestures of bad faith on the part of the White House throughout the week. Haig had already begun contradicting the published stories in private sessions with reporters.

Richardson did not ask the President why, after a week of negotiations, he suddenly had been presented with a fait accompli, an order to Cox directing him not to seek any further White House evidence through the courts. He did not remind Nixon and Haig that he had predicted the result. And neither the President nor Haig raised these issues.

They talked about the Middle East. They were back where they had been exactly a week before, with Richardson called to the White House to hear how critical was the situation and how he could help. A week earlier all he would have to do to win the peace was fire Archibald Cox. Now they asked that he publicly support the President despite all that happened in the meantime.

Richardson had announced that he would hold a farewell news conference Tuesday morning at the Department of Justice. Nixon and Haig asked him to be careful that nothing he did or said would fan the flames of political dissent at home, further weakening the President in his dealings with the Russians over the Middle East.

Elliot Richardson reassured the President. His resignation letter had made clear that he was still a devoted follower of Nixon policies, and whatever he said at the meeting on Monday convinced the President and his chief of staff that Richardson was "on board," that he would help the President. Several White House aides passed that word to the White House press corps.

So on Tuesday morning Nixon's aides continued a counteroffensive. Charles Alan Wright appeared on the *Today* show to repeat his version of events: how surprised and overjoyed he had been when he found out that the President seemed to have settled the issue by a generous compromise, but Cox rejected it.

Bryce Harlow and William Timmons went to Capitol Hill to plot strategy with the Republican leaders of the House. As Harlow began a lecture on how the Republicans should defend the Stennis compromise and the firing of Cox, Timmons passed around "fact sheets" containing the White House defense, the party line to be used by Republican congressmen in speeches before their colleagues.

John Anderson of Illinois, leader of the House Republican conference, told Harlow coldly, "If you want Republican members to support you, tell the President he has to turn over the tapes."

Although Anderson was the most liberal member of the Republican leadership, and strongly disliked by the White House, he spoke for the other leaders. Party whip Leslie Arends of Illinois and Representative John Rhodes of Arizona quickly agreed. "Damn all this executive privilege," Representative Jack Edwards of Alabama said. "People are saying the tapes have to be turned over."

Nixon and Haig were watching television at 11:00 A.M. when all three networks switched to the Great Hall at the Department of Justice. Elliot and Anne Richardson, followed by William Ruckelshaus, stepped from behind the blue velvet curtains and the room erupted into prolonged waves of applause that lasted for two minutes. Elliot Richardson stood with a tight smile. His eyes were glistening.

"There can be no greater privilege and there is no greater satisfaction than the opportunity to serve one's country," Richardson began when the applause finally died. "I shall always be grateful to President Nixon for giving me that opportunity in several demanding positions."

For the next few minutes he explained the events of the past week as generously as possible for the President and his men. "I have been compelled to conclude that I could better serve my country by resigning from public office than continuing in it," he said.

The fatigue and the tension were showing. The response of his Justice Department colleagues had moved him, and he was struggling for control. In the past forty-eight hours Richardson had been besieged with advice from all sides. Some of his friends and constituents in Massachusetts thought he should take the occasion to skewer Richard Nixon. The Nixon partisans wanted him to explain how he had been put in an impossible position by Cox, to defend the firing.

During the question·period Richardson denied that the White House "specifically" intruded on Cox's investigations. There were simply arguments over jurisdiction. He seemed to deny that he had been told to fire Cox on the previous Monday, although this story had been leaked by his own aides. "The only mention of firing Mr. Cox at the beginning of the week was in the context of one way of moving the case and thereby in effect resolving the Constitutional impasse," he said. This "was discussed with members of the President's staff and counsel. I might add that I made clear that I thought it was a totally unacceptable way of dealing with it."

The reporters pressed. "On what day of last week? Which employee of the White House suggested it?" a reporter asked.

"I don't believe this is a possibility that can be attributed to any one person," Richardson said. "Indeed it has been suggested at least in theory by Professor Alex Bickel of Yale Law School."

"How did Elliot do?" one insider watching this performance was asked after the news conference.

"Shallow dive," he answered.

At the White House, Nixon and Haig focused on other answers. Richardson did not suggest that he at any time agreed with the White House strategy, and noted that he disagreed with those in the White House who believed Cox had been "out to get the President." He expressed the hope that another independent special prosecutor would be appointed to carry on the case, although he had high praise for Henry Petersen's qualifications. He told the reporters that he did not believe Nixon had yet defied the court's order and added, "Indeed, I have no reason to believe the President would defy a court order."

Richardson was asked what he would have done if he "were in Cox's shoes." "I would have done what he has done," he said. Finally he was asked point blank whether Richard Nixon should now be impeached. He declined to answer. It was, Richardson said, "a question for the American people."

Congress convened shortly after Richardson's news conference ended and for an hour member after member walked to the House floor to castigate the President of the United States. One lonely man, Republican Dan Kuykendall of Tennessee, faced his colleagues and accused them of becoming "a legislative lynch mob." As he said it he lifted from a brown paper bag a rope fashioned as a hangman's noose.

Shortly after noon Richard Nixon summoned Fred Buzhardt and Leonard Garment to the Oval Office. Charles Alan Wright, busy preparing to defend the Stennis proposal in court in less than two hours, was not invited.

There was really no decision to be made, for it had been made by others. These men, who had told Nixon he had no other choice but to fire Cox, who had supported his every attempt to hide the tapes and then to keep them from the courts, agreed now that they must be turned over.

Buzhardt told Wright forty-five minutes before the latter was due in court. But even now he did not tell him vital information he had shared with the United States Attorney's office in New York the previous Friday —that there might be "technical problems" with some of the tapes, and that others were not accounted for. Wright, who had handled this case from the outset, had never inquired after the evidence.

The mood at 1425 K Street had improved quite a bit overnight. Columnists Robert Novak and Rowland Evans reported in their Tuesday column, "Mr. Nixon clearly expected Mr. Cox's dismissal would be followed by resignations of his top staff. Instead, White House aides were stunned Sunday afternoon when Mr. Cox's press spokesman announced the Cox operation was staying intact to bring Watergate wrongdoers to Justice."

The younger lawyers passed the column around. The junior staff was coming together, beginning to sense that there might be great advantage in remaining at their posts and showing a united front.

The staff gathered in the anteroom outside the special prosecutor's suite, watching Richardson on television and waiting for Cox to arrive to share a last glass of punch and some of Florence Campbell's brownies. Most of the lawyers and secretaries were standing around the desks, but a few extra chairs had been pulled up, and sitting among this group was a middle-aged man nobody had ever seen before. He was wearing one of our identification badges with his picture on it. He was a security man from the Justice Department, watching us.

Archie arrived just as the Richardson news conference ended. He tried to be cheerful and casual. "I have been thinking over something to say and never got beyond that point," he began. "Perhaps we've been saying all the things that needed to be said during these past months together. Perhaps, as in most important things, there is nothing to say.

"I don't want to tell anyone what the future should hold for any individual. I do think it important that the work go on . . . that there be a holding together of the organization. . . . I cling to the faith that its merit will appear to the American people and those who make decisions for them, and that you will be able to continue to do what you came here to do.

"One should bet on it, just as we all bet on that chance when we came here to begin with. Because life isn't a sure thing . . ."

We stood around for awhile trying to act as if this was a social occasion. After a few minutes Archibald Cox left, plunging into the crowd of reporters who waited outside. He climbed into his Falcon and drove away.

I walked back into the office and noticed the Justice Department spy sitting quietly in the anteroom. I walked up to him and said, "Say, we're out of paper towels in the men's room. Take care of that, will you?" He leaped out of his chair. "I know all about you, Doyle," he said. "We'll take care of you." By then I was halfway down the corridor.

Tuesday afternoon, October 23: John Sirica's crowded courtroom had an aura of expectation and tension. Except for Charles Alan Wright and Leonard Garment, who were seated at one of the counsel tables, nobody in the large, paneled room had any idea what was going to happen. And these two men barely spoke. During the early confusion, as the court filled with newsmen and the legal fraternity, one or another reporter approached the President's lawyers and tried to engage them, receiving only polite monosyllables in response. The only clue to their mood came in Garment's rather vacant stare at the audience as he absentmindedly ran his fingers through his thinning hair. Charles Alan Wright drank water, refilled his small cup, drank again, refilled, and drank again. He turned once to his wife in the first row of spectators and smiled.

At the opposite counsel table eleven lawyers from the prosecutor's office sat in a tight circle around a table made to fit six. Archibald Cox and James Neal were missing. Henry Ruth was barely visible in the crowd. The men and women of the special prosecutor's office seemed embarrassed by this faintly disorganized scene, squeezed together, perhaps trying to demonstrate unity. Instead what was apparent was the absence of their leaders. The old discipline seemed to be slipping away, replaced by polite elbowing.

Judge Sirica was eight minutes late. Garment's hand moved across his face. Wright drank. The prosecutors scraped their chairs, trying to get closer to the table. Finally the clerk opened the door and said simply, "All rise." John Sirica walked into the room, his face frozen.

For ten minutes he read pertinent sections of the appellate court decision, and finally the order of that court directing Richard Nixon to surrender the tapes. There was no special force to his voice as he read the words. He checked his notes. "The court will now read the order," he said, and then broke off, adding almost to himself, "I've already read an order." He turned to the table to his left. "Are counsel prepared at this time to file the response of the President to the modified order of the court?"

Charles Alan Wright stood. "Mr. Chief Judge, may it please the court. I am not prepared at this time to file a response. I am, however, authorized to say that the President of the United States will comply in all respects to the order of August 29 as modified by the order of the court of appeals."

The men and women in the courtroom were not sure they understood. All eyes studied Wright as he paused. "It will require some time, as Your Honor realizes, to put these materials together, to do the indexing and itemizing as the court of appeals calls for."

There was a loud rustling in the benches as numbers of journalists tried simultaneously to rise and tiptoe out of the courtroom. Sirica motioned them to their seats.

"You will follow the decisions or statements delineated by me?" he said to Charles Alan Wright.

"We will comply in all respects with what Your Honor has just read," Charles Alan Wright said. His slightly reedy voice was almost the only sound in the large room. In the quiet, one could hear the scratching of reporters' pens as they took down the words. "This President does not defy the law," Wright declared.

John J. Sirica allowed a smile. "Mr. Wright, the court is very happy the President has reached this decision," he said, and adjourned the hearing.

10

MISSING TAPES

"Do you think the public will believe this?"

To much of the world it appeared that Richard Nixon was in full retreat, that justice was about to triumph. To the men and women of the Watergate prosecutor's office, it appeared that the President was winning the chess game.

He was surrendering the tapes of conversations he knew were being recorded. It seemed unlikely to the embittered prosecutors that this wily man would have incriminated himself when he knew the tape recorders were running. One could assume the tapes were at worst ambiguous. But Nixon had drawn the game out, and before yielding the tapes he had raised expectations about their contents, so that all but the most incriminating statements would be taken as proof that Nixon was innocent. When the prosecutors pressed their case for other documents, the crisis-weary public would cry "Enough," and the case would be aborted before the evidence was obtained. Nixon had rid himself of Cox, Richardson and Ruckelshaus in one well-planned weekend. The malleable Henry Petersen was again in charge of the investigation, and a confused and unprepared Robert Bork was running the Justice Department. It looked like the "big play" strategy that Nixon favored to extricate himself from tight situations.

That was not a unanimous view, of course, but many of the men and women of the Watergate Special Prosecution Force held it. Henry Ruth came to the conclusion that it was only a matter of time before the mission of his office would be aborted; that it was now doomed to fail.

The perceptions were quite different at the White House.* Nixon's attorneys were discussing the possibility of a Presidential resignation as the fitting way out of an intolerable crisis of confidence. Other aides were preparing to leave the administration at the earliest moment of least embarrassment. But Alexander Haig and Ronald Ziegler successfully isolated Richard Nixon from these realities.

The rage level was high, in the prosecutor's office, even in parts of the White House, and certainly in the country. There was a pervasive sense that the country might not endure this crisis without being changed, for the worse. This was to affect people in many ways.

A few hours after the White House backed down on the tapes Robert Bork met for the first time with the prosecution force. The acting attorney general came to 1425 K Street rather than summoning the top staff to his offices, a gesture of conciliation. More than a dozen of us were assembled around the conference table in Hank Ruth's office when Bork entered along with the restored director of the investigation, Henry Petersen. Nobody rose to greet the men or shake hands.

There were traces of perspiration on Bork's face as he attempted to explain his new role, trying to be neither defensive nor belligerent. "I was given ten minutes to decide whether I would assume this job," he said. "I made my decision and here I am."

He wanted the staff to continue its work, Bork said, and then he asked Petersen to speak. The assistant attorney general tried to hide his nervousness behind a show of forcefulness.

"If you want to lose your jobs, you are going to have to quit. You won't be fired. And for you to quit would be a moral and professional disservice to yourselves and the country. This case cannot sustain another change in personnel," Petersen said in his high-pitched voice. He was wearing a jaunty blue nautical tie patterned with large yellow anchors and rope knots,

---

* Bob Woodward and Carl Bernstein have recorded the White House mood during this period in their book, *The Final Days.*

which seemed incongruous with the occasion of this meeting. He asked if there were any questions, and for a moment the silence cut like a knife. From midway across the room, Carl Feldbaum spoke, eyeing Bork with an icy stare.

"Why did you fire Archibald Cox?"

"I'll answer the question but I won't get in a debate," Bork said rapidly. "At the time I believed the decision to dismiss Professor Cox was final and irrevocable. If I did not do it, it would have led to the decimation of the Justice Department, which I did not find acceptable."

There were a few more questions, and the atmosphere in the room eased a bit. The subject of future relations with the White House came up. "Who over there is wearing the cap with the scrambled eggs?" Rick Ben-Veniste asked. It was a transparent suggestion that General Alexander Haig was acting like the leader of a military coup in a banana republic. Bork responded evenly that Haig continued to be the White House chief of staff.

Then Petersen noted that while nobody would be fired, he saw no reason for the Watergate prosecutors to have a separate public information officer. He was still miffed over my weekend comment that I planned to go home and read about the Reichstag fire, and over the fact that I had held a news conference after he had expressed his displeasure with the idea. But he didn't mention these specifics. He said only that he saw no reason to include a press officer in discussions of criminal cases.

"If this were my office, you wouldn't be here," he said.

"That's right," I said.

Henry Ruth and Rick Ben-Veniste came to my defense, noting that I had been a member of the inner circle from the beginning. Petersen said it was a question that could be settled later.* He asked if there were other questions.

"Mr. Petersen," I said, "this may sound impertinent, but could you tell us what percentage of our work is finished?" Two months earlier he had told the Senate Watergate committee that the cover-up case was "ninety percent completed" when he surrendered it to Cox. It was an extravagant claim, and he had been publicly criticized for making it.

---

* My permanent appointment as a "supergrade" federal official had cleared the Civil Service just a few days before the Saturday Night Massacre. But without any explanation I had been informed afterward that the paper work had been held up and I was still on temporary status. Thus Petersen could fire me if he desired.

"This may sound impertinent," Petersen said, mocking me, "but I haven't any idea. When I made that statement I was talking only about the obstruction case. The campaign contributions cases and most of the others hadn't even been started then."

Ruth intervened, trying to cool the atmosphere in the room. Shortly afterward the two men left. We sat there in silence for a moment. From the street below, the sound of honking car horns drifted into the room.

Rick Ben-Veniste, who delighted in making little jokes based on the last names of his adversaries, broke the mood.

"Bork if you're for impeachment," he said, and the room echoed with barely audible laughter.

The following day Robert Bork held a news conference. He desperately needed to reassure his colleagues at the Department of Justice, where the corridors echoed with rumors of impending mass resignations and hollow jokes about lawyers addressing memos to the attorney general, "To Whom It May Concern."

The first question from a reporter was, "If it's necessary to take the White House to court once again to get certain documentary evidence, are you ready to do that?"

Bork said he was, although he didn't think it would be necessary.

Would he accept the kind of deal that Cox was offered the previous Friday, transcript summaries in return for a pledge not to seek further presidential tapes and documents?

"No, I could only accept an arrangement that gives the Department of Justice all the evidence the people in charge of the prosecution think is necessary," he said.

Well then, would he have accepted the deal if he were Cox on Friday?

"If I had thought those documents were proper for the grand jury investigation, I would not have accepted any deal that precluded me from getting them," Bork said.

Well, wait a minute, a reporter said, since Cox was fired for refusing to go along with the President's order not to seek further evidence from his files, didn't Bork, who had fired Cox, think he was bound by that order?

"It didn't occur to me that I was bound by it," Bork said. "The order was not directed to me."

A reporter asked how Bork justified having violated the Justice Department regulation which said the special prosecutor could only be fired for "extraordinary improprieties." Since departmental regulations had the force of law, had Bork repealed the regulation, and published notice of repeal in the Federal Register, before he fired Cox?

"I think that is a legalism of which even I would not be guilty," Bork said. The action by the acting attorney general, he said, "obviously amends the attorney general's regulations."*

When Americans awoke on Thursday, October 25, two days after Bork's meeting with us, they learned that President Nixon had ordered a world-wide alert of all U.S. military forces. No details were available but rumors in the press were that the National Security Council had convened in emergency session and that the President, his advisers, and his top cabinet officers had been conferring much of the night on the Middle East situation. Secretary of State Henry Kissinger held a news conference the day of the alert and was asked straight out if the alert was a requirement of foreign policy or domestic policies. He answered with a long face, "It is a symptom of what is happening in this country that it could even be suggested that the United States would alert its forces for domestic reasons." He added, "We do not think it is wise at this moment to go into the details of the diplomatic exchanges that prompted this decision," but he promised a full disclosure of the details later and said it would then "be seen that the President had no other choice as a responsible leader."

When the details were forthcoming months later, it became clear that the alert was Kissinger's idea, and that it was based on a serious probe by the Soviets in the Middle East. But at this time the administration's credibility was so low that Nixon's move was greeted with the remark, "A crisis a day keeps impeachment away."

The next evening, Friday, October 26, Richard Nixon held the news conference he had promised earlier but had postponed because of the military alert. He wore a fixed smile through much of the session. The reporters were in a high state of agitation as they shouted "Mr. President" over and over and leaped from their seats after each answer. He lashed out at the press, especially television, and, perspiring and trembling with anger, he said, "The tougher it gets, the cooler I get. . . . I've got what it takes."

* Judge Gerhard Gesell disagreed a week later, and adjudged Bork's firing of Cox an illegal act. The Department of Justice did not appeal the ruling.

Nixon had two major announcements. The first was that the military alert had been an unqualified success and that the outlook for permanent peace was now better than in twenty years.

The other was that he would have the acting attorney general appoint a new Watergate special prosecutor.

Nixon's announcement was greeted with cynicism in Washington, especially at the prosecutor's office. He had rid himself of Cox, Richardson, and Ruckelshaus in one stroke and would now establish a new team and new rules more suitable to his purpose. Who could he get to serve in these positions after what had happened? It seemed a ruse. Ralph Nader had already instituted a law suit to declare the firing of Cox illegal and to have him returned to office. Nixon seemed to be trying to head off that eventuality.

By this time Henry Petersen had informed his old friend Hank Ruth that the White House was extremely angry over Ruth's performance on television during the Saturday Night Massacre, when he compared what was happening to the attempted military coup in the novel *Seven Days in May*. Petersen told Ruth not to expect to remain at his post much longer. Ruth had kept that information to himself, but his mood reflected the despair felt by many of us. The mission of the prosecutor's office appeared doomed.

Carl Feldbaum was sitting at home late one night near the end of October talking to his wife about the office morale problem. They tried to think of some gesture that would help. As Hank Ruth's "expediter," Feldbaum came to know everybody on the staff and was liked by just about everybody because he had a good sense of humor and always took time for a laugh. But he worried to himself about how things were going, how decisions were being made, and, really, about the country. He talked hopefully. Inside he had a lot of doubts.

Carl Feldbaum's father had made a lot of money in the produce business in Philadelphia and then retired to Florida. So it was natural that Carl would think of pumpkins. He called the manager of a supermarket that would be open until 1:00 A.M. and made a deal for the store's total stock of pumpkins, which came close to fifty.

Carl and Laura Feldbaum drove to the store, loaded the boxes of pumpkins in their subcompact, and made two trips to the office with them. They worked until after 3:00 A.M. putting pumpkins on desks. To each one they attached with a toothpick one of the hundreds of telegrams that had come into the office. The telegrams said things like "Congratulations on your staunch spirit and your willingness to fight from one thousand residents of Redwood City, California."

In the morning we came to work and found what we referred to as The Great Pumpkin Raid. It was several weeks before the guards told us that Feldbaum had engineered it.

Judge Sirica held a 10:00 A.M. chambers conference on Tuesday, October 30, to set up procedures for the White House tapes to be handed over. After the meeting was under way for some time J. Fred Buzhardt told Sirica, Ruth, and Lacovara that there were two recordings he would not be turning over. One was of a telephone conversation between Nixon and Mitchell on June 20, 1972. The President must have made the call from a telephone without recording capability, Buzhardt said, because there was no sign of this tape in the White House. The other was of a Nixon-Dean meeting on the evening of April 15, 1973. Buzhardt said the taping system must have malfunctioned. This conversation hadn't been recorded either. He had looked all over the place for it, but it didn't exist.

It had been more than three months since the tapes had been subpoenaed, and this was the first mention to the court that some didn't exist.

John Sirica looked at J. Fred Buzhardt. Then he looked at Henry Ruth and Philip Lacovara. He was very calm, like the school principal dealing with the boy who doesn't know how that rock got through the broken window. Sirica told Buzhardt to show up in open court the next afternoon at 3:30 P.M.; they could continue this conversation on the public record.

The next day Henry Ruth told me the news. There was one problem, he said. We could not announce the hearing to the press or disclose the fact of the missing tapes until it was revealed in court. I pointed out that if I didn't tell the press, it would be disclosed to an empty courtroom and it would be days before the story got out correctly.

Ruth was sympathetic but said there was nothing he could do. I was ordered not to mention the hearing. It was clear that my job would be up for grabs if I did.

I told Ruth I understood. Then I went back to my office, explained to my secretary that I could not be disturbed for an hour, closed my door, and got on the telephone. Between 2:30 P.M. and 3:30 P.M. I called every reporter I could trust. I told them to forget I had called but to be in Sirica's courtroom promptly at 3:30. I got the wire services to call Sirica's clerk to ask whether there were any scheduled hearings that day and then to put bulletins about the 3:30 session on their wires. Then I pointed out to Hank Ruth that the judge had announced the hearings himself. When we got to court a number of reporters were present.

It took Rick Ben-Veniste about thirty minutes from the time he heard about the missing tapes to figure out what he would do about the situation. When Sirica convened court Ben-Veniste said there were certain Secret Service agents there he would like to question. He put Raymond C. Zumwalt, the supervisor of the taping system, on the stand.

Zumwalt started out knowing exactly what had happened. Then he assumed he knew what had happened. Then he remembered that when Ben-Veniste had interviewed him earlier in the day, he had remembered things differently. Ben-Veniste asked Zumwalt to show him the log sheets used to check the tapes in and out of their super-secure storage area. Zumwalt produced a piece of wrinkled brown wrapping paper with pencil marks on it. That was the Secret Service custody record for the White House tapes that had been under subpoena for more than three months.

Judge Sirica said that he did not think these hearings could be concluded in one day. He invited everybody back the next morning. Buzhardt walked to his White House car, trailed by men holding cameras and television lights. "Do you think the public will believe this?" a reporter asked.

"I don't know," replied J. Fred Buzhardt.

Ben-Veniste had been pawing at the ground like a thoroughbred horse since he arrived in July. Bright, brash, abrasive with witnesses, he had been used to his share of the action as a prosecutor in New York. He could have become a task force head, but he had chosen instead to take the number two job, behind Jim Neal, on the Watergate obstruction case. Now Neal was gone and Ben-Veniste was the head of a team of young lawyers who were to put together a withering cross-examination of White House witnesses.

The format was a fact-finding hearing, not a trial. That meant the prosecutors needn't worry about the fine points of the rules of evidence or the possibility some judge would reverse a conviction because of their brashness. They did not need to tailor their facts or limit their case. This was simply an exercise to find out what had happened to the subpoenaed evidence.

Yet it was a trial, of Richard Nixon's credibility. The jury consisted of the reporters who sat in the spectators' seats, who listened closely, took it all down, and broadcast it to the world. Ben-Veniste and his colleagues delivered body blows to the Nixon administration.

It became a comic tennis match, with the testimony bouncing from Secret Service agents scared for their jobs; to Steve Bull, the successor to Alex Butterfield, who wanted to ease the situation as best he could; to Fred Buzhardt, now in the uncomfortable position of witness for the defense, and not doing very well.

On the second day, Thursday, November 1, Secret Service agents consulted their wrapping paper logs and testified that more than thirty tapes had been removed from the storage safe by White House aides at Nixon's request. Their return to the safe had never been recorded. Fred Buzhardt assured the court, "All the tapes made on the White House system are still in existence in their entirety."

Buzhardt revised his and Zumwalt's explanation, given the day before, of the missing April 15 tape. That had been a busy Sunday and the tape ran out before the conversation was held, he said. The machines and the system hadn't really malfunctioned.

Steve Bull testified that he did not remember ever actually seeing tapes from late that Sunday evening, that he had simply "presumed" they existed.

The prosecutors then confronted Buzhardt with Steve Bull's testimony before the Watergate committee. Bull had told the committee that on June 25 (nine days after Buzhardt wrote to Cox to deny that there was an April 15 tape) Haig had informed Bull that President Nixon wanted the April 15 tape of the Dean conversation flown to San Clemente. Bull couldn't get the tape on a courier flight until morning, so Haig instructed Bull to have the Secret Service play the tape for Buzhardt. Buzhardt then briefed the President by phone about the contents of the tape.

Buzhardt said that Bull had been mistaken when he told this to the Watergate committee, that the June 25 incident concerned a March 20 tape. Bull then backed up Buzhardt, testifying that he had been "educated that it was March 20" since his Senate testimony. (Bull also admitted that on September 29 he had arranged for Nixon to hear some of the tapes and that Nixon informed him then that two of the nine subpoenaed tapes were missing.)

Buzhardt said he had not known about the existence of the taping system until the incident on June 25 and that he hadn't asked the President about the existence of an April 15 tape on June 16, when he responded negatively to Cox's request for it.

Buzhardt, whose testimony now was laced with the phrase "I don't recall," testified that it was not until October 27 or 28, two or three days before he told Sirica about the missing tapes, that he discovered that the April 15 tape did not exist. But Bull's testimony and the logs made it clear that Richard Nixon, if not Buzhardt, had known that two of the tapes were missing when he set in motion the train of events that led to the Stennis compromise and the firing of Archibald Cox.

Buzhardt was never able to explain how he had worked on the subpoena case for four months, listening to the tapes, knowing large numbers had been made available to H. R. Haldeman and Rose Mary Woods, the President's personal secretary, without checking to see what was contained in the evidence he was defending from a subpoena, or even whether it existed. He also had difficulty explaining how he could have assured Archibald Cox, on the day that Alexander Butterfield disclosed the existence of the tapes, that they were in the personal custody of the President and completely secure. In fact neither Buzhardt nor anybody else could trace the chain of custody of some of the tapes. The present custodian, John C. Bennett, an assistant to Haig, flatly refused to vouch for the integrity of the tapes or to say that he knew none of them had been destroyed. He could only verify the custody records since July 18, two days after the White House knew that Butterfield had told the Watergate committee staff about the tapes.

11

ENTER LEON JAWORSKI

"I'm putting the patriotic monkey on your back."

The impending disclosure that some tapes were missing had made the selection of a new special prosecutor the most urgent task before Robert Bork. Al Haig kept calling him with suggestions, and Bork kept turning them down. When Haig suggested Leon Jaworski, however, Bork was receptive. Jaworski had been a president of the A.B.A. A young sixty-eight, he had good trial experience in his background; in fact he had been one of the earliest prosecutors at the war crimes trials before they were moved to Nuremberg, and he had distinguished himself.

Bork did not resent Haig's nominations and he did not ask Haig how he was qualified to recommend lawyers or where he was getting the names. Months later when the prosecutors were poring over former Treasury Secretary John Connally's law office diary, they discovered that the White House had phoned Connally to check out Jaworski's appointment but that Connally had been overseas at the time and did not receive the call. It was made just a few days after Connally was informed by Jake Jacobsen that the Watergate prosecutors had subpoenaed Jacobsen for his testimony about dairy industry money passed to Jacobsen for Connally. While I was preparing this book I interviewed a high Nixon administration official and I asked him why the White House had suggested the name of Leon Jaworski to Bork. "Because they thought he was John Connally's candidate," he said.

Other administration officials told me that Jaworski was perceived as a conservative on national security issues, a "patriot" who would be persuaded, perhaps more easily than Archibald Cox, to avoid prying into areas where the White House argued that the nation's external security was at stake.

Haig repeatedly said to Bork during this period, "We ought to get a real professional this time," and some Justice Department officials speculated after the fact that Haig saw Jaworski as a good soldier who, since he had been close to President Lyndon Johnson, would understand that the rules apply differently to Presidents than to others.

When Bork started checking out Jaworski, the Texan looked even better. He was a Democrat. And as a successful mover in A.B.A. circles he already had a national constituency among lawyers. If he would accept the job, he had as good a chance as anyone to head off the movement for a congressionally-appointed prosecutor.

Haig called Jaworski on Tuesday, October 30, the day Buzhardt disclosed the missing tapes to Sirica. At first Haig received a rejection. Wilmott Hastings, an aide to Elliot Richardson, had been in touch with Jaworski in May to discuss the requirements for a prosecutor. At the time Jaworski took the conversation to be a feeler to see if he was interested, although Hastings says it was not. Now Jaworski told Haig, "I already turned that job down once because it didn't have the proper independence. Why in the world would I change my view now?"

Haig persisted, turning on all of his charm. He said President Nixon would guarantee Jaworski total independence. He convinced Jaworski to come to Washington the following day to discuss the job further and arranged for Air Force jets and White House limousines to transport the Houston lawyer.

Jaworski agreed to come. He held a brief telephone conversation with Bork, who would be the appointing officer; but it was clear to Jaworski that this was Alexander Haig's show.

The next day Haig began by holding out the same bait he had offered

Bork the previous summer when he wanted Bork to become Nixon's Watergate counsel. "It's no secret that you're high on the list for appointment to the Supreme Court," Haig said. Jaworski smiled and said he wasn't interested. It is a felony to offer a federal position to someone in return for some benefit from them. Haig did not offer Jaworski an appointment to the Supreme Court, of course.

Then Haig took a tack to which Leon Jaworski would be more responsive. He painted a grim and accurate picture of the instability of the federal government caused by the crisis of confidence over the firing of Cox and Richardson. "I'm putting the patriotic monkey on your back, Leon," Haig said.

By the time Haig had finished making his presentation to Jaworski, Jaworski knew that if he refused the job he would always wonder whether he did so because he lacked the courage to take what looked like the toughest assignment of his life.

Haig brought Buzhardt and Garment into the meeting, and the four men talked about Jaworski's demands for independence. Jaworski wanted public assurance that, despite the President's remarks to the contrary at his Friday press conference, the new special prosecutor would be permitted to sue for evidence if it came to that. He was promised he could do so, "without reservation" in Buzhardt's words, but with an added comment that it wouldn't be necessary, because the White House would cooperate.

Haig and Buzhardt assured Jaworski that he would have a completely free hand in all areas, including the selection of staff. "After you have observed them, you may want to replace some of the present crew," Haig said, adding that some, whom he didn't name, were "inexperienced and excessively partisan," and had been talking at cocktail parties about the evidence in the cases and bragging that they would bring down the President.

Haig brought in William B. Saxbe, the recently retired Republican senator from Ohio, who was to be the new attorney general. Saxbe's only obvious qualification was that he had been known as an outspoken critic of Nixon, often with salty language. Bork, who was with Saxbe, repeated that Nixon had confirmed a pledge of independence for the new prosecutor.

Then Haig called in presidential advisers Melvin Laird and Bryce Harlow, both of whom had privately served notice to Nixon that they wished to leave the White House. Both men urged Jaworski to take the job.

After they left, Jaworski said simply, "I accept."

Haig responded, "You're a great American." Then he reminded Jaworski that the key words for him to pronounce at a news conference after the appointment was announced were that he would have the right to take the President to court if necessary.

"I'll remember," Jaworski said, and he headed back to Houston to put his private affairs in order. It was Wednesday, October 31.

When Jaworski arrived home he discovered that while he was with Haig, Buzhardt had been in Judge Sirica's courtroom disclosing that two of the subpoenaed tapes did not exist. No one had told him about that disclosure during his day of conferences in Washington.

Word of the impending appointment leaked almost immediately, and Susanna McBee of the *Washington Post* telephoned the Jaworski home. The new prosecutor's wife, Jeannette, told McBee, rather sadly, "It's a terrible job. I just feel sorry for him."

Not very much was known about Leon Jaworski in Washington except that he was the controlling force in the third or fourth largest law firm in the country. Houston had spawned three of the nation's biggest, most respected law firms, of which Fulbright, Crooker and Jaworski was the newest and most interesting. It had quadrupled in size in the past twenty years while Jaworski was firmly in control. He enjoyed a reputation as a first-class trial lawyer who could attract both legal talent and powerful clients.

Jaworski's annual income was well over $200,000 in 1973 and would have been much higher except that he refused his partners' suggestions that he take a larger share of the pie. Once when he earned a million-dollar fee for a single piece of trial work, he had divided the money among junior partners and associates rather than give most of it to the Internal Revenue Service. When Jaworski won that case a lot of young Houston lawyers paid off their mortgages.

In 1960 Lyndon Johnson asked Jaworski to represent the Vice President-elect in court challenges against him resulting from the fact that he had been on the ballot in Texas as a senatorial candidate as well as on the Kennedy ticket. The complainants wanted the Texas electoral votes thrown out in the vice presidential contest. The issue was freighted with political maneuvering, and there was the possibility that it would cast a shadow on the Inauguration. Jaworski steered the case past several Republican judges and managed to win it on appeal a few days before the Inauguration. LBJ called him, overflowing with gratefulness. "Leon, if there is anything I can do for you, just name it."

"I believe there is, Mr. Vice President," Jaworski said. "You can go on up there to Washington and get yourself inaugurated so we can be finished with this case." After that they were fast friends.

During the 1960s Jaworski, who had always been active behind the scenes in Houston and Texas politics, began to branch out. In 1962 he became a special assistant to Bobby Kennedy to try a difficult case. When Jack Kennedy was assassinated, the Texas attorney general appointed Jaworski special counsel to oversee a state investigation and prosecution. When Oswald's assassination and the Warren Commission superseded this local activity, President Johnson appointed Jaworski as the Warren Commission member who served as liaison with the state to calm some of the bitter feelings between the state and federal officials.

Later he was named by Johnson to the Crime Commission and the Violence Commission. In the meantime he was working his way up the ladder of the American Bar Association and became its president in 1971. Here was a man who had supped often with the mighty and had shown a keen attraction to power. He seemed likely to be sympathetic with the problems of the leader of the free world, sitting in the White House beset by the attacks of small people who didn't understand.

Larry Hammond, one of the young lawyers on the ITT task force, had spent a summer at Jaworski's law firm while attending the University of Texas Law School, and while he didn't much care for the conservative atmosphere of the firm and its junior associates, he remembered Jaworski's influence as a healthy one.

Jaworski was the first partner of a big Houston law firm who sanctioned, indeed pushed for, the hiring of a Jewish lawyer, who later was made a partner. He also led the way in hiring other minorities and had recently offered a black woman a position as associate, a revolutionary step for Houston.

An article about Houston's law firms that had appeared in the *Texas Monthly* just before Jaworski's appointment seemed to sum up the general view of Leon Jaworski and his firm. The author, Griffin Smith, Jr., wrote that "the eastern pretensions of the other two * are missing here. Fulbright, Crooker is Texan to the core. . . . There is no question that Fulbright, Crooker is a somewhat different genre: less sophisticated, less affected, more friendly, open and down-home. It is much less secretive than the others. . . ."

Of Jaworski himself Smith wrote: "It is impossible to dislike him. . . . He never gives you a chance. . . . Although he has never been fully accepted by the old Houston legal and social establishment, he is exempted from the reproofs that they sometimes levy against his firm. 'The colonel [Jaworski],' says one, 'is still a man who has *judgement*.' "

Archibald Cox was old family, descended from the nation's founders, his education and career at law foreordained when he was born. Leon Jaworski was a frontier American, his parents immigrants, his horizons at birth seemingly limited by the hills around Waco. What the two men shared was an attitude. Both were reachers, achievers; and both believed in the law as a kind of religion.

Jaworski was born poor, the son of an Evangelical minister who spoke five languages.† His father had been a preacher of note in Germany before marrying a Viennese woman and moving to the New World. Leon was the third child. He remembers that when his mother was pregnant with his younger sister, the senior Jaworski moved his family from Waco to "the country," the hill area beyond the town, in a vain effort to rescue his wife's health. She died when Leon was three.

His father rode a buckboard to churches in the Waco area, preaching for five dollars a sermon and earning twenty-five dollars a month, until he was able to establish his own church in the city. The Jaworski children learned to be God-fearing, law-respecting, and hardworking.

Leon finished high school at fifteen and started college at Baylor University. Baylor's president was a friend of the senior Jaworski, and he extended scholarship aid. Leon supplemented it by doing odd jobs, such as correcting papers for seventeen cents an hour. After a year at the

---

* The largest Houston law office at the time was John Connally's firm—Vinson, Elkins, Searls and Connally. The third largest and the most prestigious was Baker and Botts. Today the firm of Fulbright and Jaworski is probably preeminent.

† While Leon Jaworski told me much of his background during long sessions of reminiscing in his office at 1425 K Street, I am heavily indebted to Brock Brower for his further research into Jaworski's childhood, which appeared in *Esquire* magazine.

college he sought admission to the law school, a somewhat common practice in those days, but not for a sixteen-year-old. The dean turned him down, but the school's president overruled the decision, partly because of the family's reputation. Leon's older brother, Hannibal Joseph, was by then an honor student at Baylor Medical.

Jaworski graduated at the top of his class at the age of eighteen, then came to the District of Columbia and earned a Master of Laws degree from George Washington University, while working part-time for Representative (later Senator) Tom Connally. (Jaworski and some Texas classmates lived in a rooming house on Vermont Avenue. Forty-nine years later, when he came to 1425 K Street, if he looked from the window in his private office, Jaworski could see the old rooming house, now converted to a massage parlor.)

At nineteen Leon returned to Waco and petitioned the county courts for "removal of disabilities as a minor," which was granted. He became the youngest-ever member of the Texas Bar on October 1, 1924.

At nineteen Archibald Cox was leading his class at Harvard, preparing for The Law School and eventually a clerkship with Learned Hand. Leon Jaworski began representing bootleggers and moonshiners in bone-dry, Baptist west Texas, winning cases through his ability at cross-examining law officers and finding procedural errors. It was bootleggers or starvation for the new lawyer. The choice was easy.

While he was still a teen-ager he was a rising star at the McLennan County courthouse. He went into practice with Tom Scott, an experienced trial man, and before long he was an accomplished criminal lawyer. He had been a championship debater in high school and law school, and he took easily to trial advocacy. Once, in a capital case, he took a knife from his pocket on the day of summation and at the emotional peak of his closing argument walked to the jury box and said, "If you are going to send this man to the electric chair, then you might as well walk over there and do the deed yourself." He tried to hand the knife to one of the jurors, who instinctively shrunk back, bringing home Jaworski's point about capital punishment. The jury finally reduced the penalty.

In his fifth year of practice, 1929, Judge Richard I. Munroe appointed Jaworski defense counsel for a black tenant farmer named Jordan Scott, who was accused of murdering a white couple in their farmhouse, leaving two young children orphans. The suspect, who was illiterate, had told his story to the constable and signed his "X" to a confession. Then he took the officers to his tenant farm and turned over one of the furrows he had dug the day after the murder, unearthing a Winchester 32-20, the murder weapon.

Lynchings were still common in west Texas at this time, and the emotions in Waco were high. Twenty-four-year-old Leon Jaworski knew every law enforcement officer and court officer in the county, most of them since he was a boy, and he was the most admired young man at the courthouse. But he attacked the government's case with fury, alienating many of his Waco friends and neighbors.

The jury returned a guilty verdict within a half-hour, but Jaworski fought on and won a new trial on the basis of prosecution misconduct and racial prejudice. After a second conviction the young lawyer fought unsuccessfully against the death penalty through the Texas Supreme Court and to the governor's office.

When the emotions of the moment died away, Leon Jaworski's reputation was much enhanced by the Jordan Scott case, and because of it John H. Crooker invited Jaworski to join his Houston law firm. By age twenty-nine he was a full partner.

He became known as a man of discretion and integrity. His business clients brought him their personal troubles, and his personal friends brought him their business problems. When two of Houston's most prominent millionaires became involved in a bitter dispute over money loaned and unwritten pledges made in return, both went to Jaworski for mediation. One of the men handed over a million dollars to the other to settle their dispute quietly, because Jaworski suggested it as the best solution.

People paid large sums for an audience with him, for nothing more than his judgment on a matter. In the circumscribed world of Houston— big oil, big insurance, new money—he wielded enormous power.

The appointment of Leon Jaworski was greeted in Washington with suspicion. Jaworski's reputation was unblemished, but Washington worried about his disposition. He might be good enough to stop the congressional movement for a court-appointed prosecutor but too much in awe of the Presidency to do the difficult job of going after the evidence whatever the consequences.

A *New York Times* profile which appeared when his appointment was announced quoted *Juris Doctor,* a magazine that often spoke for young lawyers, about Jaworski's tenure as president of the American Bar Association: "There appears to be no fierce sense of moral outrage gnawing at his gut." The *Times* profile added, "Yet none who know him doubt that his reverence for the rule of law is profound."

The general attitude in the prosecutor's office was that we were now committed to carrying on the investigation, so we would simply have to wait and see what happened under this new man. Hank Ruth had worked with Jaworski on President Johnson's Crime Commission and thought well of him. We were traveling the route from Boston to Austin, as the saying had been when Lyndon Johnson replaced Jack Kennedy in the Presidency. As Cox was close to Kennedy in both friendship and style, Jaworski was close to Johnson.

It wasn't clear how a bunch of eastern Ivy League lawyers would take to a "good ole boy." More important, would Jaworski place himself in a compromising situation and force an embarrassing scene? Jaworski had been close to Jake Jacobsen, now under suspicion in the dairy industry investigation. As a foundation trustee Jaworski had once approved an $850,000 loan that helped Jacobsen get into the banking business when he was a White House aide. And it was clear, too, that Jaworski had an intolerable appearance of conflict of interest with John Connally, since each was one of the best known lawyers practicing in Houston. Connally was not a target at this time, but he was linked to the dairy investigation.

These questions of style and substance merged. Most of us were easterners to whom Texas meant big oil, quick money, rough edges, and a lack of probity. It did not seem accidental that the candidate of Nixon and Bork would be a Texas wheeler-dealer. Archibald Cox not only had been above suspicion, he had been a surrogate father to some of us, a man whose judgment and conduct could be admired at all times with no reservations. It would be impossible for Jaworski to live up to that standard, even if he wanted to.

The day Jaworski's appointment was announced, the senior staff met in Cox's vacant office. It had been twelve days since the Saturday Night Massacre. There was a good deal of gallows humor about where we were headed under the leadership of the new man.

He was due at Dulles International Airport on Monday, November 5. Hank Ruth asked me to go out and pick him up and I resented it. Ruth's reason, logical enough, was that Jaworski's immediate problem was how he would face newsmen. They would be at the airport, at the office, and at his swearing-in. Thus it was my expertise that was needed first. I suspected there was more to it. Congress was still not satisfied with the President's appointing his own man to this job, and I suspected that none of the senior lawyers, especially Hank Ruth, wanted to be publicly associated with Leon Jaworski—being photographed with him and seeming to endorse him—until opinion had formed and he had given some account of himself. That was prudent enough, I thought, but why am I asked to be the exception?

It was in that mood that I set out for the airport, with my assistant, John Barker, along to boost my morale and help with the reporters. On the trip I picked up the *Wall Street Journal* to pass the time and read a story by investigative reporter Jerry Landauer.

"The long-smoldering 'milk scandal,' no less threatening to the crippled Nixon administration than Watergate, could explode any day, and the fallout may smother John B. Connally's presidential aspirations," it said. The story told of the Senate Watergate committee's investigation of Connally, and added:

> Indeed, fellow Texan Leon Jaworski must decide, soon after taking office today as Watergate special prosecutor, whether to push a parallel criminal investigation of the milk-price increase. Mr. Jaworski's predecessor, Archibald Cox, was seeking tapes of presidential conversations about milk prices when Mr. Nixon fired him. Mr. Cox intended to discover whether the President or his lieutenants knew about the promised campaign donations when they discussed milk matters at a White House meeting on the afternoon of March 23, 1971; the price boost was announced March 25. . . .
>
> And Mr. Jaworski can expect resignations by certain members of the gung-ho Cox corps if he doesn't subpoena and go to court if necessary for Mr. Nixon's milk tapes.

Interesting, I thought to myself, that this story should greet Leon Jaworski as he arrived in Washington.

I didn't know what to make of the man who stepped from Eastern Airlines' Flight 570 onto the mobile lounge. There was no mistaking the face I had seen one newspaper picture of: receding white hair; large, broad nose; lots of lines and wrinkles; bright brown eyes. I had expected a navy blue suit and tie, white-on-white shirt, and solid gold cuff links the size of half-dollars. This man had on a sky-blue checked suit and a raincoat, and looked, well, ordinary. He was a courtly man, I could see. We chatted briefly, comfortably, as the mobile lounge headed to the terminal where the press waited. He didn't seem very nervous.

Connie Chung of CBS greeted him at the terminal. "How can you assure the American people that you will be completely independent and will carry on your investigation?" she asked.

"I tried to insulate myself in such a way when I took this assignment so that I would have complete independence," Jaworski said. "I think I'll have it."

David Schoumacher of ABC asked Jaworski about his relations with Saxbe and reminded him that Saxbe once said if the tapes were incriminating, they should be destroyed.

"I can work independently of Mr. Saxbe," Jaworski said. "He's assured me so. He's not going to give me any directions."

Jaworski stepped away from the reporters and walked over to greet the head of the Eastern Airlines ticket counter, who said, "It's great to have you back in Washington, sir." There was to be a constant series of those greetings—the bell boys at the Sheraton-Carlton Hotel, the chambermaids, the manager. "I get to Washington often," he explained. I waited for his luggage and discovered there was none, just the garment bag he carried over his arm.

As we sped through the rain toward downtown Washington, Jaworski said, quietly, "Tell me your background." I went first, then Barker.

Jaworski had a large black notebook with him and he jotted down a few notes. Then he looked out the window at the rain and talked, almost absentmindedly, about Washington, about coming there during the war on his way to Germany, and about lawyering for Lyndon Johnson. The *Wall Street Journal* lay on the seat between us.

He turned. "Now, as for John Connally," he said out of the blue, "I haven't seen him in over a year, and I haven't talked to him at any time recently. We are in the same circles, of course. But I have not entertained him in my home, nor has he done so with me. We are not close. If a situation should arise where there is the appearance of conflict, I would disqualify myself, of course." He paused. "What judge do you think I should ask to swear me in, Jim?"

I wasn't sure yet, but I thought I was going to like him.

He asked an old friend who was uninvolved with Watergate matters, Judge Byron Skelton of the Court of Claims, to offer the oath at a handsome new courthouse just across Lafayette Park from the White House. A few members of the staff and a large contingent of the press were on hand, but Jaworski was without family or close friends. He used a borrowed Bible. A reporter asked if he had brought it with him, if it was a family Bible, as is the custom.

"No," he said, "but it's, in content, very similar to other Bibles I have consulted from time to time. And I have the feeling that I will need it perhaps more so in the days to come than I've ever needed a Bible before."

He walked back to the office in the mist, and Hank Ruth called the staff together in the file room. There were eighty people in the room, standing in a ragged circle. They were silent.

Jaworski began by saying that he knew of no reasons why any staff changes should be made and that rumors to the contrary should be dismissed. He planned no changes, at least for the time being. He knew Henry Ruth and had confidence in him, and would rely on him as his deputy. Ruth had offered his resignation, and it had been declined.

"I have accepted an awesome task, a gigantic one," he said, "and I have no full answer why I did. When Bobby Kennedy called me in 1962 and asked me to try a contempt case against the governor of Mississippi, I considered it a call to duty and I did it, although some of my associates and acquaintances abused me for it. In the end most understood and came to admire my decision not to avoid that job. I think this is a similar situation."

His audience was silent.

"I have been assured complete control over the entire case," he said, "and I know that the caliber of the individuals who agree to work with me will be in direct relationship to the independence the prosecution force is guaranteed. We will be independent. I have not been precluded from taking any action against the President that I consider necessary. I have the right to move immediately if I choose.

"I believe we can get the job done because I have greater independence than Archie Cox had, and . . ."

Abruptly but quietly, Hank Ruth, who was standing near Jaworski, interrupted. "You're not implying that Archie Cox didn't consider us independent, are you?" Ruth asked.

"No, not at all," Jaworski said, and he went on to praise Cox.

"I'll be meeting with the task forces individually today and tomorrow for in-depth briefings," Jaworski continued. "I ask you to continue working with the greatest degree of fairness and thoroughness, and to give me the same loyalty you would give any superior that you serve in good conscience.

"I don't need to remind you that what you learn in these offices must be held in sacred confidence. It is not fit subject for repetition outside these walls, except in the courts or the grand jury; what I mean is that it's not fit subject for idle gossip at a cocktail party."

The silence was becoming oppressive.

"I don't know the individuals here," he said, "but I have heard good things about a great many of you. I begin by believing in you, and I hope that will be a two-way street."

Silence.

"Let me just conclude by saying that each of you shares a great responsibility with me, and if we do our best we will succeed in our task."

The staff filed out of the room without a word spoken.

Leon Jaworski is a proud man. He never mentioned that day to his staff; he never again assembled the staff to address its members.

Earlier that day, as we walked back from his swearing-in, Leon Jaworski had casually mentioned to Henry Ruth and me that everybody at his law firm, in his family, and among his friends in Houston called him "Colonel." Now, back in my office, Ruth said to me, "I think he would prefer that we call him Colonel."

"Oh, really?" I said. "Well, if he opens up a fried chicken joint in the basement, I'll call him Colonel. Until then, he's Mr. Jaworski to me."

12

AN EIGHTEEN-MINUTE GAP

"The guy got hit with his own bat."

Leon Jaworski's assumption of command was greeted with skepticism by a large segment of the press, the Congress, and his new staff. The prosecutors were polite but reserved; the Congress treated him with courtesy, but its members asked a lot of questions. And the editorials and comments in the press stated baldly what was bothering all the doubters: How could Jaworski expect to succeed when he was the President's man?

The new special prosecutor was troubled by the skeptics and the possibility that they might short-circuit his efforts. Both houses of Congress were considering a number of bills that would have revived the original idea of a Teapot Dome-type prosecutor answerable only to Congress. And the federal district court had before it a suit, initiated by Ralph Nader, seeking to rescind the action of Robert Bork in firing Cox. Jaworski was aware that if he was to have any chance of success, he must quickly demonstrate to his new colleagues and to the public that he intended to be independent and aggressive.

He had started wrong in his first meeting with the staff. The members of the Watergate Special Prosecution Force took pride in their discipline. Despite great temptations they had avoided loose talk among their friends. Despite enormous provocation after the Saturday Night Massacre they had declined to disclose information from the files that was damning to the White House.

The prosecutors had heard all the complaints from Haig and Ziegler that they were zealots who boasted at cocktail parties of bringing down a President. But no one had ever singled out an instance. No name, date, place, or quotation had ever been produced to back up the loose allegations Haig and Ziegler made, usually in off-the-record conversations with reporters.

So when Jaworski warned of "loose cocktail party talk" in his first meeting with the staff, many of the young men and women were deeply offended. Because of that Jaworski started out with an extra strike against him.

Hank Ruth thought that the best way to get the staff and Jaworski on the same wave length was quickly to show the new prosecutor the details of the cases that had already been prepared.

In his first two days in Washington, Jaworski went through a nonstop series of briefings by the five prosecution task forces. Hank Ruth had purposely set up this mind-numbing schedule because he wanted to overwhelm Jaworski with the depth of the investigations and the knowledge of the task force lawyers.

The atmosphere of these sessions was quite different from that of the meeting in the file room. Jaworski listened, sometimes writing in his black notebook. The task force directors laid out a general picture of the areas they were probing, and then individual lawyers discussed specific targets of the investigations, the evidence against them, and the possible defenses. Although they were talking about past and present leaders of the country, the tone was low-key and unemotional. The sessions usually ended with Jaworski hearing what decisions the prosecutors, and thus Jaworski, faced in the immediate future. Usually these decisions involved the need to seek evidence from the White House or an executive agency, but in some cases they concerned what tactic to use in court to forward a case.

Tuesday afternoon, Jaworski's second day, Dan Rather of CBS, who had known Jaworski in Texas, came by for an informal, off-the-record chat between briefing sessions. At one point Jaworski turned to Rather and said, "Dan, I'm impressed by two things. One is the professionalism of this staff. The other is the evidence."

Early in his tenure Jaworski had dinner with Archibald Cox, Hank Ruth, and Phil Lacovara, and said to Cox, "I hope that I can gain half the respect that this staff shows toward you." The next day, before leaving Washington behind, Cox stopped by my office to say good-bye. This brief meeting came after some nights together when we had discussed our feelings toward each other as frankly as we could. This day he had a request.

"I hope you will stay and give Leon a fair chance," Archibald Cox said. "I first met him in 1962. Bobby called on Leon to try the Ross Barnett contempt case. Leon showed me that he was a man of courage and intellect then, and a man of integrity. He will need your help, and I believe he knows that. I hope you will offer it." I said that I would.*

Leon Jaworski brought with him to 1425 K Street a strong impatience. He thought the job that lay ahead of him could be accomplished within a matter of months. He did not attempt to master the cases, as Cox had, but preferred to sit in his office and wait for decisions to be brought to him. He would study the immediate issues, worry a bit, argue a bit (he could be pugnacious when a big decision was weighing on him), and then he would decide, as much by instinct as by legal analysis.

It meant that everybody in the office had more power. The careful, analytical approach of Archibald Cox had paid off with prosecutive memoranda and legal cases that were carefully constructed by the time Jaworski arrived. Now, with the White House unable to resist as strongly, a new push began to obtain more evidence.

Jaworski's attitude was, do what you feel you should, but make sure you win. Partly because he knew any other course would be suspect, he eagerly approved the proposals brought to him by Ruth, Lacovara, and the task force leaders. In return he confidently expected the cases to move

---

* For some time after Jaworski's arrival there was talk of replacing him with a congressionally appointed prosecutor. On November 14, less than two weeks after Jaworski took over, Judge Gesell ruled in district court that Cox had been fired illegally, but he also found that past illegalities did not affect Jaworski's status. Then Judge Sirica announced that he did not want the authority to appoint a prosecutor. In mid-December the Senate Democratic leadership met and decided to shelve the bills providing for a prosecutor appointed by Congress. The debate over Jaworski ended.

into court with record speed, though none of the problems had lessened and we were still waiting to receive the subpoenaed tapes and much other evidence. Jaworski set no deadlines with the staff, but it became clear he judged the time needed as far shorter than his staff thought necessary.

He visited with Saxbe, who was still waiting to be confirmed as attorney general. Shortly after their talk, Orr Kelly of the *Washington Star* told me he had it on the highest authority in the Justice Department that the cover-up case would be over in six weeks to two months—which sounded like a bit of Texas hyperbole. In talking to the press directly Jaworski would suggest that it might take two years to conclude the work of the office. To insiders he made it clear he was in a hurry.

In his first two weeks Jaworski signed and sent to the White House four requests for tapes and documents. The list of items requested was more than twelve pages long. When he received no reply he wrote to Buzhardt on November 19, "Although I hesitate to put undue pressure on you, your failure to respond is delaying, and in some instances impeding, our investigations. . . . In light of past experience, I believe it entirely appropriate to ask you to acknowledge each of these requests and explain your current position. As to those materials you intend to produce, please let us know when you expect to produce them. . . . If there are any materials you do not plan to produce in response to our requests, please identify them and inform us why you are not producing them."

Fred Buzhardt was tied up with his own testimony in court and he found abundant reasons not to answer Jaworski's requests. That was a specialty of the law in which he was well trained. Jaworski learned that an old friend, tax lawyer Chapman Rose of Cleveland, was at that time working with the White House preparing an explanation of Nixon's past tax returns, which had come under scrutiny mostly because of stories by Nick Kotz of the *Washington Post* and Adam Clymer of the *Baltimore Sun*. Jaworski went over to the White House and took Rose under his wing. "Somebody better get word to the President that he's about to end up in more difficulty," Jaworski said. "I'm going to sue him within a few days if his lawyers don't start supplying me with these documents and tapes. I don't believe he needs that kind of problem now, and I want you to raise it with him. He's not getting the straight picture."

After the two men had talked for a while in Rose's office in the Executive Office Building, Rose walked across the White House grounds, escorting Jaworski to his car. He had Jaworski repeat his message to the President, and then he repeated it back to Jaworski. "Don't worry," Jaworski said, "General Haig is getting it in writing this afternoon. You just make sure that the President sees that letter."

The next day Buzhardt was on the telephone making arrangements to deliver documents and tapes. He asked Jaworski to have his staff ready to accept evidence throughout the coming weekend. "How did he sound?" I asked Jaworski.

"Jim," he said, "he was as friendly as a French pervert."

One of the first court papers Jaworski signed concerned Egil Krogh's national security defense in the Plumbers perjury case. The reply brief was actually written by Lacovara and his staff, but its strong language, endorsed by Jaworski, hit the front pages and sent shudders through White House aides.

"In the recent past, national security has become a kind of talisman, invoked by officials at widely disparate levels of government service to justify a wide range of apparently illegal activities," the brief said.

"Most frequently the claim has been made that the national security justifies warrantless wiretapping of domestic subversives, a claim that the Supreme Court has decisively rejected.

"Recently, however, the debate over what may be done in the name of 'national security' has taken a more ambitious turn. It has been advanced by low-level personnel to justify an illegal break-in for the installation of microphones in the offices of the Democratic National Committee."

Ehrlichman, Jaworski said, had offered it as a legal umbrella for the Fielding break-in and now Krogh offered it as an excuse for lying under oath.

"While the claim of national security gives these claims of legalized burglary and perjury a deceptively compelling ring, ultimately they rest on a wholesale rejection of the rule of law and espouse a doctrine that government officials may ignore the requirements of positive criminal statutes when they feel the circumstances dictate. . . . No government office, not even the highest office in the land, carries with it the right to ignore the law's command any more than the orders of a superior can be used by government officers to justify illegal behavior."

No sooner had the brief been read and reported in the press than

Jaworski received an urgent call from Haig to come to the White House and discuss the issue. There he was told the story of Yeoman Radford, the young man who copied papers from Kissinger's briefcase for the edification of the joint chiefs of staff. Jaworski also may have been told of White House fears of compromising the intelligence channel through which they learned that the Soviets had the Ellsberg Pentagon Papers (the suspected "triple agent" whom the FBI swore by and the CIA considered the enemy). When he returned to the office Jaworski described the briefing to his staff as "so much bullshit. I didn't pay any attention to it and you don't have to, either."

The staff was heartened by Jaworski's attitude. They were also impressed by his decision not to bring any new staff of his own with him from Texas. They had waited for his reinforcements to arrive and soon began to realize that Jaworski was indeed the lone stranger who rode into town at high noon. There would be no other troops.

Leon Jaworski's ability to reach through and touch people was to be an important part of his legacy as special prosecutor. It became clear in another context when he met with Egil Krogh late in November.

The meeting in Jaworski's office was charged with emotion. Bill Merrill, who believed Krogh to be one of the most decent men involved in the Watergate affair, opened by describing what he could prove in court was Krogh's role in the Fielding break-in, outlining what Krogh had done as the head of the Plumbers and where it had brought him. "I knew how he must have felt and I tried to make it clear that I saw him as a decent person who was caught in this vise," Merrill recalled afterwards. Merrill ended by saying that Krogh would be convicted for perjury and then tried and convicted for the Fielding break-in. Krogh would never practice law again; any chance he had for rehabilitation, and especially for keeping or regaining his law license, would depend on his decision now. If he helped the government, the perjury charge would not be pressed. If it was pressed, Krogh could never again practice law. When Merrill finished there were tears in his eyes, and tears in Krogh's eyes as well.

Jaworski listened to this recital and then began talking to Krogh about his experiences as a prosecutor of war crimes. "Those who came out of that experience whole were the ones who admitted responsibility for their own acts," Jaworski said. With some delicacy, he made comparisons between the thought processes of Nazi Germany and what Krogh found himself involved in now. He mentioned Albert Speer, who, Jaworski said, would be remembered for his repentance and his candor more than for his crimes. In a quiet voice he concluded, "It is not enough to say, 'I followed orders.' "

On November 30, Bud Krogh pleaded guilty to a felony that carried a maximum ten-year jail term, conspiracy to violate the civil rights of Dr. Lewis Fielding. The perjury charge was dropped. "My coming to this point today," he said, "stems from my asking myself what ideas I wanted to stand for, what I wanted to represent to myself and to my family, and to be identified with for the rest of my experience. I simply feel that what was done in the Ellsberg operation was in violation of what I perceive to be a fundamental idea in the character of this country—the paramount importance of the rights of the individual. I don't want to be associated with that violation any longer by attempting to defend it."

Egil Krogh's conversion was as important to the Plumbers task force as Dean's had been to the cover-up case. The train of events that led to it traced back to the weeks and months before the Saturday Night Massacre, but the timing of his guilty plea lent force to a feeling that the office had taken on new life. During Cox's tenure, the struggle with the White House had become all-consuming, and had affected every area of our endeavor. Now, the great stone wall of resistance was breached. The subpoenaed tapes would be arriving soon, and more tapes and documents promised to follow without a court fight.

What remained uncertain was the developing relationships between the Washington community and the new man in town. Jaworski's success or failure depended, not just upon his own actions, but on the reactions of the White House, Congress, the press, and ultimately the public. Those reactions were shaped in large part by events that occurred in the first month of Jaworski's tenure.

At 9:30 A.M. on Wednesday, November 21—the day before Thanksgiving—Fred Buzhardt called Jaworski and asked for an appointment "to discuss a serious problem." Buzhardt said he needed Jaworski's advice "in the strictest confidence."

Early that afternoon the White House lawyers entered the offices of the Watergate Special Prosecution Force for the first time and in private conference with Jaworski disclosed that there was yet another problem with the subpoenaed tapes. There was, Buzhardt said, an eighteen-minute-and-fifteen-second segment of the June 20, 1972, conversation between Nixon and Haldeman that was obliterated.

Buzhardt and Garment wanted Jaworski to know how concerned they were with this latest turn of events. "I see no way that this could have been done accidentally," Buzhardt said, and then he pointed the finger at Rose Mary Woods, with deadly aim. He and Garment had interviewed her, Buzhardt said, "and she has no defense." They planned to tell her to hire her own lawyer right after the holiday.

"Well," Jaworski said, "I guess we better go see the judge."

Buzhardt was horrified at the thought. He acted as if he had only found out about the tape minutes before he called Jaworski, and hadn't had time to collect his thoughts. With his Uriah Heep act in full sway, he made a pitch for not telling John Sirica until after Thanksgiving, so that he could be more sure of his facts and Miss Woods would have time to consult an attorney.

There was another reason why it was not convenient for Buzhardt to tell his story to Judge Sirica that day. The day before, President Nixon had traveled to Memphis as part of what *Newsweek* had dubbed Operation Candor. There he addressed the Republican Governors Association and said something that was not candid. Governor Tom McCall of Oregon had asked the President, "Are we going to be blindsided by any more Watergate bombs?" Nixon said, "If there are any more bombs, I'm not aware of them."

Buzhardt later testified in court that he had learned about the eighteen-minute gap, and had immediately told the President, a week before telling Jaworski. And six weeks earlier he had known there was at least a five-minute gap.

Jaworski didn't know any of this but he had no doubt about what should be done. He picked up the telephone and made an appointment to see the judge, while Buzhardt continued his objections.

Sirica had a stenographer waiting in chambers when the three lawyers arrived. Buzhardt repeated his remark that Rose Mary Woods had "no explanation and no defense" for the gap in the tape. When Sirica suggested they move to the courtroom and put the whole matter on the public record, Buzhardt pleaded once again for time to prepare a formal presentation. Sirica gave him one hour.

So as the annual Thanksgiving traffic jam piled up on the highways around Washington, J. Fred Buzhardt stood once again in the well of the courtroom on the second floor of the federal courthouse and in a barely audible voice told the latest saga of the White House tapes.

Richard Ben-Veniste suggested to Sirica that the judge get the remaining tapes into his custody without waiting any longer for the index and analysis the appellate court had ordered prepared and turned over with the tapes. Sirica agreed, and ordered the tapes turned over to himself no later than the following Monday.

"This is just another instance that convinces the court that it has to take some steps," Sirica said, "not because the court doesn't trust the White House or the President. The court is just interested in seeing that nothing else happens."

Sirica ordered more hearings to determine how a carefully guarded tape involved in a legal dispute could have been erased inside the White House. On the way out of the courthouse Hank Ruth cautioned Rick Ben-Veniste not to stop to talk with the reporters standing outside with their microphones and cameras. Ruth and Jaworski had agreed that the facts spoke for themselves and the prosecutors should avoid any out-of-court characterizations of the situation.

But Ben-Veniste was not to be contained. "Relax," he told Ruth, "I'll just stop and take their questions. I won't make any comment." But when a reporter asked him what possible charges might arise from the forthcoming hearings, Ben-Veniste couldn't resist. "Obstruction of justice," he said.

That was a news interview that never would have been given in the days of Archibald Cox. Once when Cox thought that Bill Merrill was on the verge of conversing with the newsmen arrayed in front of the two of them, Cox had reached over and pinched the sleeve of Merrill's jacket and pulled him away as the cameras rolled. The incident pointed up one of Jaworski's problems in the early days; he was being tested, by the White House and by his own staff.

"I want Rick spoken to about this," Jaworski told Hank Ruth. "And I want Jill Volner to take over the interrogation of Rose Mary Woods on Monday. Tell her to be prepared." He telephoned me from his ranch the day after Thanksgiving. "You will be getting inquiries about my meeting with Buzhardt and Garment. Let it be known, discreetly, that they asked me to sit on this situation and I refused."

On Monday morning, November 26, as a subdued Rick Ben-Veniste sat at counsel table, Jill Volner began three days of persistent and thorough questioning of the President's personal secretary. And newspaper readers around the country were greeted by an Evans and Novak column which told of Buzhardt's attempt to have the special prosecution withhold the damning news of the eighteen-minute gap in a tape from the Judge. The column said:

> That Jaworski flatly turned down the appeal powerfully reinforces his status as independent prosecutor. But far more important, the fact that the White House actually asked for a delay shows how ominously this latest fiasco looms in the wary eyes of President Nixon's lawyers. . . .
> Had Jaworski granted the delay, he would have committed a heinous offense, particularly in the eyes of zealous deputy prosecutors inherited from Cox— would, indeed, have endangered his relationship with them. Instead, without hesitation, Jaworski said no.

In Sirica's courtroom Ben-Veniste and Volner worked over the White House staff like two surgeons, beginning with Rose Mary Woods. As she described it, the erasure had taken place on Monday, October 1. She had spent the weekend at Camp David trying to transcribe the words on the tape with great difficulty. At one point President Nixon had stopped by her desk at the mountain retreat, pushed the tape recorder buttons, and listened to a bit of the tape, noting how inaudible much of it seemed. When she got back to the White House she switched to a Uher recorder equipped with a foot pedal to ease the task.

She was frequently interrupted by telephone calls—fifty or sixty that day—and after one of them she noticed that the RECORDING button had been pushed while she talked. She had meant to hit the STOP button. As soon as a signal light on her desk went off, indicating the President was alone, she rushed into the Oval Office and told Nixon of her mistake, saying, "I am terribly embarrassed." He responded, "Don't worry about it. That is not one of the subpoenaed tapes. . . . It is too bad, but don't worry about it."

Over her three days of testimony Rose Mary Woods' story changed.

In the beginning she accepted responsibility for the entire eighteen-minute gap. In the end she maintained that she could be responsible for no more than six minutes of the erasure, and even that was a supposition she was beginning to doubt. "Everyone tells me I must have done it," she said. Her lawyer accused the White House counsel of rehearsing her earlier testimony.

One reason for her change was a withering cross-examination. On the second day of her testimony, Jill Volner presented her with the tape recorder and asked her to reenact her own version of events.

As Miss Woods had told it, at the ringing of the telephone she must have jabbed at the tape machine with her right hand, missing the STOP button and hitting RECORDING instead. Simultaneously she twisted backward and to her left, grabbing a telephone five feet away from her typewriter. She tucked the receiver between her shoulder and her chin, and may even have stabbed the appropriate button on the multi-line telephone with the same hand. Then she talked for five minutes, occasionally taking notes, all the while keeping her extended left foot on the pedal of the tape recorder, which was necessary to keep it running, erasing, while she talked.

Since taking her foot off the pedal would have stopped the recorder automatically, Jill Volner observed, why would Miss Woods push any button? "Because I've done it both ways," she responded.

Miss Woods put on a pair of pale blue earphones, switched on the tape recorder and stepped down on the foot pedal. The machine started turning. Mrs. Volner told her to reach in the direction of the imaginary telephone. "Before I did anything else, I had to take these off," Miss Woods said. As she removed the earphones, the recorder suddenly stopped.

"Right, and you just picked your foot up off the pedal," Volner said quietly.

"Yes, but that's just because I'm here and not doing anything else," Rose Mary Woods said.

At Volner's suggestion, the judge agreed that the attorneys could view the operation at Miss Woods' desk in the White House. Inexplicably, a White House photographer was on hand to document the scene. Miss Woods had difficulty acting out the contortion that she had described in court, and the resulting color photograph ended up in newspapers around the country—and on the cover of *Newsweek* with a slash across it saying

"Rose Mary's Boo-Boo." The depressing shocks of Watergate turned momentarily to a national laugh.

Nobody was enjoying this sequence of events more than Richard Ben-Veniste. He was viewed by the White House and by many courtroom observers as "the little wise guy," but he was more complicated than that. He did indeed enjoy the limelight and found it difficult to pass up a wise-crack. But he was a serious lawyer who took the rule of law seriously and harbored a good deal of anger beneath his brash exterior.

Early in the proceedings I had congratulated him for his examination of an important Secret Service witness named Al Wong. "Two Al Wongs don't make a Charlie Wright," he responded. Later when there was a controversy over his nationality,* a reporter went up to him and said, "Rick, what kind of a name is Ben-Veniste?" He answered, "What kind of a name is Bork?"

When he examined a witness, Ben-Veniste moved around the courtroom, his shoulders shrugging involuntarily, his movements back and forth as aggressive as his questions. His habit of turning away from the witness at the end of a question seemed to be a gesture to gain the reaction of the courtroom. But it also had the effect of signaling the witness that the questions were more important than the answers, that after each answer there would be another question, like a mortar shell, landing in the witness box.

Jill Volner's style was the opposite. She disarmed witnesses without meaning to by her blonde bombshell appearance. They soon discovered that she was a quiet but persistent questioner who stayed at her post, working away at interrogation whatever the adversities. On many occasions she was to be treated to a male put-down, but she did not allow herself to be victimized by it.

Rose Mary Woods attempted to hide behind her "feminine helplessness" on the stand. Once Judge Sirica shut off a productive line of questioning by saying, "All right, we have enough problems without two ladies getting into an argument." But Volner declined to give way to what she considered courtroom sexism, and when she was through she was respected as a lawyer.

* Sirica at first thought Ben-Veniste was Italian. In fact his ancestors were Sephardic Jews. Sirica maintained his warm feelings toward Rick even when he discovered Ben-Veniste was not a *paisan.*

The hearings catapulted Rick and Jill to celebrity status. Both Ben-Veniste and Volner have what a television producer would call "star quality," and combined with their ambitions this made it difficult for them to resist camera lenses. It was a bit of a sore point in the office, where thirty-five other lawyers were laboring anonymously. Rick and Jill became known inside as "America's Sweethearts."

The Watergate prosecutors never came close to gaining indictments on the tape erasure. The standard set at the beginning of our work had been that no indictment should be brought unless the staff agreed there was more than just an ordinary chance of conviction. This was one means of resisting any latter-day temptations to solve problems and end criticisms by ventilating issues when the legal case seemed shaky. On the matter of the eighteen-minute erasure there was no discernible chance to prove the case against any one of the suspects beyond a reasonable doubt.

But I always took to heart John Dean's comment to some of the lawyers in the office when he first heard about the eighteen-minute gap. "Who in the White House had the most to gain?" he asked. "And who has two left hands? Who hasn't driven a car in years? Who has trouble taking the top off his fountain pen?"

In mid-December it was obvious that something was happening at the office, but exactly what was not clear. The tapes had been arriving from Judge Sirica's office in batches of two and three, as he monitored them and decided whether or not they were pertinent to the investigation. On December 12 a new batch arrived, and some of the lawyers were holed up in Rick Ben-Veniste's office with the door closed much of the afternoon. Hank Ruth was summoned to Ben-Veniste's office at one point, and then Jaworski.

I had had dinner the night before with author Theodore H. White, who wanted to get some perspective on the strange goings-on in Washington. He had been out of the country during the Saturday Night Massacre, and upon his return he had been approached by the editors of *Reader's Digest* with a proposal to write a book about the events that had overtaken the Nixon administration. He had access to Nixon's aides, but he wanted to get a sense of what was happening at our office.

We talked into the late evening. I told him that the evidence was not yet in and that the most difficult job, especially after the Massacre, would be the decision not to prosecute cases when the evidence was lacking. That had always been true, I said, but the events of October had convinced more people Nixon was trying to hide his own crimes. The President, I said, had been the victim of the "Chappaquiddick theorem," my own description of what happens when politicians try to hide bad news. Teddy Kennedy, I argued, would have been better off if he had held a news conference on Martha's Vineyard the day Mary Jo Kopechne was drowned, rather than a strategy conference with his brain trust back at Hyannisport. Every day he waited had compounded the mystery and multiplied Kennedy's problems.

I pointed out that just a few weeks ago Archibald Cox had wondered whether he was the source of a leak to *The New York Times* concerning Richard Kleindienst. He volunteered to a Senate hearing the fact that he had imparted sensitive information to four people he should not have, that this was "inexcusable," and he apologized. In fact, I said, we had since learned he was not the source of the leak. But his forthrightness had made the subsequent attacks on him by the Nixon administration a one-day event and the incident had not stained his reputation for integrity, nor his stewardship as special prosecutor.

Nixon had the same choice after the Watergate break-in, I said. It would have been the toughest decision of his career to admit that his own campaign forces had committed the break-in. In June, 1972, George McGovern had looked strong, and Nixon must have thought that this one incident could defeat him. It would have taken extraordinary courage to decide to cut his losses.

Even if he had not been able to bring himself to make a full admission at the time, he could have postponed his own investigation until after the election, and then acted. Although there would have been immediate calls for impeachment and rampant cynicism across the land, the furor would have ended before he was inaugurated.

Nixon's second term, I told White, was the Chappaquiddick theorem at work. Whatever his involvement in Watergate, most of his problems stemmed from his attempts to hide the bad news.

The next day, it was clear that whatever was going on in Ben-Veniste's office was important. The lawyers from the Watergate task force had been there an inordinate amount of time. Jaworski seemed especially preoccupied and said to me, "Jim, things are beginning to unravel at the White House."

I grabbed Rick Ben-Veniste in a corridor.

"What's up?" I asked.

"The guy got hit with his own bat," he said, and he kept walking. Next I accosted Feldbaum.

"What's going on?" I demanded.

"We've got a case against the President," he said.

CHAPTER

13

THE GUN BEGINS TO SMOKE

"The grand jury's report has got to be arrows to Toyland."

For a brief moment at year's end the nation seemed to forget its troubles. Heavy snow fell over the capital for the first time in three years. Congress went home. Mr. Nixon went to San Clemente. John Doar, newly appointed as special counsel to the impeachment committee, was seen ice skating at Rockefeller Center. Leon Jaworski joined his children and grandchildren at the Circle J Ranch in Texas.

But the quiet was an illusion. The chain reaction that would culminate in the events of the coming spring and summer—on Capitol Hill and at the Supreme Court and the White House—had begun inside 1425 K Street.

On Wednesday, December 12, Judge Sirica handed over to the prosecutors a second batch of the subpoenaed tapes for use as evidence. Six lawyers—Ben-Veniste, Goldman, Feldbaum, Frampton, Kreindler, Rient —began auditing the March 21 conversation between the President, John Dean, and, for the last part of the meeting, H. R. Haldeman.

Later they would have an office filled with sophisticated electronic equipment and six experts who could enhance the voices by electronically washing away background noises. But for now they had a single, borrowed Sony 800B (the same type of machine the White House used), a speaker, and a few sets of earphones.

Standing around Rick Ben-Veniste's desk, they listened intensely, struggling to catch every word. The taped voices, at times barely audible in the small room, were soon to send their message through the prosecutors' offices.

It was much as John Dean had depicted the scene in his testimony before the Senate—only worse. As the meeting began, Dean was reciting his presentation to Richard Nixon: "We have a cancer within, close to the Presidency, that is growing. It is growing daily. It's compounded, growing geometrically now, because it compounds itself. . . ."

Dean's voice was low and clear, but the quality of the tape in general was poor, certainly not as clear as Alexander Butterfield had indicated to the Senate. The lawyers strained to hear Nixon.

"At first we kept playing short segments and rewinding and playing, looking for phrases like 'It would be wrong,' and the key testimony about raising a million dollars," one of the team remembered. "Then we realized that the whole meeting was about raising a million dollars, that Nixon was taking the obstruction conspiracy for granted. So we played it all the way through, and it was like listening to the most private meeting you could imagine. It sent a chill through you. You wondered what would happen next. It was as if this conversation was taking place at the time, perhaps in the next room, and you were eavesdropping. It enveloped you. We just stood there and stared at each other, incredulous, wondering why they had ever sent this tape over. We played it again and again."

Every few minutes a new name or a revealing statement would be heard, an important lead to be followed. The lawyers would make a mental note. The most important point they wanted to check was the conflicting stories as to whether the President had authorized the collection and payment of hush money.

At the beginning Dean said to Nixon, "One, we are being blackmailed; two, people are going to start perjuring themselves very quickly, that have not had to perjure themselves, to protect other people in the line . . ." Then John Dean laid out what he knew and what others knew.

He told of the $350,000 that had been "borrowed" from Haldeman's cache and paid out before the election to Howard Hunt and the other burglars. "The blackmail is continuing," Dean said. "Hunt is now demanding seventy-two thousand dollars for his own personal expenses and another fifty thousand dollars to pay attorney's fees; a hundred and twenty thousand dollars." He added that it would doubtless go on after Hunt and the others were sentenced. "It will compound the obstruction of justice situation. It will cost money. It is dangerous. People around here are not pros at this sort of thing. This is the sort of thing Mafia people can do: washing money, getting clean money, things like that. . . ."

Nixon asked, "How much money do you need?"

"I would say these people are going to cost a million dollars over the next two years," Dean replied.

"We could get that," Nixon said. "On the money, if you need the money, you could get that. You could get a million dollars. You could get it in cash. I know where it could be gotten. It is not easy, but it could be done. But the question is who the hell would handle it. Any ideas on that?"

There was no suggestion that Nixon thought it would be wrong to raise the money, as Haldeman had claimed in testimony to the Senate Watergate committee.

Nixon asked, "Your major guy to keep under control is Hunt?"

Dean said that was right.

"Just looking at the immediate problem," Nixon responded, "don't you think you have to handle Hunt's financial situation damn soon? It seems to me we have to keep the cap on the bottle that much, or we don't have any options."

The prosecutors tried to jot down some of the dialogue as they went along. "I don't understand why they gave us this tape," one said.

"Can you imagine what was on the one they erased?" another said.

The lawyers played the tape through to the end, their suspicions confirmed. Someone had held out executive clemency to Hunt, and Nixon was aware of it; the national security defense had been hatched as nothing more than an alibi for burglary and perjury. Parole had been considered as an alternative to clemency because, as Dean was heard saying on the tape, "Kleindienst has now got control of the parole board and he said to tell me we could pull paroles off now where we couldn't before."

Nixon kept reminding Dean that he had to pay off Hunt right away. Near the end of the meeting he said, "That's why for your immediate things you have no choice but to come up with the one hundred and twenty thousand dollars or whatever it is. Right?"

Dean agreed, but his voice showed some lack of resolve.

Nixon pressed. "Would you agree that that's the prime thing, that you damn well better get that done?"

"Obviously, he ought to be given some signal anyway," Dean said.

"Well, for Christ's sake, get it!" Nixon said, and his voice made it clear it was a command.

The six men in Ben-Veniste's office agreed that they should say nothing to anybody outside the room until Hank Ruth had had a chance to hear the tape and inform Jaworski.

Later Jaworski listened and was most shocked, not by the crucial evidence concerning the blackmail money, but by a key passage about the grand jury investigation.

"You can't have a lawyer before the grand jury," Dean had said.

"Oh, no. That's right," Nixon responded.

"But you have the rules of evidence," Haldeman declared. "You can refuse to talk."

"You can take the Fifth Amendment," Dean said.

"That's right," the President concurred.

"You can say you have forgotten, too, can't you?" Haldeman inquired.

"Sure," Dean said, "but you are chancing a very high risk for a perjury situation."

"But you can say, 'I don't remember,'" Nixon replied. "You can say, 'I can't recall. I can't give any answer to that, that I can recall.'"

Jaworski reddened. "Can you imagine that?" he said. "The President of the United States sitting in his office telling his staff how to commit perjury." Jaworski spoke of this exchange many times over the next months. It was something he could not accept.

On the basis of the seven tapes Sirica had turned over and evidence developed from leads on the tapes, assistant prosecutor George Frampton began to prepare a memorandum that eventually ran to 128 pages. It was an analysis of crimes committed by the President of the United States.

It began:

   The evidence before the Grand Jury clearly demonstrates that President
Nixon knew prior to March 21, 1973, about the existence of a conspiracy to
obstruct justice on the part of his closest White House aides and high officials
of his Re-election Committee, and that on March 21, when the President
learned many of the material details of the cover-up and the potential criminal
liability of those involved, he joined the conspiracy (1) by urging that a cash
payment be made to Howard Hunt to "buy time" and (2) by approving a
new strategy to continue the cover-up which contemplated limited disclosure
of some information together with contained concealment of the most damaging
evidence.

Months later the President's congressional supporters would demand
to know what specific criminal laws Richard Nixon had broken. The
Frampton memo had answered that question in devastating fashion: 18
U.S.C. [United States Code] 371—conspiracy to obstruct justice; 18 U.S.C.
201(d)—bribery; 18 U.S.C. 1510—obstruction of a criminal investigation
through bribery to prevent communication to the prosecutors; 18 U.S.C. 3
and 4—accessory after the fact, misprision of a felony.*

This memorandum was passed around the office to Jaworski, Ruth,
Lacovara, and the members of the Watergate task force, who handled it
like a state secret. The first question that arose was: When will the
President's own advisers, especially Alexander Haig, tell him that his
situation is untenable and he must now plan for an orderly succession?
Perhaps such activity was already under way.

When the tapes first arrived, their contents had so surprised the
prosecutors that there was speculation that perhaps the White House did
not understand what was on the March 21 tape; that through some lapse,
or self-deception, the lawyers had missed the words. But Buzhardt knew
well what was on the tape.

Just before the March 21 tape was delivered, Haig had allowed Jaworski
to send an assistant, Chuck Breyer, to the White House, where Breyer was
given supervised access to some files to search for evidence. Breyer discovered immediately that some documents—copies of which already had
been delivered to the prosecutors by various witnesses—had been retyped

* Frampton's memorandum remains unpublished, but the substance of it appears in Leon
Jaworski's *The Right and the Power* in a chapter entitled "The Case Against the President."

and key paragraphs removed or rewritten. In other cases parts of the documents had been snipped out with scissors. No attempt had been made to conceal these alterations.

At a meeting with task force leaders on December 13 Jaworski announced, "The White House files have been gutted and sanitized and whatever. I'm certain that everybody who had a chance to get at those files has done so and removed what they could."

He told Hank Ruth to prepare a plan for calling the White House principals and their secretaries, and Buzhardt and his assistants before the grand jury to attempt to determine how supervised government files had been tampered with.

"But," he added, "before we begin those interviews, let's get as much evidence as we can out of those White House files."

Eight days later—on Friday, December 21—Jaworski held still another meeting with Alexander Haig. The two men had been cultivating their relationship. Jaworski believed he could use Haig. Haig believed he could use Jaworski. Haig would tell Nixon and Buzhardt and others that Jaworski was sympathetic to the President's problems but was a captive of the old Cox staff of zealots.

The two met in a warm, dimly lighted parlor on the first floor of the White House called the Map Room, where Franklin Roosevelt had often retired during World War II to study battle maps which told of the world situation.

Jaworski and Haig exchanged pleasantries, then bargained over more tapes and documents the special prosecutor wanted. Haig chided him gently for his insatiable appetite and Jaworski turned the remark aside. He told Haig that the White House files had been tampered with but did not add that he intended to begin a grand jury investigation of the matter.

Jaworski brought up the March 21 tape and how serious it was for the President. There was the discussion of clemency and, far more damning as criminal evidence, the discussion of raising a million dollars, and the order to Dean to get the money and pay Hunt quickly.

Haig agreed that the taped conversation was inexcusable but added he had been assured by White House counsel that the President had not committed a criminal offense. Jaworski disagreed.

Jaworski later repeated to me something he said in this meeting. He looked at Haig and said, "If you were going to block out eighteen minutes and clip out passages from documents and lose a couple of tapes, then why in the goddamned hell was this thing allowed to remain?" He told me Haig answered, "I wish I knew the answer to that myself."

It was the special prosecutor's way of bringing home the point—that despite blatant efforts to obstruct justice the White House conspirators had failed and had turned over the instrument of Richard Nixon's destruction.

Haig protested that the White House lawyers had assured him there was no criminal case against the President on the tape. Those lawyers had spent long hours listening to the tapes. Perhaps Jaworski should look at the transcripts they had made. Haig thought they would be better, more accurate than the ones Jaworski's staff prepared.

Jaworski quickly accepted the offer. The White House's own transcripts might someday lend corroboration to the prosecution's case in a court. But Jaworski had listened to the tape himself. He told Haig again that the general was wrong in his assumption that Nixon was not criminally liable.

"Al, I think you should get the finest criminal lawyer you can find and let him listen to that tape," Jaworski said. Then he added that he had other evidence that corroborated the tape.

They talked a few more moments. Haig rose and walked with the prosecutor to the south portico, to the door under the Truman balcony, where Jaworski's car was waiting. Jaworski saw tears in Haig's eyes.

Later that day Haig telephoned Jaworski, excited and buoyant. "There was no overt act that followed the meeting of the twenty-first," he said.

Someone had given Haig a quick lesson in conspiracy law. On the basis of what he had been told he was prepared to ignore the implications of the President's words on March 21.

Under the law those who join in a criminal conspiracy are not guilty of a crime until some overt act flows from their planning. For example, if four men meet and devise a plan to rob a bank, and after the meeting one of them rents a getaway car, the conspiracy is a crime even if they never actually commit the robbery. If they take no action to forward their plan, the essential elements of a conspiracy are not present.

The White House believed that Nixon's words in themselves could not be used to accuse him of criminality. This argument was based on the mistaken testimony of E. Howard Hunt before the Senate Watergate committee that he probably had received a $75,000 payment through his lawyer, William Bittman, on the morning of March 21, and thus before the President's orders to Dean.

In fact, as the prosecutors were to prove after a great deal of detective work, the payment to Bittman was not made until the evening of the twenty-first, after a series of telephone calls implicating Haldeman, LaRue, Mitchell, and Dean (and through Dean, Nixon) in the plan to make the payment.

Even if the payment had been made before the meeting, Nixon's involvement probably constituted a crime because of other overt acts—the telephone calls and subsequent meetings—which flowed from his conversation with Haldeman and Dean on March 21.

And even without such overt acts, Nixon was probably guilty of conspiracy. As numerous court cases make clear, once the existence of the conspiracy was established, Nixon needed only to be shown to have cast his lot with the conspirators and to have had a stake in the successful outcome of their plans to be adjudged a conspirator.

As Phil Lacovara subsequently wrote to Jaworski, all of this was "hornbook law," recognizable by any competent criminal lawyer. That Haig could be so easily turned aside by the "no overt act" theory was a reflection on his own sense of honor and a measure of the quality of legal advice available to the White House.

Throughout this period, as the special prosecutor struggled to find the proper way to handle the case of Richard Nixon, Leon Jaworski hoped against reason that the President would resign and save the country the anguish that lay ahead. But before that could happen, Nixon and his top aides had to be convinced that the men and women charged with bringing the President to account would perform their jobs.

Jaworski's staff immediately set about to shape the boundaries of the prosecutor's options. What developed was a debate, emotional and even furious at times, shaped by the values and experiences of the people involved. For the first two months of 1974 the tension in the prosecutor's office matched the intensity of those days just before the Saturday Night

Massacre. The city outside was quiet, waiting. But for those within the compound at 1425 K Street every day was a new exercise in frustration and, before it was over, recrimination.

At the center of it all was the new special prosecutor. His values, his experiences, his view of his responsibilities would shape the debate and decide the final outcome.

He was not Archibald Cox, and that was one of his sins to many members of Cox's army. They did not speak of it, but it was a factor. Phil Lacovara never brought back the pictures that had graced his office walls before he took them home during the Saturday Night Massacre. I asked why one day. "Because," he said, "it will never be the same here."

That was the emotional factor. There were differences of style and of intellect that came into play, perhaps in more important ways. "There are two kinds of lawyers," someone remarked one day. "One sees a problem. That's Archie Cox. The other sees a solution. That's Leon."

Cox could be autocratic when it came to making a decision. But beforehand he would engage anyone and everyone in debate, for as a teacher that was his life. Jaworski instinctively made the decision he thought would lead most directly to the goal he sought and shaped his arguments afterward. He could become very frustrated when others forced him to defend his position.

A debate began shortly after the March 21 tape arrived. Hank Ruth sent Jaworski a confidential memorandum that reduced the choices to three: Indict Richard Nixon; decline to indict him because of Constitutional doubts or simple discretion, but list him as one of the unindicted conspirators in the Watergate cover-up case; do neither, and turn over all the evidence pertaining to Nixon's alleged criminal activity to the House impeachment committee.

Ruth said that Archibald Cox, early in his tenure, had reached the tentative conclusion that it would not be proper to indict a sitting President. Ruth added that this view had been his own firm conviction since his second day on the job. However, naming Nixon an unindicted co-conspirator was no solution, Ruth said, because it prolonged the period of limbo for the President without giving him a legal forum in which to defend himself against the charges. (Cox had once said of that solution, "That is just a backhanded way of sticking the knife in.") The proper course of action, Ruth said, was to begin at the earliest possible date to work with John

Doar, counsel to the impeachment committee, who was fully capable of handling the explosive evidence in strict confidence and with sensitivity. Ruth suggested that Peter Kreindler be assigned as a liaison officer with the House Judiciary Committee to effect the transfer of information to that group and to help them evaluate the evidence.

Jaworski thought Ruth was right in concluding that a sitting President should not be indicted or named in an indictment, but he was against the idea of turning the evidence over to the House when "the objectives and particularly the procedures of the House Judiciary Committee regarding impeachment are unknown to us." His attention was on the defendants who would be indicted, whose trials would be immensely complicated by a House inquiry that publicized the evidence of the conspiracy. Jaworski told Ruth, "If we are to participate in jeopardizing the fairness of their trials, we have no business even indicting these individuals. It may be that some carefully worded observation regarding the President's actions or non-action could be included in a grand jury report, and this may be sufficient to inform the public of the existence of factual situations that should be brought to light." But he quickly added that he did "not for a moment commit myself to it." Kreindler was never assigned to work with Doar.

Jaworski's attitude was greeted with a mixture of dismay and suspicion by the staff. Many of the lawyers disagreed with the conclusion that a sitting President either could not or should not be indicted when there was overwhelming evidence of his involvement in a criminal conspiracy while in the White House. But if that was to be the office policy, then Ruth's proposed alternative seemed compelling to them; the evidence must be turned over to another tribunal with authority to act.

The new strategy at the White House was to make a public display of cooperating with the special prosecutor while resisting any cooperation with the House. Having retreated from his attempt to defy the courts, Nixon was back to his old line of leaving the entire matter up to the courts, hoping that this would give him an acceptable political position when he stonewalled the impeachment inquiry, now perceived as his greatest threat.

Jaworski's cautious attitude in cooperating with the impeachment inquiry, while based on valid objections, was all the more annoying to many on the staff because of his general attitude toward the lesser cases at this time. He had been so impressed, on his first two days in the office, by the initial presentations made to him that he found it hard to understand why indictments could not be returned immediately. Wasn't that the biggest complaint of the White House, after all, that the prosecutors were deliberately dragging their feet?

Ruth went over the reasons for moving slowly—the necessity to exhaust efforts to obtain the rest of the evidence (including any exculpatory material) from the White House; the need to examine carefully every document when it arrived, and to analyze every taped conversation, so that as many questions as possible were answered before the indictments came down; and finally the need to discuss at length just exactly who would be included in each indictment to assure that the cases, as complicated as they would be, were not weakened by the inclusion of any suspects against whom the evidence was marginal.

Jaworski recognized all these considerations but he still wanted to "go public with the lesser cases" as quickly as he could. He had not forgotten the suggestion that he was appointed to hinder the investigation rather than complete it. He felt that the longer we waited, the greater chance the indictments would have to be further delayed because of the actions of the House impeachment inquiry or the publicity attending the release of the Senate Watergate committee's final report.

Many of the lawyers concluded that inadvertently Jaworski was playing exactly the game the White House wanted: He was so busy protecting the other cases that he was willing to ignore or at least downgrade the biggest case of all.

At the end of December Jaworski called me in and suggested that we issue an end-of-year press release predicting a series of major indictments within the next few weeks. The idea was so out of character for our office that I was taken by surprise. We had just spent months in court arguing that the grand juries were independent bodies with independent authority, and now we were going to predict what they would do when it came time to vote on the cases. It was a safe enough prediction, of course, both because the evidence was strong and because grand juries usually do follow the advice of prosecutors. But the original Watergate grand jury was independent and sensitive and could easily take offense at any such statement by Jaworski. In addition, the idea smacked too much of the self-seeking prosecutor to do us any good.

When I drew Jaworski out I found that he was motivated by an eagerness to show the press and public a sense of progress, at the same time committing the staff to bring the indictments without further delay. Some members of the senior staff became alarmed. In their minds his proposal raised questions about Jaworski's judgment.

After weighing my objections for a few days, Jaworski agreed to a year-end press release which devoted most of its space to a summary of the court actions to date, with a comment at the end that the presentation of evidence to the grand juries had progressed to the point where they should be ready to act in a number of cases in January or February. This caused us no criticism, and Jaworski was in the end careful and deliberate about its language. But in the meantime there had been a number of furtive and anguished discussions among staff members who wondered whether Jaworski was, deliberately or otherwise, joining in the White House strategy by trying to complete the cases quickly at the risk of costly errors and an incomplete investigation. The atmosphere was tense. At one point Hank Ruth went to Jaworski and told him straightaway, "Leon, you're getting too cozy with Al Haig." Jaworski rejected the criticism.

While the public was showing more confidence in the special prosecutor, his own staff was becoming increasingly jumpy. Hank Ruth began convening meetings of his own closest circle—Lacovara, Kreindler, Feldbaum, myself—to thrash out some issues and anticipate future problems. These gatherings were necessitated in part by the virtual discontinuation of the weekly staff meetings. Jaworski did not seem comfortable in such meetings, and the task force leaders were especially busy. This meant that information within the office tended to be fragmented, so Ruth called his own periodic meetings.

The first was held on Wednesday, January 9, and Ruth went around the table soliciting opinions on the problem of Richard Nixon. Even in this small group opinion varied widely.

Lacovara said that his research convinced him we had the power and the authority to indict the President. Feldbaum added, "If we have that power and authority, and we agree we have sufficient evidence, we have a duty to act without regard for external factors. It is not for us to weigh the 'political' effects or to pass off on the House because it is conveniently available."

I took the opposite view, saying that the indictment of a President is essentially a political act and should not be done by an insulated group of lawyers with no constituency; that the House of Representatives should be the court of both first and last resort. Kreindler and Ruth were uncertain and expressed no definite conclusions, but Kreindler seemed to have reservations about indictment, and Ruth seemed more and more disposed in favor of indictment.

The tenor of the meeting was that Leon Jaworski had become as big a problem as Richard Nixon. Why was Jaworski so secretive? He had recently held a long conversation with Haig by telephone, Ruth reported, and there had been no subsequent report of what had been said. Had the special prosecutor committed himself to sparing the President? Or had he decided to obtain as much information as possible from the White House and to inform the staff only at a later time?

At the next meeting, a few days later, we got down to an immediate problem. The March 21 tape was to be played for the grand jury soon, and there seemed to us a real possibility that the jurors, who had lived through the frustrations of Watergate for eighteen months and had just committed themselves to a second eighteen months, might insist on voting an indictment of Richard Nixon then and there, before the prosecutors had decided upon a course of action. It would have taken no encouragement at all for the leaders of this grand jury to propose such a vote, and we knew that if they asked the legal advice of the lawyers handling the case, those lawyers would not be able in good conscience to say they believed an indictment was unconstitutional. We decided to advise Jaworski to be present the day the tape was played so he could personally reiterate the standard advice to the jurors: Listen to the evidence and keep an open mind; don't make any decisions until you've heard all the facts from all the witnesses.

On Wednesday, January 16, Jaworski did address the grand jurors and they listened attentively. Later that afternoon the tape was played for them by a very nervous team of lawyers. Feldbaum and Frampton had spent hours arranging for the wiring of the special room with twenty-three sets of earphones and a sophisticated tape player.

As the tape began to play, one of the jurors opened a mammoth bag of potato chips and passed it along to his colleagues. The crunching grew so loud that the lawyers wondered how the voices on the tapes would be heard, even with high-fidelity earphones. But several of the jurors, including foreman Vladimir Pregelj, were registering expressions on their faces that made it clear they did indeed hear and understand what had transpired on March 21.

There was still no agreed-upon plan as to how this evidence would be used. Jaworski was receiving the unsolicited views of many of the lawyers working on the case, sometimes in great and impressive detail. Four of them—Feldbaum, Frampton, Goldman, and Rient—sent along a twenty-one-page memorandum they had worked for days to refine and accommodate to each's views. It was a polished version of what many other office lawyers were arguing.

They cited the special prosecutor's mandate: "full authority for investigating *and prosecuting* . . . allegations involving the President . . ." That mandate was established, and reestablished after the Massacre, they argued, "because of overwhelming public support for committing the decision of the President's criminal guilt or innocence to the traditional processes of law enforcement . . . [and] to do so in like fashion as in the case of allegations of criminal activity involving anyone else."

They quoted the decision in the tapes case: The grand jury "is a constitutional fixture in its own right." They quoted the jurors' pledge to "present no one from hatred or malice or leave anyone unpresented from fear, favor, affection, reward, or hope of reward." To tell the grand jury not to act against Nixon, the lawyers said, "would thus be to counsel abdication of its constitutionally sanctioned function to 'present crimes committed by any citizen, regardless of his circumstances or station.'"

They cited a crucial difference between the mandate of the special prosecutor's office and that of the House impeachment committee. The existence of the impeachment inquiry did not change the prosecutor's duty, they said. "Our criminal justice process exists . . . to prosecute crimes with reference to an apolitical code applied objectively to all citizens. For this very reason our office was created as an office of criminal prosecution, not, as it might have been, as an independent commission to determine all the facts and then to make recommendations about anyone's fitness to continue to serve in public office. Under the Constitution the one task is allocated to Congress and the other to the grand and petit juries."

As to the argument that indictment would be equivalent to forcing Nixon from office, the four lawyers argued that the disruption caused would be no greater and perhaps less than that caused by the impeachment process. The President could be tried quickly in court, while the House inquiry promised to be "terribly drawn out, divisive, and possibly inconclusive." At least some of the evidence would come out in either event, and the effect of such revelations on the conduct of domestic and foreign affairs would be less severe if the revelations were in the form of distinct allegations to be determined to public satisfaction in a traditional courtroom proceeding according to customary standards. "Of course, the President clearly could not perform the duties of his office while in jail, but the Twenty-Fifth Amendment provides a mechanism by which the vice president can govern the country should the President become 'unable to discharge the powers and duties of his office,' " the lawyers said.

"The real issue before us is not *whether* to recommend that the grand jury manifest its conclusion about the President's guilt or innocence, but how we should recommend that it do so. . . . In sum, if the grand jury finds probable cause to believe the President acted criminally, then it is essential that this simple, primary truth emerge from the action that we and the grand jury take: that but for the fact that he is President, Richard Nixon would have been indicted. This fundamental conclusion should not be allowed to be lost in a recitation of facts or sources of evidence that omits the basic judgment involved or leaves it open to public (and Congressional) speculation and debate," the memorandum concluded. As these four men saw it, the only choice was one between a standard indictment and the less common but traditional grand jury presentment which stops short of the act of indictment.

This paper was a tour de force, of course, the sort of thing that would have had Archibald Cox writing lengthy marginal notations back to the men, at the very least, and more likely would have been the occasion for convening a lengthy skull session and writing further memoranda under Cox's supervision.

Jaworski answered the twenty-one pages with one paragraph: "I read with great interest your memorandum and will re-read it studiously at my first opportunity. I thank you for giving me the benefit of your views."

To his critics this response showed that Jaworski had already made up his mind; he had his solution and was no longer interested in a discussion of the problem; he wanted only a justification for the solution he had determined.

That judgment was too harsh, for during this period Jaworski, while irritated at the constant and prolonged arguments, moderated his position a good deal. But it certainly was true that he was no theoretician and that he showed little patience with what he considered abstractions that didn't address the problem. If we indicted Richard Nixon there would be all hell to pay—a Supreme Court battle at the wrong time on the wrong question—and in the end we would lose. Nixon would not resign, and the results of the abstract legal battle would be used to shore up his position before the House. That was Jaworski's view (as it was mine), but he did not try to defend it with a lengthy rebuttal to the legal points raised by the staff. "Those fellows are still law clerks," he told me. "All they know is case-books. This is the real world."

As a blizzard of memos and a constant debate whistled in and around his office, Jaworski became testy and defensive and finally exhausted. We faced the ultimate question of how we would use the enormous power we held, and Jaworski instinctively drew away from anything that could be construed as an abuse. We were a small group with an average age of around thirty-five, operating in a political vacuum. We could not depend, in Hamilton's phrase, on "the restraints of public opinion." In my opinion, we were in danger of becoming like the Nixon White House, an island whose inhabitants acted without relation to the world around them. Perhaps there was no rebuttal in the law books, but I felt, and I believe Jaworski did as well, that the instrument of an indictment was extraordinary when the very fact of it would bring down the President before there could be a trial. One could speculate to the contrary, but the risk seemed great.

Jaworski instinctively understood that no matter how strong the evidence, we could be criticized, misunderstood, and perhaps in the judgment of history condemned if we used our power to render the final judgment on Richard Nixon. And the act of indictment in this case seemed to me an act of final judgment.

Underlying the arguments of the Feldbaums and the Framptons was a basic distrust of the political process. In my opinion they did not believe that the House of Representatives would act upon the evidence. I was not so sure it would either, but, I said, "When the evidence goes to the House, we are going to find out what kind of a country we live in."

While the internal debate raged, Ruth, Jaworski, and the rest of us tried in our separate ways to solve the problem of getting information to the

House Judiciary Committee. The Republicans were pushing Chairman Peter Rodino to "impeach him or get off his back," in the phrase first used by Senator George Aiken of Vermont. Under pressure Rodino foolishly promised a committee report by April, less than six months from the committee's establishment, although he had no idea whether he would be staffed and prepared to evaluate the evidence in that short time—or even whether he would obtain the evidence that soon.

Shortly after his appointment as special counsel to the impeachment committee was announced on December 20, John Doar began meeting with Jaworski, but the meetings proved unproductive. Jaworski did not want the evidence he had fought for to be squandered in a leaking match between Republican and Democratic members of the House. And even if confidentiality were guaranteed, Jaworski felt that Doar should go to court and seek judicial approval for transfer of grand jury material normally held inviolate under the Federal Rules of Criminal Procedure.

Hank Ruth tried to steer Doar in what we all felt was the right direction. John Doar, recently divorced and an old friend of Ruth's, was alone in Washington and working long hours, so Hank invited him to dinner as often as Doar could make it. The Ruths' house was something of a salon for Watergate insiders in those days, and Hank tried to expose Doar to various members of the prosecutor's staff who might have some friendly advice on how he should proceed.

At that point the prosecutors to a man believed that the evidence that would sink Nixon was that March 21 tape, but Doar was not an officer of the court and there was a serious question whether he was eligible to share such grand jury information. In various ways they tried to suggest this was the key to the case against the President. Without actually telling Doar, they referred to John Dean's testimony before the Senate Watergate committee or otherwise alluded to the existence of evidence on tape. Doar, a laconic Irishman from the Midwest, never indicated whether he got the message.

As Doar later told the story, "The first night I had dinner alone with Hank and Tina. When that didn't work they invited me back for dinner with them and Carl and Laura Feldbaum. The third time the Ruths and the Feldbaums were there, along with Jim Vorenberg. When that still didn't seem to get the message across, Ruth brought in a fellow Irishman to do the job; the fourth time at dinner it was the Ruths and the Feldbaums along with Jim and Ann Doyle.

"It must have seemed that the message still wasn't getting across. I rented an apartment on Capitol Hill where Phil Bakes had been living. I was having a bed delivered to the apartment and I asked Bakes to allow my thirteen-year-old son, Robert, to wait there for it. Robert and Bakes were having a big talk, the gist of which apparently was Robert asking why Bakes' office should remain open now that his father was in town to take care of Watergate. Bakes was kneeling on a sideboard in the kitchen taking glasses down from a high cabinet and passing them to a friend who was packing them, and Robert was standing in the doorway. All of a sudden Bakes looked at the boy and said, 'Robert, tell your father to ask the White House for the March 21 tape.' "

Early in January columnist Mary McGrory interviewed the new special prosecutor. She was favorably impressed by him but disturbed by his reticence toward the Rodino committee. She called me after the interview to say how much she liked my boss. "I've been trying to decide whether I should give him a pass," she said. "I could write a puff piece about him and be completely comfortable with it. But I worry about his attitude toward the House."

I encouraged her to lay out her reservations, and I made it clear that I shared them. Her first idea—a simple profile—would probably be best for my boss, I said, but the analytical piece was the one that was needed. When the column appeared it was about 90 percent favorable. But in a few paragraphs McGrory brought her message home. She told of Jaworski's groundbreaking work with war crimes trials during World War II but added, "He begged off going to Nuremberg where the big fish were caught." She predicted a vigorous performance on his part in prosecuting the Watergate underlings and added:

> But the final verdict on Jaworski may be made not on the basis of the indictments, the trials or even convictions. He may be judged instead on the outcome of the graver matter of impeachment, and the degree of cooperation he sees fit to give, to the possible detriment of his own cases, to the House Judiciary panel which is just beginning its inquiry.

Then she quoted a conclusion from his book on the war crimes trials: "No nation, however powerful and whatever be its form of government, can long withstand the stranglehold of moral deterioration in its people."

Jaworski was hurt and angry when he read the column. On the day it appeared he made his decision to explain his case to the public in some detail.

Within a few weeks he appeared on the *Today* show and *Issues and Answers,* and he held a series of on-the-record interviews with reporters, as well as background sessions with columnists and news executives. In numerous answers during this "media blitz," as the *Wall Street Journal* called it, Jaworski made clear that he possessed significant evidence which the House impeachment committee should get, and he made specific proposals as to how they could get it. First, he said, he would be happy to tell the committee what material he had subpoenaed from the White House so that they could subpoena it. Secondly, he suggested, the committee should ask Judge Sirica to intervene on their behalf to receive anything relevant, even if it had been used before the grand jury.

Jaworski also made the point that the train was leaving the station for any defendants who wanted to conclude a plea bargain. He refused to say whether some plea bargaining was going on at the time, but by his manner he made it seem that a great many prospective defendants had already come in to tell what they knew about their fellow conspirators. He used newspaper and television interviews almost as invitations to others with culpability. The message was clear to all those involved that Jaworski was ready to talk about a deal.

Jaworski did indeed have high hopes of "pleading out" enough of the major figures so that the conflict between the impeachment inquiry and the trials of others would be moot. And while the media blitz continued, serious negotiations were under way with John Ehrlichman and Herbert Kalmbach, and Charles Colson's clever lawyer was paying attention as well.

We decided that the best way to engage the press and have them understand our problems was to avoid a large news conference and hold a series of smaller sessions where it would be easier to pursue a single line of questioning and where there would be less chance of a misstep that would put us in trouble with the courts on one of our cases. For the most part it worked. This colloquy with the press had two important results. It created a spate of editorial comments that raised the public's consciousness of the evidence problem; and it caused Jaworski, in answer to the many questions, to refine his own thinking on how he should proceed.

Throughout this period Jaworski retained confidence in his own judgment, faith that everything would work out for the best, and sense of humor—although at times his patience was sorely tried by what seemed like assaults from all directions.

For the first time hints of the policy disputes within the office were dribbling forth in the press. I remember arriving at the morning briefing one day and seeing that Jaworski was mad enough to chew nails over what appeared to be a leak in the morning newspaper.

Jaworski said, "Sometimes I get up in the morning with all these things on my mind and I pick up the *Post* and I feel like coming down here and telling all you people to *shove this job*," he said.

He continued to be belligerent, or simply silent, whenever anyone suggested he was wrong to be holding back from the House impeachment inquiry. But he listened to all the arguments and he was coming around to the view that he must help Rodino's efforts. If there was a day when his conversion became noticeable, it was a busy day in mid-January when he met with the senior staff for the first time in several weeks.

The day had begun with a meeting with columnist Robert Novak, who asked whether Jaworski, having heard the tapes, still believed John Dean. "Yes, I do," Jaworski said.

After the interview I took the columnist to my office. I have known Bob Novak for ten years and I can read the expression on his face. It was obvious that he knew what he had.

"That was off the record, Bob," I said.

"No, it wasn't, Jim. Jaworski said 'This is for your guidance' at the beginning. That's not off the record."

"Come on, Bob, he doesn't know the semantics of your business. He clearly meant that nothing was to be attributed to this office, and if you report that, you attribute it to us automatically because we're the ones who heard the tapes."

Novak agreed that mine was a fair reading of the situation. "I'll work something out," he said.

"I hope so," I said. "If you don't they are going to charge us with an 'extraordinary impropriety' and they'll can his ass."

When the newspaper came out I saw that Novak had played down one of the best stories he got that year. "Though the prosecutors—including Jaworski himself in some cases—have heard the Nixon-Dean tapes," he wrote, "they are resuming interrogation of Dean. The inescapable conclusion is that they do not feel that possible differences between the tapes and Dean's Senate testimony are damaging to his credibility." The rest of the column was a thoughtful piece about the danger that the evidence against Nixon could "fall between the stools of indictment and impeachment."

Novak could have made some headlines if he had taken Jaworski's straightforward "Yes, I do," and turned it into the centerpiece of an accusation against Nixon. Instead, he filed away the information and used it to inform his subsequent reporting. From that day forward Novak was convinced Nixon could not last in office, but he never revealed the conversation to his readers. There were to be more such incidents with other reporters before the media blitz ended.

After the Novak interview Jaworski, properly chastened by his close call, set out for luncheon with the editors of the *Washington Star,* where another sharp engagement over his proposed handling of the evidence took place. Mary McGrory was at the table, which didn't add to Jaworski's pleasure. Newbold Noyes, then the *Star*'s editor, and Lyle Denniston, a respected Supreme Court reporter who was then an editor, questioned Jaworski closely. At one point Denniston noted that the House of Representatives was, in the words of the Founding Fathers, "the Grand Inquest of the nation," which meant its inquiry must take precedence over Jaworski's cases.

Jaworski responded that this did not change his own responsibility to conduct his work according to established rules and laws, and then he added, "Suppose you hold this 'Grand Inquest' as the first order of business, and there is no conviction? Do you think the lesser figures could be given a fair trial after such a proceeding?"

On the way back to the office I sensed for the first time that Jaworski had resigned himself to a basic fact of life: The evidence against the President had changed the situation. Instead of husbanding the information he had gathered to prosecute the conspirators, Jaworski might have to disclose it well before any trials to the House of Representatives. This out-of-court disclosure and the resultant publicity could jeopardize prosecution of the other conspirators.

As we drove in the car Jaworski fell into a mood of deep reflection. Speaking as if he had come to the end of the lengthy decision-making process, he said to me, "You know, Jim, as long as you do what you believe is best and you do it in good conscience and to the best of your ability, then the criticism you get doesn't count."

Back at the office he had an interview with Joseph Kraft, who in his gentle way raised all of the same issues and a new one. "Who are you counseling with for guidance?" Kraft asked. "Only my staff," Jaworski replied. Later, when he had other difficult decisions to make, the question of consulting with some elder statesmen came up. "Shoot, Jim," he said, "they don't do you any good. They can't feel the weight of that problem on *their* backs. Their advice isn't worth a damn. Anybody can advise you how to make a decision when they don't have to share the weight."

He had agreed, at Ruth's insistence, to meet the staff that afternoon. But when the hour came he said to his deputy, "Hank, I can't take another session of argument and haranguing. Do I have to go through with this?"

"You do have to go through with it," Ruth said, "and there won't be any harangues."

The session was miraculously calm. Jaworski began by going over the conflicting interests of the courts and the Congress, an exposition we had all now heard ad nauseam. Then he said, "I got a memo from Philip [Lacovara] saying that he was unclear what my understanding is with the White House. I have no understanding beyond the one you know: The evidence was given us for our confidential use with the grand jury and trials, and we agreed to those purposes alone."

There was a brief discussion of the plea bargaining that was going on. The lawyers for Ehrlichman and Haldeman had expressed interest in dealing, and Bill Merrill wondered aloud whether the plan was to plead out the conspirators so that Nixon could not be named as an unindicted co-conspirator because there would be no conspiracy trial. Given the number of potential defendants who had expressed no interest in dealing, we decided that probably was not the motivation. But Merrill's remark made the point that plea bargaining in the present situation had to be carefully weighed.

Rick Ben-Veniste reminded us that the members of the grand jury were an unusually cohesive and sophisticated group. They had been meeting among themselves to solve mutual problems arising from their lengthy tour of duty. Some had been dismissed from jobs, others had missed pay raises. They were going to ask the government to increase their daily allowances because of their unusual length of service, and they were even considering a civil suit to get their way.

Ben-Veniste pointed out that before they began working the Watergate case they had investigated a complicated conspiracy involving police corruption. They were sensitive to the subtleties of individuals joining a conspiracy to obstruct justice as an investigation goes along. They would be patient, Ben-Veniste said, as long as they knew what to expect. After they had heard all the tapes, they would expect to have an opportunity to question Nixon or at least get his side of the story. They would have other questions about how to proceed. But as long as they didn't think that the prosecutors were dodging the issue, they would not try to go public, leak, or act on their own.

After listening to Ben-Veniste's views, Jaworski indicated that he knew the time for a decision on whether to ask for an indictment of Nixon was nearing, and that he would be prepared.

"My attitude toward this case is no different than all of yours," he said, "except maybe I'm a little more detached than some of you because I didn't go through what you did when Cox was fired. I know we are going to have to find a way out of this impasse," he said, "but I'll tell you one thing. I'm not going to practice self-destruction. If my cases get blown away, it's not going to be without my best efforts to avoid it."

The meeting did much to restore our confidence in each other and our faith that we would find an acceptable way out of our problem.

Toward the end of January a consensus began to emerge from the non-stop discussions and arguments. From the beginning one option had been clear. The grand jury could make a presentment to the judge which would lay out the case against Nixon and note that the grand jury was not issuing a formal indictment only because he was a sitting President. At first this option had been rejected out of hand. It seemed to carry with it all the problems and disadvantages of an indictment and none of the legal virtues.

After the first meeting of Ruth's inner circle in January, Lacovara had raised the possibility of a presentment addressed not to the court but to the House impeachment committee. Peter Kreindler, who was uncomfortable with the idea of indicting President Nixon, took an immediate interest in this "special presentment" concept and began researching for precedents.

Kreindler and Lacovara concluded that there was ample justification for such a course, and the idea began to take a more detailed form. Perhaps the evidence, such as a copy of the March 21 tape, could be included. But exactly what form should the presentment document take? Phil Lacovara listed the requirements: It should invoke all of the evidence that had been gathered against the President, and it should do so in a way that would be sustained by the courts. To these Jaworski added a critical demand: It must not make any accusations against Nixon. The evidence must be invoked in a neutral way so that no conclusions were drawn by the grand jury or the prosecutors.

Jaworski met with Judge Sirica privately during this period, and while he never disclosed any discussions he might have had with the judge on this subject, his final, irrefutable argument against an indictment or other accusation against Nixon was, "Judge Sirica will not allow this. He will condemn the grand jury for overreaching, and he will condemn us for condoning or inspiring it. And he will dismiss the action out of hand."

One day in February Jill Volner and I were discussing the subject over a late lunch in a cafeteria on Fifteenth Street. Jill was agitated over the thought that the integrity of the office was about to be compromised, and she was talking excitedly. She would start out in a near-whisper, and then as she lost herself in the problem her voice would get louder and her sentences would come faster. I was very uncomfortable because when we walked into the restaurant Carl Bernstein tried to join us. Since Bernstein was capable of conning a monkey off a banana boat, I wasn't sure that our rebuff had made him leave. I kept looking at the empty tables around us and out the window to the street, expecting to see Bernstein eavesdropping with a pair of binoculars and a parabolic antenna.

Jill kept going over all the reasons why Nixon should be charged as one of the conspirators, and I kept listening and looking over my shoulder. Then I went into the idea of a non-accusatory presentment that was kicking around the office. "You've got to let Leon win this argument," I said, "because he'll never back down and his vote counts more than all of ours. But once you let him win the argument, you'll be able to do practically anything you want."

She asked me to run that by her again. "Look," I said, "every Christmas in Boston the Jordan Marsh Company puts signs all over every floor in its store. The signs are shaped like arrows and they say 'To Toyland.' Now Jordan Marsh's Toyland is way back on the fifth floor annex, but everybody always finds it. No matter where you are, there is a big arrow to Toyland. Even somebody who isn't paying attention would find it impossible to get lost. The grand jury's report has got to be arrows to Toyland."

She understood.

"One thing about Jaworski," I said, "he'll fight like hell and complain like hell, but if you have a strong case and marshal the facts well, he will go along. Kicking and screaming, but he'll go along. If you let him win the argument and say, 'Okay, Uncle Leon, no accusations,' he'll let you put anything you want in the report, so long as it's well done."

Jill Volner said, "In other words, we can draw the House of Representatives a road map."

"Exactly," I said.

CHAPTER

14

THE ROAD MAP
FOR IMPEACHMENT

*"The grand jury has an indictment and also
a sealed report to deliver to Your Honor."*

By uneasy agreement between Jaworski and his staff two documents were
drawn for presentation to the grand jury. One was an indictment of the
top men, save one, who had conspired to obstruct justice in the highest-
level such conspiracy known in the country's history. The other was an
unprecedented bill of particulars that would become the heart of the House
of Representatives' case against the President.

Every Saturday morning the members of the Watergate task force met
in their offices to go over the wording of the indictment. Peter Rient, an
assistant prosecutor, would write a draft. His colleagues would review it
line by line, raising questions, offering amendments. Rient would spend
much of the next week redrafting, and on Saturday the process would
begin again.

The task force had easily decided at an early point that the heart of the case would consist of a broad allegation of conspiracy to obstruct justice, with the specific substantive offenses—acts of obstruction, falsehoods told to the FBI or other investigators, perjury before the grand jury—charged as secondary counts against the various individuals.

The conspiracy statute had been much abused by government prosecutors in recent years and almost universally criticized by liberals as a symbol of political repression. Many of the most publicized trials of the late sixties and early seventies did indeed seem politically motivated, and invariably the draft resisters, antiwar demonstrators, and political radicals were tried under the looser rules provided by the law of conspiracy. When a conspiracy is charged, the government is allowed to take exception to some of the normal rules of evidence, such as the rule which prohibits use of third party testimony—hearsay—in a trial. Instead of the usual burden of proving that a defendant carried out a specific criminal act, the government has only to show that, with criminal intent, each defendant joined a conspiracy the aim of which was criminal.

The U.S. Court of Appeals for the Ninth Circuit defined the theory: "A conspiracy may be a continuing one; actors may drop out, others may drop in; the details of the operation may change from time to time; the members need not know each other or the part played by the others; a member need not know all the details of the plan or the operation; he must, however, know the purpose (and agree) to become a party to a plan to effectuate the purpose."

Such a theory invited government abuse. There were cases on the record where the FBI planted an agent provocateur within a dissident political group; the "plant" then led the group beyond legitimate protest to, for example, breaking into a draft board at night; the FBI arrested all the members of the group, immunized their own agent who had instigated the crime, and charged the others with conspiracy. This sort of accusation was made frequently during the Vietnam years, when Mitchell and Mardian and J. Edgar Hoover were in philosophical accord and in charge.

But the conspiracy law was well reasoned and on the books for good purpose. There were many cases where organized crime or plundering business groups so arranged events that the only links between those who gave the orders for a crime and the actual perpetrators of the crime were third and fourth parties whose testimony would be considered hearsay under normal circumstances. The Watergate conspiracy was a classic example. The tapes were the proof that the orders came from on high.

Yet Richard Nixon, because he was President of the United States, was not to be charged. Whatever the legal considerations, that was Leon Jaworski's choice, and it was at heart a political decision. To succeed at his job, Jaworski thought he must be perceived as extraordinarily prudent and ordinarily fair. His instincts were against charging the President in a criminal proceeding.

Having resolved that question in his mind, Jaworski wanted to concentrate on all the other cases and send the evidence against the President to the judge for transfer to the impeachment inquiry. But it wasn't that simple. A central act in the cover-up case was the payoff of hush money to Howard Hunt, and a crucial piece of evidence was the tape of that March 21 meeting where Richard Nixon presided. How could one delineate the outlines of this conspiracy without involving Nixon in the charging process?

It had been an early presumption that, whatever course the prosecutors took, it would be unfair—"a backhanded way of sticking the knife in," as Archibald Cox had said—to name Nixon as an unindicted co-conspirator. But George Frampton followed that conclusion to its logical consequences in a series of written questions to the rest of the Watergate task force on February 15:

> If the Grand Jury fails to manifest a conclusion in the charging process that the President is a conspirator, though the evidence so shows, and we do not name the President as a co-conspirator in our bill of particulars, thus barring such proof at trial, then:
> —Will not Presidential statements be inadmissable?
> —Will not all Dean-Nixon conversations be inadmissable?
> —Will we not be subject to a defense that since the Grand Jury found that the President was not a conspirator (and indeed he gave us the tapes himself) the taped meetings in March and April were not in furtherance of the conspiracy, and our entire interpretations of those discussions must be wrong?
> —What does this defense do to the heart of our case in March and April, [1973] against Haldeman, Ehrlichman, Mitchell? What does it do to Dean's credibility?

Frampton's questions made the point: Regardless of whether he was to be charged with a crime by the special prosecutor, Richard Nixon's role in the conspiracy was so central that he had to be an integral part of the cover-up indictment. One could separate Nixon out of the charging process to let the political branches work their will. But to disregard the evidence against him would be to throw away the entire case.

Leon Jaworski did not wish to step out ahead of Congress or the American public and seem to be spearheading the move to oust Nixon. His staff felt that silence by the prosecutors made the office part of the cover-up. But the question would be resolved by the one consideration upon which they could all agree, that it was their duty to try the other defendants with all the resources and all the evidence they could summon.

Nixon would not be named in the indictment, but it would show him as the central figure, offstage. Indeed, none of the unindicted co-conspirators would be named. The prosecutors decided to postpone the publication of that list as long as possible. The defense would be entitled to such information in advance of trial, and at the trial testimony would make Richard Nixon's role in the conspiracy very clear. Hopefully, before the case reached the court the political process would have proceeded to the point where the House of Representatives and the American public would be able to view the evidence without reference to the actions of the Watergate Special Prosecution Force.

To help the process along the prosecutors would draw the House of Representatives a road map to be presented to the Judge with the indictments. It was a simple document, fifty-five pages long, with only a sentence or two on each of the pages. Each page was a reference to a piece of evidence—sentences from one of the tape recordings, quotations from grand jury testimony.

Someday the archives will be opened and what the prosecutors referred to as "the road map" will be made public. When that happens it will prove a simple and unimpressive document, for it is narrow, declaratory, without conclusions.

This is how the road map worked: One page might say, "On March 16, 1973, E. Howard Hunt demanded $120,000." Then it would list page references to grand jury testimony from witnesses who saw Hunt's blackmail note and references to the tapes where Hunt's demand was discussed. The grand jury transcripts and the tape transcripts would be included. The next page might say, "On March 21, 1973, John Dean told President Nixon that Hunt had demanded $120,000, and that he estimated Hunt and the other Watergate defendants would 'cost' a million dollars in the next two years." More grand jury and tape transcript page references. The next page might say, "President Nixon responded, 'For Christ's sake, get it' "; and there would be further references to the tapes.*

The strength of the document was its simplicity. An inexorable logic marched through its pages. The conclusion that the President of the United States took part in a criminal conspiracy became inescapable.

There remained a major investigative task, determining the precise sequence of events before and after Nixon's payoff conversations of March 21. The prosecutors now had nineteen White House tapes—seven through subpoena and twelve volunteered—and the pertinent recorded conversations made a strong legal case that Nixon had cast his lot with the conspirators no later than March 21, 1973. But what precisely had happened after the meeting of March 21? The testimony was confused.

Before the prosecutors knew about the contents of the March 21 tape, they had been working with Dean and Fred LaRue, who had worked for Mitchell at the reelection committee, to pinpoint the sequence of events. Dean knew that on Monday, March 19, he had received Hunt's demand for money from CRP attorney Paul O'Brien. Sometime between then and the afternoon of Wednesday, March 21, he had discussed it with LaRue—perhaps more than once, but neither of them could remember the precise timing of the conversation or conversations. Both agreed, though, that Dean had told LaRue that he [Dean] was "out of the money business" and would not take part in the payoff. Dean suggested that LaRue call his patron, John Mitchell, whom Dean had already alerted, in New York and discuss it with him. The sequence had not seemed so important before the extent of Nixon's direction was revealed through the March 21 tape. The prosecutors previously had assumed the final payoff to Hunt had been made without the President's involvement. Hunt had told the Senate Watergate committee that he probably received the money on the morning of the twenty-first—before the President had heard about the blackmail demand. LaRue had been uncertain of the date but basically corroborated Hunt's version.

Suddenly the precise sequence of events became important to an under-

---

* The same technique was used extensively in the preparation of the House impeachment inquiry's volumes of evidence against Nixon, which were published under the title, "Statement of Information."

standing of how the conspiracy worked and how deeply Richard Nixon was implicated in that final payoff.

Rick Ben-Veniste and George Frampton, who was the expert on the money transactions, went over LaRue's story with him time after time, trying to determine if he had picked up his laundry or signed a credit card receipt or a restaurant voucher that would be dated. LaRue remembered that on the day Mitchell told him to deliver the money he had entertained three friends for dinner. One of them, a sales and marketing executive named Manyon Millican, had worked with LaRue at the Nixon campaign committee. Millican had also delivered two sealed, unmarked manila envelopes to a mailbox in rural Potomac, Maryland, for delivery to an attorney named William Bittman (E. Howard Hunt's lawyer) without asking any questions. On this night he had taken a third such envelope from LaRue and delivered it to the same mailbox.

Millican could not pinpoint the date of this last delivery. But there were two others at the LaRue dinner which preceded it, a woman named Laura Fenwick and a friend from out of town named Sherman Unger. All four remembered one event during the evening. LaRue had started a fire in the fireplace of his new apartment and the flue was clogged. The fire smoked up the entire apartment.

Unger's hotel and airline reservations and receipts fixed the night of that dinner as March 21, 1973. With the help of these records LaRue and Millican were able to swear that the last manila envelope, containing $75,000, was delivered to William Bittman's mailbox in Potomac between 10:30 P.M. and 11:00 P.M. on the night of March 21, and that the payment had been set in motion by the Haldeman-Mitchell-LaRue telephone calls of earlier that day.

Through telephone records the prosecutors determined that thirty-five minutes after the meeting with Nixon, Haldeman called Mitchell. Shortly after that LaRue called Mitchell and was told to make the payoff. LaRue then gathered the $75,000 remaining from Haldeman's secret fund. Hunt had demanded $120,000, but $75,000 was all that LaRue could collect on such short notice. The payoff was made after Nixon had ordered it. The case against Richard Nixon now seemed airtight.

A final decision remained: Who among the panoply of figures in this conspiracy would be recommended to the grand jury for indictment? As with all such decisions, the staff and the special prosecutor went through earnest and sometimes angry argument. The list of possible targets totaled about fifteen people. The self-imposed rule of the Watergate special prosecutors was that the standards of proof for indictment should be higher than in a normal prosecution. The rule of thumb adopted was that there had to be general agreement that the government had better than a fifty-fifty chance of winning the case.

When a decision to prosecute seemed likely, the potential defendant's counsel was offered an opportunity to meet with the prosecutors, have the outlines of the case presented, and make whatever statements or arguments they could. The procedure was unusually considerate of defendants, and it was a conscious trade-off. The sessions involved exposing some of the government's witnesses, evidence, and theory of the case to the defense lawyers, information not usually disclosed until just before trial that could significantly aid the accused person in constructing a defense. Since indictment in the major Watergate cases would likely devastate a person's career, the prosecutors wanted to be sure that they were not blindly proceeding with a case that had a fatal flaw.

This deferential treatment was viewed as a necessity in cases so highly charged with political implications. The prosecutors wanted high marks in the history books for fairness and procedural correctness. They also did not want to blow any cases.

In the cover-up case the presentations of defense lawyers did not make much difference, although some of them were lengthy and detailed. Colson's lawyer, David Shapiro, presented written briefs, wall charts, and an extensive oral argument that took several days. Jaworski was not impressed.

Jaworski still hoped to dispose of Watergate with a quick stroke—guilty pleas and a presidential resignation. But his staff wondered, worried, and fretted about what he would give to gain that goal. The problem, and the fretting, grew over time. In December and early January, it appeared that Ehrlichman might "plead out." His lawyer, Joe Ball, was an old friend of Leon's and was ready to negotiate.

From the outset, but especially after the tapes had been weighed as evidence, Ehrlichman, Haldeman, and Mitchell were viewed as "the big three" who were certain to be indicted for conspiracy and for perjury. The decision about the adequacy of the evidence in their cases was an easy one.

But there had also been discussions from the outset as to what demands the prosecutors would make if one of these men plea bargained. Mitchell had been tentatively offered the mildest possible plea—one five-year felony —early in the investigation when the evidence was still thin and the tapes seemed out of reach. Now the question was whether Ehrlichman should be offered the same minimum plea.

The unanimous opinion of the staff was, No. The cases against Ehrlichman were strong, and there were two of them—the Watergate cover-up and the Fielding break-in. After some discussions Jaworski agreed with this position. But he raised the anxieties of the staff because he seemed very impatient to strike a deal and because he seemed to be playing his cards close to his vest as he dealt alone with defense attorneys such as Joe Ball as well as presidential assistant Alexander Haig.

The lawyers feared that Jaworski would give away one of the cases inadvertently. For example, if Ehrlichman pleaded guilty only in the Fielding break-in, he could be expected to be an extremely hostile witness— albeit a prosecution-sponsored witness—in the Watergate cover-up trial. His version of the "facts" would almost certainly contradict that of the other conspirators who had cooperated, for Ehrlichman remained truculent and clearly unrepentant. He would be defiant in court, and the staff lawyers preferred that he be defiant as an accused defendant rather than as an untrustworthy prosecution witness.

Jaworski seemed anxious to "plead out" Ehrlichman, perhaps in hopes of convincing Haldeman and Mitchell to plead as well. Nobody in the office was quite sure what was in Jaworski's mind because he chose not to confide in us, at least not completely.

The suspicion within the office was tangible, and one situation exemplified it. Occasionally, perhaps once a week, Jaworski would leave the office for a brief period in the late afternoon without announcing where he was going. The pattern was always the same. Shortly before 5:00 P.M. he would suddenly put on his overcoat and walk out, carrying his black attaché case. He would inform his secretary that he would be back shortly, and he always was.

But where had he been? All of his appointments were carefully recorded by his secretary in a desk diary and normally he was accompanied by a driver when he left the office. These exceptional late afternoon disappearances became the subject of an enormous amount of speculation among the staff because they were so out of the routine.

At group lunches out of the office Hank Ruth and his aides would go over the details of Jaworski's brief absences, trying to guess their purpose. What could he be delivering, and to whom? Perhaps he was taking draft copies of the forthcoming indictment to a defense attorney in the hopes of striking an unorthodox plea bargain that he could present to his staff as a fait accompli. Perhaps he was receiving from, or delivering to, the White House material he wanted concealed from his staff.

That made little sense. If he wanted to spirit material out of or into the office, the easiest way to do so was simply to take it home in the evening and have his contact meet him at his hotel.

Was he visiting a business establishment that closed at 5:00 P.M.? Perhaps he was having material photocopied for his own use later in writing a book. But he would hardly risk delivering highly sensitive material to a commercial printing shop when he could have had any papers in the office photocopied by his own clerical staff without raising suspicion.

One popular theory was that Jaworski continued to do work for his old Houston law firm, which had an office in Washington, and that he was picking up and delivering papers to a secretary before the office closed. Aside from the fact that such conduct would be unethical, it seemed unlikely that his old law firm would not have arranged for pickup and delivery from his hotel.

As the trips continued, Jaworski's assistants began considering countermeasures. One day at lunch, with Ruth, Lacovara, Kreindler, Feldbaum, and myself present, there was a discussion of whether we should follow Jaworski when he left the office. "We had to do that sort of thing during training in Army intelligence," Ruth said. "We always were seen by the people we were supposed to tail."

As far as I know, Jaworski was never followed. The prosecutors continued to wonder about the mysterious afternoon trips, and to suspect the worst. But they did nothing about it, and we did not learn what Jaworski was doing. I asked him about it after he had left Washington.

"Frequently I realized that I would be staying at the office until seven or eight o'clock," he said. "On such occasions I thought it wise to take a little walk, which I usually did around five o'clock. Sometimes a little earlier, sometimes a little later. The attaché case was empty and remained empty. The walk was for several blocks around the building and then I returned. Why carry the attaché case? Often I would be recognized as I walked and it was much easier for me to explain that I was hurrying to an appointment than to engage in conversations with strangers who undertook to talk with me." Jaworski said he found the suspicion "laughable [but] also somewhat saddening. . . . I actually think it was more curiosity than it was a lack of trust. I like to think that after the initial month or two, the staff trusted me just as I trusted the staff."

Negotiations with Ehrlichman, Haldeman and Mitchell never came close to agreement. Even though Jaworski was more malleable than the rest of the staff, his demands for a plea bargain remained much stiffer than what the defense lawyers (or perhaps their clients) would accept. The crisis came when Herbert Kalmbach started plea bargaining.

Kalmbach, as the White House money man, was involved in a large number of cases. Although not himself a White House aide, and thus unable to make promises on behalf of the government, he was the glue that made both the campaign fund raising—and later the obstruction of justice fund dispensing—hold together. He was a private lawyer whose annual net income had climbed from $25,000 to around $200,000 since the beginning of the Nixon Presidency. To many of the prosecutors he appeared to be the classic influence-peddling man.

When Kalmbach and his lawyer came to the office to strike a deal, they dealt with Tom McBride, Hank Ruth, and Jaworski. Over several days, Kalmbach offered McBride extensive information about the Nixon fund raising operation, including effective testimony on at least two important criminal matters. The first was the so-called "townhouse operation" of 1970, in which millions were raised and dispensed secretly and illegally by the White House on behalf of congressional candidates. The second was the sale of ambassadorships, including the refund of money in at least one case when the nomination did not come through.

Kalmbach was less helpful with respect to his own fund raising for the original Watergate defendants. John Dean had told us he had informed Kalmbach what the money was for; Kalmbach insisted he never knew to what use the money would be put.

To the members of the Watergate task force, who would be either using

Kalmbach as a government witness or attacking him as a defendant, this story was patently incredible. Kalmbach had come in voluntarily, but they saw him as a witness who would yield as little as possible and could do more harm than good for the office. He had been the President's attorney, involved in a range of questionable activity, and most of the lawyers believed he should be treated harshly. If he chose to be a defendant rather than a fully cooperating witness, so be it.

Three men disagreed: Leon Jaworski, Tom McBride, and to a lesser extent Hank Ruth. They were three of the oldest and most experienced lawyers in the office, but two of them, Jaworski and McBride, had the most to gain from a Kalmbach plea. The younger lawyers were ready to go to trial and they suspected that neither Jaworski nor McBride cared if there were any trials as long as the cases could be neatly disposed of. The Watergate task force lawyers, preparing one of the biggest cases they would ever handle, had the most to lose if Kalmbach fogged over the motivations and consciousness of guilt of the conspirators. They had a skeptical view of Kalmbach's demeanor as a naïve dupe rather than a clever lawyer who operated in the shadows.

McBride went over Kalmbach's story in detail and came to the conclusion that Kalmbach really believed now—whatever he had thought at the time—that he had started raising money for the Watergate defendants without having any idea what the money was for. McBride also came to the conclusion, from Kalmbach's testimony and the facts in the many campaign contributions cases, that Kalmbach was indeed a low-level, naïve messenger who earned the misleading title of presidential lawyer by being no more than a conduit to the government officials who cut the deals and made the decisions.

Jaworski had spent his life with sharp lawyers, and he judged that Kalmbach was not one of them. Jaworski tended to take the measure of a man when he met him, and his measurement of Kalmbach agreed with Tom McBride's.

On Friday, February 8, Jaworski called a meeting of a dozen or more attorneys, the senior members of the Watergate and campaign contributions task forces, along with Lacovara, Ruth, Kreindler and Feldbaum.

Those present at the meeting knew that Jaworski had told Kalmbach and his lawyer to wait in an anteroom and decide whether Kalmbach would plead guilty to a two-year felony and a misdemeanor for the townhouse operation and the sale of ambassadorships. For McBride this would be no small accomplishment, since, in the long history of swapping money for ambassadorial appointments, the government had never brought a case. It would be a good precedent. And McBride was getting a valuable witness. But this would be the first time that the Watergate Special Prosecution Force offered less than a five-year felony plea to a major figure. And many were convinced we were doing it with a witness who was not really co-operating.

Jaworski started the meeting by reading to the assembled lawyers the American Bar Association guidelines for prosecutors when charging a defendant. Since these men had been charging defendants for much of their professional careers, some of them found the reading patronizing and offensive.

Jaworski then opened the meeting to discussion. Everybody except McBride and Ruth argued for at least a five-year felony charge and an insistence that Kalmbach be more forthright in his testimony about the Watergate payments. Ruth said he would prefer more than the two-year felony suggested by McBride, but he would agree to it. Jaworski neither argued with his colleagues nor budged from his agreement to the two-year felony. The meeting, in the opinion of all present except Jaworski, was a charade. It allowed Jaworski to say he had consulted with the staff, but his mind had been made up before the discussion began.

Immediately after the meeting Kalmbach was formally offered the bargain—a two-year felony, promising federal employment in return for a contribution, and a misdemeanor, illegal fund raising—and accepted. I drove Tom McBride home that night. (It had been a snowy winter day, infrequent in Washington, and McBride had skied to work.) On the way home I said to him, "I'll make two predictions: You've gotten the last bit of information you'll get from Herbert Kalmbach, and this deal will not go down well with the press when it is announced." *

Kalmbach's plea bargain became an issue that represented all the frus-

---

* I was wrong on both counts. The press was not very critical of the plea bargain, and Kalmbach turned out to be one of the most helpful and candid witnesses. At the Watergate trial his testimony coincided with John Dean's. He gave us more information about the dealings of the White House and CREEP than any witness except Dean. And after Kalmbach finished six months in prison, he came to the office to thank the prosecutors for allowing him to begin to put his life in order. By the time the case was over I doubt that many of the prosecutors questioned Kalmbach's sincerity, or Leon Jaworski's judgment of him.

trations and fears the staff attorneys of the Watergate Special Prosecution Force had experienced since the Saturday Night Massacre. Their distrust of Jaworski had taken root. Now that distrust grew.

The next morning, a Saturday, I went to the office hoping to spend some undisturbed hours doing paper work. A full complement of attorneys was there, interviewing witnesses, writing memos, holding meetings. This was a period of unprecedented activity in the office, with a number of cases at what the lawyers called the "threshold decision" stage.

I stopped by the soft drink machine and saw a hand-lettered note affixed to it. "This machine owes me 20¢," it said, and it was signed "John Dean." He was spending so much time around the office being debriefed on White House crimes that Hank Ruth had installed him in Jim Neal's vacant office, where Dean held court. Between interviews with lawyers Dean wrote passages in a notebook, reconstructing quotes from the prosecutors for his book. At my suggestion Dan Rosenblatt, Jaworski's driver, made a nameplate just like those the attorneys used and affixed it to Dean's door. I took Hank Ruth to Dean's office and said, "Look at that. Do you have any idea what the press would do if they saw that? They'd have a field day." Ruth burst in on Dean and chewed him out.

But it was not a very good day for the practical jokes that were becoming epidemic within the Watergate Special Prosecution Force. I soon realized that tension was high.

Tom McBride stopped by my office. "God, spare me from the Harvard Law School!" he said. "I feel like I'm negotiating with student demonstrators. Any moment now they are going to occupy my office and refuse to leave."

The Kalmbach decision of the previous day was a spark that ignited the anxieties of much of the staff, particularly the young lawyers who reserved a deep distrust for not just the Nixon administration but the whole generation of leaders who had tolerated a series of moral and political fiascoes from the Bay of Pigs through the war in Vietnam, from Billie Sol Estes and Bobby Baker to Howard Hunt and Watergate.

These youngsters had not invaded offices and disrupted campuses. They had studied while the others demonstrated, graduated at the top of the class, and accepted jobs within the system. They had ended up at the special prosecutor's office for the usual mixed reasons: They wanted the experience, and they also wanted to change things.

NOT ABOVE THE LAW

To them Herbert Kalmbach was a high roller, a lawyer to the President —it did not escape them that the same description fit Leon Jaworski— whose footprints left their mark on almost every case we investigated. They suspected he was being treated with a deference he did not deserve, that sympathy was being extended because he had been among the mighty, and that his fall meant he had "suffered enough." They feared that this was only the first of what would be a series of overripe plea bargains by Leon Jaworski. They were idealistic and they wanted justice, but they were also young and they wanted blood.

Three of the younger lawyers who worked on the eighth floor—Roger Witten, John Koeltl, Robert Palmer—were most upset because they had been working on the Kalmbach case with McBride and felt they had not been fully consulted on its disposition. Others—Ben-Veniste, Volner, Rient, Frampton, Goldman—were only slightly less disturbed. And that feeling pervaded the compound. While McBride was fielding the complaints, Jaworski was meeting with the Watergate task force to discuss other matters, but the tension over the Kalmbach decision was palpable in that meeting.

Jaworski was taken by surprise. He believed that once the decision had been made, his troops would fall in line behind him like good soldiers. They continued to question him.

Jaworski thought they were magnifying Kalmbach's importance to the conspiracy, and his cleverness in evading responsibility as well. He judged the President's lawyer "easygoing, shallow, and in love wth his title." McBride had checked Kalmbach's logs and discovered that most of the lawyer's time had been spent on errands: getting a zoning variance or a building permit for construction at Nixon's San Clemente home.

Interviews disclosed that while he had raised and dispensed huge amounts of cash, Kalmbach had declined to take part in a number of other questionable ventures. And despite enormous pressure he stopped the hush money payments once their purpose was unmistakable. McBride contrasted him to Jake Jacobsen, the money conduit in the dairy industry operations, who had worked for various principals, including Lyndon Johnson and John Connally, in a long career in politics. "Herb Kalmbach is not by any means in that category," McBride said. Yet he had been the man who delivered the money, and without his deliveries the criminal deals might not have taken place.

I thought of the many Herbert Kalmbachs I had met in twenty years of watching politicians. Nice, affable men in expensive clothes with no visible means of support; lawyers who never argued a case, public relations men with mysterious clients. They were always around, always friendly, but not quite willing to talk to reporters. Their acquaintances were the contractors, purchasing agents and company owners who wanted to do business with the government. They had been in the lobbies of the Massachusetts legislature, the corridors of Boston City Hall, and at the tables of expensive Washington restaurants late at night with their sponsors, the congressmen and senators whom they served. It wasn't often that one of them got caught, and I hated to see this one talk his way out of fit punishment. But I also believed the disagreement over Kalmbach's fate was an honest difference of opinion about his willingness to cooperate, not a moral issue.

Jaworski took the challenges to his judgment with alternating good and bad humor. At this time Senate Republican leader Hugh Scott of Pennsylvania, known without affection in our office as "the senator from Gulf Oil," was conducting a public attack on John Dean's credibility, under the orchestration of Alexander Haig. Jaworski was becoming increasingly combative with the White House over such tactics. Rumors spread in Washington that he was about to be removed.

Nixon's new lawyer, James St. Clair, met with Jaworski and said, "I want you to know that you are in no danger of being fired."

Jaworski shot back, "That would be the biggest favor you could do me."

On Sunday, February 11, Jaworski attended services as usual with his wife Jeannette at the New York Avenue Presbyterian Church in downtown Washington. He was surprised to see Secret Service men in the vestibule and to find Richard Nixon sitting in a front pew. The sermon that day was on moral courage.

The next day he resumed a series of intensive meetings on the cover-up indictment, then interrupted his work to entertain a delegation of the eighth-floor dissenters organized by Roger Witten, an intense young man from Atlantic City, New Jersey, by way of Dartmouth College and Harvard Law School. "I figured if I could spend all day Saturday running around the eighth floor ranting about Kalmbach, I should spend twenty minutes making the same points to him," Witten said.

I asked Witten afterward how the meeting had gone. "It's like Red Auerbach at the Boston Garden," he said. "It won't change the decision but it might make a difference on the next one."

Jaworski, Ruth, and I had lunch at the Lawyers Club. The special prosecutor was fuming. I told him it was an honest difference of opinion and would work out all right.

"The first time there is a difference I'm faced with disloyalty," he said. "By God, I defended this staff when it was under attack."

"Yes, and they defended you," I said.

"That was quite different, my dear man," he said. "I took this job with no hope for any personal gain and performed it conscientiously. There was no justification for any criticism."

It wasn't different at all, I thought.

I said, "The problem is to have this thing out now so that it doesn't spill over into everything else, and people don't start airing their criticisms publicly."

"The only gainers in all of this will be the White House," Jaworski said. "They'll say, 'We warned you about those people, Leon.' "

Ruth and I proposed a meeting of the entire professional staff. He refused.

"It's my responsibility to make these decisions," Jaworski said. "It's the responsibility of these people, once the decision is made, to be loyal and to end their criticisms."

"That was true in your age and mine," I said, "but there really is a generation gap now. They know what your responsibilities are and they are not denying them. What they are saying is that it is their responsibility to criticize you."

Hank Ruth had been making many of the same points with Jaworski during the morning. "It's the new participatory democracy," he said. "Everyone gets to have their say."

I told Jaworski that Tom McBride had been taking even more heat from his own task force than Jaworski had received. "And he isn't even a newcomer," I said. Jaworski agreed to write a memorandum detailing his reasons for accepting the plea and to put a covering note on it addressed to each attorney, inviting each of them to visit him and discuss the case. Slowly Leon Jaworski's anger dissipated.

"Just the same," he said, "it's a damn good staff."

He reminisced for a while about fights he'd been in during his career and his buoyancy returned. As we walked to the street, he was engrossed in a story. "I'll walk in the middle," he said as we started back toward the office.

((302   ))

"You might as well," I said, "because that's where you are."

"Doyle, you've always got something to say, don't you," he said, and he smiled.

That night on the way home I heard a radio bulletin about Aleksandr Solzhenitsyn, who was being expelled from the Soviet Union because of his views. John Barker, who was in the car with me, commented, "They really shouldn't do that, you know. Dissent is what makes the world go around."

Nowhere was the distance between Leon Jaworski and his staff more evident than in the discussion of who should be charged with criminal activity in the Watergate cover-up. There was general agreement that six men should be charged—Mitchell, Haldeman, Ehrlichman, Colson, Robert Mardian, and Gordon Strachan. All were considered principals in the conspiracy. But three others, all of them hired as lawyers for principals during the cover-up, caused long discussion and much disagreement.

Paul O'Brien and Kenneth W. Parkinson had been hired as attorneys for the Committee to Re-elect the President. William O. Bittman had been hired to represent E. Howard Hunt. The three men had not been targets of the investigation, but their demeanor when questioned raised suspicions. Eventually a view developed among most of the prosecutors that some of the defense lawyers had become the sine qua non of the conspiracy once the efforts of the original White House conspirators had proved inadequate.

Bittman particularly became the focus of a spirited debate. He was strongly recommended for inclusion in the cover-up charges by all the lawyers of the Watergate task force and by counsel Philip Lacovara. Jaworski, alone, decided to exclude Bittman.

Bittman had been inextricably involved in the passing of requests from Hunt and the passing of money to Hunt. His evasive testimony, his demeanor, and gradually developing information contradicting his story on small points made him a more and more suspicious figure. Bittman was a friend and former colleague of Jim Neal, and a partner in Sirica's old law firm after Sirica's time there. His indictment would complicate the prosecution of the case in more ways than one. It was possible that the trial judge might disqualify himself if Bittman were indicted. And it would end all possibility that Jim Neal could return to head the prosecution. While this point was not argued, it again raised suspicions about people's motives, not only those of Jaworski for excluding the man, but those of staff members who might have found their positions on the prosecution team elevated by Neal's disqualification. The participants in the discussions of Bittman became offended whenever there was a suggestion that they were affected by personal considerations, but the suspicions made the debate all the more spirited and at times personal. Jaworski argued that it was not justifiable to view the lawyer's bare acts without regard for the lawyer-client relationship. He believed that the lawyer's conduct had been such that it would be appropriate for review by a grievance committee of the bar, but not a criminal indictment. Besides, he noted, the principal witness against Bittman was O'Brien, whose own role was just as questionable. In Bittman's case, Jaworski argued, the evidence and the witnesses did not warrant a reasonable expectation of conviction, the standard which had been set for indictment.

Jaworski may also have been affected by Bittman's lawyer, Herbert J. Miller, Jr., who made his presentation to Jaworski alone, with none of the task force members present. In such a setting Miller's low-key and persuasive manner could be most effective. In any case, the decision to exclude Bittman was to be one of the most bitterly regretted within the office, at least partly because the other lawyers felt that he had brought great shame on their profession.

Paul O'Brien was passed because Silbert, Glanzer, and Campbell had told him he would be treated as a witness not a defendant. Kenneth Parkinson was included in the cover-up indictment. (The jury found him not guilty.)

Another crucial decision involved the omission from the overt acts listed in the indictment of the attempts to use the CIA to obstruct the FBI's investigation of the Watergate break-in. There was a general belief in the prosecutor's office that the motivation for the cover-up included a desire to keep the Fielding break-in secret, and that pressure on the CIA by Nixon, Haldeman, Ehrlichman, and Dean had been a deliberate attempt to end the investigation of both crimes. But the CIA became a problem because of a memo of June 28, 1972, written by CIA Director Richard Helms. Despite Helms' testimony that he had resisted White House pressure to obstruct the investigation of the Watergate break-in, the CIA director indicated that he may have been more receptive to the White House overtures than he had admitted.

The memorandum had been written to Helms' deputy, Lieutenant General Vernon E. Walters, who owed his CIA appointment to the Nixon White House and was seen in the agency as a White House stooge. In the second paragraph Helms had written, "We still adhere to the request that they [the FBI] confine themselves to the personalities already arrested or directly under suspicion and that they desist from expanding this investigation into other areas which may well, eventually, run afoul of our operations."

That language was strangely inconsistent with Helms' testimony that no CIA operations had been threatened by the Watergate investigation. The former CIA director explained that he meant only to suggest that there was a danger of FBI leaks endangering various CIA cover operations. But that explanation was as puzzling as some of the Helms testimony under oath before various bodies and his actions during the early Watergate period.

A month after the memo was written, on July 29, 1972, James McCord sent the first of a series of letters to his old agency warning that officials of the campaign committee planned to contend that the Watergate break-in had been a CIA operation. In a subsequent letter McCord wrote, "I have the evidence of the involvement of Mitchell and others sufficient to convince a jury, the Congress and the press."

At the time these letters were received by the CIA—while Earl Silbert was conducting his original investigation of the Watergate break-in—the information about McCord's state of mind would have been invaluable to the prosecutors. Helms and the CIA were at the time under subpoena to forward to the Justice Department "all communications" related to the Watergate case. But Helms overruled one of his assistants and did not disclose the letters. He also withheld the fact that John Dean had asked the agency to provide bail funds for the original defendants. The original prosecutors were not informed of the McCord letters until May, 1973, when the new CIA director, James Schlesinger, ordered all relevant material unearthed.

Shortly afterward Silbert was supplanted by Archibald Cox. Helms defended his failure to turn over McCord's letters by saying that he had called in his counsel, Lawrence Houston (the same man Elliot Richardson was to suggest would be a perfect "consultant" to Archibald Cox), and that Houston had ruled the CIA had no legal obligation to turn over the letters.

In August, 1973, before these facts were made public, Helms testified before the Senate Watergate committee, and the following exchange took place:

Q—(by Watergate committee counsel David M. Dorsen)—And to your knowledge was any relevant information withheld by the CIA to the FBI and Justice Department, information that you were aware of while the events were taking place in June, July or August of 1972?
A—(by Helms)—Sir, I do not believe so. Does the record show that there was anything of this kind?
Q—No. I am not suggesting that at all. I am just asking for your knowledge. I have no knowledge to the contrary.
A—Well, I do not either, but I just wanted to be sure that my recollections tracked with the facts.

Later it seemed clear that Richard Helms compared with the other Richard—Kleindienst—in his attitude toward truthfulness while under oath before congressional committees.

After being displaced at CIA Helms was nominated to become ambassador to Iran. The following exchange took place between him and Senator Stuart Symington of the Foreign Relations Committee at Helms' confirmation hearings:

Q—Did you try in the Central Intelligence Agency to overthrow the government of Chile?
A—No, sir.
Q—Did you have any money passed to the opponents of Allende?
A—No, sir.
Q—So the stories you were involved in that war are wrong?
A—Yes, sir. I said to Senator Fulbright many months ago that if the agency had really gotten behind the other candidates and spent a lot of money and so forth, the election might have come out differently.

The following spring CIA Director William Colby told the House Armed Services subcommittee on intelligence that under Helms the CIA had spent eleven million dollars for "covert action" in Chile aimed at blocking Salvador Allende's elections in 1964 and 1970.

It was clear that Richard Helms would not be a prosecution witness. In fact he spent a fair amount of time in 1974 commuting from Iran to the prosecutor's office for other purposes, before jurisdiction of the CIA investigation was formally handed to the regular agencies of the Department of Justice. At Christmas Helms sent his interrogator, Richard Ben-Veniste, a twenty-five-dollar tin of Iranian caviar. Ben-Veniste ate it, then reported the gift to his superiors.

The prosecutors reserved judgment as to whether they would use, in trial arguments, the attempts to have the CIA obstruct the investigation, and decided the indictment as drawn was broad enough to include this aspect of the conspiracy. Given the evidence available to them in February, they felt that to include the subject in the indictments would allow the defense to argue that obstruction was a perfectly proper exercise because even the CIA agreed with it. Later, when the June 23, 1972, tape-recorded conversation between Nixon and Haldeman became available, the attempt to use the CIA to obstruct the FBI investigation became an integral part of the case.

At 10:00 A.M. on Monday, February 25, reporters crowded into Judge Sirica's courtroom to witness Herbert Kalmbach's plea of guilty to a felony and a misdemeanor. Four floors above in the same courthouse, unknown to any of the reporters, a very nervous Leon Jaworski walked into the grand jury room and proceeded to argue his case against indicting the President of the United States.

The jurors had heard all the evidence, and the cases against the seven who were to be indicted had been summarized. "I am prepared to discuss with you the status of matters relating to the President and to make recommendations to you in this regard," Jaworski said.

He was convinced that he did not have to review the tape-recorded conversations and other evidence the nineteen grand jurors had already heard. "The questions that lie before you," he continued, "involve not only their interpretation, but also the legally responsible action they call for you to take."

His own recommendation, Jaworski said, came after exhaustive legal research and consideration of the grave Constitutional issues involved. "It will not be necessary to weigh the evidence to determine whether there is probable cause to indict. The legal doubt that a sitting President is indictable for offenses of the type considered by you is so substantial that indictment of the President should be ruled out. It would not be re-

NOT ABOVE THE LAW

sponsible conduct in my opinion to return an indictment against the President in the present uncertain state of the law, only to learn in the end that the United States Supreme Court holds such action to be unconstitutional. The trauma the nation would suffer in the interim, let alone the scars such actions would leave on the institution of the Presidency, renders such action inadvisable, regardless of whether the evidence otherwise would warrant it."

Jaworski added that there was another sound reason for not proceeding against the President. The House impeachment inquiry was well under way, he said, and "this is the appropriate body under the Constitution, in my view, for examining in the first instance evidence relating to the President to determine whether he should be charged with conduct justifying impeachment and removal from office.

"I deem it inadvisable to name unindicted co-conspirators at this time," Jaworski continued. "At a later date, when a bill of particulars is filed, the individuals who participated in the acts forming the conspiracy will be discussed with you and your permission to name them in the bill of particulars will be sought.

"The question has been raised whether you can transmit to the House Judiciary Committee for its consideration the evidence that you have before you. This seems to me to be proper and responsible action for you to take. If you determine to follow this course, it should be done by way of a report to Judge Sirica. It may contain your views and recommendations in addition to transmitting any evidence you consider to be appropriate for review by the House impeachment inquiry. It is the view of the special prosecutor that you are authorized to make such a report to Judge Sirica. Once the report is made by you, it is up to him to determine whether to accept and act upon your recommendations."

The foreman, Vladimir Pregelj, an archivist at the Library of Congress and a very active member of the grand jury, made it clear that he was not convinced that Jaworski's recommendation was the best choice. He argued briefly, through a series of questions, for taking the question to the Supreme Court. The foreman was seeking an indictment of the President so that the Supreme Court could then judge the constitutionality of the procedure. In response Jaworski made two points: First, what would the country do about the national political crisis that would ensue while the issue was being debated? Second, Jaworski told the foreman, "In my opinion you are misjudging the likely result." He did not believe that the Supreme Court would uphold the validity of such an act.

Despite this contretemps, the mood in the grand jury remained calm and friendly, and it soon became clear that despite Vladimir Pregelj's reservations, the grand jury would approve Jaworski's proposals. A blond woman spoke up and said, "Mr. Jaworski, we appreciate what you are doing. I have to admit that I had reservations about you when you first came."

"I want you to know that you were not the only one," Jaworski said.

That day the grand jury voted, 19–0 (with four absent), to authorize Jaworski to name President Richard Nixon an unindicted co-conspirator in the bill of particulars at the time of the trial.

By the end of February it became clear that the only matter delaying the indictment of the major conspirators was selection of a jury in the Vesco case in New York, where John Mitchell and Maurice Stans were co-defendants. The news of the indictment in the Watergate case would so saturate the media that the Mitchell-Stans defense would argue for a further delay (the men had been indicted nine months earlier) because of prejudicial publicity. When the jury for the Vesco case was finally selected and sequestered on February 28, it was clear Indictment Day had arrived. By 9:00 A.M. on Friday, March 1, the reporters covering Watergate were in a frenzy. At one point that morning I made the mistake of walking through a corridor at the courthouse and found myself almost pulled apart by the surging crowd of newsmen seeking bits of information.

Normally we would have asked the Justice Department printing office to print copies of a document as big as the fifty-page indictment, but to insure secrecy John Barker directed a small team of men and women who made four hundred copies on the office photocopy machines. When the three machines broke down we used the National Endowment for the Arts' photocopiers, which were located on another floor.

Barker had arranged for federal marshals to escort us as we transported the copies of the indictment to the courthouse in the morning, and the two men chosen, both of whom looked like veterans of the Minnesota Vikings front four, were conscientious to a fault.

When the elevator arrived on the ninth floor of 1425 K Street, there were several people on board. The marshals decided that the boxes of indictments might be in danger, so they announced to the passengers, "This elevator is impounded. Everybody off," and they wheeled their cart aboard. A thin young man in the back of the elevator looked wide-eyed as he quickly exited, exclaiming, "Far out, man."

At the courthouse the indictment procedure took less than thirteen minutes to unfold. Twenty-one grand jurors (two were absent) filed into the courtroom, most of them dressed in their best clothes. Promptly at 11:00 A.M. Judge Sirica took the bench and Leon Jaworski rose and said, "The grand jury has an indictment and also has a sealed report to deliver to Your Honor." Vladimir Pregelj, a tall man with dark, white-streaked hair and a handsome goatee, rose from his front-row seat and carried a large black briefcase to the clerk's desk. It contained the requisite number of the fifty-page indictments and the original copy of "the road map," the presentment for the House impeachment inquiry.

The crowded courtroom was so still that in the back you could hear the sound of Judge Sirica using a letter opener to slit a manila envelope he took from the briefcase. He removed the "road map," and read a brief covering letter that said:

> The Grand Jury has heard the evidence which it regards as having a material bearing on matters that are within the jurisdiction of the House Judiciary Committee in its consideration of impeachment proceedings related to the President of the United States. The Grand Jury has listed these items of evidence which it is herewith handing to the Court. The Special Prosecutor has advised us that most of these items of evidence, if not all, will be used in the trials of the individuals against whom indictments are being returned.
>
> It is the Grand Jury's recommendation to the Court that the evidence referred to above be made available to the House Judiciary Committee for such use as is appropriate in the impeachment proceedings but under such orders of the Court regarding their use as will avoid jeopardizing the rights of the individuals to be tried on the ground of undue pre-trial publicity.

Then Richard Ben-Veniste handed up the brown briefcase containing all the evidence which John Doar later turned into his summary against Richard Nixon.

The essentially anonymous ten men and eleven women of the nation's most celebrated grand jury filed from the courtroom, their task completed.

CHAPTER

15

THE FINAL COVER-UP

*"A criminal conspiracy is criminal only after it's proven
to be criminal."*

In the final days, between the Watergate indictments and the resignation
of the President, yet another cover-up was attempted. It failed. Perhaps
it was a special power of Richard Nixon, or the mystique of the "im-
pregnable" Presidency; Nixon was able to surround himself with lieutenants who would fight to the end to retain him in office, whatever his
misdeeds or the consequences for their country.

On December 26, 1973—five days after Leon Jaworski advised Alexander Haig to find the best criminal lawyer he could for Nixon—James
Draper St. Clair and his wife, Billie, were checking into a resort hotel in
Tarpon Springs, Florida, when Haig telephoned. It took St. Clair only a
few days to decide that at this point in his life the job of defending the
President of the United States was right for him. He cut short his
vacation, flew out to San Clemente after New Year's Day, and had started
work in the Executive Office Building by January 4.

From the outset, St. Clair was a contradiction. A superb trial lawyer, his appointment was widely advertised as a sign that Nixon was finally turning his Watergate defense over to a highly competent and ethical man who would take charge, pay close attention to details, and eliminate any future possibility of suspicious conduct on the part of the presidential legal team. St. Clair encouraged this view. He told Lesley Oelsner of *The New York Times* that he had come to Washington, not to represent Mr. Nixon "individually," but to represent "the office of the President."

Fred Buzhardt was to maintain control of all the tapes and most of the sensitive documents. If St. Clair found this inhibiting, he did not protest enough to have the system changed. His ignorance of the contents of the tapes was to enable him to get out of town with his reputation intact.

Alexander Haig and Richard Nixon continued to direct the case, and St. Clair did not object strenuously enough to have that changed either. He was often caught by surprise and embarrassed by events and disclosures. One of his assistants, an attorney named Cecil Emerson, from Dallas, left in the spring with a public blast at the "obstructionists" in the White House who were hindering the lawyers. St. Clair said nothing.

St. Clair found it necessary to ask one of the young lawyers on the White House staff to accompany Buzhardt whenever Buzhardt went to the restricted files for a sensitive document. St. Clair wanted to be sure that no documents disappeared during his tenure at the White House.

Once a St. Clair assistant had been with a White House lawyer who went to a file cabinet, looked briefly for a wanted file, and said, "It's not here." The St. Clair man brushed past the lawyer and snatched the file before it could be shoved out of sight. After that incident St. Clair could have caused a showdown and insisted that he be given control of the case, as he certainly would have done with any other client. He did not do so.

Despite his boast to the contrary, St. Clair represented Richard Nixon, not the Presidency. He fought to withhold evidence; when he could no longer hide it, he tried to deny its meaning. This was not done in the name of a criminal defendant on trial for his freedom, but on behalf of a man seeking to retain power. When Nixon left office and needed a criminal lawyer for the usual purposes, James St. Clair resigned and Herbert J. Miller, Jr., took over.

Perhaps it was coincidence, but an immediate change in the White House attitude toward Jaworski took place when St. Clair arrived. For two months there had been open, if incomplete, cooperation, as Bork, Haig, and Nixon had publicly pledged. Some tapes had been turned over voluntarily, and Chuck Breyer of the prosecutor's office had been allowed to cull through a number of White House files. The prosecutors discovered that there were deletions from both tapes and documents, far more than the few that had been publicized through court hearings.

There was a fifty-nine-second gap in a cassette recording the President had dictated, reconstructing his March 21 meeting with John Dean. The obliteration came at a crucial point in Nixon's recollections, just as he told Dean that to "hunker down" without making any statement on the cover-up would be "too dangerous as far . . . [fifty-nine-second gap]."

Other tapes contained audible blips that lasted a few seconds and that as a result obliterated key words. Listening to them was like watching the Johnny Carson show during its raunchier moments. One understood what the speaker was saying, but the blips kept the incriminating words from being heard.

On January 15, 1974, FBI agents visited the homes of White House secretaries and asked for details of how the White House files were supervised, and whether any precautions were taken when transcripts were made from the White House tapes.* Haig telephoned Attorney General Saxbe the following day to complain about the harassment of White House staff members, and Saxbe immediately called Jaworski.

"Why, Bill, I would think Al would have agreed with that decision completely," Jaworski said. "What did he want me to do, disrupt the White House with visits by FBI agents during working hours?"

Less than a week later Jaworski had an appointment to see St. Clair, and the White House guards detained him at the gate, refusing to let his car into the compound. Finally they escorted him on foot.

"What is this all about?" Jaworski asked.

"Sir," a guard replied, "we have orders not to allow any representative of your office on the grounds without an escort."

At their meeting St. Clair raised the possibility that the President give his side of the story to the grand jury by way of a written "interrogatory," a device normally used in civil suits. The grand jury could submit written questions, and the President would then attest to the accuracy of the written answers. But as Jaworski said at the time, "The trouble with

* A grand jury inquiry was launched at this time and continued sporadically for a year, but it gathered insufficient evidence to charge anyone with obstruction of justice.

((313))

interrogatories is that the replies are written by lawyers with the aim of *not* answering the questions."

Jaworski asked St. Clair, "Why don't we bring the grand jury on down here in a bus, bring them right in the back gate like tourists, and we can question the President in some room down here?" St. Clair was less than enchanted with the idea.

Subsequently Jaworski made an offer. He would accept a written interrogatory providing that along with it the prosecutors got all the tapes and documents they had asked for. St. Clair rejected that proposal, so the prosecutors sent the White House a letter signed by foreman Vladimir Pregelj requesting that the President appear before the grand jury and tell his story. Nixon rejected the secret invitation and, a few days later, blurted out at a news conference that one had been extended.

Soon after the Jaworski-St. Clair meeting, Haig called and asked Jaworski to drop by his office for a chat. "I'm sorry, you'll have to come over here, Al," Jaworski said. "That really was a chickenshit operation you pulled over there last week." Haig professed surprise that Jaworski had been detained at the gate but surmised that it was because of the FBI interviews with the White House secretaries. "Well Godamighty," Jaworski said, "what has that got to do with it? Why should that cause such an order to be issued?" The order was subsequently amended to except Jaworski.

Haig met Jaworski at the White House and told him it probably would not be possible to supply the special prosecutor with more tapes and documents, including some that had already been promised. Jaworski responded that he would immediately tell the chairman and members of the Senate Judiciary Committee.

Haig was taken by surprise and told Jaworski that whether he was to receive more documents and tapes would be "a presidential decision," because Nixon had taken complete control of the case. Subsequently St. Clair informed Jaworski that "There has been a Cabinet meeting," apparently a reference to a summit meeting between Nixon and his lawyers, and that Jaworski would be given the material already promised. St. Clair later took pains to make it clear to Jaworski that he did not make final decisions.

If Nixon decided to stonewall, St. Clair seemed to have no great difficulty in accepting that tactic and indeed showed some creativity in implementing it. Late in January he wrote to Judge Sirica challenging the adequacy of the Preliminary Report by six court-appointed experts—people chosen by the White House and the prosecutors together—which concluded the eighteen-minute gap was a deliberate erasure. The experts said this conclusion was unanimous but that several months would be needed to write a definitive technical report. St. Clair insisted the report be finished before the experts went on to other tapes.

This delay would prove significant because the prosecutors wanted the experts to start testing all the other tapes that contained gaps and blips, and a delay of several months could effectively stall the grand jury investigation of the tapes, begun on Sirica's orders. Perhaps more to the point for St. Clair, it would forestall any public disclosure that there were more deliberate erasures. By the time the panel had submitted its exhaustive report on the eighteen-minute gap, Sirica had decided that the court budget could not sustain the further expense of examining the other gaps and blips, and they were not analyzed. Although there were rumors of such gaps in the press, the White House always denied them, and was never contradicted.

On Wednesday night, January 30, Richard Nixon stood before the House of Representatives, on the occasion of the annual State of the Union address, and concluded his speech by saying, "As you know, I have provided to the Special Prosecutor voluntarily a great deal of material. I believe that I have provided all the material that he needs to conclude his investigations and to proceed to prosecute the guilty and to clear the innocent. I believe the time has come to bring that investigation and the other investigations of this matter to an end. One year of Watergate is enough."

Two days later Haig invited Jaworski to the White House. The President and his lawyers, Haig said, were extremely unhappy with Jaworski. The complaint was prompted by a subpoena given to Ron Ziegler, ordering him to appear before the Watergate grand jury. In fact the prosecutors had little interest in Ziegler and few questions to ask him. But the grand jurors, who had been reading Ziegler's statements on Watergate for nineteen months and knew that he was close to the President, insisted on interrogating him. "Look at the position you put Ziegler in," Haig said. "He has publicly criticized Ben-Veniste and now he is called before the grand jury to be interrogated by Ben-Veniste." Jaworski told Haig, "That's no problem. Just tell him to be sure to tell the truth."

Haig said the White House staff thought Jaworski had played "dirty pool," and they were generally dissatisfied with the way he had conducted himself in the last several weeks. Jaworski responded that he was the one who had been badly treated; he had been promised cooperation, and the promises had not been kept.

Haig said this was a political decision, that the White House had to be consistent and had to protect itself against the burgeoning impeachment inquiry. They couldn't afford to supply Jaworski with any more material because the House of Representatives would use this cooperation with Jaworski as an argument for receiving the same material.

"Al," Jaworski said, "every time you get a little bit ahead of the game you make some decision that plunges you behind again. I'm going to have to go to the Hill and tell them about this, and then I'm going to litigate the piss out of you."

Haig ended by telling Jaworski a story about the Middle East. According to Haig, the Soviet military were very dissatisfied with their government's showing in the war there. "If Nixon falls, Brezhnev will fall shortly afterwards, and the entire world will become unstable," Haig said.

That afternoon St. Clair called Jaworski and said, "Things have changed again. I'm not going home this weekend. I'll be working, and you'll be hearing from me on Monday."

"Well, am I going to hear from you, or am I going to get some material?" Jaworski asked. St. Clair implied that either more evidence would be handed over or a definitive reply to the requests would be made; the decision would be made after St. Clair reviewed the material.

No evidence was forthcoming. Instead St. Clair joined in the White House-sponsored campaign publicly to discredit John Dean's testimony. "He's not a lawyer," Jaworski said of St. Clair, "he's a mouthpiece."

On the weekend of April 8 to 10, 1974, Nixon and his advisers met in Key Biscayne and decided to go public. Over the next seven weeks the White House prepared its own transcripts of forty-six tapes, most of them tapes that had been subpoenaed by the House. The strategy was to gain political support for the idea that, as bad as the transcripts were, they contained no evidence of a crime committed by the President and represented all of the tapes of any relevance that existed within the White House.

That was a lie, of course, and one participated in by the men around the President. Someone in the White House had removed the June 23, 1972, tape from its vault. That was the tape in which Nixon and Haldeman planned to use the CIA to obstruct the FBI. Had none of the President's men listened to this tape? That was to be their story, that only the President heard it. The House of Representatives unfortunately had not subpoenaed it.

The transcripts the White House released contained numerous omissions. According to the introduction to the transcripts written by James St. Clair, "The attached transcripts represent the best efforts accurately to transcribe the material contained on the recording tapes. Expletives have been omitted in the interest of good taste, except where necessary to depict accurately the context of the conversation. Characterization of third persons, in fairness to them, and other material not relating to the President's conduct has been omitted, except where inclusion is relevant and material as bearing on the President's conduct."

When the prosecutors checked the White House transcripts against the tapes, they found appalling omissions:

—April 14, 1973, according to the Nixon transcripts: "material unrelated to presidential action."

April 14, 1973, on the tape: President: *"And before I leave office and they'll get off. You get them full pardons. That's what they have, John."* Ehrlichman: *"Right."* President: *"Do you agree?"* Ehrlichman: *"Yep, I sure do."*

—March 21, 1973, according to the Nixon transcripts: President: "But at the moment, don't you agree it is better to get the Hunt thing that's where that . . ." Dean: "That is worth buying time on."

March 21, 1973, on the tape: President: *"Well, at this moment, don't you agree that we better take the Hunt thing. I mean, that's worth it at the moment."* Dean: *That's worth buying time on, right."*

At another point near the end of the March 21 conversation, the tape had Richard Nixon saying, *"The main point is now the, the people to, uh, get the money together.* Of course, you've got the surplus from the campaign. Is there any other money hanging around?" The transcripts omitted the first sentence entirely.

Any number of presidential exclamations at critical times— *"That's right," "Yeah, I know."*—were omitted without any notation.

The original cover-up, designed to protect the President's men and to lead the investigation away from the White House, had now led to a second cover-up designed to hide evidence that the President ordered, approved, or knew about specific criminal acts that were part of the original cover-up. If these sorts of omissions occurred before a tribunal in any case not involving the President, you could expect the person to be charged with contempt and his lawyers subject to disbarment. In fact there was a grand jury investigation of the deletions from the transcripts, an attempt to discover whether those who prepared the transcripts were guilty of obstructing Congress. But the situation was too complicated to prove criminality beyond a reasonable doubt. The transcripts were prepared by a large number of persons, from lawyers and public relations men to secretaries and typists. It is unlikely that the principals *ordered* any incriminating sentences removed; they undoubtedly blue penciled the sentences themselves, without explanation. And the original typescripts, according to St. Clair, were destroyed.

No congressional committee, no bar association, no other authority has held a public inquiry into the actions of the President's aides involved in editing the transcripts. A grand jury did seek to determine any basis for an obstruction of justice, but it returned no indictments. Thus it is likely that only after those involved have passed from the scene, if at all, will we learn exactly how the evidence against the President was doctored before it was published by the Government Printing Office.

The White House gambit of releasing the transcripts surpassed even the firing of Archibald Cox as a measure of desperation. The shock and outrage that had hit the prosecutors when they heard the tapes in December now spread across the nation. Kenneth Clawson of the Office of Communications orchestrated the release of the transcripts to factor in the maximum possible distortion in favor of the White House, and it took most of the press twenty-four hours to realize the enormity of the contents of the 1,308-page "blue book" that was handed out just before the evening television shows.

The reaction gathered each day, as more and more reporters read more and more pages. The news magazines digested the conversations and their meaning, *Newsweek* in a seventy-five-page section, *Time* in twenty pages. Newspapers began publishing the entire text. In less than two weeks *The New York Times* and the *Washington Post* had published paperback editions, and three million copies were printed.

The politicians recoiled with horror. Hugh Scott read the transcripts Alexander Haig had neglected to show him and said, "It's a shabby, disgusting, immoral performance by each of those persons according to what he said." Haig telephoned and pointedly reminded Scott that he had many times advocated that the White House get the whole story out. "That's right," Scott said, "but I didn't have the slightest inkling that it was anything like this."

The collapse was total; no trips to Capitol Hill by White House lobbyists would help, no further explanations were possible. The Nixon adminstration had lost its last shred of self-respect.

Even H. R. Haldeman joined in the sport of making fun of his old boss. He was at the prosecutor's office listening to some of the tapes that were to be introduced as evidence against him when he engaged one of the prosecutors in conversation during a break. "Do you know how a Polish President would have handled Watergate?" Haldeman asked Ruth. Tell me, Ruth said, how would a Polish President have handled Watergate? "The way that Nixon did," Haldeman said.

We could not expect Ron Ziegler or Fred Buzhardt or Pat Buchanan to tell Nixon to resign. But why not Alexander Haig, the man who so often and so sincerely talked of patriotism? Why not James St. Clair, the recent arrival who came to town paraphrasing Justice Brandeis, suggesting that he would be a lawyer who would represent the situation, not merely a client? It was not to be. Haig, the moving force behind the Saturday Night Massacre, would fight on. St. Clair would read the sleazy conversations in the transcripts and write a fifty-page apologia. "James St. Clair," said Yale chaplain William Sloane Coffin, a former client, "is all case and no cause."

At Boston's Pemberton Square, where men in gray Homburgs and felt collars lounge outside the courthouse admiring the fancy footwork of colleagues in hit-and-run cases, "Jimmy" St. Clair is known as "the silver fox," and he is much admired, though not universally. Another leading Boston trial lawyer, Richard Donahue, told *Time* magazine what he thought of his colleague's representation of the President of the United

States. It was, Donahue said, as if he were representing "a drunken driver." He added, "If you have a guilty client, you make them prove everything every inch of the way. Attack everyone in the room—the judge, the court officers, the witnesses. But you always smile."

In the earlier stages of the legal battle Charles Alan Wright had confined himself to respectable legal arguments while Fred Buzhardt lurked in the background, stalling Cox and planning for his demise. Now St. Clair was conducting what amounted to a legal street brawl, where anything goes until the cops arrive, at which time you run for the alleys. Leon Jaworski was up to the challenge.

Two weeks before the White House transcripts were made public Jaworski had sent a subpoena to Richard Nixon for sixty-four tapes needed as evidence in the case of *U.S.* v. *Mitchell.* The second item on the list was dated June 23, 1972, and listed the conversations that day between H. R. Haldeman and Richard Nixon.

The prosecutors had not singled out this tape as the most important but they knew it was essential to their case. Haldeman had admitted that on June 23 he and the President had discussed the suggestion that the CIA might have been involved in the Watergate break-in. And the logs of Haldeman and Ehrlichman showed that together they had met with General Walters, the Nixon man at CIA, that afternoon.

The fifth item on the list was the tape of a "Meeting or telephone conversation in or about late January, 1973, between the President and Mr. Colson in which E. Howard Hunt, Jr., was discussed." Both Colson and John Dean had told the prosecutors that at some point in January Colson and Nixon had discussed clemency for Howard Hunt. Nixon had later remarked to Dean that he should never have held the conversation.*

* Even after the Supreme Court decision and the surrender of the fatal June 23 tape, this Colson-Nixon tape, of January 8, 1973, was not turned over to the prosecutors. J. Fred Buzhardt maintained that no such conversation existed. After Nixon resigned and Philip Buchen took over the office of White House counsel, the tape was discovered and made available for the Mitchell trial. It showed that Nixon had indeed suggested clemency for Hunt. "Hunt's is a simple case," the President said. "I mean, after all, the man's wife is dead . . . we'll build, we'll build that son of a bitch up like nobody's business. . . . We'll have [William] Buckley write a column and say, you know, that he, that he should have clemency if you've given eighteen years of service."
That tape, as it turned out, was even more incriminating to Richard M. Nixon than his words of June 23, but by the time it became public he was a disgraced civilian pardoned for his crimes and nobody paid much attention to its contents.

When James St. Clair received Jaworski's subpoena on April 16, he and his legal staff were engrossed in the editing of forty-six presidential conversations for public consumption. The return date on the subpoena was May 2. On May 1, as he appeared on national television to defend the Richard Nixon of the transcripts, St. Clair announced that he would move into court to quash Jaworski's subpoena.

The White House was in a far weaker position now to take its case to the Supreme Court. All the events that had transpired since the resolution of the Cox suit had weakened the credibility of Nixon's assertions that he sought to withhold the evidence only to protect the Presidency. After the release of the transcripts it was unlikely that any court would find need to protect presidential confidentiality as far as the Watergate cover-up was concerned.

Nevertheless Leon Jaworski wanted to avoid a court fight if possible. The Supreme Court was due to adjourn in a month. A fight over the subpoena might put off the Mitchell trial until 1975, and by then the effect of the impeachment inquiry would have complicated that trial considerably. Jaworski decided to play his trump.

On Saturday, May 4, the special prosecutor returned from Texas, where he had made several Law Day speeches, to meet with Ruth, Lacovara, Ben-Veniste, and Kreindler. All week they had been discussing the legal brief that would be filed to support the subpoena for sixty-four tapes. Peter Kreindler pointed out that the strongest argument for the relevance of the sixty-four tapes as evidence was the fact that Richard Nixon had been named by the grand jury as a member of the conspiracy. He proposed that the fact be included. For five months, from December until May, the staff of the special prosecutor's office had held confidential the explosive information on the tapes they possessed. Despite Nixon's deliberate lies through the weeks of Operation Candor, the attacks on John Dean's credibility by Hugh Scott, other provocations, and the constant prodding of a curious press, none of the staff had succumbed to the temptation of leaking the criminal contents. It had been a matter of discipline and professional pride, but also a cause of tension. Every day the lawyers picked up the *Washington Post* with trepidation, knowing that any leak would hurt their cause.

Jaworski could envision a situation in which as long as impeachment dragged on so would his fight for the tapes. As a result there would be an intolerable delay on a resolution of the issues. The special prosecutor decided to offer the White House a compromise. Ben-Veniste was to go through the list of sixty-four tapes and cull out those that were absolutely essential. Jaworski would offer to drop his subpoena—and consequently his disclosure that Nixon was named a co-conspirator—in return for the voluntary release of a smaller number of tapes. Ben-Veniste already knew which tapes he really wanted for trial. They amounted to eighteen new tapes, including June 23 and the January Colson tapes.

Jaworski telephoned Al Haig in Spokane, Washington, where Nixon had gone to open the 1974 Exposition. Could Jaworski come to the White House to see Haig the next afternoon at 3:00 P.M.? He wanted to be sure that Haig would have sufficient time to get settled after the return flight across country. "I know you are going public in the morning and will be busy," Jaworski said, a reference to the fact that Haig and St. Clair were guests on two of the Sunday television talk shows. Haig agreed to the afternoon meeting, and said he would have St. Clair there.

Later that day President Nixon appeared at the dedication of the Expo '74 fair grounds. An angry crowd stood under a huge white banner imprinted with "Impeach The (Expletive Deleted)." Nixon referred to his host, Governor Dan Evans, as "Governor Evidence."

On Sunday morning, Haig called Jaworski, obviously concerned about the upcoming meeting. Could Jaworski be specific? Not on the telephone, Jaworski said. He added that he would be bringing Phil Lacovara and Rick Ben-Veniste with him.

Early that afternoon Haig appeared on *Issues and Answers*. The transcripts in the blue book, he said, "cover the full spectrum of the operative discussions in the President's office which would give the American people, which would give the Judiciary Committee, and indeed give Mr. Jaworski, the full picture of the operative aspects of what the President knew about Watergate and what actions he directed with respect to Watergate."

ABC-TV correspondent Sam Donaldson said, "Let me ask you an easy question. . . . You are a military man. That was your career. You have studied the problem of 'just following orders,' which many people now believe is not an excuse. . . . Can I take it correctly that you wouldn't follow orders in any sense, or do anything that you believed had some aspect of criminal wrongdoing to it?"

"You are absolutely right, of course," Haig said.

James St. Clair appeared on *Meet the Press*. Carl Stern of NBC-TV said, "I am sure you would be the first to agree that the members of the House Judiciary Committee are all honorable men. Why not simply give them everything that they think they need?"

St. Clair said, "I am sure the President has given them everything that he thinks they need."

Columnist George Will wanted to know how Nixon could say that he "had no information when payments were made" to the blackmailers, when the transcripts showed that Dean told him "about leaving hush money in mailboxes for Mr. LaRue to pick up."

"*Where* payments are made and *when* payments are made are two different things," St. Clair said.

Will was momentarily taken aback. "The President was saying he didn't know the mailbox? Is that it?"

"As I understand your question, that would be a clear explanation in my view," St. Clair said.

Columnist Nick Thimmesch asked, "Are you your own man in your relationship with the President on this?"

St. Clair said, "Mr. Thimmesch—yes. As a lawyer. I am not the President of the United States. I have noticed a lot of people feel I should be making presidential decisions. I don't have that authority nor do I have the real capability. But in terms of, am I able to function as a lawyer? Yes. Of course."

Carl Stern said, "Mr. St. Clair, you are a fine lawyer. I know you love the legal profession as few things in life. The canons of ethics say that a lawyer should strive at all times to uphold the honor and maintain the dignity of the profession and improve not only the law but the administration of justice. Do you believe Richard Nixon has upheld that canon?"

"Yes," St. Clair said.

At three o'clock the five men—Jaworski, Haig, St. Clair, Lacovara, Ben-Veniste—met in the White House map room. Jaworski was cordial and somewhat circumspect. He had with him the brief that he proposed to file, and a copy of the grand jury minutes of the deliberations at which the jurors voted to name Nixon a co-conspirator. He showed both documents to Haig and St. Clair. They looked at the grand jury minutes showing

Ben-Veniste's entering the grand jury room and saying to the foreman, "Have you decided?" and the foreman's saying, "We have decided en bloc," and the vote was listed: 19–0.

St. Clair apparently misunderstood what he was reading. He turned bright red. "Has this been signed?" he asked Jaworski. After a few more questions it became clear that St. Clair thought there was a sealed indictment of Nixon in existence somewhere. Jaworski explained in more detail his compromise proposal. On the next day he would file papers disclosing that Nixon was an unindicted co-conspirator unless an accommodation could be reached.

Haig was concerned about the timing. If the White House announced that Jaworski was getting more tapes, there would be no chance that the Judiciary Committee would accept the "blue book" as best evidence. On the other hand, if Jaworski announced his news, Nixon's situation would worsen.

Haig asked Jaworski to join the White House in seeking to delay presentation of the briefs in the subpoena case until Wednesday, and he and St. Clair promised that if the delay was agreed upon, it would be to use the time to change President Nixon's position and to gain release of the eighteen tapes Jaworski demanded as a minimum offering.

Jaworski agreed to ask Judge Sirica for the delay. Together with his aides, the special prosecutor left the White House shortly before 4:00 P.M.

White House logs subsequently showed that the eighteen tapes Jaworski sought were checked out of their White House storage area shortly after the special prosecutor departed the map room. No White House aide admits to learning the contents of the June 23 or January 8 tapes at that time. On Monday the President began listening to the tapes personally. At 9:15 A.M., St. Clair called Jaworski and asked that the delay be extended until Friday. "I'll check with Rick Ben-Veniste," Jaworski told Haig, "and we will go along unless he has a major point of objection."

"I hope you will," St. Clair said. "You can believe me that this request is made in good faith."

As St. Clair spoke with Jaworski, Nixon was listening once again to the June 23 tape. He heard Bob Haldeman say, "Now, on the investigation, you know the Democratic break-in thing. We're back in the problem area because the FBI is not under control."

And then he heard Haldeman say, ". . . the way to handle this now is for us to have Walters [the White House man at the CIA] call Pat Gray [head of the FBI] and just say, Stay the hell out of this. This is, ah, business here we don't want you to go any further on it. That's not an unusual development and, ah, that would take care of it."

Then Nixon heard his own voice ask a series of questions about the traceable money and suggest the answers that Kenneth Dahlberg, who had been a finance chairman of Nixon's reelection campaign, and the Texas fund raisers would have to give as their cover stories. Haldeman said, "Well, if they will. But then we're relying on more and more people all the time. That's the problem. And they'll stop if we could take this other route."

And then Richard Nixon heard his own voice say, "Right, fine . . . How do you call him in? I mean you just—well, we protected Helms from one hell of a lot of things."

And on the next portion of tape, later on June 23, Nixon heard himself say, "Just say it's very bad to have this fellow Hunt, ah, he knows too damned much, if he was involved—you happen to know that. If it gets out that this is all involved, the Cuba thing, it would be a fiasco. It would make the CIA look bad and it is likely to blow the whole Bay of Pigs thing . . ."

On Monday at 2:00 P.M. Jaworski, Ben-Veniste, and St. Clair met with Judge Sirica in his chambers to discuss the reason for delaying the briefs in the subpoena case. Sirica reluctantly agreed, announcing to the press that the parties would seek an accommodation during the interim.

When the lawyers returned from court Ben-Veniste mentioned to me that St. Clair was shaking badly during the session in chambers. I thought this strange, since the man had always seemed the epitome of aplomb. I asked Jaworski, "Was St. Clair shaking at the conference?"

"Shaking like a dog crapping peach pits," Jaworski said.

On Tuesday St. Clair called and told Jaworski he was about to hold a press briefing to announce that the White House would turn over no further tapes or documents to the special prosecutor or the House Judiciary Committee. Four days before the new deadline, with no further negotiations, the compromise was dead.

Jaworski hung up the telephone. "That's it," he said. "Those tapes must be devastating."

There never has been a credible explanation of why neither Haig nor

St. Clair became suspicious at this point that perhaps Richard Nixon still had more to hide. Their story is that nobody except Nixon listened to the tapes. But if that is true, then the next question is, Why not? J. Fred Buzhardt had general access to the tapes. Haig and St. Clair already had seen their judgment and even their integrity questioned. For the sake of their own reputations, why didn't they seek to find out what was on those tapes? Because they wanted "deniability"? Because they were afraid of what they would hear and what they then knew they would have to do?

Richard Nixon deserved the best defense available, and his advisers owed him their loyalty as long as they remained his aides and he insisted on clinging to office. But the collusion or acquiescence of high-level government officials in the second cover-up—the last minute effort to abridge or hide the evidence—remains one of the shabbier chapters in Watergate history.

The signs of instability in Washington were never greater during Watergate than in early May, 1974. The House Judiciary Committee was still weeks away from formulating formal impeachment charges, yet the publication of the damning transcripts summoned forth a widespread demand for a palpable reaction from someone in government. It was not enough that the *Chicago Tribune,* William Randolph Hearst, the *Omaha World-Herald,* the *Cleveland Plain Dealer*—all the remaining conservative voices from the heartland who had not spoken earlier—now called for Richard Nixon's removal. The Congress was seized by a wave of sentiment that something must happen to resolve the situation quickly. But what? There could be no quick resolution unless Richard Nixon acted himself, tendering his resignation to the Secretary of State after providing for an orderly transfer of power. To Nixon and his inner circle this remained unthinkable. Nixon's game plan was to ride out the storm created by the release of the transcripts, hide the rest of the evidence, and take his chances with the House.

Rumors began on Capitol Hill and soon spread throughout the federal bureaucracy: Nixon was resigning. In a city of words the rumors created a conditioned response; the signs of Richard Nixon's imminent departure were everywhere. Yet there were no facts, and there could be none, to support that conclusion.

In this setting Leon Jaworski had to decide whether to argue in court, and thus before the nation through its press, that his subpoena should be honored because Richard Nixon was an alleged co-conspirator in obstruction of justice.

He convened a meeting of his top staff to discuss the question. Jim Neal, who had just returned to the staff for the Watergate trial, was shocked at the strong wording of the brief draft that Kreindler had prepared. "We need to ask ourselves if this is necessary," he said. "We are dealing with the President of the United States, and the President is not like any other respondent in court."

Peter Kreindler said, "We have a very good chance of losing this case if we neglect this argument. We may not get the tapes if we withhold the main reason we are asking for them. If we don't get the tapes, our evidence is weakened and the defense has an excellent chance of dismissal."

"Doesn't it come down to whether the judge accepts or rejects executive privilege as a defense?" Neal asked. He suggested that the co-conspirator argument could be implicit, leaving the judge to read between the lines.

Henry Ruth interrupted him. "Jim, you don't ask the judge to rule on an argument you didn't make." Lacovara noted that Sirica had previously addressed the executive privilege argument in Cox's case and the prosecutors had been less than thrilled with his restrictive decision.

"It's up to you to suggest an alternative, Jim," Hank Ruth said. "We met on this subject all last week. Leon came back on Saturday to join the conversation. We have been through all the arguments, and the result was the extraordinary offer we made Sunday. It was rejected. If you have a specific proposal, let's hear it."

Jaworski had been listening calmly throughout the debate. "It seems to me that it has to be done," he said. "There is no avoiding it without risking loss of the tapes. But we can make a representation to Judge Sirica that he might want to accept the briefs under seal and hear the arguments *in camera.*"

The next day Jaworski, Neal, Lacovara, and Ben-Veniste, along with St. Clair, went to see Sirica. The judge listened to the proposal and agreed to accept the briefs under seal, reserving judgment on what he would do about oral arguments. St. Clair urged him to hold them in secret. "This is an act of legal statesmanship on the part of Mr. Jaworski," St. Clair said.

The next day Jim Neal took the current draft of our brief and ripped it apart. "This is too strong," he said. "It reads like the final argument summing up the trial of Richard Nixon." So the authors—Kreindler, Goldman, and Frampton—went back to the drafting boards, removing whenever they could the hard language and legal hyperbole.

On Friday morning, May 10, the lawyers for Nixon, and the prosecutors met in Sirica's chambers along with the defense attorneys for the seven men already indicted in the Watergate cover-up. The defendants' lawyers had to be shown the government's brief; the subpoena it defended was directed toward the trial of their clients. The men sat in a wide semicircle reading the thirty-nine-page brief that was handed to them. The prosecutors watched as they flipped the first page and on page two saw this paragraph:

> On February 25, 1974, in the course of its consideration of the indictment in the instant case, the June 5, 1972, Grand Jury, by a vote of nineteen to zero, determined that there is probable cause to believe that Richard M. Nixon (among others) was a member of the conspiracy to defraud the United States and to obstruct justice charged in Count One of the instant indictment, and the Grand Jury authorized the Special Prosecutor to identify Richard M. Nixon (among others) as an unindicted co-conspirator in connection with subsequent legal proceedings in the case.

Mouths dropped open involuntarily, and brows wrinkled. The defense arguments to exclude the presidential tapes as evidence at the cover-up trial, and the emotional argument that the chief figure in the case had been spared, appeared to have been lost.

William Hundley, Mitchell's lawyer, argued for a continuance. Jaworski should have been more diligent in getting those tapes before the grand jury acted, not afterward, he said.* Judge Sirica was more interested in seeking their opinions on whether the oral arguments should be open to the public. If one of the defense attorneys had argued for an open session it would have been done. But all agreed to the prosecutor's motion for secrecy.

Only Judge Sirica was against the idea. He thought it would be viewed in the press and among the public as a suspicious proceeding. After all, the grand jury had spoken, and the accusations were now supposed to be

---

* On the way out of court Jaworski said to Neal, "You tell your friend the next time I hear him make an argument like that I'm going to kick him in the ass. I've known old Bill for years, but I like him, you know. But as long as I've known him I've never heard him make an argument except 'continuance, continuance.' "

public. The conduct of the case from now on should be under public scrutiny. Reluctantly he agreed to close the hearing.

At the end of the meeting the lawyers brushed past reporters waiting in the hallway, offering no comments. A month would pass before the accusation against Nixon would leak to the press.

But it was obvious something important was happening. Here were lawyers for all seven defendants along with St. Clair, Buzhardt, Jaworski, Neal, Lacovara, Kreindler, Ben-Veniste, and Volner.

The next day's *New York Times* registered the extent of Washington's anxiety. A black headline on page one said: "Nixon Loses More Backing; Rumors That He'll Resign Sweep Capital, Are Denied." The story quoted Ronald Ziegler, who had telephoned the *New York Times* bureau to say, "The city of Washington is full of rumors. All that have been presented to me today are false, and the one that heads the list is the one that says President Nixon intends to resign." But as the *Times* pointed out, each denial had given rise to new rumors. One was that Vice President Gerald Ford had emerged from a meeting with Nixon and was overheard telling his chauffeur to put his entire staff on "red alert." Ford, reached on his arrival in Buffalo where he was to make a speech, called the report nonsense. As John Barker commented, "He probably said, 'Did you pack my red shirt?' "

Within three weeks the prosecutors had won an order from the district court demanding the sixty-four additional tapes from the President. Bypassing the court of appeals, Jaworski asked the Supreme Court to take the case directly because of its urgent nature. A sense of inevitability grew. Charles Colson's lawyer began plea bargaining in earnest.

On Friday, May 31, Colson came to terms and the Supreme Court became the last branch of the government to engage the Watergate scandal, agreeing to accept Leon Jaworski's petition. Jaworski said nothing, just smashed a fist into his hand and smiled.

He had remained cool in the preceding weeks, during a dramatic meeting with Haig and St. Clair and tense conferences in Sirica's chambers. Exactly three weeks before, in fact, the tension in Washington was so high and Jaworski was so much in the thick of it, that some of us were beginning to wonder how long a sixty-nine-year-old man could hold up under such pressure. Carl Feldbaum had stopped Jaworski in the corridor that day and said, "How are you doing?" Jaworski gave him a gimlet-eyed look and said with a trace of amusement, "I'm sitting up and taking nourishment."

Now his cultivated sense of calm was giving way to a contagious feeling that big days were approaching. It had been a gamble to bypass the appellate court. If the Supreme Court had said no, it would have been a psychological defeat—a misjudgment that might have ruffled the feathers of the appellate judges and would certainly have led to speculation that the Supreme Court wanted no part of Jaworski's tape case—the type of ruling that leads to further speculation and further maneuvering. But Jaworski had won the gamble, and the pressure on his adversaries was now multiplied. The timetable now meant that the Supreme Court might order the tapes turned over just as the House of Representatives began debating articles of impeachment.

St. Clair had his back to the wall. He began to swing wildly. Before he arrived on the scene, the White House had announced that the President would of course obey a definitive decision of the Supreme Court. St. Clair deliberately withdrew from that position, saying only that it was a hypothetical question. This view was perceived as an attempt to plant in the minds of the justices the suggestion that Nixon might defy an order to hand over the tapes—a test of the court's power with which the justices would have to reckon.

St. Clair also raised anew the contention that Jaworski, a creature of the executive branch, had no right to sue the chief executive. Jaworski worried that the Supreme Court might seize upon this jurisdictional question to avoid the real issues in the case. He considered St. Clair's position a shabby betrayal of his, Jaworski's, agreement with Bork and Haig that he would have the right to sue the President.

Jaworski and other staff members had a low opinion of St. Clair's sense of propriety. It sunk further on July 1 when the White House filed its reply brief. In a footnote on page 26 the brief seemed to say that twenty of the sixty-four tapes under subpoena were not at issue before the court because they had been made public in transcript form. Immediately Jaworski wrote to the White House and asked if that meant the tapes would be turned over.

St. Clair, in response, was careful not to offer the tapes. He proposed that a conference be held with Judge Sirica "to verify the accuracy of the public transcripts." Jaworski wrote back noting that it was "highly questionable whether transcripts would be admissible as evidence," and asked that St. Clair so inform the Supreme Court before oral arguments were held.

On Friday, July 5, St. Clair telephoned Jaworski from Boston, where he was working on his oral argument. He wanted to assure Jaworski "that I am not trying to cheat you." He repeated the remark three times during a short conversation, and each time it was greeted with silence on Jaworski's end of the line. Finally St. Clair said, "You know it is up to the President whether you will get tape as well as the transcripts."

"Well, fine then. I'll see you at ten o'clock on Monday morning," Jaworski said.

Spectators began to gather in front of the Supreme Court on Saturday morning, forty-eight hours in advance. The guards told them they would not be allowed to form a line until Sunday at midnight, so the early arrivals began to gather across the street, where they were allowed to stretch out on the lawn of the Capitol. By Sunday evening the crowd had grown to more than a hundred and had formed itself into a committee, issuing its own tickets and arranging to have the guards across the street recognize those pass holders at midnight Sunday. There were to be seats for 136 members of the public, plus another twenty-seven seats whose occupants would be changed every five minutes. At midnight the people filed quietly across the street to begin a nine-hour wait on the stone plaza under the etched inscription, "Equal Justice Under Law."

Lacovara and Kreindler had been urging Jaworski to wear a morning suit, and he had declined. The two young lawyers thought this a serious mistake, since by long tradition the government counsel always appeared before the justices in morning suit. Jaworski was adamant. Finally he said, "If you keep it up, I'll show up in cowboy boots and jeans."

"We'll never mention it again," said Lacovara.

Jaworski was serene before going to court. "Our brief is one of the strongest I've ever seen," he said. "We have by far the best of the argument, if we can get by the jurisdictional question." He and Lacovara were dressed in very expensive-looking, nicely tailored dark blue suits as they left the office. Jaworski had a large black notebook containing his oral argument. The rest of us shook their hands as if they were departing on a long voyage, and tried not to show our nervousness.

The prosecutors arrived shortly before 10:00 A.M. and began the long walk across the plaza and up the white marble stairs of that massive cathedral to the Constitution. There were still hundreds of people in a quiet and orderly line under the muggy Washington sky, and they began to applaud, a noise that undulated across the plaza like the sound of a small boy running a stick along a distant picket fence. Then a lone voice was raised in a simple cheer.

"Go, U.S.," the voice said.

Inside it soon became clear that the highly charged atmosphere of Washington extended to the men on this bench as well. The justices would frequently interrupt with questions. Justice Felix Frankfurter had once said the court saw itself, not as "a dozing audience for the reading of soliloquies, but as a questioning body, utilizing oral argument as a means for exposing the difficulties of a case with a view to meeting them." That would certainly be true this day.

Jaworski tried to bring home the point of his special charter and the fact that he was, unlike an ordinary U.S. Attorney or ordinary prosecutor, "quasi-independent." The justices seemed uninterested in finding a jurisdictional quarrel in this case.

The rest of Jaworski's time would be spent answering questions, jumping from executive privilege to separation of powers. When he raised Nixon's countersuit to expunge Nixon's name from the grand jury's list of co-conspirators, Justice Byron White said rather crisply, "I thought we had put that case aside. I just don't understand what the relevance of that is to this case." There followed an exchange on the issue among the justices, and Jaworski's time was up.

St. Clair launched immediately into what would be his main point, that the impeachment inquiry under way across the street in the Capitol made this a political question and non-justiciable, and that the tapes were protected by executive privilege.

Justice Thurgood Marshall referred to the footnote in which St. Clair stated twenty of the tapes were not at issue because their contents was now public—the footnote that had caused the confidential exchanges between St. Clair and Jaworski. Marshall asked if the White House was willing to release the twenty tapes as well as the transcripts. St. Clair gave the judge a different answer than he had offered Jaworski three days before: "As soon as the judge approves some method of validating the accuracy of these tapes, they can have the tapes. But you have to understand, the tape is part of a reel. A reel may cover a dozen conversations. So there is a mechanical problem of trying to validate or be sure that this is correct. But it is only a mechanical problem. Once that is solved, subject to the approval of the judge below, they have the availability of that."

Justice Lewis Powell asked, "Mr. St. Clair, what public interest is there in preserving secrecy with respect to a criminal conspiracy?"

"The answer, sir, is that a criminal conspiracy is criminal only after it's proven to be criminal," St. Clair responded. He smiled. Justice Powell did not.

Lacovara used the government's final thirty minutes for rebuttal. He began by quickly clearing up the several technical points raised but not answered to the court's satisfaction. He knew that judges often took away impressions from oral arguments which could not be overcome during their conference discussions. He tried now to clear away the small stumbling blocks that might hurt the prosecutor's case.

He discussed the specific manner in which the case had gotten to the Supreme Court (Justices Harry Blackmun and Potter Stewart both raised suggestions of a flaw in the procedure); whether Judge Sirica was properly represented before the Supreme Court (Stewart had raised the point. Lacovara informed him of a letter on file from Sirica designating the special prosecutor his counsel); the non-Constitutional issue which the court must decide first (whether the subpoena was relevant to the trial of the men indicted in the Watergate cover-up).

One of the justices raised St. Clair's point, that the prosecutor didn't really know whether the subpoenaed items were relevant.

> LACOVARA: Oh, well, that obviously we don't think is a proper legal standard . . . we go back to Chief Justice Marshall's opinion in the *Burr* case, where exactly the same suggestion was made by the United States Attorney . . . and Chief Justice Marshall replied, with his eloquent common sense, "Of course not, because he hasn't seen the letter yet. But he's made a sufficient averment that it does contain something material, that at least it should be brought into court."
>
> Now, we, as I say, have gone much further than Colonel Burr did.

Then the justices launched Lacovara into a discussion of two court cases that dealt with this "relevance" issue, *U.S.* v. *Iozia* and *Bowman Dairy Co.* v. *U.S.* When he was finished, he raised a question he sensed was still bothering many of these men: What was the relevance of the grand jury's finding that the President was a co-conspirator?

He was immediately deluged with questions, and it became clear that this issue had the potential of dividing the court. Lacovara mentioned the charge that the prosecutors might have had the President so named in order to prejudice Nixon's rights and that this was a highly unusual procedure.

Justice Powell asked whether this action by the grand jury did not set a dangerous precedent.

> LACOVARA: . . . our democratic system is based on several fundamental propositions, one of which is that Grand Juries usually are not malicious. Even prosecutors cannot be assumed to be malicious. We also assume, as this court regularly holds in first amendment cases dealing with public officials, that we have a resilient society where people can be trusted to sort out truth from falsehoods. We have a robust debate.
>
> I submit to you, sir, that just as in this case a Grand Jury would not lightly accuse the President of a crime, so, too, the fear that, perhaps without basis, some Grand Jury somewhere might maliciously accuse a President of a crime is not necessarily a reason for saying that a Grand Jury has no power to do that. I think the system may be vibrant enough to deal with that. And I think the inherent dignity of the presidential office on any incumbent provides him with a notable check against being defeated, or as my colleague says, impeached by the action of a Grand Jury. This is perhaps the most notorious event, notorious case, in recent times. When the Grand Jury's action was disclosed, I venture to say that although it was a difficult time for all concerned, including the prosecutors as well as other counsel and the country—the President has not been displaced from office, he still is President, he still functions in accordance with his constitutional powers.

Lacovara's argument was brilliantly constructed and smoothly executed. He and Kreindler left the courtroom, took off their best suits, and departed with their families for a week's vacation on the beach in Delaware.

Two weeks went by. Jaworski sunk into the only real depression that overtook him during his tenure as special prosecutor. He had been tense about the Supreme Court case, impatient for a decision. In the humid heat of Washington summer, his hotel suite and the constrictions of his life seemed especially harsh. He was angry with James St. Clair and what he considered sharp practices on the part of men who had given him their word. (He said to Haig at one point, "Al, this isn't what we agreed upon," when his right to sue the President was challenged. Haig protested that it was a valid legal point. "You're just parroting St. Clair," Jaworski said. "I'm going to get your Jesuit brother after you.") Most of all, he was homesick.

The despondence was triggered by what he saw as press criticism that his oral argument had not been perfect. I told him it was nothing more than a kind of sportswriting, the writers pretending they could have played the game better. But the stories hurt him very much, and for the first time he talked of resigning. The staff rallied around him, sometimes counseling, sometimes cajoling. For several days he received an inordinate amount of attention. Jill Volner stopped by to share a long cup of coffee with him. Tom McBride took an hour to tell of a recent vacation and to talk, casually, about his cases. Carl Feldbaum dropped by twice a day with the latest batch of letters and telegrams supporting Jaworski. It must have been a transparent effort to this canny man, but he was no less touched by it for its lack of subtlety.

In early July Richard Nixon returned from his Mideast tour and the Moscow summit meeting that followed, to find a sense of further deterioration in Washington. Both trips had been, by any normal measure, overwhelming successes, but they had done him no good. Within days of his arrival he witnessed the conviction of John Ehrlichman. Colson had toppled just before he left. The Senate Watergate committee's final report was published, containing new evidence of Bebe Rebozo's role as a presidential money man misdirecting campaign funds to Nixon's personal use. The House Judiciary Committee published the first eight volumes of its encyclopedic Watergate evidence, and described in the four thousand pages were fresh examples of the President's relentless malfeasance.

On July 11 Nixon's lawyers had been called by Judge Sirica (at the urging of Jaworski) to state whether they would turn over the twenty tapes, as St. Clair had assured Justice Marshall they would. The lawyers balked and Sirica, now disgusted, sent the transcript of the proceeding to the Supreme Court to inform the justices, as they wrote their decision, that the President's brief and St. Clair's oral argument had misrepresented the President's intentions.

On July 19 John Doar rose before the House Judiciary Committee and ended his role as neutral purveyor of evidence. Acting like a prosecutor, he laid before the committee a theory of prosecution, a broad obstruction of justice case that relied on no single date or meeting but tied together both the President's actions and his failure to act in specific situations from June of 1972 through the spring of 1973. Doar recommended that articles of impeachment be drawn. As the case was laid out in more detail, Republicans started to defect. White House lobbyist Bill Timmons noticed a steady erosion in support among the members of the House.

On Wednesday morning, July 24, 1974, a twisting line of people formed once again before the door of the Supreme Court, down the marble steps, and out of sight around the corner. It was fourteen months less one day from the time Archibald Cox took the oath of office as special prosecutor. It was judgment day for Richard Nixon. There were just sixteen days left of his Presidency.

On the day of oral arguments the eight justices of the Supreme Court had conferred and voted to order Richard Nixon to turn over the sixty-four tapes subpoenaed by Leon Jaworski. Chief Justice Warren Burger then wrote an opinion which displeased his seven colleagues for the shallowness of its legal analysis as well as its lack of candor toward the President's position. Justices Stewart and White set about rewriting large portions of it. When they presented their version to Burger, he went to his close friend Justice Blackmun for support. Blackmun sided with the others. The final opinion was a hybrid of several justices' work including Blackmun, who rewrote Burger's statement of facts. To save face, Burger would read the opinion from the bench as if it were his own.

James St. Clair was not present when the court convened at 11:00 A.M. He was in San Clemente making strategy when, on the previous afternoon, the court had announced it would sit the next morning to deliver an opinion. Since an important Detroit busing case was also pending, lingering from the court's regular term, it was not certain which case the court would announce. St. Clair chose not to fly back for what he must have known would be a defeat. Three young lawyers sat at counsel table in his place.

The justices appeared on the marshal's cue, and they looked rather more relaxed. The Chief Justice began solemnly by noting the death of Earl Warren, which had occurred several days earlier. Then Burger launched into the reading of the opinion. He brushed aside the jurisdictional questions. "The mere assertion of a claim of 'intra-branch dispute,' without more, has never operated to defeat federal jurisdiction," he said. "The courts must look behind the names that symbolize the parties. . . ." In this case it was clear that the special prosecutor's authority "is to represent the United States as a sovereign, and it includes express authority to contest any privilege asserted by the Executive Branch."

He affirmed the relevance of the subpoenaed material to the Mitchell trial and the sufficiency of the prosecutor's showing in that regard, noting that the prosecutor had used White House logs and the testimony of some participants to make his showing.

On the question of the separation of powers and the court's power to adjudicate questions of executive privilege, Burger reached back, as Jaworski and Lacovara had suggested, to the first great case, *Marbury* v. *Madison,* quoting, "It is emphatically the province and the duty of the judicial department to say what the law is."

Finally, reaching the question of privilege, Burger affirmed what had been until now only a presumed principle of American law: "Neither the doctrine of separation of powers nor the need for confidentiality . . . can sustain an absolute, unqualified Presidential privilege from judicial process under all circumstances . . . the legitimate needs of the judicial process may outweigh Presidential privilege . . ." Only recently, Burger noted, the court had restated the ancient proposition that the public "has a right to every man's evidence."

Every question was raised and answered in the prosecutor's favor. St. Clair's tactic had backfired. Because of the pressure on them to write a "definitive" opinion and to support it unanimously so that Richard Nixon would be less inclined to flout it, the court had come down hard on Jaworski's side of every issue—jurisdiction, confidentiality, executive privilege, separation of powers. Later scholars would find criticism with this opinion. It was overly broad, they would say; it invoked John Marshall's sweeping dicta without distinction or reservation; it failed to mention the specific evidence of criminality in this case which might have helped draw a narrower ruling; it accepted executive privilege without adequately discussing its justification. The opinion, many predicted, would prove unfortunate as precedent. Some argued that in later years it would be seen as a mistake to have cut short the impeachment inquiry.

But none argued it now, for the reality was that Richard Nixon, despite the distintegration of his moral authority and of his government, was going to hang on until some strong force acted decisively. The decision of the court would be welcomed in Washington and across the land.

Leon Jaworski was surrounded by well-wishers and members of the press as he made his way from the courtroom. Word had preceded him to the crowd on the plaza, as newsmen broke through to tell the waiting television crews, "Eight to nothing! Eight to nothing!"

Jaworski emerged and the crowd applauded, the handclapping echoing quietly across the nation over television. How did he feel? "I feel right good over it," he said, and he smiled. "If I had to write it myself, I couldn't have written it any better."

Nobody rushed to inform Richard Nixon that his Supreme Court case had been lost by unanimous vote. It was 8:45 A.M. in California—11:45 A.M. Washington time—when Alexander Haig broke the news to the man who waited alone in his office across the parking lot from his lovely villa in San Clemente.

CHAPTER

16

DEPARTURES

"Colonel, good-bye. You're a good man."

Richard Nixon thrashed about in San Clemente, seeking a way out. It took the White House eight hours to respond to the Supreme Court decision. The President considered defying the high court, and some of his aides considered having Nixon destroy the evidence and resign, claiming that he was doing so to protect the integrity of presidential files.*

It wasn't possible. The game was up, although it took Nixon, Haig, St. Clair, and Buzhardt a day of agony before they were ready to admit it.

Jaworski spent little time on deciding his next step. He left the Supreme Court and had a leisurely lunch at the Lawyers Club with author Theodore H. White, who was working on his book *Breach of Faith*. The special prosecutor reminisced about his youth and about his present mission, White was to write, "in phrases which on any other day and occasion would have sounded trite, but now carried meaning." The famous author was impressed as well by Jaworski's sense of detachment. He wrote,

* The story has been recounted by John Osborne in *The New Republic* of August 24, 1974, and in brilliant detail in Woodward and Bernstein's *The Final Days*.

"Unless he was dissembling, it seemed to this reporter that Jaworski had no inkling, no fore-echo, of what it was that Richard Nixon had been concealing, what the subpoenaed tapes would soon reveal."

As we walked back to the office, Jaworski said, "All right, now it's time to strike." He knew, as he had observed when the President rejected his compromise offer, that the contents of one or more of the sixteen tapes Nixon audited in May would be devastating. He also knew that St. Clair would stall as long as he could before turning them over to the special prosecutor. So that afternoon, while Nixon and his aides agonized over how to react, Jaworski's staff prepared legal motions to be presented in the morning to Judge Sirica, showing why there need be no further delay in handing the tapes to the judge.

James St. Clair appeared on television at seven that evening to say he had been instructed by the President to comply with the court order. As if to assure Jaworski that he had not misjudged his adversary, St. Clair added, "The time-consuming process of reviewing the tapes . . . will begin forthwith." In answer to reporters' questions St. Clair said it could take a month to comply with the court order.

Sirica called a hearing for Friday, July 26, allowing St. Clair a day to fly back from San Clemente. The President's attorney arrived in the courtroom exhausted. He had been informed by Buzhardt two days earlier that one of the June 23, 1972, tapes in which Nixon and Haldeman discussed blocking a Watergate investigation would be considered extremely damaging to the President. "St. Clair looks as if he is watching his life pass before him," commented Lesley Oelsner of *The New York Times*.

Jaworski rose and made his case. The White House record of compliance with prosecution requests for evidence was sad and disappointing, and he would be happy to furnish the court the exchanges of letters showing White House intransigence. When the present case was still in litigation, he had asked St. Clair please to begin his analysis of the tapes in the eventuality the court directed the President to turn them over.

St. Clair had rejected that request, Jaworski said, but there was no reason to delay now. Twenty of the tapes were of conversations included in the published White House transcripts, and they obviously had been reviewed already. There was another group of thirteen that Jaworski considered crucial. All but one of them had been part of a compromise offered to the White House on Sunday, May 5. "The President of the United States listened to a number of these tapes on that Monday and Tuesday. I can't say he listened to all of them, but I think it is true that he did," Jaworski said.

St. Clair objected. The record was also sad from the President's point of view, he said, because of the way material he turned over to the special prosecutor seemed to end up in the newspapers. "The President feels quite strongly that he should know what he is turning over." St. Clair could not promise all of the tapes "in x number of days," because the President wanted to listen to those he hadn't heard, because of the mechanical problems involved, and because an index of what the President considered privileged had to be written.

Sirica reminded St. Clair that two months earlier, on May 20, he had ordered the tapes produced along with the indexes. Had St. Clair read the Supreme Court decision? Had he noted the vote? Yes, St. Clair repeated. What was it, the judge persisted, toying with the lawyer. "Eight to zero," St. Clair said. Wouldn't St. Clair say that the court had backed up Sirica's order of May 20? Smiling in embarrassment, St. Clair said he would certainly say that was so.

The judge told St. Clair to retire to the jury room along with the special prosecutor and work out a timetable. "If you are unable to, I will set the time limits myself," he said.

The discussion in the jury room was low-key. St. Clair said that he didn't care if the prosecutors obtained all the sixty-four tapes that day, "but it's not realistic to expect the President to turn them over that fast." He agreed to release the first twenty by Tuesday, and to furnish as many as possible of the next thirteen within a week. They returned to the courtroom.

With the canniness he had shown in the past, Sirica asked St. Clair if he had not himself listened to these tapes in preparation for defending the President before the House impeachment committee. St. Clair repeated what he had now said publicly several times, that he did not himself listen to tapes and did not know their content.

Sirica calmly directed the lawyer to begin listening to tapes. This act would formally place St. Clair under obligation to correct the record of his past representations. He objected that he was personally "a poor listener" and that he preferred to have assistants do this work so that he was free to pursue other obligations. Sirica insisted, saying that the court wanted the President's chief lawyer to know what the tapes contained when he argued further motions or consulted with the court. Reluctantly St. Clair agreed. "All right, now I think we're getting somewhere," Sirica said, and he adjourned court.

Exactly two weeks later, Richard Nixon was flying on *Air Force One* to California as a civilian. Judge Sirica's insistence that James St. Clair become intimate with the White House tapes quickened the process that culminated in a presidential resignation.

There were other factors as well. The day after the court session, the House Judiciary Committee voted for impeachment of the President on grounds of obstruction of justice in the Watergate case. The second and third articles of impeachment were voted early the next week. The White House staff knew the full House was ready to send Nixon to trial before the Senate.

But what set the timetable for the President's resignation was a series of decisions by St. Clair, Haig, and Buzhardt that related to their own growing jeopardy. The lawyers focused quickly on the June 23 tape, which showed Nixon's awareness of the cover-up five days after the Watergate burglary. To many this tape was less specifically criminal than some others, and only slightly more suspicious than the tape of June 20, which had an eighteen-minute erasure. But the June 23 tape contradicted a defense that Buzhardt and Leonard Garment had written and released on May 22, 1973, as well as the version of events St. Clair had given the House impeachment inquiry at the end of June, 1974.

Buzhardt, Garment and later St. Clair had asserted constantly that the President first learned of the Watergate cover-up in March of 1973, and that his orders to the CIA immediately after the Watergate break-in had been motivated by concerns for national security alone.

Now they were to be confronted publicly with the President's voice on tape, hearing and responding to the details of the break-in, and the early success of the FBI in tracing it as a political operation funded by the Committee to Re-elect the President. There was Haldeman's voice rattling off the names of those involved, and explaining that some of the investigators and much of the press thought the break-in was some kind of a Cuban operation. Nixon could be heard readily agreeing that the whole affair had to be covered up, and instructing Haldeman to have the CIA tell the FBI, "Don't go any further into this case period!" The only discussion of national security was, transparently, a discussion of how it could be used to justify a cover-up motivated by political jeopardy.

Thus it was not Nixon's position that was made untenable by this tape. The President's position was already untenable, as the votes of a federal grand jury and the House Judiciary Committee showed. But now the rationale of ignorance was no longer available to James St. Clair, Alexander Haig and J. Fred Buzhardt. They had no further room to maneuver.

The excellent accounts of this period which appear in *The Final Days,* in Theodore White's book, and in John Osborne's reporting indicate that the President first raised the "problem" of the June 23 tape himself, apparently with the idea that the lawyers would need to construct an explanation based on that old reliable, national security. Buzhardt, the most vulnerable of Nixon's remaining aides because of his long and checkered career as Nixon's Watergate defender, immediately suggested that this was the "smoking gun" and that "school was out." In fact there were many other tapes just as incriminating to the President, some of them already published. At this point Nixon was holding onto office almost totally through the devices of Haig, Buzhardt, and St. Clair. The smoking gun was anything those three said it was.

St. Clair refused to listen to the tape until four days after Sirica had served notice on him that he would be responsible for knowing its contents. By then the tape was due in court in three days. Woodward and Bernstein report that St. Clair heard the tape twice without seeing in it the importance that Buzhardt had seen. It was only when Buzhardt suggested that St. Clair listen to the tape as a direct contradiction of St. Clair's own statements before the Judiciary Committee that St. Clair began to see the "smoking gun" quality of this piece of evidence. The next day—Wednesday, July 31—Haig, Buzhardt, and St. Clair held their first planning session to bring about the resignation of Richard Nixon.

The June 23 tape changed the equation for those around Richard Nixon. The President would soon be out of office, his aides knew. His other lieutenants would soon be on trial for obstruction of justice. The Supreme Court had ruled that not even the President, much less his appointed staff, could operate above the law. It was too late for another tape to be lost or accidentally erased, or for another subpoena to be misunderstood. Shortly after James St. Clair put on earphones and listened to the tape that Fred Buzhardt claims to have heard for the first time the previous week, the charade was over.

Five days later—Monday August 5—Alexander Haig alerted the leaders of the government and "Operation Resignation" was under way. Haig called Jaworski in Texas and suggested that in the next few days Jaworski should return to Washington. He explained that the June 23 tape did indeed show the President's early knowledge of the cover-up and his effort to use the CIA to stop the investigation. The tape would be released to the public later that day. Haig did not predict a presidential resignation but he made it clear that he expected the situation to come to a quick resolution. St. Clair was on the line as well, and Jaworski, when he called his office to inform aides of the event, said that St. Clair had sounded uncharacteristically assertive, declaring he had threatened to resign if the President did not release the tape.

There seemed little for Jaworski or anybody in the prosecutor's office to do until the situation developed further. He decided to stay in Texas one more day.

By Tuesday morning, after the evening news shows had announced the release of the crucial tape and the morning newspapers had carried all the damning words on it—along with the reactions of the President's die-hard supporters—official Washington began to think about the orderly transfer of government.

By Wednesday morning a principal topic of discussion was immunity. Republican Senate leaders Robert Griffin and John Tower announced that they favored "absolution from criminal prosecution" for the President and might draft immunity legislation. There were grave Constitutional doubts whether Congress could perform this normal function of the executive branch. Asked about immunity Attorney General Saxbe said the question was in the special prosecutor's hands. Jaworski was on an airplane, en route to Washington.

Leon Jaworski had said many times that Richard Nixon would never seek immunity, was too proud to bargain away his Presidency to avoid his day in the defendant's dock. But as he returned to Washington, Jaworski knew he must be ready for the inevitable role he would play in bringing about an orderly succession.

He arrived at the Jefferson Hotel in the late afternoon, called his office, declined an invitation to meet with members of his staff. He was tired, he said, would stay at his hotel and see his aides in the morning.

The eleven members of the Judiciary Committee who had supported Nixon now sought his removal. The joint leadership of Congress spoke. Though only a few favored a Senate trial, all made it clear that enough votes existed for dismissal from office. Nixon's own staff was preparing the way.

The President's Monday statement, written with the help of St. Clair, asserted that Nixon had not informed "my staff or my counsel" of the tape's contents when he reviewed it in May, an omission, the statement said, that Nixon deeply regretted.

Hank Ruth had left on vacation a few days earlier. Jaworski called Jim Vorenberg, who was running the office in Ruth's absence, and suggested that Vorenberg come to the Jefferson at 9:30 A.M. Thursday for breakfast, bringing Jim Neal and Phil Lacovara along. Jaworski was now prepared for an expected call from the White House.

The three lawyers met briefly at the prosecutor's office in the morning, then continued their conversation as they walked the few blocks to the Jefferson. Crowds of newsmen clustered at the White House and on Capitol Hill, but the streets of Washington were sleepy. The Jefferson, only a few blocks from the White House, seemed cool and quiet.

The three lawyers agreed that Jaworski ought to decline to negotiate with Richard Nixon or his agents. They reasoned that a plea bargain with a sitting President was too great a matter to be handled alone by a special prosecutor. Senator Edward Brooke of Massachusetts had filed a sense of Congress resolution calling for immunity for Nixon. Jaworski should, if asked, say that he would be guided by such expressions of opinion but that he could make no commitments. They felt Jaworski should do nothing to preempt the legislative branch, which was then prepared to vote on impeachment.

"When we started discussing it with Leon," one of the participants recalled, "we took the position that there should be no participation of any kind in a deal. Leon listened, seeming noncommittal, but we sensed that he disagreed with us. Certainly he didn't say or do anything to indicate he acquiesced in the judgment. We thought, in fact, that he was leaning the other way. Then we mentioned the middle ground, waiting on the advice of Congress. We mentioned the Brooke resolution, and he was interested in that and asked questions about it."

Jaworski called the White House, then informed the three men that Haig was sending a car for him and the two men would meet at Haig's house on Edmunds Street in suburban Wesley Heights, twenty minutes from downtown Washington. Haig said that reporters were swarming around the White House and Jaworski's presence there would cause hysteria. The Jefferson seemed no better, since Haig would be seen entering. The meeting was set for 11:30 A.M.

A few hours later Jaworski called the prosecutor's office and told the three lawyers to come back to his hotel room. Haig had informed him that Nixon would announce his resignation that evening on television and would leave office at noon Friday. Then he would fly directly to California. Ford would be sworn in as President while Nixon was airborne. Haig was worried about Nixon's emotional and physical health and about how the Nixon family was taking events. Nixon would refuse to testify at the Watergate cover-up trial if called, and would take the Fifth Amendment. Haldeman and Ehrlichman had both "made passes" at the White House in hopes of getting pardoned but had been rebuffed by Haig. Jaworski said that Haig had felt he owed it to the special prosecutor to let him know what was about to transpire; that was the sole purpose of the meeting. There had been no request for any consideration, Jaworski said. Jaworski had begun the meeting, he said, by telling Haig, "Al, I think we should agree at the outset that there will be no understandings from this meeting." Haig had said that was absolutely the way he wanted it too.

"Come on, Leon," Vorenberg said. He was smiling, and the remark was passed off as jocular. But according to some of those present, it was clear that Vorenberg was not really kidding, that he was expressing doubt that the meeting had been that simple. Jim Neal later said, "Well, if Leon did make a deal, good for him! It helped the country."

When John Barker heard this report from Vorenberg, he proposed that a statement be drafted for release after the President's resignation was announced, confirming that no deal had been asked for or offered. Vorenberg agreed, drafted the statement, and read it to Jaworski over the telephone. He approved its release.

That night Barker told the press:

There has been no agreement or understanding of any sort between the

President or his representatives and the Special Prosecutor relating in any way to the President's resignation.

The Special Prosecutor's Office was not asked for any such agreement or understanding and offered none. Although I was informed of the President's decision this afternoon, my office did not participate in any way in the President's decision to resign.

While the statement was accepted by the press and the public, there were many staff members who did not believe that Alexander Haig, as an act of courtesy, would take two hours out of such a climactic day to go to his suburban home simply to inform Leon Jaworski of events about to transpire.

There was no evidence to the contrary, but the subsequent handling of Nixon's pardon by President Ford kept speculation alive within the office. The most popular theory was that Haig had already received implicit assurances from Ford that Nixon would be pardoned after a decent interval. Ford himself has testified that Haig had met with him on Thursday, August 1 (a week before Haig's meeting with Jaworski) and told him to be prepared to assume the Presidency, and that the subject of a pardon was raised but not resolved at that meeting. As Ford related the conversation before a House Judiciary subcommittee, Haig indicated that various options were being discussed, three of which included a pardon— Nixon pardoning all the Watergate defendants and himself, then resigning; Nixon pardoning only himself and then resigning; Nixon resigning and being pardoned after the fact by Ford.

It was not too difficult to believe that Haig came away from that meeting knowing that Gerald Ford understood what was expected of him and that he would comply at the proper time. If that was the case, Haig would need some reassurance from Jaworski that there would be no precipitous action immediately after a resignation, especially if the family, and Nixon himself, were worried about the legal consequences of surrendering the Presidency.

Some members of the prosecutor's staff assumed that Haig communicated to Jaworski the anxieties of the President or his family and indicated that he, Haig, needed time to work out the problem. Jaworski might then have indicated that he wanted no understandings of any kind to come from this meeting, but he could have spelled out his own sincere belief that it would be months or years, if ever, before Nixon could get a fair trial. He could also have told Haig quite confidently that the way in which the prosecutor's office worked was such that it would take months before any decision could be readied on the prosecution of Richard Nixon.

Partly from his southern manner and partly from his horse-trading instincts, Leon Jaworski is very good at being agreeable without agreeing to anything. Haig had often told White House aides that Jaworski was completely sympathetic to the President's problems but was unable to control the staff he had inherited from Cox.

In his memoir, published in 1976, Jaworski lent credence to the theory that he may have led Haig into thinking he was sympathetic. He discloses there for the first time that at the August 8 meeting Haig informed him that Nixon planned to take his tapes and papers to San Clemente but that no "hanky panky" was involved—the prosecutors would still have access to them. In fact, when the Ford White House tried to move some of the papers to San Clemente a week after the resignation, the special prosecutor's office vociferously objected. Ford's staff had been assured by Buzhardt that Jaworski approved the move, but the prosecutor's aides denied any consent and threatened court action if documents were taken away. Buzhardt was pushed out of his office shortly afterward, in good part because Ford's aides were convinced he had misrepresented a situation and embarrassed the new President.

Columnist Joseph Kraft raised another question stemming from the Haig-Jaworski meeting on August 8. Kraft reported that the first draft of Nixon's memoirs claimed that when Haig returned from the meeting that day he informed the departing President that Nixon "had nothing to fear from the special prosecutor." Kraft concluded that this could have been simply Haig's deduction, "but another interpretation is open. It is that Haig improperly raised the issue of letting Nixon off, and that Jaworski gave him assurances."

This speculation was the natural consequence of a private meeting between Haig and Jaworski, of which there is no public record. The suspicions were not shared by the press and the public for the most part. But the degree to which doubt prevailed within the prosecutor's office can be seen by those who read carefully the Watergate Special Prosecution Force report of October, 1975. On page 128 the recounting of the Haig episode includes the sentence, "Jaworski later told members of his staff . . . that no promises or understandings of any kind had been requested or offered." Nowhere else in the report is any meeting in which the special prosecutor was a party reported with the qualification that this was what the special prosecutor *said* happened at the meeting, as opposed to a flat statement of what transpired.

Jaworski and Haig deny that any agreement, spoken or unspoken, was made; and there are indications that Richard Nixon thought he was in jeopardy, that Haig had not reassured him. On the night he resigned, Nixon, unable to sleep, called a number of his aides. To several of them he expressed fears that he would be pursued by the prosecutors. To at least one he said, "Some of the best political writing is done from jail." Three weeks later Nixon made a brief "Thank you" telephone call to Representative Dan Kuykendall of Tennessee. When Kuykendall asked how Nixon was getting along, the former President said, "We've got problems with that fellow, uh, uh . . ." Kuykendall said, "Jaworski?" and Nixon said, "Yes." Then he added, "Do you think people want to pick the carcass?"

Again, Joseph Kraft has told me that in the draft of his memoirs, Nixon discloses that while Haig flatly stated the resigned President was in no jeopardy from the special prosecutor, Nixon did not believe him because of contrary advice he purportedly received from Buzhardt. According to Kraft's report, Buzhardt reminded Nixon that Jaworski would be "going back to Texas to make money" and would leave the "zealots" of the prosecutor's office behind to do what they would with Nixon.

After Nixon's departure Leon Jaworski called together his senior staff for a general discussion of his own future. He was anxious to get back to Texas, he said, and he had set himself an informal deadline of the end of October. He would have been in office a full year come November 5, and he had never expected to be away that long. Those at the meeting got the sense that despite his wealth, Jaworski was finding the loss of more than $200,000 a year in income and the cost of living in Washington a financial strain. He would not resign, he said, until "the big decision" was made. But departure was on his mind.

The staff quickly decided that Jaworski must move to prosecute Nixon. There were no dissenters, and, as far as I could tell, only two people besides myself had any serious doubts. One was Jim Neal, who basically agreed with my argument that a prosecution would tear apart the country, though he did not suggest that this was a valid legal analysis. The other doubter was Leon Jaworski.

On the day of the resignation Kreindler and Feldbaum had listed the factors to be considered in deciding whether to prosecute Nixon. The presumption must be that Nixon was subject to the rule of law. The evidence was sufficient to indict, but there were arguments against indictment: His resignation was punishment enough; the impeachment inquiry and the vote of the House Judiciary Committee (now on the record as unanimous on the first article of impeachment) established the record of his guilt; prosecution would aggravate the political divisions in the country, and it was time for conciliation, not recrimination; a fair trial would be difficult because of the intense publicity.

Then there were the factors in support of indictment: Equal justice required that Nixon be prosecuted for the same offenses as his aides, who acted upon his orders and in what they conceived to be his interest; the country would be further divided if there was no final disposition, and the former President could argue, as he had, that he had left office simply because he had lost his political base; Article I, Section 3, clause 7 of the Constitution specifically provided for prosecution after impeachment; it was not sufficient retribution for crimes simply to surrender one's office; the courts would properly judge as to whether and when a fair trial could be held despite the publicity.

Finally, one had to consider the following points favoring delay of the decision: The prosecutors, the Congress, and the public had not had time to absorb and consider the cataclysmic events that had transpired during the week just ending; the sixty-four tapes had not yet been monitored, and their evidence must inform the decision; there might be events in the coming days—in Congress or at the Mitchell trial, or events involving Nixon himself—which would affect the decision.

Jaworski made it clear that his inclination was to wait a substantial period—weeks, if not months—before deciding whether to prosecute. Yet he wanted to be gone by November. So the staff had time to fret over the burden. One of the more thoughtful of a second wave of memos was written by Richard Davis. He rehearsed the arguments, agreeing that the decision should be based on the law and not the country's instant sentiments.

A prosecutor must consider the consequences of proceeding, Davis said.

The available examples were many. Assuming that the evidence was sufficient, a prosecutor could properly decide not to prosecute the Chicago Seven, or to re-try Doctor Spock, or not to pursue an investigation of the resigned Abe Fortas, on the basis that it did not serve the public good to pursue these cases to their ultimate possible conclusions. The same might be true with rioting prisoners or violent protestors. It was a similar national interest, perceived by the attorney general, that caused him to accept an extremely lenient punishment for Spiro Agnew, thus avoiding bitter and protracted proceedings while the President was himself the subject of serious investigation.

If a given course of action would cause national crisis or even turmoil, "it seems absurd to say that the decision-maker must bind himself from considering that risk," Davis wrote.

Yet, he continued, ". . . it seems inescapable to me that allowing M:. Nixon to go free while prosecuting all others—from Haldeman to Segretti —would mean that our laws are not being applied evenly to all our citizens . . . our history is unfortunately filled with instances of justice being applied with an uneven hand [but] it is rare indeed that one decision has the potential to so boldly demonstrate the unfair and unequal manner in which our system of justice can operate."

Under a section entitled "The Personal Factor" Davis wrote, ". . . while his suffering has been more public it was no greater on a personal level than that endured by John Mitchell, Donald Segretti or many of the thousands of criminals prosecuted every year. . . . Richard Nixon has, in his actions over the last two years, done nothing at all to justify mercy on this basis.

"No office has ever been required to make a more difficult and inevitably controversial public decision than that confronting this office. To some extent the entire performance of this office will be evaluated on the basis of this judgment alone."

In conclusion he declared, "I suggest that it is now impossible to weigh these factors with any accuracy. More time is needed so that the long range reaction of various segments in our society can be given a chance to develop. But equally as important, since our evaluation of these factors must by their nature be affected by our own emotions, it is important that we allow more time for our own feelings to stabilize."

He recommended that the trial of those already indicted, which was scheduled to begin in the fall, be allowed to go forward, that any decision on Nixon be postponed a month. If the decision was to prosecute the former President, he could be tried separately.

The office was further divided on this last point, whether the Watergate cover-up case should be delayed for a superseding indictment that would include Nixon.

The most exhaustive analysis was done by the counsel, Philip Lacovara. It was cold and clinical, and yet behind some of its sentences there seemed to be the strongest passion of all.

Lacovara began by citing the opinions of the Founding Fathers which had resulted in the Constitutional provision that an impeached official was still subject to indictment: Alexander Hamilton in *The Federalist Papers* (three different citations); Justice James Iredell, later of the Supreme Court, in the North Carolina Ratification Debates; George Nicholas at the Virginia Ratification Convention; Gouverneur Morris at the Federal Convention of 1787.

Then he examined current public opinion and found it uninstructive one way or another. Few writers seemed to suggest that prosecution would be vindictive, yet there was no strong consensus in its favor. He noted that the American Bar Association had just passed a resolution at its annual convention recording that organization's opposition to immunity for Richard Nixon, without mentioning his name.

As a former President, Jaworski cared about the views of the A.B.A. He had recited the A.B.A. standards for prosecutors to his staff. Now Lacovara cited them back to Jaworski to show that they argued for prosecution in the Nixon case: The evidence was overwhelming, the harm of the crimes was grave and continuing, the authorized punishment was suitable.

"You are not really confronted with the specter of sending a former President to prison, with all of the awkwardness and possible unseemliness of such a course," he said. "I regard it as unlikely that upon conviction President Nixon would actually be sentenced to confinement and we need not press for imprisonment. In any event, that is primarily a decision to be made by the sentencing court. You should be aware, however, that under federal law even when a judge wants to sentence an offender to prison the judgment must provide simply that he is committed to the custody of the Attorney General for the specified term. It is then up to the Attorney General to 'designate the place of confinement where the sentence shall be served.' There is ample administrative discretion to provide for the unique problems that would be created by the 'confinement' of a former President, even if such a course were directed. I would regard it as appropriate to make a recommendation, upon conviction, that a former President not be confined in any established federal correction institution."

Other factors made it fair and just to proceed, Lacovara said.

> Even though [the impeachment] process was aborted by the President's resignation, I might have been inclined to recommend against criminal prosecution if Mr. Nixon had acknowledged his complicity in the events at issue. Although I can understand why he would be reluctant to confess his guilt on national television, when he had received no commitment against prosecution, the simple fact is that President Nixon chose to leave office, not as a remorseful person who faced up to the offenses he committed, but as a noble peacemaker who was driven out of office by a hostile Congress. This tone led to the quick evaporation of any sentiment in Congress in favor of a concurrent resolution urging non-prosecution.
>
> Furthermore, upon his resignation, Mr. Nixon promised he would continue to play an active part in American political life. Thus, it is to be expected that he will remain a public figure and will attempt to capitalize on the absence of a definitive adjudication of his role by contending that he was "hounded" out of office as a result of a political cabal rather than as the result of his own criminal abuses. I regard this prospect as a strong reason for bringing to a head the issue of the former President's guilt or innocence through the only process that now remains for adjudicating that question. While the majority and minority reports from the House Judiciary Committee will be categorical in accusing the former President of having committed impeachable offenses, those reports constitute only accusations and not adjudications.
>
> Finally, I regard it as extraordinarily unjust that the former President's aides are serving time in prison or are exposed to prison sentences and to professional and financial ruin, while he benefits from the perquisites accorded to a former President who left office honorably.

He named them: $900,000 for a transition period, $60,000 in salary, and $96,000 for staff each year; Secret Service protection; continued participation in the affairs of the national government under a 1969 executive order, including "a direct channel to the incumbent President, the Secretary of State, the Secretary of Defense, the Director of the Central Intelligence Agency, the Executive Secretary of the National Security Council and other government agencies."

Nixon's files were valued at between three and five million dollars according to published reports, Lacovara noted, and the current White

House position was that the tapes belonged to the former President. "There is certainly something bizarre," Lacovara wrote, "in Mr. Nixon's earning a handsome profit by his control over files that include important evidence of his own crimes and those of his aides."

It was, he said, "naïve and unfounded" for anyone to suggest, under those circumstances, that Nixon had suffered enough simply by losing his office. "The office was not 'his' but was a public trust that he violated and forfeited."

Finally, Lacovara argued for a quick decision and a superseding indictment which would place Nixon with the other cover-up defendants in the *U.S.* v. *Mitchell* cover-up case, to stand trial alongside them when a court decided the time was appropriate.

Jaworski received these memos and said little. He did not respond in writing to any of them but made it clear that he considered the problem of a fair trial an almost insurmountable objection. He dispatched Kreindler to research the law on this subject.

My own relationship with Jaworski had grown over the months we had worked together. I had long ago overcome my initial resentment toward him for supplanting Archie Cox, and I had become genuinely fond of the man. Frequently there was not much for the special prosecutor to do as he waited for one or another party in one or another case to react to his moves or to the court. His staff took care of all the paper work. Sometimes he sat in his office just reading the Houston newspapers. Most mornings I would visit with him for a half hour or longer, supposedly to brief him on the news but more often to listen sympathetically to whatever was on his mind, seldom offering any argument, simply letting him know that there was a great reservoir of personal respect and affection for him within the office, whatever the current differences might be over some policy decision.

In mid-August, I found him refreshed from a recent stay at his ranch and in a genial mood. To hear him tell it, he was not bothered by the prospect of having to make a decision that was sure to cause bitter dissent whichever way it went. "I don't worry about these things," he said. "You have a decision to make, you make it and forget about it.

"Jim, the ranch is as beautiful as I've ever seen it," he said. "Because of all the rain it's as green as can be and the water is flowing over the dams in the ponds." A little while later he said, "Every night on the way home I pass by the Hotel Burlington, where I spent my first night in Washington. *Lord, how lonely I was that night.*"

Washington was deserted. Officials and newsmen who had been trapped there—in 1972 by the presidential campaign, in 1973 by the Watergate hearings, and earlier in 1974 by the impeachment inquiry—fled the heat and the bad memories, joined their families at Cape Cod or the Virginia mountains or the Delaware beaches. The White House staff was already changing. St. Clair was back in Boston. Buzhardt had been fired when he misled the new press secretary, Jerald terHorst, telling him the prosecutors had agreed that Nixon's unsubpoenaed papers and tapes could go to San Clemente. Others of the old crowd were still in their offices but looking for posts outside of government. At the prosecutor's office nothing had changed, except that the situation was more complicated. I returned refreshed from a vacation, and the old weariness was a shock to see.

Jaworski asked me to put together an analysis of the news reports during the week of Nixon's resignation to determine how pervasive had been the depiction of Nixon's guilt. He wanted Peter Kreindler to help.

"What's the use?" Kreindler asked me. "First of all, it is not for us to decide if the climate is too prejudicial for a fair trial—that's the judge's decision. Secondly, what are we going to find? A massive, unprecedented amount of publicity, the likes of which have never been seen before. He knows that. We know it. The only value of this will be to justify a decision not to prosecute, to convince the public that he couldn't get a fair trial."

Jaworski was not asking to see draft indictments, to pinpoint what the case against Nixon would look like, Kreindler noted. "Whatever the immediate good may seem to be for the country, whatever may seem to create the most healing at this time, the decision that will be seen in history as the correct one will be the decision to prosecute."

If this was essentially a political decision, then Jaworski should not make it, Kreindler said. He should limit himself to two choices—either to prosecute or to decline to decide the issue on the grounds that it was a political decision. Jaworski's answer to that was, "If he can't get a fair trial, I'm not going to pass it off onto a judge or the Congress."

Jim Vorenberg spent a long time with me, analyzing my view that a prosecution would only prolong a national agony. My suggestion that Nixon simply not be prosecuted would be the most serious arrogation of power a prosecutor could commit, Vorenberg said. We would be far more criticized for that abuse than for doing our duty, even if it was politically painful and divisive. "The pardoning power is not ours to exercise," he said. "The decision to judge the prejudicial atmosphere at a trial does not belong to the prosecutor." If we were to live up to our duties, Vorenberg declared, we had to follow the standards that existed when we took the job, and not make up standards of our own. "I sat down and tried to make a case on paper for not prosecuting Richard Nixon," Vorenberg said. "I wasn't able to do it, even as an intellectual exercise."

"I'm hoping the decision will go away," I said lamely.

I found Jim Neal taking a different view. "You know, Jim," he said, "when Leon and I rub up against the people from our part of the country, we get a lot different view of things than you get in the Northeast." Neal thought there were serious problems with the idea of Leon Jaworski's deciding on his own that Richard Nixon should not be prosecuted, but he also thought that the perceptions of people across the country were properly a factor to be considered.

Lacovara was comfortable with his own carefully thought-out position. I told him I believed his concept of retributive justice was harsh. "Retribution is an important part of justice," he said. I was becoming more and more concerned that this decision, whichever way it went, would nullify all the work we had done. "Don't worry, Jim," Lacovara said. "The world will go on in any case."

The press was flooding the prosecutor's office with questions about how the decision was being made, who was being consulted, and what were the factors under consideration. We retreated into our compound like monks, unable to get the subject off our minds, unwilling to discuss it with outsiders.

Jaworski's mood remained chipper, although this new burden was having its effect. During a long August weekend in Texas Jaworski developed chest pains, shortness of breath, a general feeling of fatigue. He went to see his doctor, who said he showed no signs of heart involvement and was in good physical shape, then added, "Leon, you are an old man. You can't endlessly operate under continual tension. I suggest you start wrapping up your affairs in Washington and come home."

One day I met Bob Woodward on the street, and we talked for a long time. "I'm not going to write it," he said, "but the best possible source has told me that Jaworski told the people closest to him that he has made up his mind, that he is going to indict Nixon."

I looked him in the eye and said, "Bob, there is at least a fifty percent chance it could go the other way." He didn't believe me. It sounded exactly like the kind of answer a press agent would give when he didn't want to disclose any information.

I called up the Gallup and Lou Harris organizations to get all their available data on the public's perception of Nixon's guilt. I talked to two of the best men in those organizations, who were very helpful and promised to keep the calls confidential. Later that day George Gallup, Jr., had an appointment with executives of ABC news. Afterward David Schoumacher of ABC called me. "I understand you people are commissioning a poll to see whether the people want Nixon indicted," he said. I denied it, and as we talked he admitted that he didn't really believe it himself, but some ABC executives had passed the rumor on.

On Thursday, August 22, Jim Neal went to Leon with a proposal; Leon should make a presentation of the evidence to the grand jury, state his own views of whether Nixon should be indicted and his reasons for those views, and then agree to abide by the decision of the jurors. Jaworski rejected it. "They can't answer the question of whether Nixon can get a fair trial," Jaworski said. "It is beyond their scope."

On Monday, August 26, Fred Buzhardt called Jaworski, saying that he was at San Clemente and was about to return to Washington. He would be in communication with Nixon's new lawyer, he said, who would want to set up an early meeting.

Jaworski told all this to the senior staff and added that he did not intend to meet with this still unnamed lawyer in the prosecutor's offices; nor would he tell us about meetings with Nixon's new attorney. He said that he would begin negotiations by finding out whether Nixon planned to plead the Fifth Amendment; if so, he would request a letter stating that from the lawyer. Then he said he would ask this lawyer to spell out any arguments as to why Nixon should not be indicted.

That day a man from Columbus, Ohio, sent a huge bedsheet to Jaworski through the mail. Inscribed on it in block letters was NIXON—NO AMNESTY, and the peace sign. Two secretaries stapled it up in the rear of Jaworski's office, facing his desk. It covered the entire wall. Jaworski laughed when he saw it, but he was not really amused. It stayed up only a few hours.

The next morning Jim Neal had a puzzling phone conversation with an old friend. It was Herbert J. Miller, Jr., the same Jack Miller who had gotten George Spater of American Airlines off without a plea for an illegal campaign contribution; and had then represented William O. Bittman, Hunt's lawyer, and Richard Moore of the White House staff, neither of whom were charged. He had gotten a misdemeanor plea for Richard Kleindienst, who had lied under oath at his Senate confirmation hearings to become attorney general.

"Small world," Miller said to Neal. Since they were old friends, Neal passed this off. Then Miller said, "How about a misdemeanor?" and he laughed. Neal joked with him but didn't really know what the conversation was all about.

Shortly afterward Jaworski left his office and told his secretary he would be at his hotel apartment for a few hours. He told Hank Ruth and Phil Lacovara that he was going to meet Nixon's new lawyer, Jack Miller, but he wanted this kept confidential.

Shortly after that the press began calling my office and informing me of the news. Lawyers started drifting in as the word spread. They were surprised and apprehensive. Hank Ruth said, "Jack Miller is the only lawyer that Leon Jaworski ever meets with alone. When he met with him on Kleindienst, his mind was completely changed, and he was never able to articulate why."

Jim Neal wandered in to see what the crowd was all about. "If you were Richard Nixon who would you hire as your lawyer?" someone asked. Neal came up with the names of a few top criminal trial lawyers.

"How about Jack Miller?" someone asked. Neal thought a moment.

"Naw," he said. "Jack is a superb lawyer, but he doesn't have that much trial experience."

"Well, that's who he hired," I said. "Maybe he doesn't expect to go to trial."

Neal got Miller's office on the phone. "Tell him it's El Casa Pacifico calling," he said to the secretary.

"Jack?" he said, when Miller got on the line, "Nixon couldn't have gotten a worse lawyer. You used up every chit you had on the Kleindienst thing. Maybe you ought to associate Kleindienst in this one. I told these boys here, 'Nobody knows if Jack Miller's any good because nobody has ever seen him inside a courtroom.' Jack, you know I'm just kidding. We're gonna treat your client just the same as we treat Gordon Liddy."

He hung up the phone. "That man will skin Leon Jaworski alive," Neal said.

Jack Miller is a Republican who worked in a Democratic administration, a conservative who surrounded himself with liberals in his law firm, a serious man who liked to keep the mood light when negotiating. He laughed a lot, usually at his own jokes. In the late 1950s Miller became the lawyer to a court-appointed board which was monitoring the affairs of the Teamsters Union during the scandal-ridden days following the administration of Dave Beck. Robert Kennedy, who was then counsel to the Senate committee investigating the Teamsters, was so impressed with Miller's ability to handle that dismal nest that when he became attorney general he appointed Miller head of the criminal division, despite Miller's impeccable Republican credentials.

In that job Miller successfully supervised the Hoffa prosecutions (which Neal handled), as well as the Bobby Baker case and other examples of corruption. His aides once made a presentation to Robert Kennedy of a copy of his own book, *The Enemy Within*. When he opened it, there was a picture of Jack Miller pasted inside.

Miller knew Neal, Ruth, Vorenberg, and McBride from his old Justice Department days. He was highly respected, which made the staff all the more apprehensive that he might convince Leon Jaworski to reach a decision that history would condemn.

Would Miller try to arrange a plea? "I sure as hell wouldn't if I were Nixon's lawyer," Neal said. "There's too big a chance that he won't be charged; or if he's charged, that he won't go to trial; or that his case would be thrown out; or that he'd be found not guilty; or if he was found guilty, that he would never be sentenced; or if he was sentenced, that he would never serve his sentence."

Neal had come to the conclusion that Nixon should be indicted and tried along with the other defendants in the case now entitled *U.S.* v. *Mitchell.*

"What about the delay?" Hank Ruth asked. We all knew that a superseding indictment would mean another postponement that could last a full year. The longer a trial is delayed, the less chance the case will ever reach court, that a prosecutor can keep witnesses together, that events do not overtake the prosecution's case. Delays serve only the defense. There was also a personal consideration. Jim Neal could not try the case if it was postponed for a long period of time. He had a commitment to defend a client in a jury trial early in 1975.

"What about the delay?" Neal shot back. "The delay doesn't mean anything."

Lacovara said, "It's frightening to have those two men dealing alone with so much at stake."

Neal said, "What's at stake?"

"Richard Nixon's soul," Lacovara said.

"The hell with that," Neal said. "My writ doesn't run to his soul. Only to his ass."

Early the next morning, Tuesday, August 27, I wandered next door to Carl Feldbaum's office, interrupting his work to unburden my fears that our office was about to make the wrong decision in the wrong way. He felt as gloomy as I did.

Peter Kreindler, who shared the office with Feldbaum, came in, took a look, and said, "What's the matter with you two?" He joined the discussion, adding to our skepticism about the validity of the process being followed by Jaworski. Soon Hank Ruth wandered in, followed by Phil Lacovara and Jim Vorenberg. All of a sudden the room was charged with a sort of doomsday tension, a sense that after all we had been through our efforts would be discredited by a single, illegitimate act.

Jaworski's Texas friends were advising him that the former President had been punished enough. He even received a message from a former sweetheart he had known as a young lawyer in Waco, a woman he had not seen or heard from in almost fifty years. Only his own staff urged that Nixon should stand trial. Most of us tried to be very low-key in the advice we gave. During the past nine months we had had too many confrontations with our boss and we felt he would view too strenuous opposition as a sign that we lacked objectivity when it came to Richard Nixon. Subjectively I was still against prosecuting Nixon. But the arguments of my colleagues convinced me that it was the *legitimacy* of the process that mattered, and we had no legitimate way of not prosecuting the former President. I was even thinking of resigning if we failed to bring Nixon to trial.

Vorenberg said to me, "You are really on an emotional roller coaster. You came back from vacation convinced that Nixon should not be prosecuted. Now, in a matter of days, you are ready to resign if he is *not* prosecuted. Maybe you better slow down and see if there isn't a middle ground here. Your job is to do what you can, before the decision, to change it, and if you lose, you lose. You don't resign. You can have great influence because Leon listens to you and because you come to the question in basic sympathy with Leon's view."

The meeting broke up with nothing decided. Kreindler submitted an extensive legal memorandum on the question of pretrial publicity, which was forwarded to Jaworski with a strong covering memo from Lacovara. The two lawyers noted that not a single precedent held, or even suggested, that dismissing a prosecution was a legitimate remedy for dealing with prejudicial pretrial publicity. On the contrary, the courts repeatedly and uniformly had treated as adequate the traditional remedies—postponing the trial, changing its location, allowing the defendant latitude in questioning, and challenging prospective jurors.

I went to see Leon, accepting Vorenberg's challenge, but I was so depressed that much of the conversation consisted of Jaworski's telling me not to be overwrought. "You can't *worry* a decision like this," he said. "When I was thirty-eight years old I was making decisions whether men should be hung by the neck until they were dead and now, thirty years later, this decision isn't any harder. If you want to know, it's a damn sight easier."

I responded that one of the good things that had come out of Jaworski's war crimes trials was that they helped to establish an accepted rule of law for the world, and this was another case where the rule of law might be at stake.

"I know, I know," he said, "but you have to look at the negative aspects of what you do as well as the positive. And you can't worry about it in any case. Especially *you* can't get your spirits down now—thirty days or more before we decide. I need you to keep *my* spirits up."

He told me that he would not make any decision until the jury in the cover-up case was chosen and sequestered, which was a decision in itself. It was now clear he had rejected the idea of joining Nixon to the conspiracy trial.

He also told me that Jack Miller had reported he was shocked by Nixon's appearance when he accompanied Buzhardt to San Clemente, and that he was worried about Nixon's mental state. Miller asked for time before Jaworski acted, saying he needed to master the facts in the case. In response Jaworski had said, "You can't argue the merits with me, Jack. I made up my mind about that when we listed your client as a co-conspirator." Miller was perceptive enough to know that his best approach would be on questions such as the fair trial issue.

After my conversation with Jaworski I called up Tony Lewis of *The New York Times,* the journalist most respected by Jaworski (as he was by Cox). Over the months Lewis had come to Washington on more than one occasion to talk through legal issues with Jaworski and to give him a sense of how informed opinion outside the office felt about issues. Jaworski saw many journalists during his tenure, but only three maintained a special relationship with him. Philip Geyelin and Meg Greenfield of the *Washington Post* editorial page saw him regularly on a confidential basis, and as a result they were the best-informed journalists in Washington on the workings of the office. Neither ever violated this confidence by turning their information into a news story, although their editorials were consistently better informed than others. In a similar manner Lewis would frequently fly down from Boston to see Jaworski, and while he would write well-informed columns (and sometimes drop hints to reporters in the Washington bureau about matters to be pursued), he did not try to scoop his colleagues with perishable news items which would have spoiled in a day or two and ruined his relationship with Jaworski as well.

"Tony," I said, "can you come down some time in the next week or so?

It would be very useful to interview Leon." Lewis asked if there were particular subjects to be pursued. "You might be thinking about the arguments of prejudicial publicity preventing a fair trial in notorious cases and how a prosecutor should respond to that problem," I said. That puzzled him, since the question of pretrial publicity was considered the exclusive concern of the judge, but Lewis promised to think about the issue before he arrived.

That same day, Wednesday, August 28, Gerald Ford held his first news conference as President, which Jaworski watched on television in his office, along with a few aides. We had all assumed that Ford had ruled out a pardon for Nixon. At his vice presidential confirmation hearings Ford had been asked whether he considered it possible to pardon his predecessor, should he accede to the Presidency. He had answered indirectly but emphatically by saying the public would never stand for such an act.

Now that the situation was no longer hypothetical, Gerald Ford took a different, and puzzling, position. "In this situation, I am the final authority. . . . I am not ruling it [a pardon] out. It is an option and a proper option for any President. . . . I think the Special Prosecutor, Mr. Jaworski, has an obligation to take whatever action he sees fit in conformity with his oath of office, and that should include any and all individuals. . . . Until the matter reaches me, I am not going to make any commitment during the process of whatever charges are made." Jaworski correctly read these answers as Ford's way of signaling that he would pardon Nixon some time after he was indicted.

Although Ford's statements seemed to imply that Nixon had suffered enough, they were open to other interpretations. I suggested to Jaworski that Ford's remarks could also be read as an invitation to prosecute, a recognition that Jaworski must fulfill his duties.

"That's bullshit," Jaworski said. "That's not what the courts were meant for, some kind of a charade where you take the steps to prosecute and then somebody else pardons."

The events of the next eleven days are still shrouded in conflicting and misleading statements on the part of the President and some White House aides, but I believe that the chain of events leading to Nixon's pardon for the most part did not involve the special prosecutor's office. Before the President's August 28 news conference Ford and his advisers had prepared what they thought would be an acceptable position with which to deflect pardon questions; since no specific charges had been made against Nixon, Ford would not decide the question in advance. Only afterward did Ford consult with his legal counsel, Philip Buchen, and discover that the pardon power, although usually exercised after a charge, could be employed at any time. Thus the question of pardon could be considered whenever the President wished to do so.

After his news conference Ford also spoke to Alexander Haig, who during this period urged a quick pardon for Nixon. Haig had planted the seed with Ford before Nixon resigned. Now he was upset with Ford's indications that a pardon would have to wait. He had already received a memorandum from Leonard Garment arguing that Nixon's physical and mental condition was at low ebb and that he could not face a long period of suspense about his future. Garment also argued that the political sentiment against a pardon would intensify as the legal process moved forward.

Garment had given one copy of his memo to Buchen, who returned it, saying that he would not take it up with the President because it was premature. The other copy was given to Haig, who reported to Garment and several other White House aides around this time that a pardon seemed assured.

Two days after the press conference Ford met with Haig, Buchen, and two other White House counsels, Robert T. Hartmann and John O. Marsh, to begin immediate consideration of the pardon question. Once Buchen reported to him that sufficient precedent existed for a pardon before indictment, Ford moved ahead rapidly to make the decision. Jack Miller smoothed the way by assuring Buchen that Nixon would never agree to plead to anything. Miller also said Nixon would issue a contrite statement acknowledging his errors in Watergate and that Nixon's tapes and papers could be removed from the White House in a way that would keep the Ford administration from becoming endlessly involved in civil and criminal litigation over Watergate.

But the prosecutor's office knew none of this, and a whole separate set of discussions took place there, which were to have a profound effect on the people involved.

On the next day, Thursday, August 29, Lacovara wrote a memorandum to Jaworski which complicated his own position. Those who know Phil Lacovara and what motivates him gave two reasons why this memorandum was written. Lacovara was annoyed that he had been completely left out of the decision-making process and wanted to get back in. He also was convinced that Jaworski had decided not to prosecute Nixon. Lacovara saw in Ford's press conference a way to save the reputation of the Watergate Special Prosecution Force by our demanding that Ford act before Jaworski.

His memorandum cited the legal precedents which allowed Ford to exercise the pardon power before any criminal charges were pending, and then said:

> I believe President Ford has placed you in an intolerable position by making his public announcement. I see no reason why the matter should not be put squarely to him now whether he wishes to have a criminal prosecution of the former President instituted or not. I believe you should not make a decision not to prosecute when the record has been muddied in this way and when it will appear to many, regardless of what you may say, that such a decision merely responded to informal "signals" from President Ford. Conversely, I do not believe it is in the public interest, in the interest of former President Nixon, or the interest of this Office to initiate serious criminal charges against the former President (whether they are joined with the charges against the present Watergate defendants or are filed separately) when the new President has decided to abort such charges.
>
> I recommend that you put this matter squarely to President Ford or to his counsel, either personally by contacting one of them, or less formally by authorizing me to contact Mr. Buchen. Since President Ford is now publicly on record as having expressed willingness to assume the responsibility for the exercise of the ultimate constitutional powers that are his, I believe he should be asked to face this issue *now* and make the operative judgment concerning the former President, rather than leaving this matter in the limbo of uncertainty that has been created.

This memo was to cause Lacovara a good deal of embarrassment when other members of the staff learned of it much later. For months there had been a standing joke among Hank Ruth's inner circle—Kreindler, Lacovara, Feldbaum, Barker, me—about Jaworski's penchant for passing off tricky situations to other agencies or parties whenever possible. The staff members had noted that both Jaworski and Judge Sirica were fond of saying in private, "I don't want that monkey on my back." Once during a staff meeting, when Jaworski suggested temporizing on some matter, Carl Feldbaum drew a large monkey on his yellow legal pad, folded the paper, and passed it to the lawyer next to him. Slowly the monkey made its way from lawyer to lawyer around the circle in Jaworski's office. After that, whenever the lawyers thought Jaworski was avoiding a problem during a staff meeting, it was common for one or another to casually brush his hand across his shoulder, thrusting away an imaginary monkey. Lacovara had joined in this sport along with everyone else and was often more critical than the others when he judged Jaworski to be shirking his duty.

Whatever Lacovara's motivations might have been, the advice seemed to coincide with Jaworski's feelings. To those who read the memo for the first time after the pardon was issued on September 8, it seemed that Lacovara had offered to convince Ford to make a decision Lacovara considered wrong. A week later Lacovara attempted to modify its message drastically, but events were moving too fast.

The day he received Lacovara's memorandum Jaworski was invited to the office of Senator James Eastland of Mississippi, chairman of the Judiciary Committee. Senator Roman Hruska of Nebraska, the ranking Republican member of the committee, was also present. Eastland told Jaworski he had received a call from "the President"—he was referring to Nixon —from San Clemente. "It was just a friendly call," Eastland said, "and he is a friend. He is in terrible shape. I thought you ought to know that. He cried on the phone."

Jaworski said, "Mr. Chairman, I had thought that I would have heard from the Committee of Eight." This was a reference to the eight members of Congress—chairmen and ranking members of the two Judiciary committees, and the top leaders of the House and Senate from each party— who had veto power over any dismissal of Jaworski under Robert Bork's guidelines.

Eastland responded that he was leaving that day for Mississippi, would be back after Labor Day, and would be in touch. He did not say so but he seemed to imply that he would be sounding out the other members of the Committee of Eight to see if they would agree that Richard Nixon should not be prosecuted. Jaworski responded that he would be returning from Texas around the time Eastland came back to Washington. But Eastland never called Jaworski again.

Philip Buchen worked through the Labor Day weekend. On Friday, August 30, President Ford commissioned him to research the pardon question thoroughly, to find out if there were any legal reasons for Ford not to act immediately, and to learn, if he could, what Jaworski planned to do. Haig had been advising the President that the prosecution of Nixon might drag on for years.

When Leon Jaworski returned to Washington on Tuesday, September 3, he knew that he was off the hook. Sufficient forces were at work to prevent the prosecution of Nixon, and enough time was available, so his instincts told him, that the situation would be resolved to his satisfaction. It is possible that Buchen gave him some signal over the phone of what the White House planned to do. If so, Jaworski did not mention it. But he had forewarned us that he would not discuss his conversations concerning Nixon that occurred outside the office.

He was bubbling with good cheer, carrying on about the new foals at his ranch, some sired by his champion quarter horse Magnolia Pay, and about his own grandchildren as well. I asked him if he would see Philip Geyelin and Meg Greenfield and Tony Lewis that week, and he readily agreed. "We need people's goodwill," he said. "I don't know what's going to happen, I promise you I don't. But I have an intuition—and I have spent my life acting on intuition—that something is going to happen. Ford is going to act." When I mentioned that journalist Brock Brower hoped to interview Jaworski during the coming cover-up trial, Jaworski said the appointment should not wait. "There may not be a trial," he said. "You never know."

When I set up specific appointments, Jaworski agreed to them but noted rather casually that they might have to be canceled or changed around, which I took to be a suggestion that he was on call to meet with Nixon's lawyer or Ford's counsel.

The next day, Wednesday, September 4, Jaworski met separately with Philip Buchen and with Jack Miller. Neither Miller nor Jaworski wanted the White House to know that there was any doubt about a prosecution, and Buchen did not want Jaworski to know that intensive negotiations were beginning to couple a deal on delivery of the tapes and documents with a pardon.

Miller gave Jaworski a written brief arguing against prosecution on the grounds that a fair trial was impossible. He relied heavily on the uniqueness of the case rather than any persuasive legal citations. Miller also made the argument that public sentiment in favor of a pardon was already such that it would deny Nixon due process. His reasoning was that the usual constraints on jurors would be lifted by the belief that Nixon would be pardoned in any case and thus a guilty verdict would not be a ticket to jail. He also argued that Jaworski should take into consideration the impact of an indictment on "the domestic spirit" of the country as well as on its international relations.

Jaworski, in turn, gave Buchen two documents. One was an internal memorandum he had requested the day before from Hank Ruth. It outlined the ten areas, besides the Watergate cover-up, in which Nixon would be under investigation (even though, Ruth noted, at present no case against him existed). The other document was a letter, based on an opinion by Lacovara, which argued that it would be nine months to a year or longer before selection of a jury could begin in the event Nixon was indicted. Lacovara had made it clear that he was against a separate indictment and thought the Nixon case and that of the seven men already indicted should be joined, but Jaworski distinguished Nixon from the other defendants.

Jaworski's negotiations with Miller and Buchen were held secretly and caused great bitterness in the prosecutor's office. The staff feared that without any consultation with them the special prosecutor was reaching a compact with Miller and Buchen. Jaworski, however, had not acted, except possibly to subtly encourage the White House along a path it had already chosen. Buchen has said that he did not seek Jaworski's opinion on the question of a pardon, or even solicit Jaworski's intentions toward the former President. Jaworski later told me that he had simply told Buchen that if the White House was going to leave this decision to Jaworski, he did not want the White House interfering before or after the fact. Other than that, he indicated it would be a while before any action was taken.

On Thursday Jaworski saw the two editorial writers from the *Post*, Geyelin and Greenfield, and later in the day he spoke to Tony Lewis. Geyelin raised all the usual arguments against indicting Nixon and asked Jaworski if he gave any of them credence. "None of that bothers me too much," Jaworski said, "but I have real problems concerning his ability to get a fair trial, problems which I think can be solved eventually." It was the first time I had heard him make such a concession.

Tony Lewis, who was fully briefed and prepared on the question, went over the fair trial question in greater detail, and Jaworski seemed even less resistant by the time Lewis was through. I began to suspect that he was softening his position and would finally come around. Lacovara, on the other hand, had a different sense of what was about to happen.

Lacovara was simmering that day and he stayed late to write another memorandum on the pardon question. He left it on Jaworski's desk so that the special prosecutor would see it first thing Friday morning.

It was clear that Lacovara was having second thoughts about his advice of a week earlier. He now recommended that a Nixon pardon follow the "not uncommon practice" of setting conditions: first, that Nixon publicly acknowledge his complicity in the Watergate conspiracy; second, that the special prosecutor be guaranteed continued access to Nixon's tapes and documents. Finally, Lacovara wrote, Jaworski might recommend, although it was "beyond the ambit of our official interest," that a pardon be conditioned on Nixon's agreeing never to run for public office again.

Lacovara had a problem. Jaworski had already met with President Ford's counsel and had followed his own instincts, which happened to coincide with the advice of Lacovara's earlier memo. He had encouraged the President to make his decision soon, before the prosecutors acted. Neither Jaworski nor Lacovara had much doubt about what that meant. Lacovara had written in his earlier memo, "President Ford seems inclined to exercise his pardon power on behalf of the former President."

The second Lacovara memo came too late. Jaworski responded to it immediately, saying, "If conditions were to be mentioned, this should have been done at the Buchen meeting of [September] fourth if at all." He added that he thought it would have been inappropriate to propose conditions. "The President has not undertaken to tell us how to prosecute and I do not regard it proper to tell him how to pardon, if he has this in mind," Jaworski wrote.

It was Friday morning, September 6, when Lacovara received Jaworski's answer. At lunch that day he seemed distressed. "It's going to happen," he said. "It's going to go down."

That afternoon deputy spokesman John Barker received calls from reporters he knew. They told him that Jack Miller had been seen at the San Clemente compound with another Washington lawyer named Benton Becker. Nobody in the office seemed to know any Washington lawyer by that name. We checked the lawyers' directory, but his modest general practice did not offer much of a clue.

Then we heard that the senator closest to the new President, Robert Griffin, had told a group of Michigan reporters that Jaworski had a "locked" case against Nixon and that he intended to put him away for a long time. According to Griffin, Jaworski had informed the White House that he was poised to bring Nixon before the courts at any moment. In fact the prosecutors were in a panic trying to be ready for the cover-up trial and had not even prepared the first memorandum outlining the case against Nixon. Most of them doubted it would ever be needed.

I went to see Jaworski to tell him about the rumors that were circulating and to ask whether I could play the role of peacemaker. He was not aware of the mounting unrest in the office over his failure to consult with his staff.

He had no idea who Benton Becker might be or why he was seen with Jack Miller. The Griffin report puzzled him. He had never given the White House any idea of his intentions, he said. It sounded as though Griffin was either trying to show how knowledgeable he was on the basis of no facts or launching a trial balloon for the White House to arouse sympathy for Nixon.

I told Jaworski that his senior aides were very unhappy with the lack of consultation over the Nixon decision and suggested that for the good of the office, to avoid future trouble, he ought to meet with them and invite their complaints.

"Jim," he said, "I would never make a decision affecting this office without conferring with those people, and I never have done so. But I feel very uncomfortable sharing information which is given to me in the strictest confidence." He said that at the present time he was not being asked to make any decisions, he was simply being asked for information. "You can't share information with just one person around here," he said. "It never stays there."

He was right. We each tended to compare notes after talking with him to see if we could piece together what he might be planning, in order to have more leverage so that we could change his views. This, perhaps, was a penalty he paid for taking over someone else's staff.

Earlier that day Jaworski had disclosed to Hank Ruth that Buchen had asked him for an estimate of how much time would elapse before Nixon could be tried. He told Ruth he had given Buchen a letter with an estimate of nine to twelve months. A few minutes later Jaworski went to Ruth's office to ask a question and found Ruth meeting with Lacovara, Kreindler, and Feldbaum, apparently sharing this information. "Oh," Jaworski said, "the committee is meeting." He walked out of the room.

Jaworski told me that the White House had not consulted him, but from his one meeting with Buchen he believed that Ford was going to pardon Nixon and was going to do it within a few days. Jaworski said that Ford had rehearsed an answer to the pardon questions at his news conference, "But he got it all screwed up, and that brought the matter to a head."

The next morning Jaworski met with his top staff members and tried to calm them. The problem was not really soluble by a meeting because it was a difference over what the prosecutor's role should be. Jaworski was glad to have Ford make the decision sooner rather than later, if he was going to make it at all. The others were against a pardon and would have tried to head it off if they had been in Jaworski's position.

That day Tony Lewis wrote a column for publication in Monday's *New York Times*. The column had been written for one reader, Leon Jaworski. Lewis killed the column Sunday morning after the pardon. It never appeared.

MR. JAWORSKI'S DUTY: I

by ANTHONY LEWIS

Washington—It is a month since Mr. Nixon left. The nightmare of his presidency is already dimming in memory. But the person of Richard Nixon is not so easily dismissed from the national consciousness.

Some of his principal aides go on trial in three weeks for obstruction of justice. Mr. Nixon's words, on tape or from the witness stand, will be crucial evidence. He has already been gravely implicated by the published transcripts, and more will come out at the trial. Yet Mr. Nixon, acknowledging no wrongdoing, seems to expect all the perquisites of an honorably retired President. And so the question will not down: Should he be prosecuted?

Initially, it is a question for Leon Jaworski, the Watergate special prosecutor. He is in a curious and difficult position, a prosecutor with no real base in the political system facing a case of high political import. Some thought Congress would provide guidance, but it shied away from involvement. President Ford has indicated that he will wait upon the special prosecutor.

Leon Jaworski is no brooder. He is prepared to decide the Nixon issue as a responsibility of his office, though he will do nothing before the cover-up trial starts and the jury is chosen, to avoid any risk of interference with that case. But he evidently has concerns about the idea of prosecuting the former president.

One question troubling Mr. Jaworski—a matter hardly mentioned in outside commentary—is whether Mr. Nixon, if indicted, could get a fair trial. That is, could a reasonably impartial jury be found to try him?

Mr. Nixon's new lawyer, Herbert J. Miller Jr., has already raised that very point with Mr. Jaworski. He argued that the American public had been so saturated with the evidence against Mr. Nixon in the impeachment proceedings that no fair jury could be found—and that no prosecution should even begin. Mr. Miller cited a case decided 20 years ago by the U.S. Court of Appeals for the First Circuit, *Delaney v. U.S.*

Denis Delaney was Collector of Internal Revenue for Massachusetts. He was indicted on corruption charges. Then, shortly before his trial, a congressional committee held public hearings on his derelictions. He was convicted, but the Court of Appeals reversed, saying that the trial should have been postponed until the prejudicial effects of the hearings had dissipated. It said "the United States" had had "a choice" of which process to use, legislative or judicial.

The case of Mr. Nixon presents one obvious difference at once. It is a situation in which the Constitution uniquely provides for both legislative and judicial process. The impeachment provision says explicitly that, upon conviction by the Senate, an official "shall nevertheless be liable and subject to indictment, trial, judgment and punishment, according to law."

In this case, Mr. Jaworski advised the grand jury that it would be constitutionally doubtful to indict a President before the impeachment process. If the grand jury now sought to indict, and Mr. Jaworski declined to let it do so, a clause would effectively have been written out of the Constitution.

Conditions have changed since 1787. Television can now bring prejudicial details of an impeachment proceeding into every home. Yet the judgment of those who framed the Constitution is not irrelevant. If a President had been impeached in those early days, the details would probably have been well known to most Americans—and certainly to the men of property who served on trial juries.

Of course the issue of fairness in jury consideration of criminal charges against Mr. Nixon must be considered. Mr. Jaworski should and would agree to delay of a trial, and to a change of venue from the District of Columbia if Mr. Miller asked, but it would be a very different thing to exclude a prosecution altogether. The *Delaney* court rejected dismissal of the charges, calling only for delay, and no court has ever suggested that some cases can never be tried fairly anywhere in the United States.

The Supreme Court has said that jurors need not be "ignorant of the facts and issues involved" in a notable case. To exclude jurors as prejudiced because of "the mere existence of any preconceived notion as to guilt or innocence of an accused," the Court said, "would be to establish an impossible standard. It is sufficient if the juror can lay aside his impression or opinion and render a verdict based on the evidence."

That legal standard should make it possible to draw a qualified jury for a Nixon trial in due course. Mr. Jaworski wonders what he can answer if a judge asks him: when? But he need not make such a prediction. The answer is that the legal process must go ahead, dealing with each problem as it arises. Motions will be made, and jurors questioned as to their fairness; a trial judge will rule and appellate courts pass on the fairness of the proceeding.

The fair trial issue is not for a prosecutor alone to decide at a preliminary stage, foreclosing the process of criminal justice. I believe Leon Jaworski will come to that conclusion, seeing his role as part of a system of criminal justice. And that is the point about the larger question of whether to prosecute Mr. Nixon: its importance lies in what the decision will say about our attitudes toward the system of law.

On Sunday morning I picked up the Washington Star-News and read a story by Barry Kalb which reported that a deal was under negotiation among Ford, Nixon, and Jaworski to end the former President's jeopardy. One of Kalb's usual sources was Lacovara. A few of Leon Jaworski's top aides were the only people in Washington who thought that such a deal was under consideration. One day over lunch I had discussed with them the possible uses of the leak as a device to head off a policy decision that was wrongheaded. I hadn't leaked this story, but somebody had.

Shortly before 10:00 A.M., Jaworski called. "I'm sorry to bother you on a Sunday morning, Jim, but this is important," he said. "It looks like President Ford is going to pardon Nixon."

"Okay," I said.

"The announcement is going to be made at ten forty-five," he said. "Phil Buchen just called me. I'm just leaving for church."

"Did you see the story in the Star?" I asked.

"Phil Buchen told me about it," Jaworski said. "There was no deal of any kind. There is nothing to the story."

"Okay," I said.

"Jim, I'm very relieved," he said.

"Right," I said, and I hung up. I was relieved, too.

My first reaction to the pardon was that Gerald Ford had rid the special prosecutor's office of an enormous burden, for I was convinced that the indictment and trial of Richard Nixon would have caused a national trauma greater than that caused by the Watergate scandal itself. And if he were assassinated during the trial, or a mistrial or hung jury occurred, that hardly would have vindicated the system or laid to rest any lingering doubts that the man was a criminal conspirator. As it is, he accepted the pardon, at least implicitly acknowledging guilt. As presidential counsel Philip Buchen said, the pardon had nothing to do with justice, it was meant as an act of mercy for the country as much as for Richard Nixon. Ford was not abusing the pardon power much more than his predecessors with their Christmas clemency for politicians, labor racketeers, and powerful hoodlums.

But that opinion has within it a lack of faith in the strength of our people to have seen Watergate through to the end even if it meant the trial and imprisonment of a former President who soiled the office's escutcheon. Gerald Ford did great damage to the American ideal of equal justice under law that Sunday morning. He ignored the long-established procedures of review before granting the pardon, and he sprang it on an unsuspecting nation because he was fearful of what would have happened if there had been a careful review or a public debate. And he showed a lack of the necessary moral stature for his new job when he avoided confronting Richard Nixon and demanding, as a prerequisite, that the former President admit explicitly his culpability in the Watergate crimes, and beg the nation's pardon for those acts.

Nothing indicated the poor caliber of Ford's decision more than the quality of Benton Becker, the young lawyer—really nothing more than a messenger boy—who was dispatched to San Clemente to play the role of awed supplicant while Nixon and his attorney, Herbert J. Miller, Jr., worked out incredible, unilateral terms for the turnover of Nixon's tapes and papers to the former President. That part of the deal was so outrageous that the courts, at the initiative of the special prosecutor, had little trouble nullifying it.

After the Nixon pardon the Watergate Special Prosecution Force began to dissolve. There was still a great deal to be done, of course, court cases to be won and lost, investigations to close out. But the "tight little island" atmosphere dissipated, and the team that had held together for seventeen months began to break up.

Jaworski kept his own timetable to himself until the jury in the cover-up trial was sequestered. Then he departed with his wife for New York City on a Friday afternoon, leaving behind in a sealed envelope his letter of resignation, effective in two weeks. It was delivered to the attorney general's office on Saturday morning.

The New York Times editorial page, which had been unfriendly to Jaworski from the outset and never got over its early suspicions, greeted him that Sunday with an editorial that began, "After nearly a year of exemplary performance as Special Watergate Prosecutor, Leon Jaworski is leaving office under conditions that border on desertion of duty."

It seemed a graceless piece of writing but it was a faithful representation of a minority view. Herblock of the *Washington Post* made the same point the following day. His cartoon depicted a jubilant Jaworski, fitted out in football togs, standing out of bounds at the twenty-yard line, holding a football aloft and saying, "Touchdown!"

The work of the prosecutor's office had not been completed when Jaworski decided to leave, and it would be harder to finish without him. But one had to balance that judgment against what the circumstances had been when Jaworski took the job, what had been asked of him at the time, and how those expectations had been met. It was not necessary to reflect upon his age, or to know the advice of his personal physician, to look at his accomplishments and judge that he had done well, that he deserved the thanks of a nation and the right to retire from an assignment he had not sought.

The criticisms were few if not always muted. They had less to do with whether Jaworski had conscientiously followed his duty than with whether the dissenters agreed with his decisions. Most argued that he should have indicted President Nixon, if not before he left office then after, and that he should have challenged the pardon in court. Perhaps. There were many among his own staff who thought so. After the fact, many of his former staff members came to the view that some of Jaworski's judgments may have been wiser than they seemed at the time.

For the most part he took the dissenters in stride. Normally Leon Jaworski is thin-skinned about criticism in the press, but now he was so delighted to return home that he developed a new toleration for it. In his one act of vengeance he declined to receive Lesley Oelsner from *The New York Times* for a departing interview, despite the fact that Jaworski held the attorney-reporter in high regard.

NOT ABOVE THE LAW

Leon Jaworski left Washington as he had arrived, on an Eastern Airlines flight from Dulles International Airport, with the same garment bag that had accompanied him on the inbound trip.

His resignation was to become effective at the close of business Friday, October 25, but he left town secretly twenty-four hours earlier so that he would miss the formalities of a going-away party as well as the reporters who would be waiting at the office and the airport.

He wanted to make the ride to the airport alone, but John Barker insisted that he and I would go along. "We brought you into this and we'll deliver you out of it," Barker said. Dan Rosenblatt, who had acted as Jaworski's driver, arranged with the Jefferson Hotel to borrow three crystal wine glasses. Barker selected two bottles of fine Chablis for the trip to the airport. Jaworski was like a youngster on his last day of school. In the car he rehearsed his entire year's experiences, good and bad, characterizing friends and enemies in ranch-style colloquialisms. After a while he and I dispensed with the fine crystal and started swigging. Barker retained the savoir faire of his Cambridge college days and managed to balance his glass in the swaying government car.

Jaworski was almost a teetotaler during his days as prosecutor, sometimes taking a small glass of wine at lunch. But when we arrived at Dulles we headed for the Braniff lounge and continued our deliberations over abundant quantities of sherry.

At flight time we walked slowly to the gate and he said good-bye to the three of us. He was wearing a pair of dark glasses I had never seen before. At the last moment I hugged him.

"Colonel," I said, "good-bye. You're a good man and we're going to miss you."

He turned around and headed for home.

The next morning he called me from the ranch. We talked for about fifteen minutes about the weather in Texas, his foals, the ranch. Finally he said, "Jim, what the hell did I do with my garment bag?"

EPILOGUE:
WATERGATE JUSTICE

Henry Swartley Ruth, Jr., became the third Watergate special prosecutor, sworn in before the same judge in the same courtroom where Jaworski had taken the oath a year before. We were gratified that our second-in-command had been elevated to a position that would carry with it a bit of history. But the team was beginning to break up in some dissension.

The Saturday morning of the swearing-in, October 26, 1974, two days after Jaworski's departure, the *Washington Post* carried a long interview with our latest critic, Philip Lacovara, who resigned in protest when the Nixon pardon was announced. He predicted that the Watergate trial jury would probably be unable to agree on convictions because of the inequity of the Nixon pardon. The judge had just spent weeks interviewing prospective jurors, trying to assure that those empaneled would judge the other conspirators only on the merits of the evidence. But Lacovara reminded *Post* readers, "It only takes one juror who might be reluctant." Lacovara was one of the guests at Ruth's oath-taking, and the interview caused some tension.

There was further bitterness over Jaworski's precipitous departure. Jim Neal was upset because Jaworski had urged that he return to try the cover-up case and then had resigned without informing Neal of his plans. Ruth was displeased with Jaworski's letter of resignation, which told Attorney General Saxbe, "The bulk of the work is finished." In fact the prosecutors had many miles of litigation to go. Ruth declared, "I said this was a no-win situation when I came here, and I still say it will turn out to be that for me." The strong cases had already been moved into court. It would be Ruth's task to drop many of those that remained.

Elliot Richardson had emphasized to Archibald Cox that the hardest part of the job would be making and living with decisions *not* to prosecute. Richardson had even envisioned the possibility of asking Congress to appoint a "post-audit" group to go over the decisions and check on what was done. That did not happen but there was much criticism of Ruth for every case he did not bring to trial and every damaging fact about Nixon he refused to disclose out of court.

The public's curiosity about the special prosecutor declined rapidly, except when specific cases came to trial and a flurry of news stories momentarily reignited interest in Watergate. In March the quiz show *Jeopardy* offered contestants a ten-dollar question: Who succeeded Leon Jaworski as special prosecutor? None knew the answer.

Hank Ruth encouraged newsmen to ignore him. He rarely allowed himself to be interviewed and declined to offer much news when he was. He would refuse to comment on criticism of the office or about criticism of a specific decision within the office.

The press quickly lost interest, and Ruth remained anonymous. Sometimes he would alight from the government car at the courthouse and no one would be in sight. Hank Ruth would say, "No comment, fellas, no comment." It became a standing joke. Sometimes his driver, a young man named Mark Peabody, would park the car, run around to the passenger side and say, "Say, aren't you the special prosecutor? Could I have your autograph?"

The thrill was gone at 1425 K Street, and much of the sense of purpose as well. It became increasingly difficult, after eighteen months of living in the vortex of a national scandal, for staff members to adjust to the normal workaday world.

Life had gone on, and we had barely noticed. Marriages had broken up, others had begun. Babies had been born, illnesses suffered; some joy and some sadness had fallen into many of the lives of our loved ones. Now it was time to begin living again—except for the Watergate trial team.

On Monday, October 14, 1974, nearly two and a half years after the burglary and three prosecutors later, the prosecution began to present its case in the big Watergate trial against Mitchell, Haldeman, Ehrlichman, Mardian and Parkinson.* For the next three months the expended passions of the scandal would be rekindled in the plain, blond-paneled courtroom on the second floor of an undistinguished concrete building at the foot of Capitol Hill. Much of the evidence had been published long before, mounting up week after week in newspaper stories, Senate hearings, House testimony, White House transcripts, Supreme Court decisions. Now it must be arrayed according to the rules of the criminal trial and presented to the nine women and three men who would decide the question of guilt. This would be an esoteric battle, where the correctness of procedures would be at least as important as the verdict in deciding whether the defendants would be punished.

Perhaps the point would be that justice is equal, but nothing about this trial was "equal" to the normal standards. The prosecutors were all well trained, seasoned, and motivated. They had the resources they needed. The judge was unhurried, with no case backlog to worry about. The defendants were not awaiting a verdict in a cell in the District of Columbia jail, and their attorneys were not the dregs of the system, making a quick buck without worrying about their clients' rights. Most unusual of all, the public was paying attention.

Prosecutor James Neal, just turned forty-five, dominated the courtroom. He was composed and confident, his walk and his posture exuding aggression, his courtroom manner drawn in, coiled. One watched his eyes and saw that he was alert to every sound, every movement, every nuance in the room. In the evenings he would have stomach spasms, but they would wait until he was offstage, accommodating his enormous will. His manner reflected the easygoing southern man, but he was cold and calculating, never doing anything to hurt his case, never allowing anyone else to hurt his case.

Haldeman's attorney, John J. Wilson, at seventy-three years of age was the most experienced lawyer in the room. Crusty, contentious, his mouth turned down in a perpetual scowl, his manner was consistently

---

* Colson had negotiated a reduced charge and was dropped from the case. Gordon Strachan was severed from the other defendants after a warning from the appellate court. The prosecutors eventually dropped the charges against him. Mardian's conviction was overturned because his case wasn't severed.

combative. His motions, he explained to Sirica, were made for his "error bag"; each time Sirica made an alleged mistake Wilson would "put it in my error bag."

Judge John Sirica, just turned seventy, was, like Wilson and Neal, somewhat short with an athletic frame and an unusual intensity about his lined face. His dark hair and brows made him look ten years younger than his age, but he was tired by the time the trial began. He had lived with Watergate as long as the defendants. A federal trial judge has the most demanding job of any member of the judiciary. There are no law clerks available during the courtroom battles to substitute their intelligence for a lesser or a lazy mind; there are no reprieves from the instant when the decision must be made. And there is the appellate court, waiting in relative leisure to check the record and score the judge a success or failure.

As chief judge, Sirica had assigned this case to himself, causing consternation among the defense lawyers, who felt he should have allowed another judge to preside, since he, as much as anyone, had made this trial possible. Sirica had also caused some hard feelings among his fellow judges. Judge George Hart had said to several of the prosecutors just before the trial got under way, "John Sirica will never make it through the trial. He's about to have a nervous breakdown."

Sirica presided over the court in a vigorous fashion but he often seemed unsure of himself as the battle erupted and raged beneath his bench. The lawyers noticed that if he gave a point to the prosecution early in the day, he could be expected to give one to the defense later. The merits of the legal point did not always decide the issue. Wilson and his colleagues crouched, waiting for the "reversible error." Neal and his team perched, alert to head it off. Sirica tried to make it through each day without too much delay, too much fighting, too many side issues.

One of the nervous kibitzers from the prosecutor's office, a man with no immediate tasks on the trial team but whose heart was in the case, sat with me in the courtroom one day, waiting to see if Sirica would finally topple into John Wilson's error bag, the case irretrievably lost by some important technicality. "This is awful," the attorney said after watching for a while in excruciating anxiety. "It's like watching a drunk on a tightrope."

Wilson, Neal, Sirica. One could see that they respected each other. But the courtroom was filled with others bearing less respect and more animus.

John Wilson and Rick Ben-Veniste did not get along. Before the trial started, Wilson had stood eye to eye to the thirty-one-year-old Ben-Veniste at a meeting of counsels and said, "Sonny, you'll be an old man before you're through with this case." Ben-Veniste stared at this still vigorous but faltering old man, smiled, and said, "Don't worry, John, I have the time."

Rick Ben-Veniste is a born clown who amused his colleagues at the office with Groucho Marx imitations and victimless practical jokes. (When Jill Volner ended up in a tiny office without a window, Ben-Veniste got her a poster of a window with a Peeping Tom leering in.) The defense attorneys tried to capitalize on Ben-Veniste's somewhat deserved reputation as a wise guy by objecting when he smiled during testimony or arguments.

The mood shifted from day to day and sometimes from moment to moment. On October 17 the tapes were introduced for the first time, the courtroom equipped with stereophonic "listening stations" and sixty-dollar headsets for everyone in the room. As they were being distributed, Mitchell's lawyer, Bill Hundley, said, "Which version would you like, regular or X-rated?" and "That will be two dollars, please." Ben-Veniste suggested that the judge charge a rental for the headsets. "We can use the money to pay for Nixon's flight." Hundley became noted for reminding the judge if Sirica seemed to be running past the normal time for a midmorning recess. His reason, he would say, was that the defense attorneys could not afford the expense of the daily transcripts and were getting writer's cramp from trying to keep up. In fact, Hundley was desperate for a cigarette.

John Dean appeared as the government's first and star witness. Sirica suppressed a smile as the tapes played Dean's voice telling Richard Nixon that Judge Sirica was "a peculiar animal . . . a son of a bitch."

Dean was kept on the stand for two weeks. Wilson spent so much time in tedious and repetitive cross-examination that the press began debating whether the old man had lost his touch or was purposely trying the patience of Judge Sirica in hopes of provoking error. Sirica allowed Wilson great latitude, and at times, Neal as well. "I'm not trying this case strictly according to the strict rules of evidence," he said. "What we are trying to get in this case is the truth of what happened. T-R-U-T-H," he spelled, looking at the jury. "Remember that word."

The government's case piled up evidence, the tapes devastating the defendants' chances as the conspiracy unfolded, like the old radio drama, right before the jury's ears. The question of Nixon's appearance as a witness continually arose. The defendants wanted him, hoping to convince the jury of the essential unfairness of having him roam free while his subordinates stood trial, an anomaly that seven jurors had noted with displeasure during their selection interviews. Each had said he could put the point aside, however, and judge the men in the dock fairly. Sirica, too, was anxious to have the former President appear. When Jack Miller appeared in chambers to tell Sirica that Nixon remained a gravely ill man—he had had an attack of phlebitis—but had been released from the hospital because the doctors reported there was nothing more they could do for him, Sirica responded that he was glad to hear the former President was getting better, and he would send three doctors out to examine him to see when he could appear. At a bench conference over the choice of the three doctors, Bill Hundley suggested the choice of the Washington Redskins' physician. "Doctor Palumbo will get him back in the game, Judge," Hundley said.

On Monday, November 4, James Neal rose at the start of the day to inform the court of a weekend development. He was pale and even more tense than usual. He told Sirica he would speak from a prepared statement "in order that I am not, by speaking extemporaneously, allowing my emotions regarding this matter to color the essential facts."

The story that unfolded then and in the following days, mostly at late afternoon sessions after the jury had been dismissed, offers an insight into the easy morality of some Washington lawyers and the reason why Nixon and his top aides could expect to be successful in obstructing justice with the help of the right attorneys.

When Watergate began to unravel, the prosecutors had obtained the tape of a conversation between Chuck Colson and Howard Hunt that took place in the fall of 1972 in which Hunt spoke of a memo he had written that his lawyer, William Bittman, was "going to lay on Parkinson [lawyer for the Committee to Re-elect the President]." This memo was crucial because it was supposed to have made financial demands on the part of the burglars.

Hunt denied writing such a memo, and Bittman denied ever seeing it or receiving it for relay to Parkinson. Such an extortionate document, prepared for delivery to a third party, would not be covered by any attorney-client privilege. If Bittman had seen it, his responsibility to disclose this evidence of blackmail and obstruction of justice would have been clear. Bittman knew the law. He had been a topflight government prosecutor, had prosecuted one of the biggest Hoffa trials and later the case of Bobby Baker, Lyndon Johnson's friend and flunky at the Senate. Furthermore, Bittman was practicing in one of Washington's large, prestigious firms—Hogan and Hartson—where the senior partners and the members of the firm's executive committee could be expected to oversee the aggressive lawyer to be sure that his conduct did not cross the ethical line. In the summer of 1973 the Senate Watergate committee had subpoenaed Bittman's files on the Hunt case from Hogan and Hartson, and they found no such memorandum included.

Still, doubts persisted. Bittman had received $156,000 in legal fees just to plead Hunt guilty to the burglary charges. Some of the money, $41,000, was in cash—large numbers of fifty- and one-hundred-dollar bills—dropped at a public telephone booth for Bittman by a mysterious telephone caller named Mister Rivers, who turned out to be Anthony Ulasewicz. Hogan and Hartson's executive committee voted to accept all this anonymous money as fees, although after the first payments the members ruled that in the future cash payments should come only from Hunt himself. After that, $210,000 in small bills was delivered to Bittman's home mailbox in unmarked envelopes. He would turn the envelopes over to Hunt. Hunt paid the rest of his legal fees by check.

In the summer of 1973 Jim Neal was working on the Watergate case, and he kept asking Bill Bittman, his old friend from the Justice Department, about that memo. By this time Bittman's involvement was serious, and his law firm advised him to get himself a lawyer. Bittman chose his old Justice Department boss, Jack Miller, and furnished him a copy of the supposedly nonexistent memo. In August Bittman went before the grand jury and said, "I had no knowledge of any memorandum that was to be laid on Mr. Parkinson." He also reported, time and again, that Hunt had denied to him that he ever received any hush money, and said that he had no personal knowledge that any of the money Hunt received had any strings attached to it.

When the Watergate prosecutors drafted the indictment in the cover-up case, William Bittman was one of the lawyers listed as a co-conspirator, his activities inextricably linked to the progress of the cover-up. However, he insisted he had no knowledge of either blackmail or conspiracy, and the prosecutors could not prove otherwise. The prosecutors removed his name from the final indictment.

Then when Hunt testified at the trial on October 28, he confirmed for the first time what he had always denied, that he and his late wife had indeed composed a memorandum demanding "support" from his superiors. The prosecutors had never seen this memo, and Hunt could not supply it. He had given it to Bittman, he said, and Bittman later told him that he had read it to Parkinson, who said he would do what he could. Shortly after that Hunt got an anonymous packet of cash. Throughout the case, Bittman had denied all knowledge of such a memo.

By the time Hunt testified, William Bittman had left the prestigious Washington firm of Hogan and Hartson. A few days after Hunt's testimony, on November 1, when it was not clear whether the government now had a copy of the "nonexistent" Hunt memo, senior members of Bittman's old firm made two telephone calls. The first was to Bittman, to warn him. The second was to James Neal.

The Hogan and Hartson lawyers informed Neal that at least two members of the firm had seen the Hunt memo in the firm's files. They had chosen not to disclose it either to the Senate Watergate committee, which had a specific subpoena out for the Hunt files, or to the Watergate Special Prosecution Force. Recently when they looked for the memo in the firm's microfilm library, it was not there.

The next day, Friday afternoon, November 2, Bittman met with Neal and produced the memo. He had obtained it in the fall of 1972, he said, but he hadn't read it until the spring of 1973. Members of his old law firm testified that Bittman told them of its contents on May 1, 1973. When he finally did read it, he rejected its contents as false, and withheld the fact of its existence because of attorney-client privilege, Bittman said.

The memo, three pages long, was dated November 14, 1972. It remains one of the most explicit documents of the entire Watergate affair.

It pointed out that civil suits and congressional investigations of Watergate would be continuing long after the seven defendants were tried, and that the "wash hands attitude" of the higher-ups, now that the presidential election was over, would not do. "The media are offering huge sums for the defendants' stories," Hunt wrote, $745,000 to one man alone. "The Watergate bugging is only one of a number of highly illegal conspiracies engaged in by one or more of the defendants at the behest of senior White House officials. These as yet undisclosed crimes can be proved."

The memo proved less important now, given all the subsequent evidence. Its greater significance lay in what it said about the standards of at least one large Washington law firm at the time of Watergate. Judge Sirica, himself a former partner at Hogan and Hartson, was outraged. He scheduled a series of evidentiary hearings to determine the circumstances surrounding the long absence of Hunt's memo.

Bittman was called to testify out of the presence of the jury, warned of his rights, and confronted with a withering barrage of questions by Rick Ben-Veniste. He sat on the edge of the witness chair in a crouch, leaning well forward, sweating profusely, elbows resting on the chair arms, hands knitted together, ankles crossed and thrust back under the chair.

It was a courtroom version of the cobra and the mongoose. Ben-Veniste feinted, then thrust forward in attack. Bittman stood his ground, refusing to stray from his story. He laced his answers with "to the best of my recollection." The judge interrupted.

SIRICA: Didn't you think that was a pretty important memorandum delivered to you? You know, about the talk of clemency and all that business? You mean to say to this court you didn't look at that memo when you received it?

BITTMAN: That is correct.

SIRICA: Is that what you are telling this court?

BITTMAN: That is my recollection.

Near the end of Bittman's second day on the stand, Jim Neal, who had been fidgeting in his seat while Ben-Veniste interrogated his old friend, sought the court's permission to ask a question.

NEAL: Bill, didn't you tell me during the summer of 1973, "Jim, I have no knowledge or information that Mr. Hunt contends he was doing anything or maintaining silence in exchange for funds." Didn't you tell me that?

BITTMAN: I indicated—

SIRICA: Wait a minute. Did you tell him that, that is the first question. If you did, you can answer. If you didn't, you can answer. If you have an explanation, you may explain.

BITTMAN: In substance, I told you that, exactly.

NEAL: That is all.

But Bittman continued, explaining that he had not believed the information in the memo, that it was counter to his client's sworn testimony, and that his partners at Hogan and Hartson, and Jack Miller, his attorney, advised him not to divulge its contents. Ben-Veniste asked why Bittman had not, in that case, simply refused to answer Neal's questions during the summer of 1973 because of the lawyer-client privilege. As Bittman struggled for an answer, Neal stood up, slowly turned his back to the witness and walked from the courtroom. Bittman was dismissed by Sirica, who cut him off with, "I think we have had enough examination on this."

The next witness was Bittman's closest friend and former associate at Hogan and Hartson, attorney Austin Mittler, who hesitantly testified that on November 14, 1972, the date of the memo, he conferred with Bittman and was shown a document that, while he did not read it all the way through, contained disturbing information. He stopped reading it and said to his partner, "Why are we receiving documents like this? Why don't you tell Howard to stop sending them?" Bittman had testified he had not read the memo until the following spring.

Bittman left the courtroom before Mittler testified. A number of reporters who had known him well for years, since his prosecution of Jimmy Hoffa and Bobby Baker, confronted Bittman in the hall. They stood around him for a long moment. None asked a question. They just looked at their notebooks. Bittman waited a while, then said, "Excuse me, gentlemen," and walked toward the elevator.

Bittman appeared later to explain why he had accepted his fees in the form of bags of cash from strangers on Hunt's behalf. He was exceedingly uncomfortable and denied that the money he handled was hush money. Every cent of his portion went into the Hogan and Hartson kitty. Sirica asked, "When was the last time you ever went to a telephone booth and got twenty-five thousand dollars in cash without knowing where the money was coming from, outside of this? . . . Didn't that arouse your suspicion somehow?"

Bittman responded that the executive committee of Sirica's old law firm had approved the transaction.

Bittman was reinvestigated on perjury charges, but Ruth found the case too shaky, considering Bittman's careful answers. He continues to practice in Washington.

After nearly nine weeks of testimony Neal began his summation late on a Thursday afternoon, December 19, the worst possible time, since the jury is always tired and distracted. Within a few minutes he had their attention, for over the weeks James Neal had taken command of the courtroom, and it was now his stage.

He began softly. "Justice, and its pursuit, is an elusive goal," he said. "The court system is a delicate instrument which works only if it is not impeded, not tampered with, and if it gets the facts and the evidence."

He launched into a scathing denunciation of the defense attempts to pass off the hundreds of thousands of dollars paid to the burglars as innocent attempts to help with living expenses and attorneys' fees. "There has been an effort to beguile you, repeated over and over again," he said.

The case was complicated, he agreed, and the testimony, from twenty-eight government witnesses and another fifty for the defense, seemed almost too voluminous to comprehend. But all the jurors had to do was to keep asking, "Why?"

"Why were documents destroyed? Why was the CIA used to obstruct the FBI's investigation of Watergate? Why was a cover story (for the burglary funds) developed? Why were veiled, camouflaged offers of clemency made without using that word? And why was nearly a half-million dollars paid for seven people caught wiretapping and burglarizing Democratic National Committee headquarters? Why?"

He wheeled and pointed to the various defendants, slumped in their chairs, as he came to parts of the story that involved them. By the time court adjourned for the day, he was less than halfway through.

The next morning his timing and theatrical presence were heightened as he mimicked the defendants, quoting lines of praise from the White House tapes for John Dean, then the changed attitude after April 15, when, Neal said, "nice, good, fine John Dean became mean John Dean," because he went to see the prosecutors and told them the truth.

At the trial, he said, the finger-pointing had spread to others. "Mitchell blames Colson. Ehrlichman blames the President. Mardian blames the White House and Mr. Haldeman can't recall enough to blame anybody." The one common note, he said, was that all blamed the government's star witness, John Dean.

"Members of the jury," he said, "tragically these conspiratorial conversations have happened in the hallowed halls of the White House of the United States, where once strode such giants as Jefferson, Jackson, Lincoln, the two Roosevelts, Eisenhower, Kennedy.

"Can you compare the White House, perhaps when Jefferson was drafting his second inaugural, or Lincoln writing, 'With malice toward none and charity for all,' with the tapes you have heard in this courtroom? Or Roosevelt saying, 'We have nothing to fear but fear itself,' with 'Give 'em an hors d'oeuvre and maybe they won't come back for the main dish?'"

His voice was flat with the twang of Tennessee, and a little hoarse. He quoted Nixon's telling Ehrlichman that John Dean should be reminded that only the President could save his law license. Ehrlichman's response, Neal reminded the jurors in a prolonged singsong, was "Um hum, um hum."

"He objects to the way I read it," Neal said of the flushed, silent Ehrlichman. "He says it's a negative Um hum. You'll have to decide whether it's a negative Um hum or a positive Um hum." The jurors, who had resisted laughing until now, could not contain themselves.

Neal recalled the delivery of the "humanitarian" money from Haldeman's White House safe to Fred LaRue at his apartment. "Let me tell you something about the compassionate, humanitarian purposes. . . . When he [Gordon Strachan] gets there, Fred LaRue is wearing gloves! I don't know what gloves have to do with compassion, but they do have something to do with keeping your fingerprints from showing up."

Finally in a low voice Neal told the jurors that it had never been his practice as a prosecutor to ask a jury to bring in a guilty verdict. "I ask you to decide this case without prejudice, without sympathy to either side, solely on the evidence. Both sides deserve no less. Neither side can ask for more."

On December 30 Judge Sirica spent two hours giving final instructions to the jury, speaking from extensive notes and not deviating much from long-accepted standard instructions. The jury had been informed that Nixon might be called as a witness in the case, but the judge had never explained that three doctors had found the former President too ill even to give a deposition. Now Sirica simply told them to draw no conclusions from the fact that some prospective witness had not appeared.

The judge spent much of his time instructing the jury on the theory of conspiracy law, as he had done several times in the course of the testimony. Then he told them that the word verdict came from a Latin word meaning "to speak the truth," and he sent them to their deliberations.

All of New Year's Eve was spent in the traditional courtroom vigil, and much of New Year's Day as well. The defendants were given a room in the deserted courthouse where they could pass the time watching football games. The lawyers alternated between viewing television and mingling with reporters in the press room. In midmorning someone hit upon the idea of recording for history the entire cast, and most of the newsmen and attorneys gathered on the courthouse steps for a "class photo."

In the late morning of January 1 the jurors asked for a repeat of Sirica's instructions concerning perjury. After lunch they asked for a complete list of documentary evidence introduced during the long trial. The corridor speculation grew that a verdict was near.

At 4:25 P.M. Sirica was in his chambers chatting with a group of reporters, when a deputy marshal hurried in with a note from the foreman. "The jury has completed its work and has reached verdicts," it said.

The jurors filed in, staring straight ahead without a glance at the defendants. Their faces were sober. None of them showed even a trace of a smile. Lawyers say that this is the sign of a guilty verdict, the jurors not wanting to look at the faces of the condemned.

The foreman had a sealed manila envelope in his hand, which he gave on command to James Capitanio, Sirica's gray-haired clerk. Capitanio opened it and removed five sheets of white paper and handed them to Sirica, who read silently and handed them back. It took Capitanio two minutes to read, in a shaking voice, what was on the papers. In a singsong he read the names of the defendants and each count, starting with John Mitchell: "Count one, guilty; count two, guilty; count three, guilty; count four, guilty; count five, guilty; count six, guilty."

Fifteen times he intoned the word, through four white sheets: Mitchell, Haldeman, Ehrlichman, Mardian. Finally he reached the last sheet. "Defendant Parkinson: Count one, not guilty; count two, not guilty."

The defendants did not move or change expression. Defense lawyer

Bill Hundley was obviously shaken. After a while Mitchell whispered to him, "Don't take it so hard, Bill." Throughout the trial Hundley had winced whenever he talked to reporters about how strong the government's case seemed. But all that time he nurtured his hopes and his dreams that luck and a sharp defense might turn fortune around.

Only Robert Mardian appeared stricken, unable to control his emotions. He sat down heavily and stayed in one position, staring at the table, trembling.

Sirica thanked the jury and wished them a Happy New Year, then dismissed them. As they filed from the courtroom, a demure-looking, white-haired woman who had sat quietly each day in the second row of spectator seats gave the jury the Bronx cheer and stuck out her tongue. It was Dorothy Mardian. "We'll get you, Sirica," she said in a voice loud enough to be heard from counsel table. The defendants and the lawyers began to file out amidst the melee of the press corps. Dorothy Mardian walked up to Neal and Ben-Veniste. "We'll get you, too," she said. They walked away, but Ben-Veniste was shaken and he was still talking about the confrontation an hour later.

The courtroom emptied. The pale blond benches and the brown cork floors and the glaring white ceiling reflected no sound. Mardian still sat at a table in the front of the room, his head down.

After fourteen weeks there was nothing more. The lawyers greeted each other at the doors of the courthouse, praised and thanked each other. The defendants walked through the gauntlet of the press and made their statements. A freak storm brought a few minutes of lightning and dark clouds and rain and noticeably high winds, and it seemed a little too melodramatic really to be happening. The television technicians donned their bulky, brightly colored raingear and played more lights on the front of the courthouse. The storm was gone almost as quickly as it had come.

Jim Neal went up to the prosecutor's office on the sixth floor of the courthouse, had a drink of Jack Daniels, closed his attaché case, and headed for his hotel. Within an hour he was on a plane for Nashville, his tour of government service over.

A year and five days later—January 6, 1976—Peter Kreindler, as a private lawyer working only part-time for the government, would appear in the same courthouse again to argue the cover-up case before the U.S. Court of Appeals for the District of Columbia. Long after that the case would still be in the courts. But Watergate had at last been exorcised from the American spirit by the trial of *U.S.* v. *Mitchell et al.*

On Friday, February 21, 1975, Judge Sirica sentenced Mitchell, Haldeman, and Ehrlichman to two and a half to eight years. Mardian was given ten months to three years.*

Except for the original burglars, these were the toughest sentences given to Watergate defendants. Hank Ruth thought they were too tough. Others I spoke to—FBI and IRS agents, reporters, secretaries—thought the sentences were too lenient.

Just before Judge Sirica acted, John Ehrlichman's lawyer requested "alternative service" for his client among the Pueblo Indians in New Mexico. But there had never been any chance that Judge Sirica would give such a sentence to the man who told the head of the IRS he wanted to see Democratic Chairman Lawrence O'Brien in the penitentiary by Election Day and who had never expressed the slightest remorse publicly for his role in the Watergate affair. At the end of 1976, Ehrlichman would be the first of these defendants to begin serving his sentence while the appeal process continued.

Of twenty-seven corporate executives guilty of injecting dirty money into the 1972 presidential campaign, none of those associated with American industrial companies received jail sentences, even those convicted of felonies. Three corporate executives or lawyers did receive short jail terms, but each was associated with the discredited dairy cooperative which flagrantly and openly tried, with success, to buy the government's policy toward milk price supports, tariffs, and import quotas. Their mistake was a lack of subtlety that made it difficult for the judge to wink at their crimes.

* Defendant Gordon Strachan had been severed from the case before it went to trial, after a veiled warning from the appellate court that it doubted the propriety of joining Strachan to the larger case, and that some of the evidence against him might have been nullified by the rules of immunity. The prosecutors eventually dropped Strachan's case, reinforcing John Dean's argument that he might well have won on technicalities if he had declined to plead guilty. The appellate court eventually reversed Robert Mardian's conviction as well, and ordered that he be tried alone under more restrictive rules of evidence. This too proved ironic, since Mardian while at the Justice Department was one of the forces behind the profligate use of the conspiracy statutes to bring suspects before grand juries, and to indict such a figure as Philip Berrigan and others who won acquittals because of what amounted to government misconduct. The convictions of Mitchell, Haldeman and Ehrlichman were upheld.

All the others were told, in words or through leniency of sentence, that they had "suffered enough" by their exposure. Some lost their titles and jobs, at least temporarily. But almost all ended up with generous settlements from companies whose officers knew that these men were no more guilty than many others—just more caught.

But compare their treatment with the upright citizens like Joe Rose, a lawyer who went to work for the Associated Milk Producers, Incorporated, and discovered a rats' nest of corruption created by those who had preceded him. His colleagues warned him he would be ruined if he reported the crimes. He went straight to the FBI—and has not worked as an attorney since that time. And then there is Alexander Butterfield, the former Nixon aide, who volunteered nothing but refused to lie to the Senate Watergate committee about the existence of the tapes. For that historic revelation Butterfield was unable to find a job for more than a year.

Alexander Haig was allowed to resume his military career, despite the tradition that politics and a military career should not mix, and despite his blemished record as Nixon's proconsul. CIA Director Richard Helms, who lied under oath to congressional committees and destroyed CIA tapes after being ordered not to do so by the Senate majority leader, became ambassador to Iran. Henry Kissinger, who fled Nazi Germany for the freedom of America, then used his power to help set up warrantless wiretaps which by their nature subvert the American Constitution, continued to serve as Secretary of State and became a Nobel Laureate.

Watergate justice was just as erratic as the criminal justice system has always been: deferential to the mighty, blind to inequities. It is a system for elitists, illustrated by a conversation Hank Ruth and his aides had one day at lunch with John Oakes, then the editorial page editor for *The New York Times*. Oakes observed that Spiro Agnew deserved to go to jail far more than did Haldeman, Ehrlichman, and Mitchell. A few of us, long bemused by the published views of Oakes on questions of criminal justice, urged him to explain.

"The man is a common grafter," Oakes said. "His crimes were those of the common criminal."

Carl Feldbaum looked at him. "The law locks up the man or woman," Feldbaum said, "who steals the goose from off the common. It turns the greater felon loose, who steals the common from the goose."

"All Agnew was caught stealing was money," someone said in explanation, but not defense. "The others were caught trying to steal our Constitution."

No one was more elitist than the deferential judges, and none was more deferential than George Luzerne Hart, Jr., the man who succeeded John Sirica as chief judge in federal district court and thus assigned many of the Watergate cases for disposition.

Hart proves the saying, "A judge is a member of the Bar who knew a politician." His father was a partner in the stenographic firm of Hart and Harkins, which was the official reporter for the Republican national conventions. Hart went to Virginia Military Institute and Harvard Law School, practiced in Washington, and spent many years as a Republican party worker. He finally became chairman of the Republican party in Washington and a delegate to the 1952 convention, after which Eisenhower made him a district judge.

Three days after he became chief judge, Hart called me to his chambers and asked if it was true that I had made free copies of indictments available to the press after they were handed down. I told him that was true. "In my courthouse," he said, "reporters are no different from Negras or whites, Protestants, Catholics, or Jews. If you give out free copies, you better have enough for everybody in the courthouse and every member of the public who wants one. Otherwise you don't give out any." His racial and religious analogies to reporters seemed curious.

One quickly gathered that George Hart didn't especially care for the Watergate Special Prosecution Force. His sentencing of the Watergate-related defendants who had come before him might be considered eccentric by some, since his reputation had him a law-and-order judge for his sixteen years on the bench.

On May 3, 1974, Tom McBride brought before Hart the first campaign contributions case that resulted in a plea to a felony count. The case was important to McBride for two reasons. The defendants were Thomas V. Jones, chief executive officer of the Northrop Corporation; and his assistant, Northrop vice president James Allen. Northrop, an aerospace firm dependent on government contracts, was hit especially hard by Kalmbach and the Nixon men during the 1972 campaign, and contributed $150,000 in three installments, using the usual foreign consultants to launder the money. Jones had thought fifty thousand dollars would be enough but was told by Herbert Kalmbach, Maurice Stans, and Leonard Firestone that they expected $100,000. Later Kalmbach came for the last fifty thousand to finance the cover-up.

When the illegal contributions to CRP started to become public knowledge, Jones first decided to construct records to cover up Northrop's money. He and his assistant, Allen, told their false story to the Senate Watergate committee and the FBI. Jones also testified before the campaign contributions grand jury before McBride and his task force caught up with the facts. As the facts started emerging, Jones' lawyers started plea bargaining.

McBride insisted that Jones must plead to a felony. In this case he offered a plea to a pertinent statute that had gone unenforced since it was put on the books in 1940: 18 U.S.C. 611, which made it a crime for firms that were government contractors to contribute to political campaigns. McBride wanted to create a precedent for enforcing this law in the future, and at the same time show other corporate executives that if they covered up their illegal contributions and got caught, it would go harder on them. Judge Hart did not see things quite that way.

As soon as McBride began to introduce the case, Hart asked him how long the law had been on the books and how many prosecutions there had been. Hart commented that "it has been outrageous, actually, the way that particular law has been permitted to be violated over the years. No one paid any attention to it at all. So I think it is fine you are applying it. I hope you will apply it impartially to both parties and to everyone concerned."

Normally in a felony case, the judge who takes the guilty plea waits for reports from the prosecutor and the probation officer before sentencing the defendant. Hart had indicated to counsel for both sides during a chambers conference that he would follow that procedure.

Hart accepted the guilty plea and then this exchange took place:

THE COURT: Counsel, would you like to waive a pre-sentence report in this case, you and your client?
COUNSEL FOR JONES: Your Honor, we believe that there is relevant information regarding the defendant's background, his community service and other information that may be pertinent to the Court's judgement.
THE COURT: Can't you make that to me?
COUNSEL: I can represent that to you, Your Honor, that Mr. Jones is—

THE COURT: Let's don't go into details at the moment. *Stop and think a minute.*

COUNSEL: Yes, Your Honor, we are prepared to waive the pre-sentence report.

Hart then told the amazed courtroom that the charge was a very serious one, but since this law had not been enforced before, he was sentencing Jones to a five-thousand-dollar fine. The penalty under the law could have been five years in prison.

He sentenced Allen to a one-thousand-dollar fine. "But let me say this, if ever there comes before me a case of a violation of . . . this statute . . . *committed on or after this date,* somebody will most certainly go to jail." It seemed to be an announcement that any other defense contractors hiding an illegal 1972 contribution had no worry. They would be free for a small percentage of their original contribution, if the case came before Hart.

The prosecutors were surprised and disheartened. Hart had telegraphed to the business community that resisters could expect to be treated as leniently as those who came forward with the incriminating facts in the campaign contributions cases.

A few hours after the Northrop affair, Judge Hart presided over a pre-trial hearing in the perjury case of Jake Jacobsen, who was a central figure in the expanding investigation of the dairy industry. The prosecutors had been methodically following the leads given them in October by officials of Associated Milk Producers, Incorporated, and had caught Jacobsen in a clearly false statement when he testified before the grand jury. He had claimed that from the date he first put it in his safe deposit box, he never touched the $10,000 allegedly given to him for John Connally. Some of the bills the prosecutors found in that box were too new to have been there since the date Jacobsen said.

The perjury count charged that Jacobsen had lied when he testified as follows:

Q—And it is your testimony that that $10,000 which you put into that box within a number of weeks after it was given to you by Mr. [Bob] Lilly [an Associated Milk Producers, Inc., lobbyist] —and it was untouched by you between then and the time you looked at it with the FBI agent [on Nov. 27, 1973]?

A—That is correct.

Q—You are certain about that?

A—Yes, sir.

Hart threw out the indictment on the argument of defense counsel that Jacobsen's answer was literally true, that it *was* his testimony, albeit false testimony, that the money went untouched.

The ruling was not appealed. The official reason given—the indictment could be redrafted using a different set of false answers.* But the unstated reason was that George Hart had become chief judge of the federal trial court for the District of Columbia, and by whim he could sink the special prosecutor's chances in any number of decisions. The prosecutors had to get along with him.

The day he threw out the Jacobsen indictment Hart said privately to an attorney from the special prosecutor's office, "When are you fellows going to bring in some Democrats and some labor unions?"

Hart gave his general philosophy on white collar crime in chambers on July 23, 1974, in talking with David Parr of the milk producers, one of the men who handled the huge dairy industry slush fund. "This is a serious matter," the judge said. "These laws were designed for burglars, robbers, and muggers but they have to be applied equally to situations like this." Parr got four months and a ten-thousand-dollar fine for conspiracy to make illegal contributions.

Hart's sentencing formula was highly personal. Once, he had before him an attorney who had mingled his own funds with those of an estate for which he was an executor, later making full restitution. Hart sentenced him to eighteen months in jail "for violating a lawyer's trust." Later a forty-two-year-old black Baptist minister who worked for the District of Columbia was caught certifying ineligible persons for food stamps. Hart sent him to prison for three months. A twenty-five-year-old black woman, a clerk at the Department of Labor, was brought before him. Like the minister she had an unblemished past record. When she was demoted she began stealing money sent to the department to pay for booklets. She took over two thousand dollars in the course of a year. Hart sent her to prison for four months. "You violated your trust to the government," Hart told both defendants. He took a different view with Richard G. Kleindienst, former attorney general of the United States.

The Kleindienst case became a cause célèbre within the prosecutor's

---

* Before this occurred Jacobsen pleaded to a different charge and became the prosecution force's most controversial witness in the case of *U.S.* v. *John B. Connally.*

office. Kleindienst had clearly, specifically, and categorically denied receiving any orders from the President telling the Justice Department to drop the ITT antitrust cases. He was questioned closely during hearings on his nomination as attorney general that ran several days and he kept repeating his false testimony; he had had no contact at all with the White House on the case, and had not consulted with or reported to any administration official, including John Mitchell.

Even under the loose ethical standards that seem to apply when officials of the executive branch testify under oath before congressional committees, the bald deceptions and outright falsehoods of the witnesses in the Kleindienst hearings registered a new low. Committee members were incensed and referred the complete transcript of the hearings to the Justice Department for investigation to determine whether any witnesses had lied under oath. The case eventually landed in the special prosecutor's lap.

By August, 1973, Kleindienst had received any number of signals, from newspaper headlines, congressional testimony and the implications of his colleagues' appearances before the Watergate grand jury, that the prosecutors were on the trail of the ITT case and its false testimony. Through lawyers William Hundley and Herbert J. Miller, Jr., he offered to talk to Cox with the understandings that the session would be off the record and Kleindienst would be entitled to some unspecified consideration when it came to criminal charges. Cox readily accepted.

Eventually Kleindienst's admission of false testimony became the subject of news stories, and Cox admitted that he had told Senators Edward Kennedy and Philip Hart and two of their aides about it. Kleindienst's lawyers argued that because of Cox's indiscretion, their client should not be charged.

The ITT task force lawyers wanted to charge Kleindienst with a multitude of perjuries as well as with obstruction of the Senate. After first seeming to agree, Jaworski changed his mind following a session with Hundley and Miller. He accepted Miller's suggestion of a plea to a misdemeanor—2 U.S.C. Section 192, refusal to answer pertinent questions before Congress (meant to cover witnesses who flatly refused to testify before a congressional committee). Three of the four members of the ITT task force considered this reduced plea so improper that they planned to resign in protest if it was consummated.

Jaworski and Cox exchanged telephone calls and correspondence on the subject. Cox argued emphatically that Jaworski was free to charge Kleindienst according to the evidence. Kleindienst fully expected to be charged when he dealt with Cox, the former special prosecutor said, and the implicit offer of consideration was certainly no diminution of that.

As to Hundley's argument that Cox worsened Kleindienst's prospects by telling two senators of their conversation, Cox made two points. First, he had assurances from two sources within *The New York Times* that his indiscretion with the senators was not, directly or indirectly, the source for the *Times* story which publicized Kleindienst's admission of misleading testimony. Second, the information was exactly the same as that which Kleindienst agreed to tell a grand jury.

"I am perfectly certain that you are free to do the right thing . . . [with] an obligation to decide *for yourself* [Cox's emphasis]—free from any commitments or even intimations—what weight you would give to Kleindienst's coming forward when he did," Cox wrote in a final, handwritten note to Jaworski.

Jaworski now had only one ally within the office, but it was a powerful one. Jim Vorenberg had not been involved in the Kleindienst situation. He heard the various versions of events from Cox, Jaworski, and Jim Neal. "My understanding," he said later, "is that for anybody in Kleindienst's position we would have been very happy to agree to a plea to one five-year felony count, and we all would have thought for a variety of extenuating circumstances that it was on the high side; that if there was a three-year felony count or even a two-year felony count it would have been more appropriate, because even though he was attorney general and in a position of obligation, he was also somebody who was really not involved in the worst aspects of the case."

Vorenberg gave great weight to the fact that Cox had pursued Kleindienst. "It's sort of like contract negotiations where the two parties are negotiating but there's some basic misunderstanding between them, so that they are actually negotiating on different terms," he said. "It is possible that Archie was being conned, but we have never been able to establish that it was the case. And it is clear that Archie said, 'If you will cooperate now you certainly will be entitled to some consideration.' I thought it would be terrible if the office could be seen as going back on an understanding—going back on a misunderstanding, if you will. If there *was* a misunderstanding, it was partly Archie's fault."

Richard Davis, the one ITT task force member who chose to see the case through despite his disagreement, was the most forceful and articulate in arguing against the misdemeanor. "So far as I know," he wrote, "we have only given such pleas [single felony counts] to people who have cooperated. More importantly, I believe it likely that we would have been more insistent that the one count be a count drafted in our terms. This would mean a plea to one of the main perjury counts or to an obstruction of the Senate count which listed all aspects of the offense."

That was not possible given the offense being charged. If Kleindienst were to plead guilty to "refusal to answer pertinent questions," detailing the actual offenses committed would emphasize the inappropriateness of the charge.

As this debate continued, Jaworski began to consider not charging Kleindienst at all, and he might well have resolved the case in that way if Lacovara had not argued that the misdemeanor plea was at least legally defensible, even if inappropriate.

To reach this conclusion, Lacovara overruled one of his own staff members. Kenneth Geller had been assigned the task of researching the legal applicability to this case of a statute designed to cover instances where witnesses before Congress refused to answer questions. Geller found no case that construed the statute as to include the giving of false or evasive testimony as a refusal of the witness to testify. But Lacovara concluded, "It is a close question whether a charge based on false or evasive answers would be proper under the statute, but I conclude it could be attempted."

On Wednesday, May 15, 1974, Kleindienst and attorneys for both sides met with Judge George L. Hart in his chambers to rehearse the plea. Miller had tried to get Jaworski to agree to a recommendation of leniency, but Jaworski refused. In chambers, Miller asked the judge to sentence Kleindienst as soon as he took the plea because, he said, Kleindienst was on the verge of a nervous breakdown. Jaworski told the judge he did not believe it was advisable to sentence immediately, that Hart should follow normal procedure and wait for the usual pre-sentencing report.

"The man is a former attorney general of the United States," Hart said. "Why do we need a pre-sentence report?" But the more Miller talked, the more Hart came to realize that an immediate sentence, if it was lenient, would look like an old-fashioned fix.

Under the statute the minimum sentence called for was thirty days in jail and a fine of a hundred dollars. If that sentence had been levied, some in the prosecutor's office still would have felt that Kleindienst had got off too easily for his actions (and many would still have argued that the statute had been bent out of shape to accommodate him). But from the beginning the presumption was that the sentence might be suspended, and Hart's attitude in chambers confirmed it.

By the time Kleindienst appeared in court—Thursday, May 16, 1974— the controversy within the prosecutor's office had ended and the staff had gone on to other concerns. But the case was just beginning for the press and the public.

Kleindienst stood before Judge Hart looking ill at ease, his back ram- rod straight. The proceeding was mercifully short. The press did not notice that three members of the ITT task force, including its co-leader, were not present. They soon resigned in protest.

Hart took the plea and continued the case for sentencing. Then, in an unusual act of deference to a defendant in his courtroom, Hart ordered the press and all other spectators to remain in their seats while his clerk ushered Kleindienst and his attorney out through the judge's exit and safely away from the reporters.

Hart met with newsmen in front of the building afterward. The judge told them that Kleindienst would be issuing a statement. He also noted that he could suspend the minimum sentence called for by the statute.

Jaworski was asked why he had not brought a perjury charge against Kleindienst, and he said, "The decision was that this was the appropriate charge, and that is as far as I can go."

The initial press reaction turned out to be mild, as Jaworski had pre- dicted. There were a few articles and editorials critical of Jaworski's decision and some thoughtful pieces about plea bargaining in general. But the press' attention was fixed to the impeachment struggle and Nixon's survival, and most reporters thought that Kleindienst was cooperating with Jaworski and providing major evidence, as was the case with others who had bargained for reduced pleas.

From the beginning an unspoken factor in this case had been that Richard Kleindienst was a lawyer. Were he found guilty of perjury, he would certainly be disbarred and deprived of a lucrative livelihood. To his supporters such an outcome seemed especially harsh treatment for a man who had only defended his President. But to his critics Kleindienst's position at the head of his profession, as attorney general of the United States, made his testimony before the Senate more reprehensible. One side argued that it was enough for Kleindienst to be the first attorney general found guilty of a crime. The other side argued that with the power and authority he wielded went a higher responsibility, and a higher debt to be paid for failing it.

In a six-minute proceeding on Friday, June 7, 1974, Hart placed Kleindienst on one month's unsupervised probation, suspending the minimum penalty of thirty days and even the hundred dollars minimum fine.

The pre-sentence reports from the probation office and the special prosecutor's office, Hart said, "reflect a defendant of the highest integrity throughout his personal and official life . . ."

Kleindienst, Hart said, was pleading guilty "to a technical violation . . . not the type of violation that reflects a mind bent on deception. Rather, it reflects a heart that is too loyal and considerate of the feelings of others."

Richard Davis was sitting at the government's counsel table along with Henry Ruth, but he looked very much alone. He began frowning with Hart's first sentences. Then he just stared at his shoes.

"Had the defendant answered accurately and fully the questions put to him in this case, it would have reflected great credit on this defendant, but would have reflected discredit upon another individual," Hart said.

Kleindienst was in tears as the ceremony ended. "The tears a man sheds," Davis said, "when he has been awarded the Congressional Medal of Honor." That night, Kleindienst was photographed smiling at an embassy party.

The public reaction to the Kleindienst sentence was caught best, as always, by the editorial cartoonists. Herblock of the *Washington Post* showed a prisoner reading Hart's words in a newspaper while his cellmate explained, "You see, he's not a common criminal like us. He was the chief law enforcement officer of the U.S."

Immediately after the sentencing Kleindienst was interviewed by Ronald J. Ostrow of the *Los Angeles Times*. "Kleindienst explained in the interview why he had decided to disclose to the special prosecutor that Mr.

Nixon had called him on the ITT case," Ostrow wrote. "He said he understood the special prosecutor had obtained logs of White House calls and that the calls to him from Ehrlichman and Mr. Nixon would show up on the log of April 19, 1971. That was about the time the Justice Department had obtained a thirty-day extension from the Supreme Court in the ITT case."

Leon Jaworski was at his Texas ranch the day Hart delivered his encomium. We called him with the news and he said simply, "I think the judge went too far." Later, as the outrage spread and the entire rationale of plea bargaining by our office came under increasing scrutiny, Jaworski fought back and managed to convince the most important segments of the press, correctly, that what he was doing as a plea bargainer was precisely what prosecutors were authorized and expected to do.

He continued to believe that his leniency with Kleindienst was necessary under the circumstances. Justice Oliver Wendell Holmes once wrote that "It is less evil that some criminals should escape than that the government should play an ignoble part," and that was the Jaworski rationale in this case. To which I would answer with a quote from Justice Felix Frankfurter, "Justice must satisfy the appearance of justice."

Leo Rennert, a reporter for the *Sacramento Bee,* compared the cases of three men caught in the backwash of Watergate, each accused of falsehoods under oath before a Senate committee.

One was Lieutenant Governor Ed Reinecke of California, who also testified about ITT at the Kleindienst nomination hearings. He is not a lawyer and not schooled in the fine points of perjury. He cooperated with the prosecutors but had no standing in Washington. He was charged with three counts of perjury and convicted of one. He received an eighteen-month suspended sentence.* The second was Richard Kleindienst, a nominee for United States attorney general, well-schooled in the law and well-connected in Washington. He pleaded guilty to an obscure misdemeanor and was praised by the judge. The third was Henry Kissinger, the President's national security adviser and later secretary of state, not a lawyer, but the most schooled of the three in testifying under oath, and the best-connected in the nation's capital. He was not charged

---

* The appellate court voided the conviction because the prosecutors did not prove a quorum of the Senate Judiciary Committee was present for the false testimony. The same technicality would have applied to Kleindienst and had been raised during negotiations by Miller.

at all, and when the question of perjury was raised publicly, the Senate voted to accept the discrepancies in his testimony and his own explanation that the truth "very often has intangible aspects." When he threatened to resign at a famous news conference in Salzburg, Austria, the Senate overwhelmingly passed a resolution declaring him a patriotic American "whose integrity and veracity are above reproach."

"Are we witnessing a fulfillment of George Orwell's prophecy," Rennert asked, "of a society strongly professing egalitarianism while also acknowledging that some people are 'more equal' than others?"

The disciplinary board of the District of Columbia Bar recommended that Richard G. Kleindienst be suspended from the practice of law for one year. "Misrepresentation by a lawyer, like obstruction of justice in every form, goes directly to the heart of the lawyer's function and his role in society," the board wrote. "In the present case we are confronted with a lawyer who rose to the highest legal position in the land and who had a correspondingly high obligation to set an example of truth."

Three months later the District of Columbia Court of Appeals, which has the final power in cases of suspension from the Bar, suspended Kleindienst for one month. The vote was four to three. The majority included three men who had been appointed to that court while Kleindienst was serving as deputy attorney general with jurisdiction over judicial selections. The judges agreed that Kleindienst had engaged in "conduct involving dishonesty, fraud, deceit or misrepresentation," but they noted Judge Hart's disposition of the case with a suspended sentence and said, "Any further attempt to punish in this proceeding inferentially would carry with it an implied expression of disagreement with [Hart's] sentencing judgement."

It was logical that plea bargaining in the Watergate cases would raise suspicion and controversy because the country was paying attention to its system of justice, for a welcome change. Leon Jaworski's motivations in February, 1974, were no different from Archibald Cox's in October, 1973; he wanted to quickly resolve the guilt, and gain the cooperation, of some figures in order to establish his cases against others. "Dealing up," prosecutors called it, but making a deal with a principal like John Dean or Herbert Kalmbach raises inevitable questions about the good sense and the motivations of the man entrusted with such power.

NOT ABOVE THE LAW

Every day across the United States, thousands of men and women have their future freedom decided by two lawyers in the process of plea bargaining, a necessity if there is to be any justice in the complicated, sprawling, and snarled system of the criminal courts. That system is like a huge pyramid. At the bottom are the ten million crimes reported each year. These crimes result in perhaps two million arrests, less than a quarter-million formal charges, half again as many cases that get to the sentencing stage, until finally, at the top of the structure are the one hundred thousand or so people (well less than 2 percent of that bottom figure) who end up in penal institutions. There are miscarriages of justice all along the way, and many believe that the biggest miscarriage is leniency for certifiable criminals. Watergate seemed no different from that pyramid.

There was another model that Carl Feldbaum called "the Hearing pyramid." George Hearing was the stooge hired by Donald Segretti to help distribute scurrilous literature about Senators Humphrey, Muskie, and Jackson during the 1972 Florida primary campaign.

The United States Attorney in Tampa had ignored Senator Jackson's complaints at the time, but when Watergate broke he made an all-out effort to track the Segretti operation. A cooperating witness, in return for immunity, delivered evidence against Segretti, and against Hearing, the lowest man of all in the Watergate hierarchy. Segretti had his own information to deliver and entered into negotiations with the Watergate prosecutors. Hearing cooperated but had little to offer. He pleaded guilty, and the judge, aware of the public spotlight, sentenced him to a year in prison.

When Segretti's turn came months later, he was sentenced to six months. It seemed that the higher up the ladder of power and responsibility the prosecutors reached, the more prevalent became the reduced sentences and the likelihood that the defendant would serve less time than George Hearing. At the top of the ladder, of course, was a former President of the United States named Richard Milhous Nixon.

✤ INDEX ✤

Rogers, William P., 35, 121, 147
Rollenhagen, Judy, 172
Roosevelt, Franklin D., 267
Rose, Chapman, 250-251
Rose, Joe, 392
Rosenblatt, Daniel N., 27, 376
Rothberg, Don, 103
Ruckelshaus, William D., 27, 64, 143, 153, 160, 168, 183, 187, 190-191
    resignation of, 192, 209, 219
Ruff, Charles F., 27
Russell, Ken, 201
Ruth, Henry S., Jr., 27, 61, 98-99, 109, 115-116, 121, 130, 131, 137, 161, 165-166, 168, 174, 179, 195, 196, 205, 210-211, 213-215, 216-217, 222, 225-227, 229, 230-231, 246, 248, 255, 265, 266, 267, 284, 365, 401
    anonymity of, 378
    appointed special prosecutor, 377
    as deputy special prosecutor, 64
    Jaworski and, 242-243, 245, 273, 295, 370-371
    Kalmbach and, 296-298
    in mediating Special Prosecution staff relations, 248, 283, 302
    Nixon's impeachment and, 277-278
    Nixon's indictment and, 270-272, 274, 358-360, 368
    opinion on Watergate conspiracy sentences, 391-392
    in tapes subpoena case, 321, 327
Ruth, Tina, 115, 204, 278

Sadat, Anwar, 167
Safire, William, 181
St. Clair, Billie, 311
St. Clair, James D., 20, 27, 64, 301, 311-355 *passim*
    Jaworski and, 312-315, 316, 320-321, 323-326, 330-331, 334-335, 344
    knowledge of tapes by, 18, 341-342, 343
    in Nixon's resignation, 342-345
    Supreme Court and, 332-333, 336-337

Sakkaf, Omar, 152
Sale, Jon, 212-213
Saturday Night Massacre, 125, 141, 186-215 *passim*
    "firestorm" after, 205-209, 215
    see also Richardson, Elliot L.; Ruckelshaus, William D.
Saudi Arabia, 152, 166-167
"saving string" technique, 71
Saxbe, William B., 236, 244, 250, 313, 344, 377
Schlesinger, James R., 84, 121, 305
Schorr, Daniel, 80-81
Schoumacher, David, 244, 357
Schweiker, Richard, 178
Scott, Hugh, 18, 301, 319, 321
Scott, Jordan, case, 240-241
Scott, Tom, 240
Sears, John, 181
SEC (Securities and Exchange Commission), 31
Secret Service, 95, 109, 231-232
Segretti, Donald H., 27, 50-51, 61, 80, 130, 136, 404
Senate Judiciary Committee, 50, 51, 130, 163n., 175n., 183, 314, 366
    ITT investigations of, 60, 130
    in Richardson appointment, 40, 41, 44, 47
Senate Labor and Public Welfare Committee, 88
Senate Watergate Committee, 13
    Bittman's files subpoenaed by, 383
    Cox's opposition to televising of, 67-68, 98
    dairy investigation by, 243
    Dean's testimony before, 67, 79, 97, 127, 147, 278, 282
    establishment of, 33
    final report of, 272, 335
    Helms' testimony before, 306
    Hunt's testimony before, 269, 291
    immunity grants of, 67
    news media pressures on, 68
    Rebozo and, 131
    tapes and, 96, 97, 98-99, 101-103, 145, 152, 154, 156, 172, 175, 181, 232